Lecture Notes in Computer Science 6900

Commenced Publication in 1973
Founding and Former Series Editors:
Gerhard Goos, Juris Hartmanis, and Jan van

Kurt Jensen   Susanna Donatelli
Jetty Kleijn (Eds.)

Transactions on Petri Nets and Other Models of Concurrency V

 Springer

Editor-in-Chief

Kurt Jensen
Aarhus University
Faculty of Science
Department of Computer Science
IT-parken, Aabogade 34, 8200 Aarhus N, Denmark
E-mail: kjensen@cs.au.dk

Guest Editors

Susanna Donatelli
University of Turin
Computer Science Department
Corso Svizzera 185, 10149 Turin, Italy
E-mail: susi@di.unito.it

Jetty Kleijn
LIACS, Leiden University
P.O. Box 9512, 2300 RA, Leiden, The Netherlands
E-mail: kleijn@liacs.nl

ISSN 0302-9743 (LNCS)   e-ISSN 1611-3349 (LNCS)
ISSN 1867-7193 (ToPNoC)   e-ISSN 1867-7746 (ToPNoC)
ISBN 978-3-642-29071-8   e-ISBN 978-3-642-29072-5
DOI 10.1007/978-3-642-29072-5
Springer Heidelberg Dordrecht London New York

CR Subject Classification (1998): D.2.2-4, D.2, I.6, F.3-4, H.2.3, C.2, C.4

Typesetting: Camera-ready by author, data conversion by Scientific Publishing Services, Chennai, India

Printed on acid-free paper

Springer is part of Springer Science+Business Media (www.springer.com)

Preface by Editor-in-Chief

The fifth issue of LNCS Transactions on Petri Nets and Other Models of Concurrency (ToPNoC) contains revised and extended versions of a selection of the best papers from the workshops and tutorials held at the 31st International Conference on Application and Theory of Petri Nets and Other Models of Concurrency, in Braga, Portugal, June 21-25, 2010. It also contains a paper that was submitted to ToPNoC directly through the regular submission track.

I would like to thank the two guest editors of this special issue: Susanna Donatelli and Jetty Kleijn. Moreover, I would like to thank all authors, reviewers, and the organizers of the Petri net conference satellite workshops, without whom this issue of ToPNoC would not have been possible.

November 2011

Kurt Jensen
Editor-in-Chief
LNCS Transactions on Petri Nets and Other Models of Concurrency (ToPNoC)

LNCS Transactions on Petri Nets and Other Models of Concurrency: Aims and Scope

ToPNoC aims to publish papers from all areas of Petri nets and other models of concurrency ranging from theoretical work to tool support and industrial applications. The foundation of Petri nets was laid by the pioneering work of Carl Adam Petri and his colleagues in the early 1960s. Since then, an enormous amount of material has been developed and published in journals and books and presented at workshops and conferences.

The annual International Conference on Application and Theory of Petri Nets and Other Models of Concurrency started in 1980. The International Petri Net Bibliography maintained by the Petri Net Newsletter contains close to 10,000 different entries, and the International Petri Net Mailing List has 1,500 subscribers. For more information on the International Petri Net community, see: http://www.informatik.uni-hamburg.de/TGI/PetriNets/

All issues of ToPNoC are LNCS volumes. Hence they appear in all large libraries and are also accessible in LNCS Online (electronically). It is possible to subscribe to ToPNoC without subscribing to the rest of LNCS.

ToPNoC contains:

- revised versions of a selection of the best papers from workshops and tutorials concerned with Petri nets and concurrency;
- special issues related to particular subareas (similar to those published in the *Advances in Petri Nets* series);
- other papers invited for publication in ToPNoC; and
- papers submitted directly to ToPNoC by their authors.

Like all other journals, ToPNoC has an Editorial Board, which is responsible for the quality of the journal. The members of the board assist in the reviewing of papers submitted or invited for publication in ToPNoC. Moreover, they may make recommendations concerning collections of papers for special issues. The Editorial Board consists of prominent researchers within the Petri net community and in related fields.

Topics

System design and verification using nets; analysis and synthesis, structure and behavior of nets; relationships between net theory and other approaches; causality/partial order theory of concurrency; net-based semantical, logical and algebraic calculi; symbolic net representation (graphical or textual); computer tools for nets; experience with using nets, case studies; educational issues related to nets; higher level net models; timed and stochastic nets; and standardization of nets.

Applications of nets to: biological systems, defence systems, e-commerce and trading, embedded systems, environmental systems, flexible manufacturing systems, hardware structures, health and medical systems, office automation, operations research, performance evaluation, programming languages, protocols and networks, railway networks, real-time systems, supervisory control, telecommunications, and workflow.

For more information about ToPNoC, please see: www.springer.com/lncs/topnoc

Submission of Manuscripts

Manuscripts should follow LNCS formatting guidelines, and should be submitted as PDF or zipped PostScript files to ToPNoC@cs.au.dk. All queries should be addressed to the same e-mail address.

Guest Editors' Preface

This issue of ToPNoC contains revised versions of contributions selected from workshops and tutorial presentations held in conjuction with the 31st International Conference on Application and Theory of Petri Nets and Other Models of Concurrency, and the 10th International Conference on Application of Concurrency to System Design (ACSD 2010), co-located in Braga, Portugal, 21-25 June 2010; in addition it contains a contributed paper selected through the regular submission track of ToPNoC.

We are indebted to the Program Committees of the workshops and in particular their chairs. Without their enthusiastic work this volume would not have been possible. Many members of the Program Committees participated in reviewing the new versions of the papers selected for this issue. The strongest contributions were submitted from the following workshops:

- APNOC 2010: 2nd International Workshop on Abstractions for Petri Nets and Other Models of Concurrency
- ART 2010: Applications of Region Theory
- BioPPN 2010: International Workshop on Biological Processes and Petri Nets
- PNSE 2010: International Workshop on Petri Nets and Software Engineering
- SUMo 2010: Scalable and Usable Model Checking for Petri Nets and Other Models of Concurrency

The best papers of these workshops were selected in close cooperation with their chairs. The authors were invited to improve and extend their results where possible, based on the comments received before and during the workshop. The resulting revised submissions were reviewed by three to four referees. We followed the principle of also asking for fresh reviews of the revised papers, i.e., from referees who had not been involved initially in reviewing the original workshop contribution. All papers went through the standard two-stage journal reviewing process and eventually nine were accepted after rigorous reviewing and revising. This special issue is completed by two tutorial papers and by an article selected through the standard submission procedure of ToPNoC. Presented are a variety of high-quality contributions, ranging from model checking and system verification to synthesis, and from foundational work on specific net classes to innovative applications of Petri nets and other models of concurrency.

Four papers of this issue are in the area of model-checking and state space exploration. The tutorial paper by Gianfranco Ciardo, Yang Zhao, and Xiaoqing Jin entitled *Ten Years of Saturation: A Petri Net Perspective* carefully reviews the use of decision diagrams to represent state spaces. The topic is tackled with particular attention to a technique for state space generation called *saturation* that was developed ten years ago in the context of Petri nets and that has gained wider applicability in the verification world. The result is an in-depth treatment that constitutes a not-to-be-missed bulk of knowledge on decision diagrams and Petri nets. The (regular) paper by Silien Hong, Fabrice Kordon, Emmanuel Paviot-Adet, and Sami Evangelista, *Computing a Hierarchical Static Order for Decision Diagram-Based Representation from P/T Net*, addresses the well-known problem that the efficiency of decision diagrams may strongly depend on variable ordering. They show how the state space explosion problem can be dealt with for large Petri nets by mixing heuristics for variable ordering with a hierarchical form of decision diagrams. The work of Michał Knapik and Wojciech Penczek deals with *Bounded Model Checking for Parametric Timed Automata*. In parametric model checking, property verification relies on parameter synthesis. The paper shows how bounded model checking can be applied to parameter synthesis for parametric timed automata with continuous time leading to a theory useful for the parametric verification of a range of temporal formulae. Finally, the tutorial paper by Lars M. Kristensen and Michael Westergaard, *A Graphical Approach to Component-Based and Extensible Model Checking Platforms* presents JoSEL, a graphical language for the specification of executable model checking jobs, which allows a user to work at different levels of abstraction when interacting with the underlying components of a model checking tool. The tutorial uses the model checking platform ASAP as a reference to illustrate the use of JoSEL with an existing model checking tool.

Another group of papers is concerned with synthesis, the construction of a system (e.g., a Petri net of a certain type) from a given behavioral specification. In *Synthesis Problem for Petri Nets with Localities*, Maciej Koutny and Marta Pietkiewicz-Koutny consider Petri nets with localities. In such nets the transitions are partitioned into disjoint groups within which execution is synchronous and maximally concurrent. This idea is generalized to overlapping causalities for which different semantical interpretations are given. It is shown how the resulting net classes, as instances of the general framework of τ-nets, are synthesizable from behavioral specifications given in terms of finite step transition systems. Marc Solé and Josep Carmona, in their paper *Incremental Process Discovery*, are concerned with control-flow process discovery, meaning that given a representation of (part of) the behavior of a system in the form of a log (a set of observed sequences) or an automaton, an event-based formal model, here a Petri net, is generated as an underlying model for that behavior. Algorithms for this problem are often based on the theory of regions, but space requirements form an impediment for this approach. The paper discusses incremental derivation and exploration of a basis of regions, which makes it possible to split large inputs in fragments of tractable size. The resulting algorithm has been implemented in a tool that is experimentally tested and compared to other applications. As argued by Robin Bergenthum, Jörg Desel, Andreas Harrer, and Sebastian Mauser in *Modeling and Mining of Learnflows*, the area of workflow management has a lot in common with the field of learning and teaching processes (learnflows). Based on workflow modeling ideas, Petri net modeling languages for learnflows are introduced. Workflow mining methods are adapted to obtain a method for the synthesis of learnflow models from log files of learning systems.

Dorsaf Elhog-Benzina, Serge Haddad, and Rolf Hennicker discuss modal Petri nets (i.e., with distinguished may- and must-transitions) in *Refinement and Asynchronous Composition of Modal Petri Nets*. They provide procedures to decide whether such Petri nets are weakly deterministic and whether two modal language specifications generated by weakly deterministic modal Petri nets are related by the modal refinement relation. Asynchronously communicating modal I/O-Petri nets are studied as an application scenario.

Petri nets are gaining increasing attention as a formalism for the analysis of biological networks. The paper by Murad Banaji, *Cycle Structure in SR and DSR Graphs: Implications for Multiple Equilibria and Stable Oscillation in Chemical Reaction Networks* illustrates two graph-based formalisms, a labeled bipartite multigraph termed an SR graph, and its directed version, the DSR graph, for the analysis of oscillation behavior in chemical reactions. These objects are closely related to Petri nets, and the author discusses similarities and differences.

An innovative application of Petri nets to grid computing is the topic of the paper by Marco Mascheroni and Fabio Farina, *Nets-Within-Nets Paradigm and Grid Computing*. Nets-within-nets have been used to model the architecture of a Grid tool for High Energy Physics data analysis, and the paper provides evidence of how the modeling activity has led to the identification and solution of a number of defects in the tool implementation. Nets-within-nets can be found also in the paper *Providing an Agent Flavored Integration for Workflow Management* by Thomas Wagner, José Quenum, Daniel Moldt, and Christine Reese. It discusses the introduction of software agents, and their related concepts, into workflow management. Petri net based technologies are used to achieve a common basis for the integration and combination of workflow and agent technologies. The paper by Juan-Pablo López-Grao and José-Manuel Colom, *A Petri Net Perspective on the Resource Allocation Problem in Software Engineering*, starts from the observation that classical approaches to resource allocation analysis, as for flexible manufacturing systems, cannot naturally extend to software engineering, since the concept of resource is different (resource may be services that may be created or destroyed by the processes). The paper proposes therefore a generalization of the classical Resource Allocation Systems (RAS) classes, the usefulness of which is shown through the identification of a taxonomy of anomalies that can be found in the context of software systems.

As guest editors, we would like to thank all authors and referees who have contributed to this issue: not only is the quality of this volume the result of the high scientific value of their work, but we would also like to acknowledge the excellent cooperation throughout the whole process that has made our work a pleasant task. Finally, we would like to pay special tribute to the work of Lars Madsen of Aarhus University who has provided technical support for the composition of this volume, including interactions with the authors. We are also grateful to the Springer/ToPNoC team for the final production of this issue.

November 2011

Susanna Donatelli
Jetty Kleijn
Guest Editors, Fifth Issue of ToPNoC

Organization

Guest Editors

Susanna Donatelli, Italy
Jetty Kleijn, The Netherlands

Co-chairs of the Workshops

Natalia Sidorova (The Netherlands)
Alexander Serebrenik (The Netherlands)
Jörg Desel (Germany)
Alex Yakovlev (UK)
Claudine Chaouiya (Portugal)
Monika Heiner (Germany)
Michael Duvigneau (Germany)
Daniel Moldt (Germany)
Didier Buchs (Switzerland)
Fabrice Kordon (France)
Yann Thierry-Mieg (France)
Jeremy Sproston (Italy)

Referees

Wil van der Aalst
David Angeli
Eric Badouel
Marco Beccuti
Béatrice Bérard
Robin Bergenthum
Luca Bernardinello
Liu Bing
Josep Carmona
Ivana Cerna
Piotr Chrząstowski-Wachtel
Philippe Darondeau
Erik Flick
Giuliana Franceschinis
Serge Haddad
Xudong He
Kees van Hee

Vladimir Janousek
Peter Kemper
Victor Khomenko
Alex Kondratyev
Maciej Koutny
Lars Kristensen
Sebastian Mauser
Daniel Moldt
Marta Pietkiewicz-Koutny
Oana Prisecaru
Wolfgang Reisig
Charlotte Seidner
Natalia Sidorova
Jeremy Sproston
Enrico Vicario
Jan Martijn van der Werf
Mengchu Zhou

Table of Contents

Cycle Structure in SR and DSR Graphs: Implications for Multiple Equilibria and Stable Oscillation in Chemical Reaction Networks

Murad Banaji

Department of Mathematics, University of Portsmouth, Lion Gate Building, Lion Terrace, Portsmouth, Hampshire PO1 3HF, UK

Abstract. Associated with a chemical reaction network is a natural labelled bipartite multigraph termed an SR graph, and its directed version, the DSR graph. These objects are closely related to Petri nets, but encode weak assumptions on the reaction kinetics, and are more generally associated with continuous-time, continuous-state models rather than discrete-event systems. The construction of SR and DSR graphs for chemical reaction networks is presented. Conclusions about asymptotic behaviour of the associated dynamical systems which can be drawn easily from the graphs are discussed. In particular, theorems on ruling out the possibility of multiple equilibria or stable oscillation based on computations on SR/DSR graphs are presented. These include both published and new results. The power and limitations of such results are illustrated via several examples.

1 Chemical Reaction Networks: Structure and Kinetics

Models of chemical reaction networks (CRNs) are able to display a rich variety of dynamical behaviours [1]. In this paper, a spatially homogeneous setting is assumed, and the state of a CRN is defined to be the set of concentrations of the reactants involved, each a nonnegative real number. In addition, continuous-time models are treated, so that CRNs involving n chemicals give rise to local semiflows on $\mathbb{R}^n_{\geq 0}$, the nonnegative orthant in $\mathbb{R}^n$. These local semiflows are fully determined if we know 1) the CRN *structure*, that is, which chemicals react with each other and in what proportions, and 2) the CRN *kinetics*, that is, how the reaction rates depend on the chemical concentrations. An important question is which CRN behaviours are determined primarily by reaction network structure, with limited assumptions about the kinetics.

As will be seen below, a variety of representations of CRN structure are possible, for example via matrices or generalised graphs. Some of these representations encode weak assumptions on the reaction kinetics. Of these, a signed, labelled, bipartite multigraph, termed an **SR graph**[1], and its directed version,

---

[1] The term derives from "species-reaction graph" [2]. However, while CRNs provided the original motivation for their construction, such graphs have since proved useful in more general contexts. The construction here follows [3].

K. Jensen, S. Donatelli, and J. Kleijn (Eds.): ToPNoC V, LNCS 6900, pp. 1–21, 2012.

the **DSR graph**, are formally similar to Petri net (PN) graphs. Examples of the PN graphs associated with a single chemical reaction, and the corresponding SR/DSR graphs, are presented in Figure 1. Formal constructions and more detailed comparisons will be presented in Section 3.

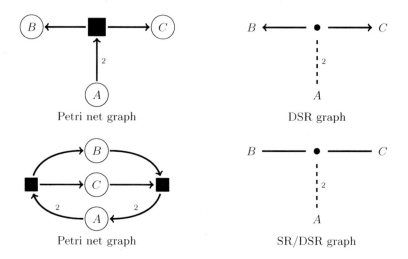

Fig. 1. *Top.* The PN graph (*left*) and DSR graph (*right*) for the irreversible reaction $2A \rightarrow B + C$. *Bottom.* The PN graph (*left*) and DSR graph (*right*) for the reversible reaction $2A \rightleftharpoons B + C$. The DSR graph in this case is undirected, and hence also the SR graph of the system. In all cases, labelled vertices correspond to reactants (or "places" in the PN terminology), while unlabelled vertices correspond to reactions (or "transitions"). Note that the SR/DSR graphs are constructed under weak assumptions on the kinetics, and actually encode information not on the flow of mass, but on the structures of influence in the system. These points are elaborated on in Section 3.

It is now well established that graphical representations can tell us a great deal about asymptotic behaviours in the associated dynamical systems. Pioneering early work on CRNs with mass-action kinetics ([4,5] for example), had a graph-theoretic component (using graphs somewhat different from those to be presented here). More recently, graph-theoretic approaches have been used to draw conclusions about multistationarity and oscillation in CRNs with restricted classes of kinetics [2,6].

The applicability of such work, particularly in biological contexts, is greatly increased if only weak assumptions are made about kinetics. Consequently, there is a growing body of recent work on CRNs with essentially arbitrary kinetics. It has been shown that examination of PNs associated with a CRN allows conclusions about persistence, that is, whether ω-limit sets of interior points of $\mathbb{R}_{\geq 0}^n$ can intersect the boundary of $\mathbb{R}_{\geq 0}^n$ [7]. Work on multistationarity has been extended beyond the mass-action setting [3,8]: some conclusions of this work will be outlined below. Finally, recent work applying the theory of monotone dynamical systems [9,10] in innovative ways to CRNs [11] has close links with some of the new material presented below.

Outline. After some preliminaries, the construction of SR and DSR graphs is presented, and their relationship to PNs is discussed. Some recent results about multistationarity based on cycle structure in these objects are described. Subsequently, a new result on monotonicity in CRNs is proved. This result, Proposition 4, is a graph-theoretic corollary of results in [12]. It bears an interesting relationship to results in [11], which provide stronger conclusions about convergence, but make different assumptions, and a somewhat different claim. Finally, several examples, some raising interesting open questions, are presented. At various points, in order to simplify the exposition, the results are presented in less generality than possible, with more technical results being referenced.

2 Preliminaries

2.1 A Motivating Example

Consider the following simple family of CRNs treated in [13,14]:

$$
\begin{array}{llll}
\textbf{SYS } 1 & \textbf{SYS } 2 & \cdots & \textbf{SYS } n \\
\boxed{\begin{aligned}
A_1 + A_2 &\rightleftharpoons B_1 \\
A_2 + A_3 &\rightleftharpoons B_2 \\
A_3 &\rightleftharpoons 2A_1
\end{aligned}} &
\boxed{\begin{aligned}
A_1 + A_2 &\rightleftharpoons B_1 \\
A_2 + A_3 &\rightleftharpoons B_2 \\
A_3 + A_4 &\rightleftharpoons B_3 \\
A_4 &\rightleftharpoons 2A_1
\end{aligned}} & \cdots &
\boxed{\begin{aligned}
A_i + A_{i+1} &\rightleftharpoons B_i, \\
i &= 1,\ldots,n+1 \\
A_{n+2} &\rightleftharpoons 2A_1
\end{aligned}}
\end{array} \tag{1}
$$

The reader may wish to look ahead to Figure 3 to see representations of the SR graphs associated with the first three CRNs in this family. This family will be revisited in Section 6, and the theory to be presented will imply the following conclusions (to be made precise below): when n is even, **SYS** n does not allow multiple positive nondegenerate equilibria; when n is odd, **SYS** n cannot have a nontrivial periodic attractor. Both conclusions require only minimal assumptions about the kinetics.

2.2 Dynamical Systems Associated with CRNs

In a continuous-time spatially homogeneous setting, a chemical reaction system in which n reactants participate in m reactions has dynamics governed by the ordinary differential equation

$$\dot{x} = \Gamma v(x). \tag{2}$$

$x = [x_1,\ldots,x_n]^T$ is the nonnegative vector of reactant concentrations, and $v = [v_1,\ldots,v_m]^T$ is the vector of reaction rates, assumed to be C^1. Here, a reaction rate is defined to be the rate at which a reaction proceeds *to the right* and may take any real value. Γ is the (constant) $n \times m$ **stoichiometric matrix** of the reaction system. Since reactant concentrations cannot be negative, it is always reasonable to assume invariance of $\mathbb{R}_{\geq 0}^n$, i.e. $x_i = 0 \Rightarrow \dot{x}_i \geq 0$.

The jth column of Γ, termed Γ_j, is the **reaction vector** for the jth reaction, and a stoichiometric matrix is defined only up to an arbitrary signing of its columns. In other words, given any $m \times m$ signature matrix D (i.e. any diagonal matrix with diagonal entries ± 1), one could replace Γ with ΓD and $v(x)$ with $Dv(x)$. This amounts to a redefinition of the "left" and "right" of a reaction, but the resulting dynamical system is left unchanged. The subspace $\text{Im}(\Gamma)$ of $\mathbb{R}^n$ spanned by the reaction vectors is called the **stoichiometric subspace**. The intersection of any coset of $\text{Im}(\Gamma)$ with $\mathbb{R}_{\geq 0}^n$ is called a **stoichiometry class**.

Two generalisations of (2) which include explicit inflow and outflow of substrates are worth considering. The first of these is studied in the chemical engineering context of a continuous flow stirred tank reactor (or CFSTR)

$$\dot{x} = q(x_{in} - x) + \Gamma v(x). \tag{3}$$

$q \in \mathbb{R}$, the flow rate, is generally assumed to be positive, but we allow $q = 0$ so that (2) becomes a special case of (3). $x_{in} \in \mathbb{R}_{\geq 0}^n$ is a constant nonnegative vector representing the "feed" (i.e., inflow) concentrations. The second class of systems is:

$$\dot{x} = x_{in} + \Gamma v(x) - Q(x). \tag{4}$$

Here $Q(x) = [q_1(x_1), \ldots, q_n(x_n)]^T$, with each $q_i(x_i)$ assumed to be a C^1 function satisfying $\frac{\partial q_i}{\partial x_i} > 0$, and all other quantities defined as before. Systems (4) include systems (3) with $q \neq 0$, while systems (2) lie in the closure of systems (4).

Define the $m \times n$ matrix $V = [V_{ji}]$ where $V_{ji} = \frac{\partial v_j}{\partial x_i}$. A very reasonable, but weak, assumption about many reaction systems is that reaction rates are monotonic functions of substrate concentrations as assumed in [14,15,16] for example. We use the following definition [3]:

A reaction system is **N1C** if i) $\Gamma_{ij}V_{ji} \leq 0$ for all i and j, and ii) $\Gamma_{ij} = 0 \Rightarrow V_{ji} = 0$.

Reactions satisfying this condition were originally termed "nonautocatalytic", in [14]. As discussed there, the relationship between signs of entries in Γ and V encoded in the N1C criterion is fulfilled by all reasonable reaction kinetics (including mass action and Michaelis-Menten kinetics for example), provided that reactants never occur on both sides of a reaction.

3   SR and DSR Graphs

3.1   Construction and Relation to Petri Nets

SR graphs are signed, bipartite multigraphs with two vertex sets V_S (termed "S-vertices") and V_R (termed "R-vertices"). The edges E form a multiset, consisting of unordered pairs of vertices, one from V_S and one from V_R. Each edge is signed and labelled either with a positive real number or the formal label ∞. In other words, there are functions sgn : $E \to \{-1, 1\}$, and lbl : $E \to (0, \infty) \cup \{\infty\}$. The quintuple $(V_S, V_R, E, \text{sgn}, \text{lbl})$ defines an SR graph.

DSR graphs are similar, but have an additional "orientation function" on their edges, $\mathcal{O} : E \to \{-1, 0, 1\}$. The sextuple $(V_S, V_R, E, \text{sgn}, \text{lbl}, \mathcal{O})$ defines a DSR graph. If $\mathcal{O}(e) = -1$ we will say that the edge e has "S-to-R direction", if $\mathcal{O}(e) = 1$, then e has "R-to-S direction", and if $\mathcal{O}(e) = 0$, then e is "undirected". An undirected edge can be regarded as an edge with both S-to-R and R-to-S direction, and indeed, several results below are unchanged if an undirected edge is treated as a pair of antiparallel edges of the same sign. SR graphs can be regarded as the subset of DSR graphs where all edges are undirected.

Both the underlying meanings, and the formal structures, of PNs and SR/DSR graphs have some similarity. If we replace each undirected edge in a DSR graph with a pair of antiparallel edges, a DSR graph is simply a PN graph, i.e. a bipartite, multidigraph (albeit with some additional structures). Similarly, an SR graph is a bipartite multigraph. S-vertices correspond to variables, while R-vertices correspond to processes which govern their interaction. The notions of variable and process are similar to the notions of "place" and "transition" for a PN. Edges in SR/DSR graphs tell us which variables participate in each process, with additional qualitative information on the nature of this participation in the form of signs, labels, and directions; edges in PNs inform on which objects are changed by a transition, again with additional information in the form of labels (multiplicities) and directions. Thus both PN graphs and SR/DSR graphs encode partial information about associated dynamical systems, while neither includes an explicit notion of time.

There are some important differences, however. Where SR/DSR graphs generally represent the structures of continuous-state, continuous-time dynamical systems, PNs most often correspond to discrete-state, discrete-time systems, although the translation to a continuous-state and even continuous-time context is possible [17]. Although in both cases additional structures give partial information about these dynamical systems, there are differences of meaning and emphasis. Signs on edges in a DSR graph, crucial to much of the associated theory, generally correspond to directions on edges in a PN, in that it is signs in DSR graphs which provide information on which substrates occur on the same side of a chemical reaction. For example, in an irreversible chemical reaction an arc from a substrate to reaction vertex in the PN would correspond to a negative, undirected, edge in the SR/DSR graph (assuming the substrates were chosen to be on the left and the products on the right).

Apart from formal variations between PNs and SR/DSR graphs, differences in the notions of state and time lead naturally to differences in the questions asked. Most current work using SR/DSR graphs aims to inform on the existence, nature, and stability of limit sets of the associated local semiflows. Analogous questions are certainly possible with PNs, for example questions about the existence of stationary probability distributions for stochastic PNs [18]. However, much study, for example about reachability, safeness and boundedness, concerns the structure of the state space itself, and has no obvious analogy in the SR/DSR case. In the discrete state case, the state space itself is a directed graph, and questions regarding its finiteness, connectedness, etc. are nontrivial. This explains why markings (i.e., vertex-labellings representing the current state) are important in the study of discrete-state systems. On the other hand, in the case of SR/DSR graphs, the state space is a closed connected subset of Euclidean space, and the aim is to draw conclusions which are largely independent of initial conditions, except perhaps on the boundary, where the graphs themselves may change structure.

It is interesting that despite the formal differences between the discrete-state, discrete-event and continuous-state, continuous-time approaches to CRN dynamics, some questions find similar answers. Both such points of convergence, and the difficulties in extending results between different formalisms, are discussed in the conclusions.

3.2   SR and DSR Graphs Associated with CRNs

SR and DSR graphs can be associated with arbitrary CRNs and more general dynamical systems [3,8]. For example, the construction extends to situations where there are modulators of reactions which do not themselves participate in reactions, and where substrates occur on both sides of a reaction. Here, to avoid an excessively technical discussion, the construction is presented for an N1C reaction system[2]. Assume that there is a set of substrates $V_S = \{S_1, \ldots, S_n\}$, having concentrations $x_1, \ldots, x_n$, and reactions $V_R = \{R_1, \ldots, R_m\}$ occurring at rates $v_1, \ldots, v_m$, and that the system has $n \times m$ stoichiometric matrix Γ. The labels in V_S and V_R will be used to refer both to the substrate/reaction, and the associated substrate/reaction vertices.

- If $\Gamma_{ij} \neq 0$ (i.e. there is net production or consumption of S_i in reaction j), and also $\frac{\partial v_j}{\partial x_i}$ is not identically zero, i.e. the concentration of substrate i affects the rate of reaction j, then there is an undirected edge $\{S_i, R_j\}$.
- If $\Gamma_{ij} \neq 0$, but $\frac{\partial v_j}{\partial x_i} \equiv 0$, then the edge $\{S_i, R_j\}$ has only R-to-S direction.

The edge $\{S_i, R_j\}$ has the sign of Γ_{ij} and label $|\Gamma_{ij}|$. Thus the labels on edges are just stoichiometries, while the signs on edges encode information on which substrates occur together on each side of a reaction. A more complete discussion of the meanings of edge-signs in terms of "activation" and "inhibition" is presented in [8]. Note that in the context of N1C reaction systems, the following features (which are reasonably common in the more general setting) do not occur: edges with only R-to-S direction; multiple edges between a vertex pair; and edges with edge-label ∞.

SR/DSR graphs can be uniquely associated with (2), (3), or (4): in the case of (3) and (4), the inflows and outflows are ignored, and the SR/DSR graph is

---

[2] The construction can be regarded either as of the DSR graph at an interior point of the state space, or as the superposition of all DSR graphs throughout state space. The two are equivalent since the DSR graph at a point on the boundary is always a subgraph of that in the interior.

just that derived from the associated system (2). The construction is most easily seen via an example. Consider, first, the simple system of two reactions:

$$A + B \rightleftharpoons C, \qquad A \rightleftharpoons B. \tag{5}$$

This has SR graph, shown in Figure 2, *left*. If all substrates affect the rates of reactions in which they participate then this is also the DSR graph for the reaction. If, now, the second reaction is irreversible, i.e. one can write

$$A + B \rightleftharpoons C, \qquad A \rightarrow B, \tag{6}$$

and consequently the concentration of B does not affect the rate of the second reaction[3], then the SR graph remains the same, losing information about irreversibility, but the DSR graph now appears as in Figure 2 *right*.

Fig. 2. *Left.* The SR (and DSR graph) for reaction system (5). Negative edges are depicted as dashed lines, while positive edges are bold lines. Unlabelled edges have edge-label 1. These conventions will be followed throughout. *Right.* The DSR graph for reaction system (6), that is, when B is assumed not to affect the rate of the second reaction.

3.3   Paths and Cycles in SR and DSR Graphs

In the usual way, **cycles** in SR (DSR) graphs are minimal undirected (directed) paths from some vertex to itself. All paths have a sign, defined as the product of signs of edges in the path. Given any subgraph E, its size (or length, if it is a path) $|E|$ is the number of edges in E. Paths of length two will be called **short paths**. Any edge-set E of even size also has a **parity**

$$P(E) = (-1)^{|E|/2}\text{sign}(E).$$

Given two disjoint, even-sized edge-sets E_1 and E_2, it is immediate that $P(E_1 \cup E_2) = P(E_1)P(E_2)$. A cycle C is an **e-cycle** if $P(C) = 1$, and an **o-cycle** otherwise. Given a cycle C containing edges $e_1, e_2, \ldots, e_{2r}$ such that e_i and $e_{(i \bmod 2r)+1}$ are adjacent for each $i = 1, \ldots, 2r$, define:

$$\text{stoich}(C) = \left| \prod_{i=1}^{r} \text{lbl}(e_{2i-1}) - \prod_{i=1}^{r} \text{lbl}(e_{2i}) \right|.$$

---

[3] Note that this is usually, but not always, implied by irreversibility: it is possible for the product of an irreversible reaction to influence a reaction rate.

Note that this definition is independent of the starting point chosen on the cycle. A cycle with stoich(C) = 0 is termed an **s-cycle**.

An **S-to-R path** in an SR graph is a non-self-intersecting path between an S-vertex and an R-vertex. **R-to-R paths** and **S-to-S paths** are similarly defined, though in these cases the initial and terminal vertices may coincide. Any cycle is both an R-to-R path and an S-to-S path. Two cycles have **S-to-R intersection** if each component of their intersection is an S-to-R path. This definition can be generalised to DSR graphs in a natural way, but to avoid technicalities regarding cycle orientation, the reader is referred to [8] for the details. Further notation will be presented as needed.

Returning to the family of CRNs in (1), these give SR graphs shown in Figure 3. If all reactants can influence the rates of reactions in which they participate, then these are also their DSR graphs (otherwise some edges may become directed). Each SR graph contains a single cycle, which is an e-cycle (resp. o-cycle) if n is odd (resp. even). These cycles all fail to be s-cycles because of the unique edge-label of 2. Conclusions which follow immediately from these observations will be presented in Section 6.

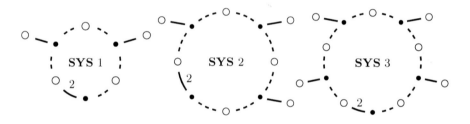

Fig. 3. The structure of the SR graphs for **SYS** 1, 2 and 3 in (1). For simplicity vertices are unlabelled, but filled circles are S-vertices while open circles are R-vertices.

4   Existing Results on CRNs, Injectivity and Monotonicity

4.1   Injectivity and Multiple Equilibria

A function $f : X \to \mathbb{R}^n$ is **injective** if for any $x, y \in X$, $f(x) = f(y)$ implies $x = y$. Injectivity of a vector field on some domain is sufficient to guarantee that there can be no more than one equilibrium on this domain. Define the following easily computable condition on an SR or DSR graph:

Condition (∗): All e-cycles are s-cycles, and no two e-cycles have S-to-R intersection.

Note that if an SR/DSR graph has no e-cycles, then Condition (∗) is trivially fulfilled. A key result in [3] was:

Proposition 1. *An N1C reaction system of the form (4) with SR graph satisfying Condition (∗) is injective.*

Proof. See Theorem 1 in [3].

In [8] this result was strengthened considerably and extended beyond CRNs. In the context of CRNs with N1C kinetics it specialises to:

Proposition 2. *An N1C reaction system of the form (4) with DSR graph satisfying Condition (∗) is injective.*

Proof. See Corollary 4.2 in [8].

Proposition 2 is stronger than Proposition 1 because irreversibility is taken into account. In the case without outflows (2), attention must be restricted to some fixed stoichiometric class. The results then state that no stoichiometry class can contain more than one nondegenerate equilibrium in the interior of the positive orthant [8,19]. (In this context, a degenerate equilibrium is defined to be an equilibrium with a zero eigenvalue and corresponding eigenvector lying in the stoichiometric subspace.) The case with partial outflows was also treated.

4.2 Monotonicity

A closed, convex, solid, pointed cone $K \subset \mathbb{R}^n$ is termed a **proper cone** [20]. The reader is referred to [20] for basic definitions related to cones. Any proper cone defines a partial order on $\mathbb{R}^n$ as follows: given two points $x, y \in \mathbb{R}^n$:

1. $x \geq y \Leftrightarrow x - y \in K$;
2. $x > y \Leftrightarrow x \geq y$ and $x \neq y$;
3. $x \gg y \Leftrightarrow x - y \in \text{int}\, K$.

An extremal ray is a one dimensional face of a cone. A proper cone with exactly n extremal rays is termed **simplicial**. Simplicial cones have the feature that unit vectors on the extremal rays can be chosen as basis vectors for a new coordinate system. Consider some linear subspace $\mathcal{A} \subseteq \mathbb{R}^n$. Then any closed, convex, pointed cone $K \subset \mathcal{A}$ with nonempty relative interior in $\mathcal{A}$ is termed $\mathcal{A}$-proper. If, further, K has exactly $\dim(\mathcal{A})$ extremal rays, then K is termed $\mathcal{A}$-simplicial.

Consider some local semiflow ϕ defined on $X \subseteq \mathbb{R}^n$. Assume that there is some linear subspace $\mathcal{A} \subseteq \mathbb{R}^n$ with a coset $\mathcal{A}'$ with nonempty intersection with X, and such that ϕ leaves $\mathcal{A}' \cap X$ invariant. Suppose further that there is an $\mathcal{A}$-proper cone K such that for all $x, y \in \mathcal{A}' \cap X$, $x > y \Rightarrow \phi_t(x) > \phi_t(y)$ for all values of $t \geq 0$ such that $\phi_t(x)$ and $\phi_t(y)$ are defined. Then we say that $\phi|_{\mathcal{A}' \cap X}$ **preserves** K, and that $\phi|_{\mathcal{A}' \cap X}$ is **monotone**. If, further, $x > y \Rightarrow \phi_t(x) \gg \phi_t(y)$ for all values of $t > 0$ such that $\phi_t(x)$ and $\phi_t(y)$ are defined, then $\phi|_{\mathcal{A}' \cap X}$ is **strongly monotone**. A local semiflow is monotone with respect to the nonnegative orthant if and only if the Jacobian of the vector field has nonnegative off-diagonal elements, in which case the vector field is termed **cooperative**.

Returning to (3), in the case $q = 0$, all stoichiometry classes are invariant, while if $q > 0$, there is a globally attracting stoichiometry class. Conditions for monotonicity of ϕ restricted to invariant subspaces of $\mathbb{R}^n$ were discussed extensively in [12]. Here the immediate aim is to develop graph-theoretic corollaries of one of these results, and to raise some interesting open questions.

Given a vector $y \in \mathbb{R}^n$, define

$$\mathcal{Q}_1(y) \equiv \{v \in \mathbb{R}^n \mid v_i y_i \geq 0\}.$$

A matrix Γ is **R-sorted** (resp. **S-sorted**) if any two distinct columns (resp. rows) Γ_i and Γ_j of Γ satisfy $\Gamma_i \in \mathcal{Q}_1(-\Gamma_j)$. A matrix Γ' is **R-sortable** (resp. **S-sortable**) if there exists a signature matrix D such that $\Gamma \equiv \Gamma' D$ (resp. $\Gamma \equiv D\Gamma'$) is R-sorted (resp. S-sorted).

Proposition 3. *Consider a system of N1C reactions of the form (3) whose stoichiometric matrix Γ is R-sortable, and whose reaction vectors $\{\Gamma_k\}$ are linearly independent. Let $\mathcal{S} = \mathrm{Im}(\Gamma)$. Then there is an $\mathcal{S}$-simplicial cone K preserved by the system restricted to any invariant stoichiometry class, such that each reaction vector is collinear with an extremal ray of K.*

Proof. This is a specialisation of Corollary A7 in [12]. $\square$

Systems fulfilling the assumptions of Proposition 3, cannot have periodic orbits intersecting the interior of the positive orthant which are stable on their stoichiometry class. In fact, mild additional assumptions ensure strong monotonicity guaranteeing generic convergence of bounded trajectories to equilibria [9,10].

5   Graph-Theoretic Implications of Proposition 3

Some more notation is needed for the results to follow. The **S-degree** (**R-degree**) of an SR graph G is the maximum degree of its S-vertices (R-vertices). Analogous to the terminology for matrices, a subgraph E is **R-sorted** (**S-sorted**) if each R-to-R (S-to-S) path E_k in E satisfies $P(E_k) = 1$. Note that E is R-sorted if and only if each R-to-R path E_k of length 2 in E satisfies $P(E_k) = 1$.

An **R-flip** on a SR/DSR graph G is an operation which changes the signs on all edges incident on some R-vertex in G. (This is equivalent to exchanging left and right for the chemical reaction associated with the R-vertex). An **R-resigning** is a sequence of R-flips. An **S-flip** and **S-resigning** can be defined similarly. Given a set of R-vertices $\{R_k\}$ in G, the closed neighbourhood of $\{R_k\}$ will be denoted $G_{\{R_k\}}$, i.e., $G_{\{R_k\}}$ is the subgraph consisting of $\{R_k\}$ along with all edges incident on vertices of $\{R_k\}$, and all S-vertices adjacent to those in $\{R_k\}$.

Proposition 4. *Consider a system of N1C reactions of the form (3) with stoichiometric matrix Γ, and whose reaction vectors $\{\Gamma_k\}$ are linearly independent. Define $\mathcal{S} = \mathrm{Im}(\Gamma)$. Associate with the system the SR graph G. Suppose that*

1. *G has S-degree ≤ 2.*
2. *All cycles in G are e-cycles.*

Then there is an S-simplicial cone K preserved by the system restricted to any invariant stoichiometry class, such that each reaction vector is collinear with an extremal ray of K.

The key idea of the proof is simple: if the system satisfies the conditions of Proposition 4, then the conditions of Proposition 3 are also met. In this case, the extremal vectors of the cone K define a local coordinate system on each stoichiometry class, such that the (restricted) system is cooperative in this coordinate system. This interpretation in terms of recoordinatisation is best illustrated with an example.

Consider **SYS** 1 from (1) with SR graph shown in Figure 3 *left*, which can easily be confirmed to satisfy the conditions of Proposition 4. Define the following matrices:

$$\Gamma = \begin{pmatrix} -1 & 0 & 2 \\ -1 & -1 & 0 \\ 0 & -1 & -1 \\ 1 & 0 & 0 \\ 0 & 1 & 0 \end{pmatrix}, \quad T = \begin{pmatrix} -1 & 0 & 2 \\ -1 & 1 & 0 \\ 0 & 1 & -1 \\ 1 & 0 & 0 \\ 0 & -1 & 0 \end{pmatrix}, \quad T' = \begin{pmatrix} 1 & -2 & 2 & 0 & 0 \\ 1 & -1 & 2 & 0 & 0 \\ 1 & -1 & 1 & 0 & 0 \end{pmatrix}$$

Γ, the stoichiometric matrix, has rank 3, and so Proposition 4 applies. Let $x_1, \ldots, x_5$ be the concentrations of the five substrates involved, v_1, v_2, v_3 be the rates of the three reactions, and $v_{ij} \equiv \frac{\partial v_i}{\partial x_j}$. Assuming that the system is N1C means that $V \equiv [v_{ij}]$ has sign structure

$$\text{sgn}(V) = \begin{pmatrix} + & + & 0 & - & 0 \\ 0 & + & + & 0 & - \\ - & 0 & + & 0 & 0 \end{pmatrix}$$

where $+$ denotes a nonnegative quantity, and $-$ denotes a nonpositive quantity. Consider now any coordinates y satisfying $x = Ty$. Note that T is a re-signed version of Γ and $\text{Im}(T) = \text{Im}(\Gamma)$. Choosing some left inverse for T, say T', gives $y_1 = x_1 - 2x_2 + 2x_3$, $y_2 = x_1 - x_2 + 2x_3$ and $y_3 = x_1 - x_2 + x_3$. (The choice of T' is not unique, but this does not affect the argument.) Calculation gives that $J = T'\Gamma V T$ has sign structure

$$\text{sgn}(J) = \begin{pmatrix} - & + & + \\ + & - & + \\ + & + & - \end{pmatrix},$$

i.e., restricting to any invariant stoichiometry class, the dynamical system for the evolution of the quantities y_1, y_2, y_3 is cooperative. Further, the evolution of $\{x_i\}$ is uniquely determined by the evolution of $\{y_i\}$ via the equation $x = Ty$.

It is time to return to the steps leading to the proof of Proposition 4. In Lemmas 1 and 2 below, G is an SR graph with S-degree ≤ 2. This implies the following: consider R-vertices v, v' and v'' such that $v \neq v'$ and $v \neq v''$ ($v' = v''$ is possible). Assume there exist two distinct short paths in G, one from v to v' and one from v to v''. These paths must be edge disjoint, for otherwise there must be an S-vertex lying on both A and B, and hence having degree ≥ 3.

Lemma 1. *Suppose G is a connected SR graph with S-degree ≤ 2, and has some connected, R-sorted, subgraph E containing R-vertices v' and v''. Assume that there is a path C_1 of length 4 between v' and v'' containing an R-vertex not in E. Then either C_1 is even or G contains an o-cycle.*

Proof. If $v' = v''$ and C_1 is not even then it is itself an o-cycle. Otherwise consider any path C_2 connecting v' and v'' and lying entirely in E. C_2 exists since E is connected, and $P(C_2) = 1$ since E is R-sorted. Since G has S-degree ≤ 2, and $|C_1| = 4$, C_1 and C_2 share only endpoints, v' and v'', and hence together they form a cycle C. If $P(C_1) = -1$, then $P(C) = P(C_2)P(C_1) = -1$, and so C is an o-cycle. □

Lemma 2. *Suppose G is a connected SR graph with S-degree ≤ 2 which does not contain an o-cycle. Then it can be R-sorted.*

Proof. The result is trivial if G contains a single R-vertex, as it contains no short R-to-R paths. Suppose the result is true for graphs containing $k \geq 1$ R-vertices. Then it must be true for graphs containing $k+1$ R-vertices. Suppose G contains $k+1$ R-vertices. Enumerate these R-vertices as $R_1, \ldots, R_{k+1}$ in such a way that $G_- \equiv G_{\{R_1, \ldots, R_k\}}$ is connected. This is possible since G is connected.

By the induction hypothesis, G_- can be R-sorted. Having R-sorted G_-, consider R_{k+1}. If all short paths between R_{k+1} and R-vertices in G_- have the same parity, then either (i) they are all even and G is R-sorted; or (ii) they are all odd, and a single R-flip on R_{k+1} R-sorts G (note that an R-flip on R_{k+1} does not affect the parity of any R-to-R paths in G_-); or (iii) there are two distinct short paths of opposite sign, between R_{k+1} and R-vertices $v', v'' \in G_-$ ($v' = v''$ is possible). Since G has S-degree ≤ 2, these paths must be edge-disjoint, and together form an odd path of length 4 from v' to R_{k+1} to v''. By Lemma 1, G contains an o-cycle. □

PROOF of Proposition 4. From Lemma 2, if no connected component of G contains an o-cycle then each connected component of G (and hence G itself) can be R-sorted. R-sorting G corresponds to choosing a signing of the stoichiometric matrix Γ such that any two columns Γ_i and Γ_j satisfy $\Gamma_i \in \mathcal{Q}_1(-\Gamma_j)$. Thus the conditions of Proposition 3 are satisfied. □

6   Examples Illustrating the Results and Their Limitations

Example 1. The Systems in (1). It is easy to confirm that **SYS** n in (1) has linearly independent reaction vectors for all n. Moreover, as illustrated by

Figure 3, the corresponding SR graphs contain a single cycle, which, for odd (even) n is an e-cycle (o-cycle). Thus for even n, Proposition 1 and subsequent remarks apply, ruling out the possibility of more than one positive nondegenerate equilibrium for (2) on each stoichiometry class, or in the case with outflows (4), ruling out multiple equilibria altogether; meanwhile, for odd n, Proposition 4 can be applied to (2) or (3), implying that restricted to any invariant stoichiometry class the system is monotone, and the restricted dynamical system cannot have an attracting periodic orbit intersecting the interior of the nonnegative orthant.

Example 2. Multistability in Enzyme-Driven Networks. We consider the possibility of bistability in the nine enzyme-driven chemical reaction networks presented in Table 1 of [21]. These nine networks are presented here again in Table 1.

Table 1. The nine chemical reaction networks in Table 1 of [21]

Entry	network	Condition (∗)?
1	$E + S \rightleftharpoons ES \rightarrow E + P$	yes
2	$E + S \rightleftharpoons ES \rightarrow E + P, \; E + I \rightleftharpoons EI$	yes
3	$E + S \rightleftharpoons ES \rightarrow E + P, \; ES + I \rightleftharpoons ESI$	yes
4	$E + S \rightleftharpoons ES \rightarrow E + P$ $E + I \rightleftharpoons EI, \; ES + I \rightleftharpoons ESI \rightleftharpoons EI + S$	no
5	$E + S1 \rightleftharpoons ES1, \; S2 + ES1 \rightleftharpoons ES1S2 \rightarrow E + P$	yes
6	$E + S1 \rightleftharpoons ES1, \; E + S2 \rightleftharpoons ES2,$ $S2 + ES1 \rightleftharpoons ES1S2 \rightleftharpoons S1 + ES2$ $\downarrow$ $E + P$	no
7	$S1 + E1 \rightleftharpoons E1S1, \; S2 + E1S1 \rightleftharpoons E1S1S2 \rightarrow P1 + E1$ $S2 + E2 \rightleftharpoons E2S2 \rightarrow 2S1 + E2$	yes
8	$S1 + E1 \rightleftharpoons E1S1, \; S2 + E1S1 \rightleftharpoons E1S1S2 \rightarrow P1 + E1$ $S2 + E2 \rightleftharpoons E2S2, \; S3 + E2S2 \rightleftharpoons E2S2S3 \rightarrow P2 + E2$ $S3 + E3 \rightleftharpoons E3S3 \rightarrow 2S1 + E3$	no
9	$S1 + E1 \rightleftharpoons E1S1, \; S2 + E1S1 \rightleftharpoons E1S1S2 \rightarrow P1 + E1$ $S2 + E2 \rightleftharpoons E2S2, \; S3 + E2S2 \rightleftharpoons E2S2S3 \rightarrow P2 + E2$ $S3 + E3 \rightleftharpoons E3S3, \; S4 + E3S3 \rightleftharpoons E3S3S4 \rightarrow P3 + E3$ $S4 + E4 \rightleftharpoons E4S4 \rightarrow 2S1 + E4$	yes

It is shown in [21] that, given mass-action kinetics, networks 1,2,3,5,7, and 9 cannot have multiple positive nondegenerate equilibria, while networks 4, 6 and 8 can. Assuming N1C kinetics, the DSR graph for the most complex of these networks, network 9, is shown in Figure 4. For reasons of space the remaining

DSR graphs are not all presented. However, it is easy to confirm that those associated with networks 1,2,3,5,7, and 9 fulfil Condition (∗). Thus, by Proposition 2 and subsequent remarks, these networks cannot exhibit multiple positive nondegenerate equilibria for arbitrary N1C kinetics (including, of course, mass-action kinetics). On the other hand, the remaining three networks violate Condition (∗): networks 4 and 6 have e-cycles with S-to-R intersection, while network 8 has an e-cycle which fails to be an s-cycle. Thus multiple nondegenerate equilibria cannot be ruled out, and indeed, particular rate constants where bistability occurs are provided in [21].

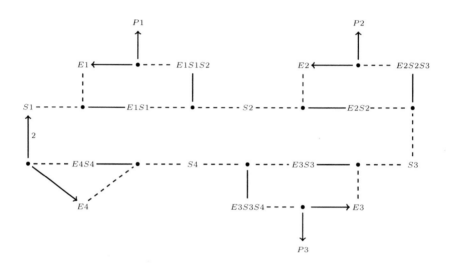

Fig. 4. The DSR graph for network 9 in Table 1. The central cycle comprising 16 edges is an o-cycle, while the remaining cycles are e-cycles which are also s-cycles. There are no intersections between e-cycles, and Condition (∗) holds.

Example 3. Direct Application of Proposition 4. Networks 1 and 5 in Table 1 have stoichiometric matrices which can be written

$$
\begin{pmatrix} -1 & 1 \\ -1 & 0 \\ 1 & -1 \\ 0 & 1 \end{pmatrix} \quad \text{and} \quad \begin{pmatrix} -1 & 0 & 1 \\ -1 & 0 & 0 \\ 1 & -1 & 0 \\ 0 & -1 & 0 \\ 0 & 1 & -1 \\ 0 & 0 & 1 \end{pmatrix}
$$

respectively. It is easy to confirm that both networks satisfy the conditions of Proposition 4, and thus the dynamics on any stoichiometry class is monotone. We remark that network 7 in Table 1 has linearly independent reaction vectors, and SR graph with S-degree ≤ 2. However its SR graph includes an o-cycle, and Proposition 4 does not directly apply.

Example 4. Generalised Interconversion Networks. Consider the following system of chemical reactions:

$$A \rightleftharpoons B, \quad A \rightleftharpoons C, \quad A \rightleftharpoons D, \quad B \rightleftharpoons C \tag{7}$$

with SR graph shown in Figure 5. Formally, such systems have R-degree ≤ 2 and have SR graphs which are S-sorted. Although Proposition 4 cannot be applied, such "interconversion networks", with the N1C assumption, in fact give rise to cooperative dynamical systems [12], and a variety of different techniques give strong convergence results, both with and without outflows [16,11,22].

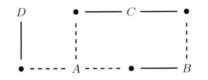

Fig. 5. The SR graph for reaction system (7). The system preserves the nonnegative orthant.

This example highlights that there is an immediate dual to Lemma 2, and hence Proposition 4. The following lemma can be regarded as a restatement of well-known results on systems preserving orthant cones (see [10], for example, and the discussion for CRNs in [11]). Its proof is omitted as it follows closely that of Lemma 2.

Lemma 3. *Let G be an SR graph with R-degree ≤ 2 and containing no o-cycles. Then, via an S-resigning, G can be S-sorted.*

Although the S-sorting process is formally similar to the R-sorting one, the interpretation of the result is quite different: changing the sign of the ith row of Γ and the ith column of V is equivalent to a recoordinatisation replacing concentration x_i with $-x_i$. Such recoordinatisations give rise to a cooperative system if and only if the original system is monotone with respect to an orthant cone.

Example 5a. Linearly Independent Reaction Vectors Are Not Necessary for Monotonicity. Consider the following motif describing, for example, phosphorylation-dephosphorylation reactions (see [11], Eq. 16):

$$\begin{aligned} S_1 + E \rightleftharpoons ES_1 \rightarrow S_2 + E \\ S_2 + F \rightleftharpoons FS_2 \rightarrow S_1 + F \end{aligned} \tag{8}$$

The stoichiometric matrix Γ and SR graph are shown in Figure 6.

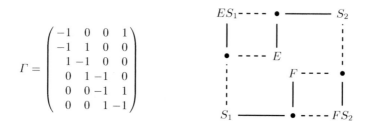

$$\Gamma = \begin{pmatrix} -1 & 0 & 0 & 1 \\ -1 & 1 & 0 & 0 \\ 1 & -1 & 0 & 0 \\ 0 & 1 & -1 & 0 \\ 0 & 0 & -1 & 1 \\ 0 & 0 & 1 & -1 \end{pmatrix}$$

Fig. 6. The stoichiometric matrix and SR graph for reaction system (8)

Note that $\ker(\Gamma)$ is not empty as it contains the vector $(1,1,1,1)^T$; in fact Γ has rank 3. Now, choose new coordinates y satisfying $x = Ty$, where

$$T = \begin{pmatrix} -1 & 0 & 0 & 0 \\ 0 & 1 & 0 & 0 \\ 0 & -1 & 0 & 0 \\ 0 & 0 & -1 & 0 \\ 0 & 0 & 0 & 1 \\ 0 & 0 & 0 & -1 \end{pmatrix} .$$

Note: i) T has rank 4, ii) $\mathrm{Im}(\Gamma) \subset \mathrm{Im}(T)$, and iii) the cone generated by non-negative combinations of columns of T has trivial intersection with $\mathrm{Im}(\Gamma)$. One can proceed to choose some left inverse T' of T, and calculate that the Jacobian $J = T'\Gamma V T$ has nonnegative off-diagonal entries so that the y-variables define a cooperative dynamical system. We remark that the argument is independent of the fact that two of the reactions in the scheme (8) are generally considered to be irreversible.

Example 5b. Linearly Independent Reaction Vectors Are Not Necessary for Monotonicity. While the kinetics in the previous scheme is generally assumed to be mass-action, in the same reference the following reduced scheme where mass-action kinetics can no longer be assumed, is also discussed:

$$S_1 + E \rightleftharpoons ES_1 \rightarrow S_2 + E$$
$$S_2 \rightarrow S_1 \tag{9}$$

The stoichiometric matrix Γ and SR graph are shown in Figure 7.

Note that Γ is R-sorted, but has rank 2. As before, let x_i be the concentrations of the four substrates involved. Now, choose new coordinates y satisfying $x = Ty$, where

$$T = \begin{pmatrix} -1 & 0 & 0 \\ 0 & 1 & 0 \\ 0 & -1 & 0 \\ 0 & 0 & -1 \end{pmatrix} .$$

Note: i) T has rank 3, ii) $\mathrm{Im}(\Gamma) \subset \mathrm{Im}(T)$, and iii) regarding the columns of T as extremal vectors of a cone K, K has trivial intersection with $\mathrm{Im}(\Gamma)$. Again, one

$$\Gamma = \begin{pmatrix} -1 & 0 & 1 \\ -1 & 1 & 0 \\ 1 & -1 & 0 \\ 0 & 1 & -1 \end{pmatrix}$$

Fig. 7. The stoichiometric matrix and SR graph for reaction system (9)

can choose some left inverse T' of T, and calculate that the Jacobian $J = T' \Gamma V T$ has nonnegative off-diagonal entries. In other words the y-variables define a cooperative dynamical system. The relationship between T and Γ is further discussed in the concluding section. As in the previous example, the fact that some reactions are generally considered to be irreversible in this scheme, plays no part in showing monotonicity.

Example 6a. The Absence of o-Cycles Is Not Necessary for Monotonicity. Consider the following system of 4 chemical reactions on 5 substrates:

$$A \rightleftharpoons B + C, \qquad B \rightleftharpoons D, \qquad C + D \rightleftharpoons A \qquad C + E \rightleftharpoons A \qquad (10)$$

Define

$$\Gamma = \begin{pmatrix} -1 & 0 & 1 & 1 \\ 1 & -1 & 0 & 0 \\ 1 & 0 & -1 & -1 \\ 0 & 1 & -1 & 0 \\ 0 & 0 & 0 & -1 \end{pmatrix} \qquad \text{and} \qquad T = \begin{pmatrix} 1 & 0 & 0 & 0 \\ 0 & 1 & 0 & 0 \\ -1 & 0 & 0 & 0 \\ 0 & 0 & 1 & 0 \\ 0 & 0 & 0 & 1 \end{pmatrix}.$$

Γ, the stoichiometric matrix, has rank 3, and the system has SR graph containing both e- and o-cycles (Figure 8). Further, there are substrates participating in 3 reactions, and reactions involving 3 substrates (and so it is neither R-sortable nor S-sortable). Thus, conditions for the results quoted so far in this paper, and for theorems in [11], are immediately violated. However, applying theory in [12], the system is order preserving. In particular, $\text{Im}(T)$ is a 4D subspace of $\mathbb{R}^5$ containing $\text{Im}(\Gamma)$ (the stoichiometric subspace), and T defines a cone K which is preserved by the system restricted to cosets of $\text{Im}(T)$.

Example 6b. The Absence of o-Cycles Is Not Necessary for Monotonicity. Returning to the system of reactions in (5), the system has SR graph containing an o-cycle (Figure 2, *left*). Nevertheless, the system was shown in [12] to preserve a *nonsimplicial* cone for all N1C kinetics. In fact, further analysis shows that with mild additional assumptions this system is strongly monotone and all orbits on each stoichiometry class converge to an equilibrium which is unique on that stoichiometry class. It is worth mentioning that this example is fundamentally different from Example 6a. While similar examples can be found in higher dimensions, it is currently unclear how commonly reaction systems

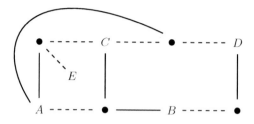

Fig. 8. The SR graph for reaction system (10)

preserve orders generated by nonsimplicial cones, and this must be an important question for future work.

7   Discussion and Open Questions

The results presented here provide only a glimpse of the possibilities for analysis of limit sets of CRNs using graph-theoretic – and more generally combinatorial – approaches. The literature in this area is growing rapidly, and new techniques are constantly being brought into play. Working with the weakest possible kinetic assumptions often gives rise to approaches quite different from those used in the study of mass-action systems. Conversely, it is possible that such approaches can be used to provide explicit restrictions on the kinetics for which a system displays some particular behaviour.

The paper highlights an interesting duality between questions of multistationarity and questions of stable periodic behaviour, a duality already implicit in discussions of interaction graphs or "I graphs" [23,24,25,26]. Loosely, the absence of e-cycles (positive cycles) is associated with injectivity for systems described by SR graphs (I graphs); and the absence of o-cycles (negative cycles) is associated with absence of periodic attractors for systems described by SR graphs (I graphs). The connections between apparently unrelated SR and I graph results on injectivity have been clarified in [27], but the results on periodic orbits are not so clear, and considerable work remains to be done.

One open question regards the relationship between the theory and examples presented here on monotonicity, and previous results, particularly Theorem 1 in [11], on monotonicity in "reaction coordinates". Note that by Proposition 4.5 in [11] the "positive loop property" described there is precisely Conditions 1 and 2 in Proposition 4 here. At the same time, the requirement that the stoichiometric matrix has full rank, is not needed for monotonicity in reaction coordinates. In some cases (e.g. Examples 5a and 5b above), it can be shown that this requirement is unnecessary for monotonicity too, but it is currently unclear whether this is always the case. On the other hand, as illustrated by Examples 6a and 6b, the positive loop property is not needed for monotonicity of the associated dynamical systems.

Consider again Examples 5a, 5b and 6a. The key fact is that their stoichiometric matrices admit factorisations $\Gamma = T_1 T_2$, taking the particular forms

$$
\begin{pmatrix}
-1 & 0 & 0 & 1 \\
-1 & 1 & 0 & 0 \\
1 & -1 & 0 & 0 \\
0 & 1 & -1 & 0 \\
0 & 0 & -1 & 1 \\
0 & 0 & 1 & -1
\end{pmatrix}
=
\begin{pmatrix}
-1 & 0 & 0 & 0 \\
0 & 1 & 0 & 0 \\
0 & -1 & 0 & 0 \\
0 & 0 & -1 & 0 \\
0 & 0 & 0 & 1 \\
0 & 0 & 0 & -1
\end{pmatrix}
\begin{pmatrix}
1 & 0 & 0 & -1 \\
-1 & 1 & 0 & 0 \\
0 & -1 & 1 & 0 \\
0 & 0 & -1 & 1
\end{pmatrix}
\qquad \text{(Example 5a),}
$$

$$
\begin{pmatrix}
-1 & 0 & 1 \\
-1 & 1 & 0 \\
1 & -1 & 0 \\
0 & 1 & -1
\end{pmatrix}
=
\begin{pmatrix}
-1 & 0 & 0 \\
0 & 1 & 0 \\
0 & -1 & 0 \\
0 & 0 & -1
\end{pmatrix}
\begin{pmatrix}
1 & 0 & -1 \\
-1 & 1 & 0 \\
0 & -1 & 1
\end{pmatrix}
\qquad \text{(Example 5b), and}
$$

$$
\begin{pmatrix}
-1 & 0 & 1 & 1 \\
1 & -1 & 0 & 0 \\
1 & 0 & -1 & -1 \\
0 & 1 & -1 & 0 \\
0 & 0 & 0 & -1
\end{pmatrix}
=
\begin{pmatrix}
1 & 0 & 0 & 0 \\
0 & 1 & 0 & 0 \\
-1 & 0 & 0 & 0 \\
0 & 0 & 1 & 0 \\
0 & 0 & 0 & 1
\end{pmatrix}
\begin{pmatrix}
-1 & 0 & 1 & 1 \\
1 & -1 & 0 & 0 \\
0 & 1 & -1 & 0 \\
0 & 0 & 0 & -1
\end{pmatrix}
\qquad \text{(Example 6a).}
$$

In each case, the first factor, T_1, has exactly one nonzero entry in each row. On the other hand, the second factor, T_2, is S-sorted. The theory in [12] ensures that these conditions are sufficient to ensure that the system restricted to some coset of $\mathrm{Im}(T_1)$, is monotone with respect to the order defined by T_1. Restricting attention to invariant cosets of $\mathrm{Im}(T_1)$, the theory in [22] can be applied to get strong convergence results, but this is not pursued here.

A broad question concerns whether techniques presented here have natural extensions when CRNs are modelled in other ways, for example as discrete-event systems. Certain basic remarks, for example that conserved quantities are associated with vectors in $\ker(\Gamma^T)$, are independent of the modelling formalism adopted. Some more nontrivial claims also generalise: in [7], there were shown to be close relationships, but also subtle differences, between results on persistence in flows describing CRNs, and results on liveness in PNs. As remarked earlier, in PNs with discrete tokens, the questions posed, for example about reachability and boundedness, tend to be different from those posed for differential equation models, for example concerning the nature, existence and stability of limit sets. The latter questions may have analogues for PNs, but their formulation depends sensitively on the firing rules: for example, questions about stationary probability distributions for stochastic PNs [18] are analogous to questions on the existence of limit sets. More closely related to the work here are continuous-state, discrete-timed PNs with deterministic firing rules. For these systems, results here on multiple equilibria and injectivity are applicable without difficulty; on the other hand, the dynamical implications of monotonicity may be quite different in the discrete-time case, and even strongly monotone disrete-time dynamical systems may have attracting k-cycles for $k \geq 2$ [28]. There remains considerable scope for further work in this area.

References

1. Epstein, I.R., Pojman, J.A. (eds.): An Introduction to Nonlinear Chemical Dynamics: Oscillations, Waves, Patterns, and Chaos. Oxford University Press, New York (1998)
2. Craciun, G., Feinberg, M.: Multiple equilibria in complex chemical reaction networks: II. The species-reaction graph. SIAM J. Appl. Math. 66(4), 1321–1338 (2006)
3. Banaji, M., Craciun, G.: Graph-theoretic criteria for injectivity and unique equilibria in general chemical reaction systems. Adv. in Appl. Math. 44, 168–184 (2010)
4. Feinberg, M.: Complex balancing in general kinetic systems. Arch. Ration. Mech. Anal. 49(3), 187–194 (1972)
5. Feinberg, M.: Chemical reaction network structure and the stability of complex isothermal reactors - I. The deficiency zero and deficiency one theorems. Chem. Eng. Sci. 42(10), 2229–2268 (1987)
6. Mincheva, M., Roussel, M.R.: Graph-theoretic methods for the analysis of chemical and biochemical networks, I. multistability and oscillations in ordinary differential equation models. J. Math. Biol. 55, 61–86 (2007)
7. Angeli, D., De Leenheer, P., Sontag, E.D.: A Petri net approach to the study of persistence in chemical reaction networks. Math. Biosci. 210, 598–618 (2007)
8. Banaji, M., Craciun, G.: Graph-theoretic approaches to injectivity and multiple equilibria in systems of interacting elements. Commun. Math. Sci. 7(4), 867–900 (2009)
9. Hirsch, M.W., Smith, H.: Monotone Dynamical Systems. In: Handbook of Differential Equations: Ordinary Differential Equations, vol. II, pp. 239–357. Elsevier B. V., Amsterdam (2005)
10. Smith, H.: Monotone Dynamical Systems: An introduction to the theory of competitive and cooperative systems. American Mathematical Society (1995)
11. Angeli, D., De Leenheer, P., Sontag, E.D.: Graph-theoretic characterizations of monotonicity of chemical reaction networks in reaction coordinates. J. Math. Biol. 61(4), 581–616 (2010)
12. Banaji, M.: Monotonicity in chemical reaction systems. Dyn. Syst. 24(1), 1–30 (2009)
13. Craciun, G., Feinberg, M.: Multiple equilibria in complex chemical reaction networks: I. The injectivity property. SIAM J. Appl. Math. 65(5), 1526–1546 (2005)
14. Banaji, M., Donnell, P., Baigent, S.: P matrix properties, injectivity and stability in chemical reaction systems. SIAM J. Appl. Math. 67(6), 1523–1547 (2007)
15. De Leenheer, P., Angeli, D., Sontag, E.D.: Monotone chemical reaction networks. J. Math. Chem. 41(3), 295–314 (2007)
16. Banaji, M., Baigent, S.: Electron transfer networks. J. Math. Chem. 43(4) (2008)
17. David, R., Alla, H.: Autonomous and Timed Continous Petri Nets. In: Rozenberg, G. (ed.) APN 1993. LNCS, vol. 674, pp. 71–90. Springer, Heidelberg (1993)
18. Bause, F., Kritzinger, P.S.: Stochastic Petri nets, 2nd edn., Vieweg (2002)
19. Craciun, G., Feinberg, M.: Multiple equilibria in complex chemical reaction networks: Extensions to entrapped species models. IEE Proc. Syst. Biol. 153(4), 179–186 (2006)
20. Berman, A., Plemmons, R.: Nonnegative matrices in the mathematical sciences. Academic Press, New York (1979)
21. Craciun, G., Tang, Y., Feinberg, M.: Understanding bistability in complex enzyme-driven reaction networks. Proc. Natl. Acad. Sci. USA 103(23), 8697–8702 (2006)

22. Banaji, M., Angeli, D.: Convergence in strongly monotone systems with an increasing first integral. SIAM J. Math. Anal. 42(1), 334–353 (2010)
23. Gouzé, J.-L.: Positive and negative circuits in dynamical systems. J. Biol. Sys. 6, 11–15 (1998)
24. Soulé, C.: Graphic requirements for multistationarity. Complexus 1, 123–133 (2003)
25. Kaufman, M., Soulé, C., Thomas, R.: A new necessary condition on interaction graphs for multistationarity. J. Theor. Biol. 248(4), 675–685 (2007)
26. Angeli, D., Hirsch, M.W., Sontag, E.: Attractors in coherent systems of differential equations. J. Diff. Eq. 246, 3058–3076 (2009)
27. Banaji, M.: Graph-theoretic conditions for injectivity of functions on rectangular domains. J. Math. Anal. Appl. 370, 302–311 (2010)
28. Jiang, J.F., Yu, S.X.: Stable cycles for attractors of strongly monotone discrete-time dynamical systems. J. Math. Anal. Appl. 202, 349–362 (1996)

Modeling and Mining of Learnflows

Robin Bergenthum[1], Jörg Desel[1], Andreas Harrer[2], and Sebastian Mauser[1]

[1] FernUniversität in Hagen, Lehrgebiet Softwaretechnik und Theorie der
Programmierung
forename.surname@fernuni-hagen.de
[2] Katholische Universität Eichstätt-Ingolstadt, Fachgebiet Informatik
andreas.harrer@ku-eichstaett.de

Abstract. This article transfers concepts and methods from business
process modeling and workflow management to the field of learnflows,
i.e. learning and teaching processes. It is first shown that these two areas
have a lot of commonalities and similarities. On the other hand, there
are also crucial specifics of learning processes that have to be taken into
account additionally. We then introduce and discuss modeling languages
for learnflows which are based on ideas from workflow modeling. Finally,
we develop an approach to automatically generate learnflow models from
log files of learning systems by adapting workflow mining methods.

1 Introduction

Learners' activity is in the focus of modern strands in pedagogy, such as con-
structivistic and self-regulated learning. Research results show that in completely
unguided learning situations productive activities like reflection and elaboration
rarely happen or are not performed successfully [1]. In contrast, structuring of
learning activities by means of scripts [2,3] and scaffolds has proven to be beneficial to learning outcomes. In most of today's learning support systems (e.g.
[4]) this type of support is hard-wired and tied to a specific learning domain
and system, especially when tightly integrated with the graphical user interface
of the system. The learning process models are given only implicitly by the respective systems. This way, re-usability and transferability to other contexts and
learning platforms is restricted.

Explicit representation of learning process models and scaffolds is one way to
make pedagogical expertise and practice re-usable, thus reducing the effort to
develop educational support systems while also stressing the underlying pedagogical design principles. This holds in particular for computer-supported collaborative learning (CSCL) systems. CSCL research investigates in the affordances
and effects of computer applications supporting groups of students in knowledge
construction and skill development.

While the initiatives to make learning processes more explicit have recently
gained scientific prominence under the terms educational modeling [5] and learning design [6], business process modeling or workflow engineering is a well-
established research field. There is a large repertoire of mature methods, rigorous

K. Jensen, S. Donatelli, and J. Kleijn (Eds.): ToPNoC V, LNCS 6900, pp. 22–50, 2012.
© Springer-Verlag Berlin Heidelberg 2012

procedures, and formal approaches that are used for definition, re-engineering, and automatic support of business processes in industry and companies [7,8,9].

Business process modeling and modeling of learning processes obviously share similar traits. We discuss in this work the similarities and differences. We also investigate potential transfer of results and methods from business process modeling to learning process modeling, or shortly from workflows to learnflows. More precisely, we first develop modeling techniques and methods for learnflows that take up approaches from workflow methodology. Then, we present specific procedures and schemas for (semi-)automated synthesis of learning process models from example scenarios and from real learning traces. These methods are based on the well-known and successful concepts of process mining and workflow mining [10,11,12].

As in the area of business processes, there are learning processes with more flexibility and with less flexibility. Too much flexibility leads to deficient structure, with the problems mentioned initially. Too little flexibility is not realistic and might frustrate learners. We concentrate on structured learning processes with limited flexibility that are supported by appropriate supporting systems, just like workflows supported by workflow systems are not those business processes with maximal flexibility.

The paper is structured as follows. In the next section, we discuss learnflows and workflows and their similarities. Section 3 is devoted to suggestions for learnflow modeling with Petri nets. In Section 4 we argue that mining techniques can be applied to derive learnflows from runs of learning processes.

2   Learnflows and Workflows

In this section we investigate similarities and differences between workflow engineering, explored intensively since the 1990s, and the challenges of the newly established strand of educational modeling.

2.1   Comparison of the Workflow Reference Architecture and Learning Design Technologies

Business information systems support workflows that define the ordering of activities to be executed. In traditional information systems these processes are integrated in the software, i.e. hard-wired. They are thus not clearly visible and can only be modified with substantial effort. Modern ERP systems make the supported processes explicit and visible, yet the modification of processes (called customization) requires a major programming effort. More flexible in this respect are workflow systems which are a stringent application of the principles of business process engineering. Workflow systems are standard software in which the respective process logic is defined in a flexible way and according to the users' requirements. The resulting formal process model is an additional input for the system with a well-defined semantics. Its representation is interpreted by the system at run-time. Thus, process logic and functionality of the application are strictly separated and can be enhanced / evolved independently of each other.

The central component of a workflow system is the workflow engine. It controls and monitors the execution of a workflow by means of an explicit process model. It ensures that the tasks are correctly accomplished by the associated actors and subsystems. Besides the core workflow engine, several other components are needed for workflow management. Among these are tools to develop, define, and analyze processes, tools for interaction with users and applications, for administration, and for cooperation among multiple workflow systems.

The Workflow Management Coalition (WfMC) was founded in 1993 and is constituted today of more than 300 institutions representing all facets of workflow management, from vendors to users, and from academics to consultants (cf. *www.wfmc.org*). The WfMC takes care of standardization of concepts, terminology, and technology to promote interoperability and establishment of workflow technology in the market.

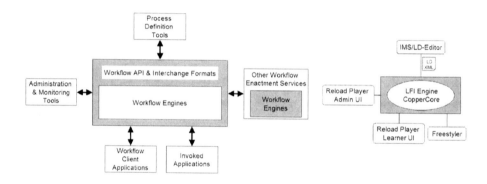

Fig. 1. Comparison of the Workflow reference architecture (left) and existing implementations of learnflow architectures (right)

Figure 1 shows on the left hand side the workflow reference architecture from the WfMC. It provides an overview of the main characteristics and components of a workflow system. We consider this reference architecture a suitable schema to compare workflow technology with the practice and technology in educational modeling and according systems.

The distinct components of the WfMC reference architecture have the following meaning:

Process Definition Tools: These include tools to edit and modify process definitions and tools for the analysis of these processes. The processes are imported into the workflow engine via a well-defined interface that takes the chosen representation format as input. A process definition specifies tasks, ordering of tasks and required resources (users / actors, external applications, etc.). Tasks can be executable concurrently or alternatively.

Workflow Engines: The workflow enactment service creates a process instance for each incoming case. Process instances are controlled by one or more workflow engines. For each case the tasks to be executed are called work items. According to the process definition, a work item gets assigned available resources.

Workflow Client Applications: User interfaces allow users to interact with the workflow system, especially by means of worklists that show the currently active work items for a user.

Invoked Applications: This component consists of technical interfaces to external applications which can process, either fully automated or interactively, specific work items.

Other Workflow Enactment Services: The protocols and the functionalities are needed for interoperability between – and cooperative use of – different workflow systems.

Administration and Monitoring: Administrators and responsible persons of processes or of specific process instances use this user interface to manipulate and configure process parameters, inspect status information, and gain data for the analysis and re-design of processes.

In the field of educational modeling, a similar distinction of components is visible, yet an agreement on a similar standard architecture has not been reached. The formal, mostly XML-based, representations such as IMS/LD [13], LDL [14], PALO [15] or MoCoLADe [16] are usually not edited directly at XML-level but rather with specific editors on a more abstract level. Some of the representations are mainly visual, some of them are tree-structured textual representations. The models are interpreted by so called learning design engines. The engine controls – depending on the concrete approach – web-based user interfaces for the learners (e.g. the web player of IMS/LD) or external learning applications. An example of the latter is the remote control approach [17] which uses the collaborative learning application FreeStyler.

Some of the approaches provide a complete implementation of editor, engine, and learning environment, while other approaches such as the Collage tool or the MoCoLaDe modeling language use a semantic mapping of the created models to IMS/LD as a target language, i.e. they use IMS/LD as an educational assembler.

To administrate and observe the learning processes configuration and monitoring tools can be used, yet currently only basic functionality and support is available.

There is no generally agreed reference model for educational modeling yet. In analogy to the WfMC reference model, the right hand side of Figure 1 presents principles and interactions of functionalities / components of process based learning systems by means of existing software / practice in the learnflow field. There are obvious similarities with the workflow architecture. This analogy supports a potential for take-up of methods and concepts from the workflow to the learnflow field.

Research groups in educational design that also have a background in CSCW (computer supported cooperative work / groupware) have recently proposed to follow service oriented approaches [18] for architecture and components. For example, the GridCole system [19] integrated the freely available Open Source

IMS/LD-engine CopperCore (cf. *www.coppercore.org*) with tools that are available as Grid-services. Approaches stressing interoperability with workflow technology, such as BPEL, have also been brought up in educational modeling [20], but they represent still isolated research initiatives.

2.2   Specifics of Learnflows

Despite of the conceptual similarities between workflows and learnflows, one can find considerable discrepancies. There are several specifics of learnflows which restrict an immediate application of existing techniques from business process engineering. In particular, the following specifics have to be regarded by appropriate adaptations and extensions.

- In business processes, so called roles of actors determine which actors are allowed to execute certain tasks [21]. This approach stems from the concept of role-based access control (RBAC) known from IT-security [22]. The concept of roles in business processes is mainly based on individual responsibility and ability for a set of tasks, which is static after an initial assignment of roles to actors. Dynamic constraints on the task execution, e.g. separation of duties and binding of duties [23,22], and special rules for an appropriate allocation of actors to tasks have been considered [23,21] on top of the static role assignments. In contrary to this rigid role concept, the usage of roles in learning processes is frequently guided by exercising specific skills. Roles are dynamically changed and acquired during a learning process (e.g. using rotating roles [4]). The changes typically depend on the learning activities accomplished by an actor. Therefore, learnflows need an extension of static role concepts to dynamic ones that can take into account the learning history.
- For business processes, the focus is on an efficient accomplishment and completion of the process and its associated tasks. The generation of a product with guaranteed quality criteria or, more generally, the achievement of a business goal is important, while the participation of individual actors is only a minor concern [7,21]. In contrast, for learning processes the priority is that the learners involved in the tasks gain knowledge and experience. Neither a product nor an efficient completion of the process is important. Consequently, the focus of learning processes is on the learners and their learning success. This requires thorough and explicit modeling of the individual actors.
- Each activity might require group work and discussion, i.e. collaboration. The same holds for the entire learning process. These group activities usually have a high importance for the learning experience. Thus, the flexible and explicit representation of groups and - if needed - the dynamic re-arrangement of groups is a requirement for learnflow modeling.
- Finally, the phenomenon of concurrency, which allows an independent and simultaneous processing of tasks in business processes has to be considered with particular care in learning processes. Due to the distinct focus of attention, usually a single learner cannot accomplish tasks concurrently.

3   Modeling Learnflows with Petri Nets

In this section we present two modeling languages for learning processes that take specifically into account the requirements identified in the last subsection. To make use of expertise and experience from business process modeling, we build the proposals upon sound existing approaches from this field [7,24,21]. Besides the intended applicability for learning and teaching processes, we consider our approaches also useful for business processes with dynamic roles or with cooperative and collaborative tasks.

Both business processes and learning processes are usually modeled and communicated via diagrams. Petri nets [25] are a very popular formalism to model and analyze systems and processes involving concurrency. In particular, Petri nets and related modeling languages such as activity diagrams, event-driven process chains and BPMN are the standard graphical modeling languages for business processes [7,24,9]. Petri nets offer an intuitive syntax and a clear semantics as well as a large repertoire of analysis, simulation and synthesis procedures together with respective tools. While place/transition-nets (p/t-nets) are well suited for modeling the control flow of processes, high-level nets offer additional modeling features to represent data and time aspects. Business processes are often modeled by so called workflow Petri nets [7] which are a special kind of p/t-nets having distinguished initial and final places. In this section we suggest to use workflow nets also for the modeling of learnflows.

In the field of business process modeling, the transitions of a workflow net represent the tasks of a business process. The places model causal dependencies between the tasks. In order to model resources and resource allocation, usually roles are assigned to the transitions of workflow nets. It is assumed that conversely each actor possesses certain roles. An actor is only allowed to execute a task if he possesses the role associated to the task.

In the previous section we have argued that such a static role concept is problematic in the context of learnflows. To account for this difficulty, we introduce a more flexible role concept for learnflows in this section. We extend the established workflow modeling concepts by mechanisms to allow the change of actor roles while performing an activity. Because of the significance of the individual learners and their learning experience, we explicitly model the dynamic roles of actors by state diagrams. To also consider learning groups and collaboration, we further introduce collaborative tasks which are performed by several actors jointly. Since Petri nets allow an intuitive representation of the interplay between concurrency and non-determinism, a differentiated consideration of concurrency is enabled by the choice of Petri nets for modeling learning processes.

There exist a wide spectrum of Petri net languages that differ w.r.t. expressiveness of the single elements, understandability and notational effort. Generally, every Petri net can be represented as a particular high-level Petri net, e.g. using the terminology of colored Petri nets [26]. However, for different purposes and in different domains, variants and dialects have proven to be more appropriate because models are better understandable for users when the respective language is specifically tailored to a particular application area. As usual in computer science, the semantics of such a domain specific language is given by translation to the more general language. Behavioral concepts and analysis methods and tools defined in the general setting thus apply to the specific one as well.

We will define two specific Petri net languages for learning processes and sketch the respective mappings to high-level Petri nets to give them the semantical foundation.

3.1 An Example

As an example we consider the following computer supported learning setting. Groups of three students use the tool FreeStyler [17] (*www.collide.info*) to learn the effect of different factors such as lightning conditions and CO_2-concentration on the growth of plants. For this purpose, FreeStyler [17] provides several tabs with different functionalities (see Figure 2). There are, for instance, tabs to formulate questions, to create simple models or to import data from a simulation tool. In this example, the set of tabs corresponds to the set of supported learning tasks. Namely, we consider the following tasks:

- **Introduction**: The students read a short textual introduction to the problem.
- **Question**: The students formulate the research questions that should be answered in experiments later on. They are guided by explanation prompts to step by step fill respective text fields.
- **Planning**: The students sketch a coarse model representing the influence of the different factors on the growth of plants. They relate nodes labeled with the different factors on a drawing area.
- **Modeling**: On another drawing area, the students first refine the previous model (from Planning) by arc labels quantifying the effect of the factors. Then they test their model in a simple simulation.
- **Hypothesize**: The students draw their hypotheses about the relationship of a factor and the growth of plants as a function in a coordinate system.
- **Experiment 1**: The students are directed to a simulation tool (e.g. BioBLAST). With the tool they can perform several experiments.
- **Experiment 2**: The students are directed to a second simulation tool.
- **Data**: The students investigate a table with precast results of lab experiments.
- **Analysis**: The students import their experimental data to a coordinate system. The resulting functions are analyzed and compared with the hypotheses.
- **Presentation**: The students summarize their results in a presentation. For this purpose a collection of text fields together with explanation prompts is provided.

In this context, a learnflow first describes the order in which the tabs have to be processed by the learners. Second, it determines the possible allocation of actors to learning tasks. It has to be specified whether a task requires a certain kind of collaboration and who is allowed to work on a tab where the latter depends on the learning history of the learners within the learning group.

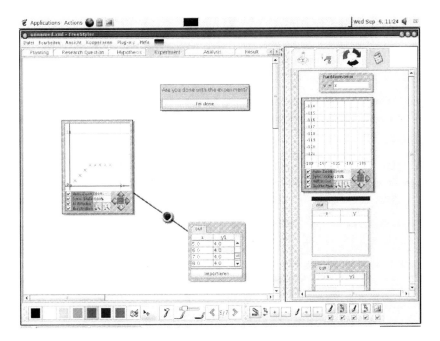

Fig. 2. Tabs in FreeStyler

The following example learning process describes groups of three learners working with FreeStyler. All three learners start with In. As soon as they have read the introduction, the two tasks Pl and Qu are executed independently. Qu requires one of the three learners. The learners have the freedom to choose who is assigned to the task Qu. In parallel to Qu, the two other learners jointly perform the task Pl. After Pl these two learners can optionally perform the task Mo which is also concurrent to Qu. When Qu, Pl and possibly Mo are accomplished, all three learners collaboratively work on Hy. Then, each of the three learners accomplishes one of the three independent tasks E1, E2 and Da. The learners can freely share these tasks among each other. When all three tasks are completed, the learners, again collaboratively, execute the task An. Subsequently, the task Pr concludes the learning process. Pr has to be performed by the learner that has initially executed the task Qu together with one of the other two learners.

3.2   Learnflow Nets

Learnflow nets present a first approach to extend the standard concepts of modeling workflows by Petri nets to learnflows. We model the control flow of a learnflow by a plain workflow net and depict actors and roles on top of the Petri net model by annotations. As in the case of workflows, we assume that there is a pool of actors possessing roles. Role annotations of transitions determine which actors are allowed to execute which tasks. However, the concept of role annotations is extended in two directions. First, to regard collaboration, instead of a single role it is allowed to specify a multiset of roles meaning that actors possessing the roles given by the multiset have to execute the task jointly. Second, for more flexibility, it is allowed to specify alternative multisets of roles meaning that different role combinations are possible for executing the task. Besides the expressivity of role annotations, we also extend the relation of actors to roles in order to model dynamic role assignments. A single actor does not anymore just statically possess a role. Instead, he has now associated a state diagram modeling the dynamics of role possession. Each state of such a state diagram represents a role. Initially, an actor possesses the role given by the initial state of the state diagram. State transitions of the state diagrams, i.e. role changes of the respective actor, are labeled by transition names of the control flow Petri net. They are triggered when the actor executes a respective task, i.e. the transitions of the state diagram are synchronized with the transitions of the net.

Syntactically, we define a learnflow net by using the definitions of workflow nets and deterministic automata. We use the following notations. $\mathbb{N}$ denotes the non-negative integers. Given a finite set A, 2^A denotes the power set of A. $\mathbb{N}^A$ denotes the set of multisets over A. For $m \in \mathbb{N}^A$ we write $m = \sum_{a \in A} m(a) \cdot a$. By $|m| = \sum_{a \in A} m(a)$ we denote the cardinality of m. The set of all words (strings) over A is denoted by A^*. This includes the empty word λ.

Definition 1. *A workflow net is a tuple $N = (P, T, F, i, f)$, where*

- *P and T are disjoint finite sets of places and transitions,*
- *$F \subseteq (P \times T) \cup (T \times P)$ is a flow relation,*
- *$i, f \in P$ are an initial and a final place fulfilling $(T \times \{i\}) \cap F = \emptyset$ and $(\{f\} \times T) \cap F = \emptyset$, and*
- *for any node $n \in P \cup T$ there exists a directed path from i to n and a directed path from n to f.*

Definition 2. *A deterministic finite automaton over the finite set of input symbols T is a tuple $M = (Q, T, \delta, q_0)$, where*

- *Q is a finite set of states,*
- *$\delta : Q \times T \to Q$ is a transition function, and*
- *$q_0 \in Q$ is an initial state.*

Definition 3. *A learnflow net is a tuple $LF = (N, R, l, S, s)$, where*

- *$N = (P, T, F, i, f)$ is a workflow net,*
- *R is a finite set of roles,*
- *$l : T \to 2^{(\mathbb{N}^R)}$ is a labeling function assigning multisets of roles to each transition,*
- *S is a finite set of deterministic finite automata over the set of input symbols T such that the sets of states of two distinct automata are disjoint and such that the union of all state sets is R (S represents a set of role diagrams), and*
- *$s \in \mathbb{N}^S$ is a multiset of role diagrams representing the learners of the learnflow.*

As usual for workflow nets, initially we have one token in the distinguished initial place. The initial state of an automaton representing the initial role of an actor can vary, depending on the actual role (learner/teacher) or on the learning states of a learner obtained so far (novice/experienced/...).

Figure 3 together with Figure 4 show a learnflow net modeling our example learning process. Figure 3 illustrates the control flow aspect in the form of a workflow net with transition annotations. The annotations refer to the roles required for a task. The state diagram of Figure 4 complements the Petri net model. It represents a role diagram, which models the dynamic roles of the three learners in the pool of actors. Each learner corresponds to one instance of the state diagram.

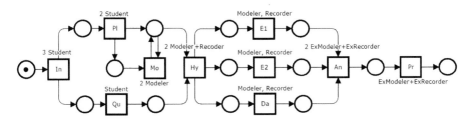

Fig. 3. Workflow net with role annotations

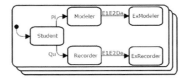

Fig. 4. State diagram representing dynamic roles

The dynamics of the learnflow net is as follows. The net gets an associated pool of actors. These actors cannot participate in other processes while the actual process is running. A task of the net can only be accomplished if this is possible in the current marking of the Petri net and if the pool of actors contains learners having the roles annotated at the transition. For instance, the collaborative task Pl requires two actors with the role Student. The roles of the learners are given by the role diagrams. In the example, the three learners may have the role Student, Modeler, ExModeler, Recorder and ExRecorder. Student is the initial role. The occurrence of a transition in the net can change the roles of the involved actors. Such a change is modeled in the role diagram by a state transition with the task name as the input symbol. Therefore, in our example the task Pl causes the two students executing Pl to switch to the role Modeler, which is later on required to perform the task Mo. When the net has received its final state (one token in the final place) the actors can take part in other learning processes, including further instances of the one just considered.

For simplicity of the role diagrams, we use the following convention. We omit transitions from a state to itself, i.e. if an actor performs a task which does not explicitly cause a change of his role in the state diagram, he stays with his role. For instance, the task Mo does not change the role of an actor with the role Modeler and therefore can be neglected in the state diagram.

While the Petri net from Figure 3 exactly represents the control flow of our example learning process, the annotations together with the associated state diagram of Figure 4 model the specified rules for the distribution of the learning tasks. The crucial aspect are the role changes. They allow to represent the given restrictions as well as the specified degree of freedom for the distribution of the tasks.

For instance, any two learners can execute the task Pl, since they all have the role Student at the beginning. The resulting role change from Student to Modeler then has two immediate effects. On the one hand the two learners are afterwards allowed to execute the task Mo which requires two Modelers. On the other hand the two learners cannot anymore execute the task Qu, since they do not anymore possess the default role Student which is required for this task.

We have a similar situation with the three tasks E1, E2 and Da. Each of these tasks can be executed by a Modeler or a Recorder. At this stage of the process, each learner has one of these two roles and can therefore be assigned to the tasks. However, the role changes associated with these tasks ensure that each learner can only accomplish one of the three tasks. A Recorder becomes an ExRecorder and a Modeler becomes an ExModeler. Finally, as desired, the role history guarantees that the learner who has formulated the question has to participate in the presentation, since he is the only learner possessing the role ExRecorder, i.e. this role stores the information that the learner has performed the task Qu. Additionally, the task Pr requires one of the two other learners possessing the role ExModeler.

The example shows that learnflow nets allow to appropriately represent collaborative activities as well as dynamic roles and the learning progress of learners within a learning process. Nevertheless, the modeling language is simple and intuitive. It naturally extends well established modeling approaches from the domain of business process management. As in the case of business process modeling, the approach supports a clear separation of the control flow perspective and the role perspective of a learnflow, but still regards both perspectives in one model.

3.3   Expressiveness of Learnflow Nets

The central new feature of learnflow nets is the concept of dynamic roles. The learning progress and the learning history of actors are encoded in role diagrams. This is an intuitive approach since, after performing a learning task, an actor often has additional knowledge, skills or responsibilities. Therefore, determined by his new status, an actor has a new role in the learning process. This role can then in a natural way be used to constrain the allocation of later tasks. This concept to represent the distribution of learning tasks allows to model in detail which tasks have to be done by certain actors and in which cases the actors can freely decide about task assignments. Using static roles, it is in many cases not possible to allow a degree of freedom for the learners. Omitting roles is also problematic, since then one learner would be allowed to execute all tasks. Therefore, without dynamic roles additional constraint specification languages, as e.g. introduced in [23,22], are necessary for an appropriate modeling of learnflows. However, we consider this more complicated and less intuitive than using dynamic roles for learners.

Formally, the behavior of learnflow nets can be defined by a translation into a special class of high-level Petri nets, namely colored Petri nets [26]. Colored Petri nets have a well-established occurrence rule which can then be applied for learnflow nets. We here do not formally define the translation. Instead we explain the ideas and illustrate them by our example learnflow net. The systematic formal translation can easily be deduced from this example.

All the standard Petri net components of the learnflow net are kept in the high-level Petri net model. The annotations of the transitions and the state diagrams are translated into one high-level place modeling the pool of resources resp. actors. The color set of this place is given by the possible roles of learners. The initial marking contains, for each instance of a state diagram, one token of the kind given by the initial state of the state diagram. The place has an outgoing and an ingoing arc connected with each transition of the net. A transition consumes tokens from the resource place as given by its annotation. For each consumed token, there are two cases. Either the state corresponding to the token type in the state diagram enables a state transfer labeled with the name of the considered transition or it does not enable such a transfer. In the first case, the transition produces a token of the kind given by the follower state of the state diagram in the resource pool. In the second case, it produces a token of the same kind as the consumed token. For classical workflow models with static role annotations, an analogous translation is possible, but in this situation the first case never occurs, i.e. each transition produces the same tokens in the resource pool that the transition consumes from the pool. Alternative role annotations of learnflow nets can be formulated by means of respective expressions of the high-level transitions.

Figure 5 illustrates the described translation for our example learnflow net. The resulting high-level Petri net does not any more show explicitly the dynamic roles and the behavior of the learners. Moreover, it is quite difficult to read and understand the high-level Petri net. Therefore, for modeling purposes, the original representation should be preferred. The high-level view is used for formal considerations.

3.4   Actor Learnflow Nets

In our second modeling approach, called actor learnflow nets, we go one step further. We remove the pool of actors and embed the role diagrams as tokens into the Petri net, representing the control flow of the process model. In this way the progress of actors within a learnflow is represented by the location of respective tokens in the Petri net. This approach is inspired by the idea of

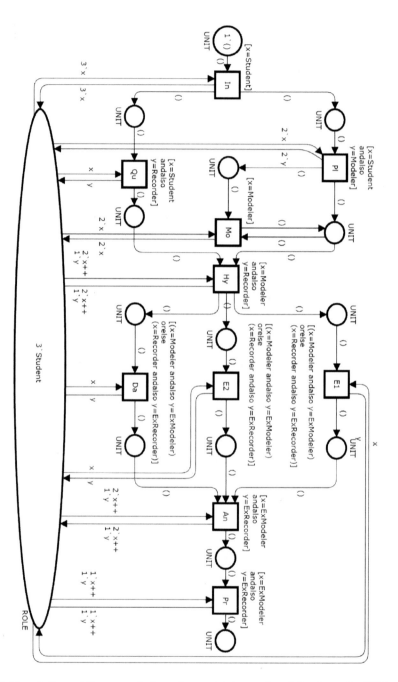

Fig. 5. Translation of the example learnflow net into a colored Petri net (in CPN tools http://cpntools.org/)

modeling with nets-in-nets and in particular by the papers about modeling of multi agent systems, inter-organizational workflows and adaptive workflows with object nets (e.g. [27]). However, our modeling concept is a lot more restrictive and simple than object nets [28].

In contrast to learnflow nets an actor learnflow net is not anymore based on a workflow net. It is a Petri net consisting of two kinds of places, "plain" Petri net places which can be marked by black tokens and role places which can be marked by role diagrams. The plain places can be considered just like places of a usual workflow net modeling control flow. The role places represent the locations of actors. They are connected to transitions by arcs having arc weights. For simplicity, we do not allow high-level arc expressions as allowed in object nets. Besides representing actors, the role places also encode control flow aspects. They are only supplemented by plain places if this is necessary for expressing advanced control flow structures.

An actor learnflow net has an initial marking assigning multisets of role diagrams to role places. The role diagrams represent the learners involved in the learning process. They are basically treated just like black tokens, i.e. they are not distinguished. Actor learnflow nets include a crucial restriction. For each transition the number of role diagrams consumed by the transition, i.e. the sum of the ingoing arc weights, has to equal the number produced by the transition, i.e. the sum of the outgoing arc weights. Since each role diagram represents a learner participating in the process, this preservation rule ensures that learners are not created or deleted, instead they are just moved forward in the learn-flow. When firing a transition, it produces the same role diagrams that were consumed by the transition. Since the arcs are annotated only by the numbers of role diagrams to be produced or consumed, only the numbers of role diagrams consumed from each place and forwarded to each place are specified. This way, the modeling language is kept comparably simple whereas the abstraction from individual identities does not harm.

An important aspect of actor learnflow nets is that they allow transition annotations modeling restrictions on the role diagrams consumed by a transition. These annotations have the same form and the same meaning as in the case of learnflow nets. The annotations specify alternative multisets of roles. The states of the role diagrams consumed overall by a transition have to match one of these combinations of roles. Therefore, the annotations again model which role combinations are allowed for executing a task. Remark that we have to require that the cardinality of the annotated multisets equals the number of role diagrams consumed by the transition. Concerning the role diagrams themselves, analogously as in the case of learnflow nets, their transitions are synchronized with the transitions of the Petri net. They cannot spontaneously change their states as in the case of object nets. The syntax of actor learnflow nets is as follows.

Definition 4. *An actor net is a tuple* $N = (P, P', T, W, F)$, *where*

- P, P' *and* T *are pairwise disjoint finite sets of role places, plain places and transitions,*

- $W : (P \times T) \cup (T \times P) \to \mathbb{N}$ *fulfilling* $\sum_{p \in P} W(p,t) = \sum_{p \in P} W(t,p)$ *is a flow relation (specifying arc weights) for the role places and*
- $F \subseteq (P' \times T) \cup (T \times P')$ *is a flow relation for the plain places.*

Definition 5. *An actor learnflow net is a tuple* $ALF = (N, R, l, S, s)$, *where*

- $N = (P, P', T, W, F)$ *is an actor net,*
- R *is a finite set of roles,*
- $l : T \to \{X \subseteq \mathbb{N}^R \mid \forall x \in X : |x| = \sum_{p \in P} W(p,t)\}$ *is a labeling function assigning roles to each transition,*
- S *is a finite set of deterministic finite automata over the set of input symbols* T *such that the sets of states of two distinct automata are disjoint and such that the union of all state sets is* R *(S represents a set of role diagrams) and*
- $s : P \to \mathbb{N}^S$ *is an initial marking assigning multisets of role diagrams representing the learners of the learnflow to the role places.*

We assume that in the initial marking plain places are unmarked.

Figure 6 depicts an actor learnflow net representing our example learning process. In addition to role places, the net includes only one (small) plain Petri net place for representing additional control flow aspects. The three learners of the learning process are all represented by an instance of the same role diagram representing the dynamic roles of the learners. In the initial marking they are located in the same role place. The transitions are annotated by labels referring to the roles required for a task.

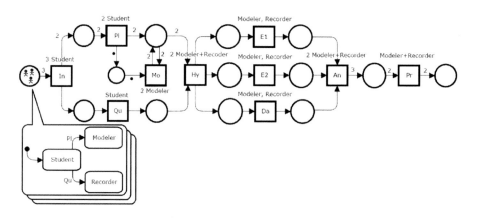

Fig. 6. Actor learnflow net

The dynamics of an actor learnflow net is as follows. A transition of the net can be fired if this is possible in the Petri net when treating role diagrams as black tokens and if the role diagrams consumed overall by the transition can be chosen in accordance to the roles annotated at the transition. These role diagrams are then distributed to the places in the postset of the transition. The distribution is non-deterministic, but it has to regard the arc weights. Moreover, the occurrence may change the states of the role diagrams analogously as in the case of learnflow nets.

In our example, we consider the transition Hy. An occurrence of this transition requires three learners, namely two Modelers and one Recorder. Two learners have to be in the upper place of the preset of the transition and one learner in the lower place. It does not matter whether the Recorder is in the upper or the lower place. Since, according to the role diagrams, neither a Recorder nor a Modeler changes its role when executing Hy, the three state diagrams are not modified and forwarded to the three postset places. One of the three role diagrams is added to each of these places. It does not matter to which place the Recorder is forwarded.

In this approach the distribution of the learning tasks is not anymore just represented by the dynamic roles. Instead, also the location of the role diagrams is important. For instance, as explained, the transition Hy distributes the three role diagrams to the three places enabling E1, E2 and Da. This ensures that each of the learners has to execute one of these tasks. Similarly, the transition In distributes two learners to the task Pl and one learner to the task Qu.

In contrast to the learnflow net from the last subsection, it is noticeable that the transitions E1, E2 and Da do not anymore trigger a role change. This is because the distribution of the learners to the three tasks is given by their location in the net and not anymore by a role change. That means, actor learnflow nets represent progress aspects explicitly by the location of role diagrams in the Petri net. As a consequence, role diagrams become simpler.

The example shows that actor learnflow nets are appropriate for comprehensibly modeling learning processes. The process perspective and the role perspective are embedded into one model. A nets-in-nets approach is applied, where tokens are role diagrams representing actors. Thereby, the role of an actor is given by the current state and the progress of the actor within the learning process is given by the location of the diagram.

We again show, using our example net, that the behavior of actor learnflow nets can formally be defined by a translation into colored Petri nets. The transitions and plain places are kept and the role places are translated into high-level places which have a color set given by the possible roles of learners. The initial marking is given by the initial roles of the state diagrams. The different non-deterministic possibilities of consuming and producing role diagrams by transitions are translated into respective firing modes of transitions. This is realized by assigning variables to respective arcs and regarding the allowed assignments of the variables by means of transition guards. These guards in particular have to regard the dynamics of roles given by the role diagrams.

Figure 7 shows the described translation by our example actor learnflow net. As in the case of learnflow nets, the colored Petri net associated to an actor learnflow net hides the dynamics of roles and is difficult to understand. Consequently, it is only useful for a formal analysis of actor learnflow nets.

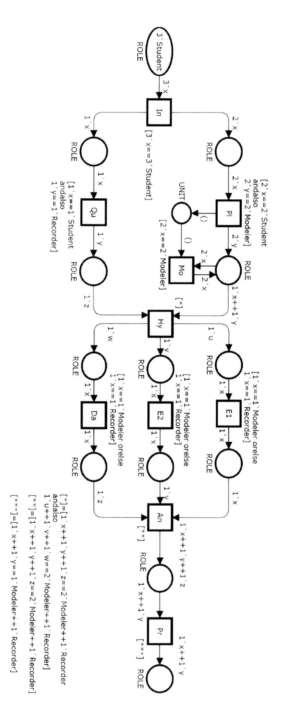

Fig. 7. Translation of the example actor learnflow net into a colored Petri net (in CPN tools http://cpntools.org/)

3.5   Discussion

Concluding, both learnflow nets and actor learnflow nets model the control flow of learning processes in a formal as well as illustrative way by means of Petri nets. They allow an appropriate representation of dynamic roles, collaboration and learning progress. The approaches differ w.r.t. their semantical clearness where none of the approaches outmatches the other one.

Learnflow nets clearly distinguish the modeling of the control flow and the resource perspective, thereby extending well-known concepts for workflow modeling. Due to the use of plain black tokens, the model is simple and allows well established formal analysis methods.

In contrast, actor learnflow nets use complex tokens represented by role diagrams having a current state. As a consequence, analysis of an actor learnflow net is more difficult and requires tailoring of known techniques. Also, the readability of the graphical representations might become worse. Finally, the role perspective is embedded into the control flow such that the clear separation known from workflow approaches is lost. On the other hand, by this approach the learning progress of each actor is explicitly represented in the control flow model. Therefore, progress dependant role changes as in the case of learnflow nets are not any more necessary. Thus, role diagrams have a more limited clear semantics and become simpler. This phenomenon becomes obvious in our example when for instance regarding the task E1. This task initiates a learning progress of the involved learner. In the learnflow net the progress is represented by a change of the role of the learner. The new role then does not allow an execution of E2 and Da by this learner anymore. In the actor learnflow net such progress-dependent role change is avoided. It represents the progress of the learner in a more elegant way by moving the actor token forward in the Petri net model.

Lastly, both modeling approaches focus on the representation of dynamic roles and regard group learning by means of collaborative activities. Thereby, a learning group is usually given by one process instance and the dynamics within a learning group is only implicitly considered. In view of representing re-arrangements of groups and an explicit modeling of group dynamics, we suggest two natural and useful extensions of learnflow nets resp. actor learnflow nets. First of all, when modeling groups by process instances, an extension of the modeling languages by global (or static [29]) places which allow to model dependencies of process instances would be helpful to regard dynamic group re-arrangements. Second, groups and group dynamics can also be modeled analogously as roles, i.e. the role diagrams of the actors can additionally capture information about group membership of actors. However, in contrast to roles it is important to represent the overall dynamics of the groups (which actors belong to a group at a particular time?). This dynamics can only implicitly be observed by group-memberships of single actors. Therefore, an extension of the modeling approach which at any time explicitly represents the learning groups is promising. This can for instance be achieved by a respective grouping of the state diagrams representing the learners.

4 Learnflow Mining

After having adapted modeling languages for business processes to learnflows, we in this section transfer the modeling and analysis technique of process mining [10,11,30,12]. The creation of a business process model can be automated or at least supported when example executions of the process are known. For this purpose, certain protocol files, so called event logs, which record the tasks executed within an information system can be used. Methods to automatically generate process models from event logs are known as process mining or workflow mining. They have recently gained a lot of attention in research and have also found their way into industrial tools [10,30,31]. We suggest to use process mining methods and tools for the generation of learnflow models in a similar way as in the case of business processes.

Teachers are not familiar with explicit modeling of learning processes. Usually, lesson plans are restricted to sequential considerations in table form. These tables cannot appropriately represent complex learnflows such as spiral approaches or learnflows including dynamic learning groups working concurrently. Moreover, the explicit definition of learning scenarios by a teacher often suffers from the so called expert blindspot [32], i.e. the teacher only considers the obvious scenarios and does not anticipate unconventional approaches. Both aspects show that real learning scenarios should be used for generation of learnflow models. We call the automatic generation of learnflow models from example scenarios learnflow mining, in analogy to workflow mining. We initiated the discussion about the application of process mining in the area of learning processes and coined the term learnflow mining in [33]. Independent work using educational mining approaches have been used to identify decision making behavior in virtual teams [34] and to identify behavior of students solving multiple choice tests [35]. While the latter uses single learner data, thus focusing on individual aspects, the first is also located in the field of collaborative learning. Yet, it concentrates on the activities and not on social or learning roles, so that both studies are similar to our work w.r.t. control flow mining while role mining is not tackled in [34,35]. Related work concerning role mining is organizational mining [12], which is however limited to static roles and organizational units.

Learnflow mining can help a teacher to construct valid lesson plans using advanced modeling languages. In particular, due to automation the effort for generating models can be reduced. For many teachers, this might be a crucial requirement for applying learnflow models. In general, analogously to experiences from the area of cognitive tutors [36] where example representations of general rules are applied, focusing on example learning scenarios instead of whole learnflows is more intuitive and less complex for teachers.

For the generation of example learning scenarios we suggest two approaches (which can also be combined), both requiring that the events of a learning system are recorded in log files.

- The teacher generates learning scenarios by demonstration on the learning system. He executes the scenarios with the learning system, thereby recording them in an event log. Then he possibly categorizes the scenarios of the log w.r.t. correctness or their potential for learning success.

– Real example scenarios of learners using the learning system are logged. The learners can freely work with the learning system such that log files are generated. For a classification, either a self-assessment of the learners in the sense of collaborative filtering can be applied or the teacher can evaluate the learning results by means of tests.

In both cases the result is a classified event log. The classification is useful to filter the relevant scenarios. The filtered event log can be used as input for process mining algorithms in order to generate a learnflow model which represents the real learning scenarios. In the following we discuss this concept in detail for learnflow nets.

The central aim of mining a process model from its specified behavior is to create a model that has exactly the behavior specified, no matter if we consider workflows or learnflows. However, we can only expect such a result if the specified behavior contains all and only legal runs. This assumption is unrealistic for larger process models because the number of legal runs can grow exponentially with the size of the model. Moreover, when starting with observed behavior, it is not easy to say whether a log is complete or whether some legal runs just never appear in the log. The situation becomes even more complicated if a log contains runs that are not legal (so called noise) or if a log contains runs that are successful, i.e., lead to a positive end, and runs that are not successful but still legal. The latter is particularly relevant for learnflows because a legal learning process can be successful or unsuccessful.

Therefore, in general it is neither possible nor desirable to gain process models that precisely have the specified behavior. The best we can expect is a model that has at least the specified behavior, is reasonably simple and has not too much additional behavior. Moreover, the model should be sound, i.e., it has no superfluous elements, does not run into deadlocks and ends with a proper end state. Roughly speaking, these are the main goals in process mining. We cannot expect to gain more than that when mining learning processes.

Usually, the generated (learning) process models are the starting point for a manual revision. At this stage, relevant properties of the model are analyzed and the model might be modified so that it enjoys desirable properties. The specified behavior is compared with the actual behavior to check whether this model is really suitable as a basis for legal processes in computer supported learning environments.

4.1   Control Flow

The methods to mine the control flow of a learning process are directly deduced from process discovery approaches known from process mining. The basic ideas of these approaches are as follows [10,11]. Every process-aware information system supports a set of tasks of a corresponding operational process. The execution of a task is an event. Typically, an event is stored together with information about the corresponding process, the process instance, the execution time, the involved actors and maybe some more information as for instance associated data elements. Within a process instance of a given process, the events can be ordered by their time stamps. Therefore, each process instance defines a sequence of events. The sequences of events associated to a certain process can then be used to identify the control flow of the process. The benefit of this approach is the following. While the manual construction of valid process models is a difficult, intricate and erroneous task, a process mining algorithm automatically generates a process model which matches the actual flow of work. The generated model can then be used for verification, analysis and optimization issues or even for controling the operational process by an engine.

For learnflow mining we formally consider an event log of one process as an ordered sequence of events where each event is a triple of the form (process instance, task, set of actors). We assume that the ordering is given by the time stamps of events. Moreover, we abstract from additional information such as data.

Definition 6. *Let T be a finite set of tasks, I be a finite set of process instances and A be a set of actors. An event is an element of $T \times I \times 2^A$. An event log is a sequence $\sigma = e_1 \dots e_n \in (T \times I \times 2^A)^*$.*

Given a log, the sequences of task occurrences given by single process instances are called control sequences.

Definition 7. *Let $\sigma = e_1 \dots e_n \in (T \times I \times 2^A)^*$ be an event log. Given a process instance $i \in I$, we define the function $c_i : T \times I \times 2^A \to T \cup \{\lambda\}$ by $c_i(t, i', U) = t$ if $i = i'$ and $c_i(t, i', U) = \lambda$ otherwise. Then $c_i(e_1) \dots c_i(e_n)$ is a control sequence of σ for the instance i.*

There are many workflow mining methods generating a Petri net model from the set of control sequences of a given event log such that the model represents the behavior given by the control sequences [10,11,30]. That means, the generated model represents the control flow of the underlying workflow. In our setting of learnflow mining, besides the control flow we also have to consider the dynamic role behavior. In the case of learnflow nets, the control flow perspective and the role models are clearly separated and can be mined one after the other. We here first consider the problem of mining the control flow given by an event log of a learning system. In the next subsection we discuss the mining of dynamic roles.

The control flow perspective of learnflow nets is given by standard workflow nets. To generate the workflow net underlying a learnflow net we can therefore apply any algorithm from workflow mining. We demonstrate this using our example learning setting. We assume that we have several learning groups processing the tabs offered by FreeStyler and thereby using an ordering and a distribution of the tasks as given by our example learning process. Each processing of a tab is recognized by FreeStyler and recorded in an event log. In this way, each learning group creates a process instance. Note that, as described before, the set of process instances can be filtered by appropriate criteria, and the teacher can also add certain desired process instances by demonstration. An extract of a respective event log is illustrated in Figure 8. We assume that the whole log (which is large and cannot be shown here) is complete for our example in the sense that all possibilities to work on the learning tasks according to the example learning process are included in the log.

Process "Plants"		
Instance	Task	Actor
Group A	In	Chuck, Wes, Susan
Group B	In	Robin, Andy, George
Group C	In	Chris, Anne, Dave
Group C	Pl	Anne, Dave
Group C	Qu	Chris
Group A	Qu	Wes
Group C	Mo	Anne, Dave
Group B	Pl	Robin, George
...	...	...

Fig. 8. Events recorded by FreeStyler

In the shown part of the example log we have the following control sequences: $In, Qu, ...$ (Group A), $In, Pl, ...$ (Group B) and $In, Pl, Qu, Mo, ...$ (Group C). Already for our small example process, the integration of the control sequences to one Petri net model exhibiting the behavior given by the sequences is not trivial. Therefore, we use the event log as input of a process mining algorithm. The workflow mining tool ProM [30] offers a lot of different mining algorithms which automatically generate a Petri net model representing the behavior of the learners as given by the log. For our complete example log file of FreeStyler we applied a mining algorithm which is based on exact synthesis methods and region theory [11]. With this tool we were able to mine the workflow net from Figure 3 (without annotations).

Thus, it is possible to mine the control flow perspective of a learnflow net which can then be used for analysis purposes.

4.2 Roles

The role names do not occur in our example log. Therefore, we cannot expect to correctly mine the role names that appear in the learnflow model of Figure 3 and 4. Our aim is to mine role diagrams and transition annotations which define the same restrictions for the assignment of tasks as given in the example process. For this purpose, the behavior of the actors recorded in the log is important. Consequently, the initial point for mining the role perspective is given by the control sequences, where now each event is stored together with the involved actors. We call these sequences learning sequences.

Definition 8. *Let* $\sigma = e_1 \ldots e_n \in (T \times I \times 2^A)^*$ *be an event log. Given a process instance* $i \in I$, *we define the function* $l_i : T \times I \times 2^A \to (T \times 2^A) \cup \{\lambda\}$ *by* $l_i(t, i', U) = (t, U)$ *if* $i = i'$ *and* $l_i(t, i', U) = \lambda$ *else. Then* $l_i(e_1) \ldots l_i(e_n)$ *is a learning sequence of* σ.

In our example, Group C defines the learning sequence $(In, \{Chris, Anne, Dave\}), (Pl, \{Anne, Dave\}), (Qu, \{Chris\}), (Mo, \{Anne, Dave\}), \ldots$

For any learning sequence and each student occurring in the sequence, we consider the sequence of task occurrences (without information about students) the student is involved in. Such a projection of a learning sequence onto a single actor is called actor sequence.

Definition 9. *Let $(t_1, U_1) \ldots (t_n, U_n)$ be a learning sequence of an event log $\sigma \in (T \times I \times 2^A)^*$. Given an actor $u \in A$, we define the function $a_u : T \times 2^A \rightarrow T \cup \{\lambda\}$ by $a_u(t, U) = t$ if $u \in U$ and $a_u(t, U) = \lambda$ otherwise. Then $a_u(t_1, U_1) \ldots a_u(t_n, U_n)$ is an actor sequence of σ.*

In our example, Anne executes the actor sequence $In, Pl, Mo, \ldots$ in Group C.

It is possible that different actors have different role behavior, i.e. different associated role diagrams. In such a case we have to divide the actors of a process instance into respective classes. Such a behavior does not appear in our example. For simplicity, we assume that all actors have the same role behavior. For instance, in our example all actors are simply learners.

Now the crucial step is to integrate all actor sequences into a deterministic state diagram in the form of a tree. That means, the states of the diagram are determined by the history of previously performed tasks (also regarding the order of the events) and are named accordingly, i.e. the states are given by the prefixes of the actor sequences. This diagram can then be used as a role diagram. Formally, we apply a very simple technique for learning a deterministic finite automaton from a set of words [37]. More sophisticated constructions such as the one of Myhill-Nerode cannot be applied here since the possible role combinations for executing a task as given by the log have to be regarded (see the Simplification Rule at the end of the section).

Definition 10. *Let AS be the set of actor sequences of an event log $\sigma \in (T \times I \times 2^A)^*$. The deterministic finite automaton $RD = (Q, T, \delta, q_0)$ where*

- $Q = \{t_1 \ldots t_i \mid t_1 \ldots t_n \in AS, 0 \leq i \leq n\}$,
- δ *is defined by $\delta(t_1 \ldots t_i, t_{i+1}) = t_1 \ldots t_{i+1}$ if there exists $t_1 \ldots t_n \in AS, 0 \leq i < n$ and $\delta(t_1 \ldots t_i, t_{i+1}) = t_1 \ldots t_i$ otherwise, and*
- $q_0 = \lambda$

is called role diagram of σ.

For our complete example log, the resulting role diagram is given in Figure 9.

The diagram encodes the complete history of each actor. In learnflow nets we assume that the role of an actor can only change in the case the actor executes a task. Therefore, when consistently defining annotations of transitions in the Petri net, it is possible to exactly represent the task allocation given in the log. To define the annotation of a certain transition we have to take the learning sequences into account. When a transition occurs in a learning sequence, the histories of the involved actors within the learning sequence define one possible role allocation. There might be different possible role combinations given

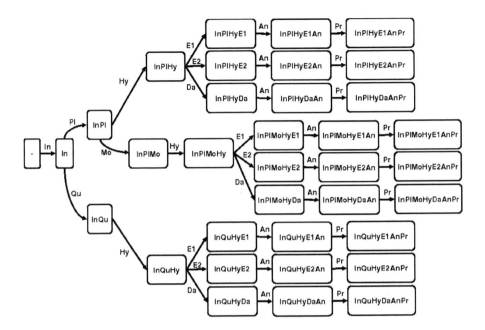

Fig. 9. Mined role diagram

by all the learning sequences. All these alternative role assignments define the annotation of the transition.

Definition 11. *Let* $(t_1, U_1) \dots (t_i, U_i) \dots (t_n, U_n)$ *be a learning sequence of an event log* $\sigma \in (T \times I \times 2^A)^*$ *and* $RD = (Q, T, \delta, q_0)$ *be the role diagram of* σ. *A possible allocation of roles for the task* t_i *is given by the multiset of roles* $\sum_{u \in U_i} a_u(t_1, U_1) \dots a_u(t_{i-1}, U_{i-1}) \in \mathbb{N}^Q$ *(*a_u *is defined as in Definition 9).*

The role annotation $l(t)$ *of a task* $t \in T$ *w.r.t.* σ *is the set of all possible allocations for* t. *The resulting function* $l : T \to 2^{(\mathbb{N}^Q)}$ *is called role labeling function of* σ.

In the example learning sequence of Group C, the task Mo is performed by Anne, who has done In and Pl before, together with Dave, who has the same learning history. Therefore, $2 \cdot InPl$ is one possible role allocation for Mo. Since Mo is always done by $2 \cdot InPl$, the role annotation $l(Mo)$ of Mo w.r.t. the given log is $\{2 \cdot InPl\}$.

Altogether, we are now able to mine a complete learnflow net from a log of a learning process. In the previous subsection we have shown how to generate a workflow net representing the control flow of the learning process. In this subsection we have shown how to mine a role diagram together with role annotations representing the resource perspective of the learning process. Combining these two models yields a learnflow net representing the behavior of the learning process. We refer to this net as the learnflow net mined from the log. The number of role diagram instances of this learnflow net is given by the maximal number of actors occurring in a learning sequence of the log.

Definition 12. *Let $\sigma \in (T \times I \times 2^A)^*$ be an event log and $N = (P, T, F, i, f)$ be a workflow net mined from σ. Let further LS be the set of learning sequences of σ, $RD = (Q, T, \delta, q_0)$ be the role diagram of σ and $l : T \to 2^{(\mathbb{N}^Q)}$ be the role labeling function of σ.*

The learnflow net mined from σ w.r.t. N is defined as $LF = (N, Q, l, \{RD\}, k \cdot RD)$ where $k = max_{(t_1, U_1)...(t_n, U_n) \in LS} |\bigcup_{i=1}^{n} U_i|$.

The examples given in this subsection illustrate that the possible distributions of tasks to actors allowed by the learnflow net mined from a log coincide with the distributions of tasks given in the log. Therefore, if the control flow has precisely been mined, the behavior of the mined learnflow net coincides with the behavior given in the log up to isomorphism and renaming of the roles. For instance, the behavior of the learnflow net mined from the example log is equivalent to the behavior given by the log and thus also equivalent to the behavior of our original learnflow net given in Figures 3 and 4.

In our example, the mined role model is by far larger than necessary. This is the case because the model represents the whole history of each learner. Therefore, an important issue is to simplify the mined role models by merging roles.

Given a mined role model, the central idea for simplification is to merge roles, i.e. states, having an equivalent future. Of course, when merging roles also the annotations in the corresponding Petri net model have to be renamed consistently. The behavior of a learnflow model is not changed by this simplification. For instance, all the leafs in our example role diagram in Figure 9 have no follower roles and can thus be merged. Also the previous nine roles have the same follower role triggered by the same task. However, we here have to consider the collaborative aspect. It is not allowed to merge two roles having the same future in the role diagram if switching the two role names changes the annotation of collaborative tasks in which both roles are involved. In our example, the task Pr is a collaborative task which is performed by two actors. Thereby, it is important that one of the actors is the one that executed Qu. Consequently, switching a role name including Qu and a role name not including Qu changes the annotation of Pr. Thus, only the upper six and the lower three roles can be merged. Altogether, we formulate the following rule:

Simplification Rule. *Let $RD = (Q, T, \delta, q_0)$ be a role diagram and $l : T \to 2^{(\mathbb{N}^Q)}$ be the role labeling function of an event log σ. Two states $q_1, q_2 \in Q$ can be merged if the following two conditions are satisfied:*

- $\forall t \in T : \delta(q_1, t) = \delta(q_2, t)$ *or* $(\delta(q_1, t) = q_1$ *and* $\delta(q_2, t) = q_2)$
- $\forall t \in T: (\exists x_1, x_2 \in l(t) : |x_1| > 1$ *and* $q_1 \in x_1, q_2 \in x_2) \implies l(t) = \{s(q_1, q_2, x) \mid x \in l(t)\}$, *where* $s : Q \times Q \times \mathbb{N}^Q \to \mathbb{N}^Q$ *is given by* $s(q_1, q_2, x) = \sum_{q \in Q \setminus \{q_1, q_2\}} x(q) \cdot q + x(q_1) \cdot q_2 + x(q_2) \cdot q_1$.

When no more roles can be merged according to this simplification rule, an additional technique can be applied. Many of the role transitions from a state to itself (which are not shown in the illustrations of role diagrams) are irrelevant. An irrelevant role transition cannot occur in the learnflow model since it is forbidden by the control flow. Therefore, changing such transitions does not affect the behavior of the learnflow net. But such changes can be used to align the future of two states in a role diagram in view of merging them.

Using this technique for our mined role diagram of Figure 9 reduces it to a diagram which is isomorphic to the original example role diagram of Figure 4. That means, with the simplification rule we are in this case able to recreate the original learning process model from a complete log file. Only the role names that are not present in the log files cannot be mined. They can be chosen arbitrarily by the teacher.

5   Conclusion

In this article we systematically carried over methods and techniques from workflow management to the modeling of learnflows. First, we worked out the similarities and differences of workflow and learning processes. In particular, we have compared relevant implementations in the two areas. As a basis for further considerations we then have developed and discussed two modeling languages for learnflows which are based on workflow modeling concepts, namely learnflow nets and actor learnflow nets. Finally, we have identified the field of process mining as particularly interesting for a concrete method and technology transfer. Under the name learnflow mining, we suggested to use mining methods for the generation of learnflow models from real learning scenarios. Using real scenarios and automatically generating more general learnflow models on the one hand disburdens the teacher when designing models and on the other hand enables the immediate usage of concrete learning experience (e.g. for supporting the learners within the learning process). We have discussed both, mining of the control flow of a learning process and mining of the role behavior of the learners within the learning process.

As in the area of workflow mining [38], for the development of learnflow mining tools a standardization of log formats of learning systems – which is already being discussed in the field of educational modeling – is an important aim. Moreover, mining tools have to support preprocessing of the event logs and postprocessing of the generated process models. For instance, an event log recording all mouse clicks is too fine grained for generating a reasonable model. In such a case, filtering and aggregation of events is necessary to prepare the log for a mining algorithm. On the other hand, a mined model usually has to be validated and possibly complemented by the teacher.

A crucial algorithmic problem known from workflow mining is that, in practical settings, we have to assume that not all possible learning sequences have been recorded in a log file, i.e. that logs are incomplete. For such log files the presented mining approach has to be extended. Heuristics can help to infer the missing sequences and to integrate them into the process model. For the control flow perspective, existing methods from the area of process mining can be used [10]. For the role diagrams we plan to use methods from the theories of structural equivalence and generalized block modeling [39] where missing information is penalized and a solution with minimal penalties can be used for the generalized role model. Moreover, it is possible that a log contains noise, i.e. behavior which should not be regarded in a process model. We think that the problem of noise can be handled by the discussed categorizations of event logs.

Finally, concerning the presented mining approach, the application of the simplification rule for reducing the mined role models has not yet been discussed in detail. In particular, the assisting technique of changing state transitions has to be done manually so far. Automatizing of this procedure is our most immediate topic of further research.

References

1. Barron, B.: When Smart Groups Fail. Journal of the Learning Sciences 12(3), 307–359 (2003)
2. Schank, R., Abelson, R.: Scripts, Plans, Goals and Understanding: an Inquiry into Human Knowledge Structures. L. Erlbaum (1977)
3. O'Donnell, A., Dansereau, D.: Scripted cooperation in student dyads: A method for analyzing and enhancing academic learning and performance. In: Interaction in Cooperative Groups: The Theoretical Anatomy of Group Learning. Cambridge University Press (1992)
4. Weinberger, A., Ertl, B., Fischer, F., Mandl, H.: Epistemic and social scripts in computer-supported collaborative learning. Instructional Science 33(1), 1–30 (2005)
5. Rawlings, A., van Rosmalen, P., Koper, R., Rodriguez Artacho, M., Lefrere, P.: Survey of Educational Modelling Languages. In: EMLs 2002 CEN/ISSS Learning Technology Workshop (2002)
6. Koper, R., Tattersall, C. (eds.): Learning Design - Modelling and implementing network-based education & training. Springer, Berlin (2005)
7. van der Aalst, W.M.P., van Hee, K.: Workflow Management: Models, Methods, and Systems. MIT Press (2002)
8. Oberweis, A.: Person-to-Application Processes: Workflow Management. In: Process-Aware Information Systems, pp. 21–36. Wiley (2005)
9. Weske, M.: Business Process Management – Concepts, Languages and Architectures. Springer, Heidelberg (2007)
10. van der Aalst, W.M.P.: Finding Structure in Unstructured Processes: The Case for Process Mining. In: ACSD 2007, pp. 3–12. IEEE (2007)
11. Bergenthum, R., Desel, J., Lorenz, R., Mauser, S.: Process Mining Based on Regions of Languages. In: Alonso, G., Dadam, P., Rosemann, M. (eds.) BPM 2007. LNCS, vol. 4714, pp. 375–383. Springer, Heidelberg (2007)
12. Song, M., van der Aalst, W.M.P.: Towards comprehensive support for organizational mining. Decision Support Systems 46(1), 300–317 (2008)
13. IMS Global Consortium: IMS Learning Design XML Binding 1.0 Specification (2003)

14. Martel, C., Vignollet, L., Ferraris, C., David, J., Lejeune, A.: Modelling collabora- tive learning activities in e-learning platforms. In: ICALT 2006, pp. 707–709. IEEE (2006)
15. Rodriguez Artacho, M.: PALO Language Overview. Technical report, Universidad Nacional de Educacion a Distancia (2002)
16. Harrer, A., Hoppe, U.: Visual Modelling of Collaborative Learning Processes – Uses, Desired Properties, and Approaches. In: Handbook of Visual Languages for Instructional Design: Theory and Practices. Information Science Reference, pp. 281–298 (2008)
17. Harrer, A., Malzahn, N., Wichmann, A.: The Remote Control Approach - An Architecture for Adaptive Scripting across Collaborative Learning Environments. Journal of Universal Computer Science 14(1), 148–173 (2008)
18. Vogten, H., Martens, H., Nadolski, R., Tattersall, C., van Rosmalen, P., Koper, R.: CopperCore Service Integration - Integrating IMS Learning Design and IMS Question and Test Interoperability. In: ICALT 2006, pp. 378–382. IEEE (2006)
19. Bote Lorenzo, M., Hernández Leo, D., Dimitriadis, Y., Asensio Pérez, J., Gómez Sánchez, E., Vega Gorgojo, G., Vaquero González, L.: Towards Reusability and Tailorability in Collaborative Learning Systems Using IMS-LD and Grid Services. Advanced Technology for Learning 1(3), 129–138 (2004)
20. Harrer, A., Malzahn, N.: Bridging the Gap - Towards a Graphical Modelling Lan- guage for Learning Designs and Collaboration Scripts of Various Granularities. In: ICALT 2006, pp. 296–300. IEEE (2006)
21. Russell, N., van der Aalst, W.M.P., ter Hofstede, A.H.M., Edmond, D.: Workflow Resource Patterns: Identification, Representation and Tool Support. In: Pastor, Ó., Falcão e Cunha, J. (eds.) CAiSE 2005. LNCS, vol. 3520, pp. 216–232. Springer, Heidelberg (2005)
22. Sandhu, R.S., Coyne, E.J., Feinstein, H.L., Youman, C.E.: Role-Based Access Con- trol Models. Computer 29(2), 38–47 (1996)
23. Tan, K., Crampton, J., Gunter, C.: The Consistency of Task-Based Authorization Constraints in Workflow Systems. In: CSFW, pp. 155–169. IEEE (2004)
24. van der Aalst, W.M.P.: The Application of Petri Nets to Workflow Management. The Journal of Circuits, Systems and Computers 8(1), 21–66 (1998)
25. Desel, J.: Process Modeling Using Petri Nets. In: Process-Aware Information Sys- tems, pp. 147–177. Wiley (2005)
26. Jensen, K.: Coloured Petri Nets. Basic Concepts, Analysis Methods and Practical Use. Monographs in Theoretical Computer Science, vol. 1-3. Springer, Heidelberg (1992, 1994, 1997)
27. van der Aalst, W.M.P., Moldt, D., Wienberg, F., Valk, R.: Enacting Interorgani- zational Workflows using Nets in Nets. In: Workflow Management Conference, pp. 117–136 (1999)
28. Valk, R.: Petri Nets as Token Objects: An Introduction to Elementary Object Nets. In: Desel, J., Silva, M. (eds.) ICATPN 1998. LNCS, vol. 1420, pp. 1–25. Springer, Heidelberg (1998)
29. Juhás, G., Kazlov, I., Juhásová, A.: Instance Deadlock: A Mystery behind Frozen Programs. In: Lilius, J., Penczek, W. (eds.) PETRI NETS 2010. LNCS, vol. 6128, pp. 1–17. Springer, Heidelberg (2010)
30. van der Aalst, W.M.P., van Dongen, B.F., Günther, C.W., Mans, R.S., de Medeiros, A.K.A., Rozinat, A., Rubin, V., Song, M., Verbeek, H.M.W(E.), Weijters, A.J.M.M.T.: ProM 4.0: Comprehensive Support for *Real* Process Analy- sis. In: Kleijn, J., Yakovlev, A. (eds.) ICATPN 2007. LNCS, vol. 4546, pp. 484–494. Springer, Heidelberg (2007)

31. IDS Scheer: ARIS Process Performance Manager, http://www.ids-scheer.com
32. Nathan, M., Koedinger, K.R., Alibali, M.: Expert blind spot: When content knowledge eclipses pedagogical content knowledge, AERA, Seattle (2001)
33. Bergenthum, R., Desel, J., Harrer, A., Mauser, S.: Learnflow mining. In: DeLFI. LNI, vol. 132, pp. 269–280. GI (2008)
34. Reimann, P., Frerejean, J., Thompson, K.: Using Process Mining to Identify Models of Group Decision Making in Chat Data. In: Proceedings of Computer-supported Collaborative Learning, pp. 98–107 (2009)
35. Pechenizkiy, M., Trcka, N., Vasilyeva, E., van der Aalst, W.M.P., De Bra, P.: Process Mining Online Assessment Data. In: Proceedings of Educational Data Mining, pp. 279–288 (2009)
36. Aleven, V., McLaren, B.M., Sewall, J., Koedinger, K.R.: The Cognitive Authoring Tools (CTAT): Preliminary Evaluation of Efficiency Gains. In: Ikeda, M., Ashley, K.D., Chan, T.-W. (eds.) ITS 2006. LNCS, vol. 4053, pp. 61–70. Springer, Heidelberg (2006)
37. Hopcroft, J., Ullman, J. (eds.): Introduction to Automata Theory, Languages and Computation. Addison-Wesley (1979)
38. Process Mining Group Eindhoven Technical University: ProM Homepage, http://is.tm.tue.nl/~cgunther/dev/prom/
39. Doreian, P., Batagelj, V., Ferligoj, A.: Generalized Blockmodeling. Structural Analysis in the Social Sciences, vol. 25. Cambridge University Press (2005)

Ten Years of Saturation: A Petri Net Perspective

Gianfranco Ciardo, Yang Zhao, and Xiaoqing Jin

Department of Computer Science and Engineering, University of California, Riverside
{ciardo,zhaoy,jinx}@cs.ucr.edu

Abstract. Due to their appealing conceptual simplicity and availability of computer tools for their analysis, Petri nets are widely used to model discrete-event systems in many areas of engineering. However, the computational resources required to carry out the analysis of a Petri net model are often enormous, hindering their practical impact. In this survey, we consider how *symbolic* methods based on the use of *decision diagrams* can greatly increase the size of Petri nets that an ordinary computer can reasonably tackle. In particular, we present this survey from the perspective of the efficient *saturation* method we proposed a decade ago, and introduce along the way the most appropriate classes of decision diagrams to answer important Petri net questions, from reachability to CTL model checking and counterexample generation, from p-semiflow computation to the solution of timed or Markovian nets.

1 Introduction

Since their definition 50 years ago [45], Petri nets have become a well known formalism to model discrete-state systems and many algorithms have been developed for their analysis [46]. However, even when the net is bounded, algorithms that manipulate the set of reachable markings usually require enormous computational resources when run on practical models.

Binary decision diagrams, introduced 25 year ago [8], have had a tremendous impact on industrial hardware verification, due to their ability to *symbolically* encode complex boolean function on enormous domains [9,39]. More precisely, while their worst-case complexity remains exponential in the number of boolean variables, many cases of practical interest have much better behavior, as attested by numerous successful verification and bug finding studies [24].

In this survey, we explore how decision diagram technology can greatly enhance our capability to analyze various classes of Petri nets. We do so in light of an algorithm we introduced 10 years ago, *saturation* [13], which tends to perform extremely well when applied to discrete-event systems having multiple asynchronous events that depend and affect only relatively small subsystems, a prime example of which is, of course, Petri nets. To provide a solid introductory treatment to decision diagrams, their manipulation algorithms, and their application to Petri net problems, this survey contains many illustrations, detailed pseudocode for representative algorithms, an extensive set of models, and memory and time results obtained when running the algorithms on these models.

K. Jensen, S. Donatelli, and J. Kleijn (Eds.): ToPNoC V, LNCS 6900, pp. 51–95, 2012.
© Springer-Verlag Berlin Heidelberg 2012

The rest of our survey is organized as follows. Section 2 discusses *reachability-set generation* for Petri nets, from safe nets up to extended Petri nets, focusing on efficient canonical forms of boolean-valued decision diagrams and the use of acceleration techniques to improve efficiency, including *saturation*. Section 3 considers *CTL model checking* for Petri nets, which benefits from the techniques introduced for reachability; to generate shortest CTL witnesses/counterexamples or bound exploration, we employ instead a form of *edge-valued decision diagrams* able to encode partial integer-valued functions, which can nevertheless be used in conjunction with saturation. Section 4 moves to non-boolean Petri net questions: *p-semiflows computation*, using zero-suppressed decision diagrams; *timed and earliest reachability* for a class of integer-timed Petri nets, using a combination of boolean and integer-valued decision diagrams; *stationary analysis of generalized stochastic Petri nets*, for which the generation of the transition rate matrix using real-valued decision diagrams is usually quite efficient, but for which an efficient fully-symbolic exact solution still eludes us; and *heuristic derivation of good variable orders* for the decision diagram variables based on the structural characteristics of the Petri net. Section 5 presents a brief list of available decision diagram libraries and tools using decision diagram technology.

2   Reachability-Set Generation for Petri Nets

This section recalls first the standard definition of Petri nets and later an extended definition for self-modifying nets, introduces the most basic classes of decision diagrams, BDDs and MDDs, and uses them to generate a symbolic encoding of the reachability set. In addition to the simpler breadth-first approach, it introduces more sophisticated fixpoint iteration strategies, chaining and saturation, which can provide much greater memory and runtime efficiency.

2.1   Petri Nets

We use the standard definition of a Petri net as a tuple $(\mathcal{P}, \mathcal{T}, \mathbf{D}^-, \mathbf{D}^+, \mathbf{i}_{init})$ where:

- $\mathcal{P}$ is a set of *places*, drawn as circles, and $\mathcal{T}$ is a set of *transitions*, drawn as rectangles, satisfying $\mathcal{P} \cap \mathcal{T} = \emptyset$.
- $\mathbf{D}^- : \mathcal{P} \times \mathcal{T} \to \mathbb{N}$ and $\mathbf{D}^+ : \mathcal{P} \times \mathcal{T} \to \mathbb{N}$ are the *input arc* and the *output arc* cardinalities, respectively.
- $\mathbf{i}_{init} \in \mathbb{N}^{|\mathcal{P}|}$ is the *initial marking*, specifying a number of *tokens* initially present in each place.

If the current marking is $\mathbf{i} \in \mathbb{N}^{|\mathcal{P}|}$, we say that $\alpha \in \mathcal{T}$ is *enabled* in $\mathbf{i}$, written $\alpha \in \mathcal{T}(\mathbf{i})$, iff $\forall p \in \mathcal{P}, \mathbf{D}^-_{p,\alpha} \leq i_p$. Then, $\alpha \in \mathcal{T}(\mathbf{i})$ can *fire*, changing the marking to $\mathbf{j}$, written $\mathbf{i} \xrightarrow{\alpha} \mathbf{j}$, satisfying $\forall p \in \mathcal{P}, j_p = i_p - \mathbf{D}^-_{p,\alpha} + \mathbf{D}^+_{p,\alpha}$. A Petri net is a special case of a discrete-state system with a *potential state space* $\mathcal{X}_{pot} = \mathbb{N}^{|\mathcal{P}|}$, a *next-state* or *forward function* $\mathcal{N} : \mathcal{X}_{pot} \to 2^{\mathcal{X}_{pot}}$ given by the union $\mathcal{N} = \bigcup_{\alpha \in \mathcal{T}} \mathcal{N}_\alpha$ of the forward functions for each Petri net transition, where $\mathcal{N}_\alpha(\mathbf{i}) = \emptyset$ if $\alpha \notin \mathcal{T}(\mathbf{i})$, while $\mathcal{N}_\alpha(\mathbf{i}) = \{\mathbf{j}\}$ if instead $\mathbf{i} \overset{\alpha}{\rightarrow} \mathbf{j}$, and an *initial state set* $\mathcal{X}_{init} = \{\mathbf{i}_{init}\}$. Indeed, we could have defined the Petri net with an arbitrary initial set of markings $\mathcal{X}_{init} \subseteq \mathbb{N}^{|\mathcal{P}|}$, and let the net nondeterministically start in one of these markings. The *reachable state space* $\mathcal{X}_{rch}$, or *reachability set*, of such a model is then defined as the smallest set $\mathcal{X} \subseteq \mathcal{X}_{pot}$ containing $\mathcal{X}_{init}$ and satisfying either the *recursive definition* $\mathbf{i} \in \mathcal{X} \wedge \mathbf{j} \in \mathcal{N}(\mathbf{i}) \Rightarrow \mathbf{j} \in \mathcal{X}$, which is the base for *explicit* state-space generation methods, or, equivalently, the *fixpoint equation* $\mathcal{X} = \mathcal{X} \cup \mathcal{N}(\mathcal{X})$, which is the base for *symbolic* state-space generation methods. Either way, we can write

$$\mathcal{X}_{rch} = \mathcal{X}_{init} \cup \mathcal{N}(\mathcal{X}_{init}) \cup \mathcal{N}^2(\mathcal{X}_{init}) \cup \mathcal{N}^3(\mathcal{X}_{init}) \cup \cdots = \mathcal{N}^*(\mathcal{X}_{init}).$$

2.2 Binary Decision Diagrams and Their Operations

An *(ordered) binary decision diagram* (BDD) over the sequence of *domain* variables $(v_L, \ldots, v_1)$, with an order $v_l \succ v_k$ iff $l > k$ defined on them, is an acyclic directed edge-labeled graph where:

- The only *terminal* nodes can be **0** and **1**, and are associated with the *range* variable $\mathbf{0}.var = \mathbf{1}.var = v_0$, satisfying $v_k \succ v_0$ for any domain variable v_k.
- A *nonterminal* node p is associated with a domain variable $p.var$.
- A nonterminal node p has two outgoing edges labeled 0 and 1, pointing to *children* denoted respectively $p[0]$ and $p[1]$.
- The variable of the children is lower than that of p, that is, $p.var \succ p[0].var$ and $p.var \succ p[1].var$.

Node p with $p.var = v_k$ encodes function $f_p : \mathbb{B}^L \to \mathbb{B}$, recursively defined by

$$f_p(i_L, ..., i_1) = \begin{cases} p & \text{if } k = 0 \\ f_{p[i_k]}(i_L, ..., i_1) & \text{if } k > 0 \end{cases}$$

(we write f_p as a function of L variables even when $k < L$, to stress that *any* variable x_h not explicitly appearing on a path from p to a terminal node is a "don't care" for f_p, regardless of whether $h < k$ or $h > k$).

We restrict ourselves to *canonical* forms of decision diagrams, where each function that can be encoded by a given class of decision diagrams has a unique representation in that class. For BDDs, canonicity is achieved by requiring that

1. There is no *duplicate*: if $p.var = q.var$, $p[0] = q[0]$, and $p[1] = q[1]$, then $p = q$.
2. One of the following forms holds.
   Quasi-reduced form: there is no variable skipping, i.e., if $p.var = v_k$, then $p[0].var = p[1].var = v_{k-1}$ and $k = L$ if p is a root (has no incoming arcs).
   Fully-reduced form: there is maximum variable skipping, i.e., no *redundant* node p exists, with $p[0] = p[1]$.

Fig. 1 shows a quasi-reduced and a fully-reduced BDD encoding the same function over (v_4, v_3, v_2, v_1), redundant nodes are indicated in grey.

Both canonical versions enjoy desirable properties: if functions f and g are encoded using BDDs, then *satisfiability*, "$f \neq 0$?", and *equivalence*, "$f = g$?",

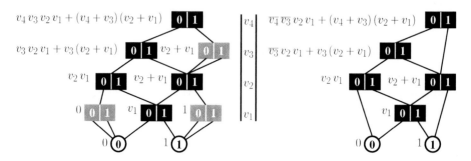

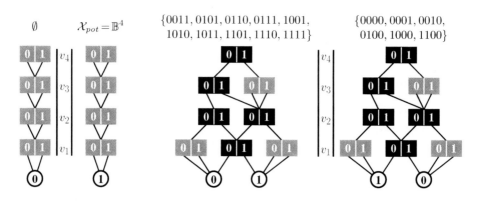

Fig. 1. Quasi-reduced (left) and fully-reduced (right) BDDs for the same function

Fig. 2. Two sets and their complement, encoded as quasi-reduced BDDs

can be answered in $O(1)$ time, while the BDD encoding the *conjunction* $f \wedge g$ or the *disjunction* $f \vee g$ can be built in $O(||f|| \times ||g||)$ time and space, if using the fully-reduced form, or $\sum_{L \geq k \geq 1} O(||f||_k \times ||g||_k)$ time and space, if using the quasi-reduced form, where $||f||$ is the number of nodes in the BDD encoding f and $||f||_k$ is the number of nodes associated with v_k in the BDD encoding f.

We can encode a set $\mathcal{Y} \subseteq \mathbb{B}^L$ as a BDD p through its *characteristic function*, so that $\mathbf{i} = (i_L, ..., i_1) \in \mathcal{Y} \Leftrightarrow f_p(i_L, ..., i_1) = 1$. The *size of the set* encoded by the BDD rooted at p is not directly related to the *size of the BDD* itself. For example, any set requires as many nodes as its complement, as shown in Fig. 2.

Algorithms for the manipulation of decision diagrams follow a typical recursive style. For example, Fig. 3 shows the pseudocode for the union operation on two sets encoded by fully-reduced BDDs p and q (i.e., the logical "or" of their characteristic functions). The pseudocode for *Intersection* or *Diff* (set difference) differs from that for *Union* only in the terminal cases. For *Intersection*(p, q), we return q if $q = \mathbf{0}$ or $p = \mathbf{1}$ and p if $q = \mathbf{1}$ or $p = \mathbf{0}$, while the case $p = q$, which might arise before reaching the terminal nodes, remains the same; for *Diff*(p, q), we return $\mathbf{0}$ if $p = \mathbf{0}$ or $q = \mathbf{1}$ and $\mathbf{1}$ if $q = \mathbf{0}$ and $p = \mathbf{1}$, while we return $\mathbf{0}$ if $p = q$. Another fundamental operation is the *relational product* which, given a BDD on $(v_L, ..., v_1)$ rooted at p encoding a set $\mathcal{Y} \subseteq \mathcal{X}_{pot}$ and a BDD on $(v_L, v'_L, ..., v_1, v'_1)$

```
bdd Union(bdd p, bdd q) is                              • fully-reduced version
 1  if p = 0 or q = 1 then return q;
 2  if q = 0 or p = 1 then return p;
 3  if p = q then return p;
 4  if Cache contains entry ⟨Union, {p, q} : r⟩ then return r;
 5  if p.var = q.var then
 6      r ← UniqueTableInsert(p.var, Union(p[0], q[0]), Union(p[1], q[1]));
 7  else if p.var ≻ q.var then
 8      r ← UniqueTableInsert(p.var, Union(p[0], q), Union(p[1], q));
 9  else since q.var ≻ p.var then
10      r ← UniqueTableInsert(q.var, Union(p, q[0]), Union(p, q[1]));
11  enter ⟨Union, {p, q} : r⟩ in Cache;
12  return r;
```

Fig. 3. The union operation on fully-reduced BDDs

rooted at r encoding a function $\mathcal{N} : \mathcal{X}_{pot} \rightarrow 2^{\mathcal{X}_{pot}}$, as the set of pairs $(\mathbf{i}, \mathbf{j})$ such that $\mathbf{j} \in \mathcal{N}(\mathbf{i})$, returns the root of the BDD on $(v_L, ..., v_1)$ encoding the set $\{\mathbf{j} : \exists \mathbf{i} \in \mathcal{Y} \wedge \mathbf{j} \in \mathcal{N}(\mathbf{i})\}$. An *interleaved order* is usually adopted for $\mathcal{N}$, that is, if $\mathbf{j} \in \mathcal{N}(\mathbf{i})$, then the BDD encoding $\mathcal{N}$ contains a path corresponding to $(i_L, j_L, ..., i_1, j_1)$ from r to $\mathbf{1}$, except that, of course, some of the values may be skipped if the fully-reduced form is used. Fig. 4 shows this function assuming quasi-reduced BDDs. As it can be seen, this results in simpler code, as the nodes in a recursive call, p and r in our case, are associated with the same variable.

We conclude this brief introduction to BDDs by observing that, to efficiently ensure canonicity, all decision diagram algorithms use a *Unique Table* (a hash table) which, given a search key consisting of a node's variable v_k and the *node_id* (e.g., the pointer to a unique memory location) of each child returns the *node_id* of either an existing node (if it exists, to avoid duplicates) or of a newly created node associated with v_k with those children. Since the manipulation is performed recursively bottom-up, children are already in the Unique Table when looking up their parent. Furthermore, to achieve polynomial complexity, the algorithms also use an *Operation Cache* (also a hash table) which, given a search key consisting of an *op_code* and the sequence of operands' *node_id*s, returns the *node_id* of the result, if it has been previously computed. These two hash tables have different requirements with respect to managing collisions on the hash value. The Unique Table must be *lossless*, while a lossy implementation for the Operation Cache is acceptable, as this at worst reduces efficiency.

2.3   Symbolic Reachability-Set Generation for Safe Petri Nets

If a Petri net is *safe* (each place contains at most one token), $\mathcal{X}_{pot} = \mathbb{B}^L$, where $L = |\mathcal{P}|$, and we can store any set of markings $\mathcal{Y} \subseteq \mathcal{X}_{pot} = \mathbb{B}^L$ for such a Petri net with an L-variable BDD, and any relation over $\mathcal{X}_{pot}$, or function $\mathcal{X}_{pot} \rightarrow 2^{\mathcal{X}_{pot}}$, such as $\mathcal{N}$, with a $2L$-variable BDD. However, for safe nets, Pastor et al. showed how to generate the reachability set [43] by encoding $\mathcal{N}$ using $4|\mathcal{T}|$ boolean functions, each corresponding to a simple L-variable BDD describing:

```
bdd RelProd(bdd p, bdd2 r) is                                    • quasi-reduced version
 1  if p = 0 or r = 0 then return 0;
 2  if p = 1 and r = 1 then return 1;
 3  if Cache contains entry ⟨RelProd, p, r : q⟩ then return q;
 4  q₀ ← Union(RelProd(p[0], r[0][0]), RelProd(p[1], r[1][0]));
 5  q₁ ← Union(RelProd(p[0], r[0][1]), RelProd(p[1], r[1][1]));
 6  q ← UniqueTableInsert(p.var, q₀, q₁);
 7  enter ⟨RelProd, p, r : q⟩ in Cache;
 8  return q;
```

Fig. 4. The relational product operation on quasi-reduced BDDs

- $APM_\alpha = \bigwedge_{p:\mathbf{D}^- p, \alpha = 1}(v_p = 1)$, i.e., all predecessor places of α are marked.
- $NPM_\alpha = \bigwedge_{p:\mathbf{D}^- p, \alpha = 1}(v_p = 0)$, i.e., no predecessor place of α is marked.
- $ASM_\alpha = \bigwedge_{p:\mathbf{D}^+ p, \alpha = 1}(v_p = 1)$, i.e., all successor places of α are marked.
- $NSM_\alpha = \bigwedge_{p:\mathbf{D}^+ p, \alpha = 1}(v_p = 0)$, i.e., no successor place of α is marked.

The effect of transition α on a set of markings $\mathcal{U}$ can then be expressed as $\mathcal{N}_\alpha(\mathcal{U}) = (((\mathcal{U} \div APM_\alpha) \cdot NPM_\alpha) \div NSM_\alpha) \cdot ASM_\alpha$, where "$\cdot$" indicates boolean conjunction and "$\div$" indicates the *cofactor* operator, defined as follows: given a boolean function $f(v_L, \ldots, v_1)$ and a literal $v_k = i_k$, with $L \geq k \geq 1$ and $i_k \in \mathbb{B}$, the cofactor $f \div (v_k = i_k)$ is $f(v_L, \ldots, v_{k+1}, i_k, v_{k-1}, \ldots, v_1)$, and the extension to multiple literals, $f \div (v_{k_c} = i_{k_c}, \ldots, v_{k_1} = i_{k_1})$, is recursively defined as $f(v_L, \ldots, v_{k_c+1}, i_{k_c}, v_{k_c-1}, \ldots, v_1) \div (v_{k_c-1} = i_{k_c-1}, \ldots, v_{k_1} = i_{k_1})$.

If we instead follow a more traditional and general approach, $\mathcal{N}$ is stored either in *monolithic form* as a single $2L$-variable BDD, or in *disjunctively partition form* as $\bigcup_{\alpha \in \mathcal{T}} \mathcal{N}_\alpha$, where each $\mathcal{N}_\alpha$ is encoded as a $2L$-variable BDD. As the reachability set $\mathcal{X}_{rch}$ is the fixpoint of the iteration $\mathcal{X}_{init} \cup \mathcal{N}(\mathcal{X}_{init}) \cup \mathcal{N}(\mathcal{N}(\mathcal{X}_{init})) \cup \cdots$, we can compute it using a *breadth-first search* that only requires *Union*, *Diff*, and *RelProd* operations. Fig. 5 on the left shows the pseudocode for a traditional implementation of this algorithm, where sets and relations are encoded using BDDs, so that its runtime is proportional to the BDD sizes, not the size of the encoded sets and relations. Fig. 5 on the right shows an alternative approach that operates on a different sequence of sets: instead of applying the forward function $\mathcal{N}$ to the unexplored markings $\mathcal{U}$ (at the dth iteration, the markings at distance exactly d from $\mathcal{X}_{init}$), the "all" version applies $\mathcal{N}$ to all the markings $\mathcal{O}$ known so far (at the dth iteration, the markings at distance up to d from $\mathcal{X}_{init}$).

The decision diagrams manipulated by these algorithms, like many of those we will see in the following, encode an increasing amount of data as the fixpoint iterations progress. However, a fundamental, and sometimes counterintuitive, property of decision diagrams is that their size can swell and shrink during the iterations, so that the *final* size of, for example, the BDD encoding $\mathcal{X}_{rch}$ is often many orders of magnitude smaller than the *peak* BDD size encountered at some point along these iterations. This means that attempts to limit exploration (e.g., using partial order reduction techniques [52]) might be beneficial, or might instead hinder, decision-diagram-based approaches. One must report both final memory (for the decision diagram encoding the desired result) and peak memory

```
SymbolicBFS(X_init, N) is

1  Y ← X_init;              • known markings
2  U ← X_init;              • unexplored markings
3  repeat
4      W ← RelProd(U,N);    • new markings?
5      U ← Diff(W, Y);      • new markings!
6      Y ← Union(Y,U);
7  until U = ∅;
8  return Y;
```

```
SymbolicBFSall(X_init, N) is

1  Y ← X_init;
2  repeat
3      O ← Y;               • old markings
4      W ← RelProd(O,N);
5      Y ← Union(O,W);
6  until O = Y;
7  return Y;
```

Fig. 5. Two versions of a symbolic BFS algorithm to generate the reachability set [15]

requirements (including decision diagrams used in the computation and the hash table for the operation cache and the unique table), as the latter determine when it is feasible to run the analysis on a given machine and strongly affect runtime.

2.4 Multiway Decision Diagrams

When v_k has finite but not necessarily boolean domain $\mathcal{X}_k = \{0,1,...,n_k-1\}$ for some $n_k > 0$, we can use multiple boolean variables to encode it. Two common approaches are a standard *binary encoding* with $\lceil \log_2 n_k \rceil$ boolean variables, or a *one-hot encoding* with n_k boolean variables, exactly one of which is set to 1 in each reachable marking. Another alternative, which we adopt, is to directly use a natural extension of BDDs, (ordered) *multiway decision diagrams* (MDDs) [34]. The definition of an MDD is exactly as that of a BDD, except that the number of a node's children depends on its associated variable:

- For each $i_k \in \mathcal{X}_k$, a nonterminal node p associated with v_k has an outgoing edge labeled with i_k and pointing to a child $p[i_k]$.

The quasi-reduced and fully-reduced canonical forms are also exactly analogous to those for BDDs, except that, of course, p duplicates q if $p.var = q.var$ and $p[i_k] = q[i_k]$ for all $i_k \in \mathcal{X}_k$, and p is redundant if $p[0] = p[1] = \cdots = p[n_k - 1]$.

MDDs open an interesting possibility: while we might know (or even just simply hope) that $\mathcal{X}_{rch}$ is finite, we might not know a priori the size of each $\mathcal{X}_k$, i.e., the bound on the number of tokens in each place. In this more general setting, we only know that the reachability set satisfies $\mathcal{X}_{init} \subseteq \mathcal{X}_{rch} \subseteq \mathbb{N}^{|\mathcal{P}|}$. Thus, we need an MDD-based reachability-set generation approach where the size of each node p associated with domain variable v_k is *conceptually* infinite, as we do not know a priori which children $p[i_k]$ might be eventually needed to store the reachable marking (i.e., whether the place corresponding to v_k might ever contain i_k tokens). However, if the net is indeed bounded, only a finite number of these children will be on paths leading to the terminal **1** in the MDD encoding $\mathcal{X}_{rch}$. We then define a *sparse* canonical form, where a node has as many children as the number of edges pointing to nodes encoding a non-empty set and only nodes encoding the empty set can be classified as redundant. Fig. 6 shows the same function encoded as a quasi-reduced, fully-reduced, and sparse canonical

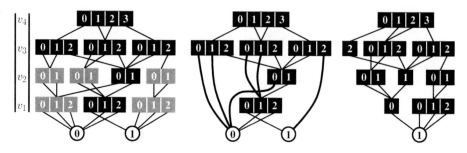

Fig. 6. Quasi-reduced, fully-reduced, and sparse canonical forms for MDDs

MDD. In the first two forms, we must know that $\mathcal{X}_4 = \{0, 1, 2, 3\}$, $\mathcal{X}_3 = \{0, 1, 2\}$, $\mathcal{X}_2 = \{0, 1\}$, and $\mathcal{X}_1 = \{0, 1, 2\}$ while, in the third form, no such assumption is required and the resulting MDD does not contain the terminal **0** nor any node leading only to it (the two leftmost redundant nodes associated with variables v_2 and v_1 in the quasi-reduced form), but it contains all other redundant nodes. As the size of the nodes associated with a given v_k is variable, this requires a slightly more complex implementation, but this is usually a small price to pay compared to the greater flexibility and generality they provide.

2.5   Extended Petri Nets

Now that we know how to encode arbitrary finite sets $\mathcal{Y} \subset \mathbb{N}^{|\mathcal{P}|}$ of markings using MDDs in sparse form, we can assume a more general extended Petri net model, for example one that allows *inhibitor arcs*:

- $\mathbf{D}^\circ : \mathcal{P} \times \mathcal{T} \to \mathbb{N} \cup \{\infty\}$ are the inhibitor arc cardinalities,

so that transition α is disabled in marking **i** if there is a place p such that $\mathbf{D}^\circ_{p,\alpha} \le i_p$, or *self-modifying* behavior where arcs cardinalities depend on the current marking:

- $\mathbf{D}^-, \mathbf{D}^+ : \mathcal{P} \times \mathcal{T} \times \mathbb{N}^{|\mathcal{P}|} \to \mathbb{N}$ are the *marking-dependent* input and output arc cardinalities,

so that α is enabled in **i** iff, $\forall p \in \mathcal{P}$, $\mathbf{D}^-_{p,\alpha}(\mathbf{i}) \le i_p$ and, if α fires, it leads to marking **j** satisfying $j_p = i_p - \mathbf{D}^-_{p,\alpha}(\mathbf{i}) + \mathbf{D}^+_{p,\alpha}(\mathbf{i})$. Both $\mathbf{D}^-_{p,\alpha}$ and $\mathbf{D}^+_{p,\alpha}$ are evaluated on the current, not the new, marking; also, these two extensions can be combined, allowing marking-dependent inhibitor arc cardinalities. It is well-known that inhibitor arcs alone suffice to achieve Turing-equivalence, while self-modifying behavior may or may not, depending on the type of functions allowed to specify arc cardinalities. However, since our approach is to simply run the symbolic reachability-set generation and "hope for the best" (i.e., for a finite $\mathcal{X}_{reach}$ that can be encoded in an MDD), these extensions are welcome from the point of view of modeling flexibility and ease.

We conclude this discussion of MDD encoding for general Petri nets by stressing that, while we have so far assumed that each Petri net place is mapped to an MDD variable, this is neither required in theory nor necessarily the most efficient approach in practice. First of all, even when MDD variable v_k corresponds to a single Petri net place a with bound B_a, not all numbers of tokens $n_a \in \{0, ..., B_a\}$ might be possible in a (in particular, even B_a itself might be just an overestimate on the real bound). It is then best to map the different numbers of tokens *observed* in a during reachability-set generation to the indices 0, 1, and so on; then, $|\mathcal{X}_k| \leq B_a + 1$ will at the end count the distinct numbers of tokens achievable in a. More importantly, if we know that the range of values for the number of tokens in a is large, we might want to *split* this number over multiple MDD variables; this is of course required if we are using BDDs, as we already observed. On the other hand, if multiple places are highly correlated, we might want to *merge* them into the same variable; for example, if two places are *complementary*, i.e., the sum of the tokens in them is a constant, we clearly want to represent them with a single MDD variable as this does not increase the complexity of the encoding but reduces instead the height of the MDD.

Unfortunately, finding a good mapping of places to variables is a difficult problem, just as the related one about finding a good order for the variables, known to be NP-hard [7]. This is especially true for the more advanced algorithms we discuss later, which strongly rely on the structural dependencies between the Petri net transitions and the MDD variables.

2.6   Running Examples for Experiments

Fig. 7 presents the Petri net models used to obtain memory and runtime results for the various algorithms presented in this paper. All experiments are run on a server of Intel Xeon CPU 2.53GHz with 38G RAM under Linux 2.6.18

To study a Petri net with MDDs, we decompose the potential state space into the product of local state spaces, by partitioning the places into L *submodels*. Each (sub)marking of the kth submodel is mapped to a local state in $\mathcal{X}_k$, so that, if the Petri net is bounded, the local state spaces $\mathcal{X}_k$ are finite. Hence, the L MDD variables correspond to the L submodels. The choice of partition affects the performance of our algorithms, and finding an optimal partition is non-trivial. In the experiments, we use a partition that works well in practice.

phils [44] models the dining-philosophers problem, where N philosophers sit around a table with a fork between each of them. To eat, a philosopher must acquire both the fork to his left and to his right. If all philosophers choose to take the fork to their left first, the model deadlocks (the same happens if all take the fork to their right). The entire model contains N subnets, the figure shows the ith one, for some $i \in \{1, ..., N\}$; place $Fork_{\mathrm{mod}\,(i,N)+1}$ is drawn with dashed lines because it is not part of this subnet. We group the places for two adjacent philosophers into a submodel, thus $L = N/2$ (with N even).

robin [28] models a round-robin resource sharing protocol, where N processes cyclically can access a resource. Again, the model has N subnets and the ith subnet (shown in the figure) can access the resource only when its place $Pask_i$ contains the token initially in $Pask_1$. Place Res, containing the resource when idle, is drawn with bold lines because it is not part of any subnet. We group the places for each process ($Pask_i, Pok_i, Psnd_i, Pwt_i$) into a submodel and assign place Res to a separate submodel. The number of domain variables is $L = N+1$.

fms [20] models a flexible manufacturing system where N parts of each of three types circulate around and are machined at stations. Parts of type 1 are machined by machine 1, of which there are three instances. Parts of type 2 are machined by machine 2, of which there is only one instance; however, when not working on parts of type 2, machine 2 can work on parts of type 3. Finally, parts of type 1 and 2, when completed, can be shipped (and replaced by new raw parts of the same type), just like parts of type 3, or might be joined by machine 3, of which there are two instances. Transitions shown in black are immediate [1] (from a logical standpoint, this simply means that they have priority over the other transitions, more details on the analysis of this type of models is given in Section 4.3). As N grows, only the possible number of tokens in (most of) the places grows, not the net itself. We group $\{M1, P1wM1, P1M1\}$, $\{M2, P2wM2, P2M2\}$ and $\{M3, P12wM3, P12M3\}$ into three submodels, and treat each remaining place as an individual submodel. Thus, $L = 16$.

slot [43] models a slotted ring transmission protocol where, as in **robin**, a token cycling around N subnets grants access to the medium. Unlike **robin**, though, this resource is not modeled, thus each subnet is just connected to its two neighbors through shared transitions, not to a globally shared place. We group the places for each subnet ($A_i, B_i, C_i, ..., G_i$) into a submodel and $L = N$.

kanban [51] models an assembly line using tokens (kanbans) to control the flow of parts to four assembly stations. Station 1, when completing work on a part, feeds that part to both stations 2 and 3 for further processing, thus transition s_{1_23} correspond to a "fork". When both stations 2 and 3 have completed parts waiting in places out_2 and out_3, the "join" transition s_{23_4} can pass them as a single token to station 4. As in **fms**, N controls the token population but not the size of the net. We group places for each station into a submodel and $L = 4$.

leader [32] models the distributed asynchronous protocol proposed by Itai and Rodeh to elect a leader among N processes in a unidirectional ring, by sending messages. The algorithm employs a randomization strategy to choose whether each process will continue running for election (my_pref=1) or not (my_pref=0). A process is eliminated from the race only if it chooses not to run and its closest active predecessor chooses to run. Once this happens, the process becomes inactive and only relays messages from active nodes. Termination is realized by having the active processes send a token around the ring to count the inactive nodes; if a process receives its own token with count $N - 1$, it knows to be the elected leader. The model contains N subnets (thus the number of places grows linearly in N, while the number of transitions grows quadratically in N) but, in addition, the token population in some places also grows linearly in N. We group places for each subnet into a submodel, thus $L = N$. We only show the automaton model due to the size and complexity of the net.

counter models a simple N-bit counter, which is incremented by one at each step, from 0 up to $2^N - 1$, then reset back to 0. We treat each place (bit) as a submodel and $L = N$.

queen models the placement of N queens on an $N \times N$ chessboard in such a way that they are not attacking each other. Places q_i, for $i \in \{1, ..., N\}$, represent the queens still to be placed on the chessboard, while places $p_{i,j}$, for $i, j \in \{1, ..., N\}$ represent the N^2 chessboard positions, thus are initially empty. The non-attacking restriction is achieved through inhibitor arcs (on the same column or either of the two diagonals, k ranges from 1 to $i-1$) plus the limitation on the row placed by having the single token in q_i be contended among transitions $t_{i,j}$, for $j \in \{1, ..., N\}$. In addition, we force the placement of the queens to happen in row order, from 1 to N, thus $t_{i,j}$ has inhibitor arcs from q_k, again for $k \in \{1, ..., i - 1\}$. The number of places and transitions grows quadratically in N. We group the places for each queen (q_i and p_{ij}) into a submodel and $L = N$.

2.7 Accelerating the Fixpoint Computation: Chaining and Saturation

So far, we have considered only breadth-first methods, characterized by the fact that reachable markings are found strictly in order of their distance from $\mathcal{X}_{init}$. If we are willing to forgo this property, enormous runtime and memory improvements can often be achieved in practice.

The first such approach, *chaining* [47], observes that, when $\mathcal{N}$ is stored in disjunctively partitioned form using one BDD or MDD $\mathcal{N}_\alpha$ for each $\alpha \in \mathcal{T}$, the effect of statements 4 and 5 in Algorithm *SymbolicBFS* of Fig. 5 is exactly achieved with the statements:

$$\mathcal{W} \leftarrow \emptyset;$$
$$\text{for each } \alpha \in \mathcal{T} \text{ do}$$
$$\quad \mathcal{W} \leftarrow Union(\mathcal{W}, RelProd(\mathcal{U}, \mathcal{N}_\alpha));$$
$$\mathcal{U} \leftarrow Diff(\mathcal{W}, \mathcal{Y});$$

However, if we do not require strict breadth-first order, we can "chain" the Petri net transitions and use the following statements instead:

$$\text{for each } \alpha \in \mathcal{T} \text{ do}$$
$$\quad \mathcal{U} \leftarrow Union(\mathcal{U}, RelProd(\mathcal{U}, \mathcal{N}_\alpha));$$
$$\mathcal{U} \leftarrow Diff(\mathcal{U}, \mathcal{Y});$$

The effect of this change is that, if **i** is in $\mathcal{U}$, thus will be explored in the current iteration, and we use a particular transition order, say α, then β, then γ, the current iteration will discover all markings reachable from **i** by firing sequences (α), (α, β), (α, β, γ), (α, γ), (β), (β, γ), and (γ). This may find more markings in the current iteration than if we used a strictly breadth-first approach, which instead just considers the individual effect of transitions α, β, and γ.

It is easy to prove that the use of chaining can only reduce, not increase, the *number* of iterations. However, the *cost* of each iteration depends on the

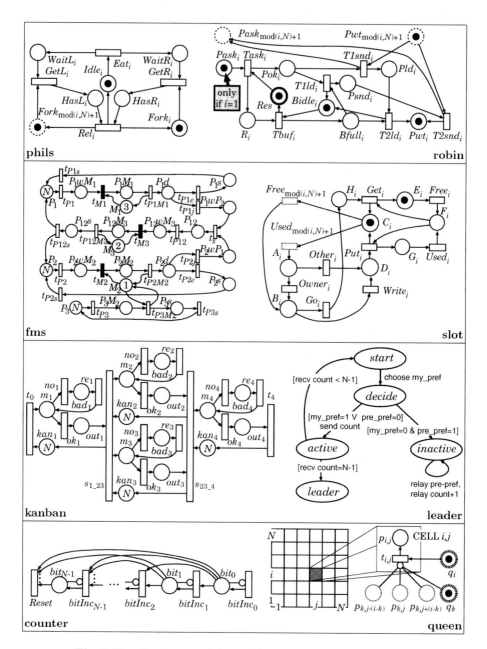

Fig. 7. The Petri net models used for experiments in our study

size of the involved decision diagrams encoding the various sets being manipulated (the encodings of the forward functions are fixed, thus independent of the iteration strategy). Fewer iterations on different decision diagrams do not necessarily imply higher efficiency in a symbolic setting. The same can be said for the

$BfSsGen(\mathcal{X}_{init}, \{\mathcal{N}_\alpha : \alpha \in \mathcal{T}\})$	
1 $\mathcal{Y} \leftarrow \mathcal{X}_{init}$;	• known markings
2 $\mathcal{U} \leftarrow \mathcal{X}_{init}$;	• frontier markings
3 repeat	
4 $\mathcal{W} \leftarrow \emptyset$;	
5 for each $\alpha \in \mathcal{T}$ do	
6 $\mathcal{W} \leftarrow Union(\mathcal{W}, RelProd(\mathcal{U}, \mathcal{N}_\alpha))$;	
7 $\mathcal{U} \leftarrow Diff(\mathcal{W}, \mathcal{Y})$;	
8 $\mathcal{Y} \leftarrow Union(\mathcal{Y}, \mathcal{U})$;	
9 until $\mathcal{U} = \emptyset$;	
10 return $\mathcal{Y}$;	

$ChSsGen(\mathcal{X}_{init}, \{\mathcal{N}_\alpha : \alpha \in \mathcal{T}\})$	
1 $\mathcal{Y} \leftarrow \mathcal{X}_{init}$;	• known markings
2 $\mathcal{U} \leftarrow \mathcal{X}_{init}$;	• frontier markings
3 repeat	
4 for each $\alpha \in \mathcal{T}$ do	
5 $\mathcal{W} \leftarrow Diff(RelProd(\mathcal{U}, \mathcal{N}_\alpha), \mathcal{Y})$;	
6 $\mathcal{U} \leftarrow Union(\mathcal{U}, \mathcal{W})$;	
7 $\mathcal{U} \leftarrow Diff(\mathcal{U}, \mathcal{Y})$;	
8 $\mathcal{Y} \leftarrow Union(\mathcal{Y}, \mathcal{U})$;	
9 until $\mathcal{U} = \emptyset$;	
10 return $\mathcal{Y}$;	

$AllBfSsGen(\mathcal{X}_{init}, \{\mathcal{N}_\alpha : \alpha \in \mathcal{T}\})$	
1 $\mathcal{Y} \leftarrow \mathcal{X}_{init}$;	• known markings
2 repeat	
3 $\mathcal{O} \leftarrow \mathcal{Y}$;	• save old markings
4 $\mathcal{W} \leftarrow \emptyset$;	
5 for each $\alpha \in \mathcal{T}$ do	
6 $\mathcal{W} \leftarrow Union(\mathcal{W}, RelProd(\mathcal{O}, \mathcal{N}_\alpha))$;	
7 $\mathcal{Y} \leftarrow Union(\mathcal{O}, \mathcal{W})$;	
8 until $\mathcal{O} = \mathcal{Y}$;	
9 return $\mathcal{Y}$;	

$AllChSsGen(\mathcal{X}_{init}, \{\mathcal{N}_\alpha : \alpha \in \mathcal{T}\})$	
1 $\mathcal{Y} \leftarrow \mathcal{X}_{init}$;	• known markings
2 repeat	
3 $\mathcal{O} \leftarrow \mathcal{Y}$;	• save old markings
4 for each $\alpha \in \mathcal{T}$ do	
5 $\mathcal{Y} \leftarrow Union(\mathcal{Y}, RelProd(\mathcal{Y}, \mathcal{N}_\alpha))$;	
6 until $\mathcal{O} = \mathcal{Y}$;	
7 return $\mathcal{Y}$;	

Fig. 8. Four simple variants of symbolic reachability-set generation [15]

difference between the two algorithms of Fig. 5, which end up encoding either the *frontier* markings at *exactly* a given distance d from $\mathcal{X}_{init}$, or *all* the markings *up to* distance d, respectively. Combining these two choices (BFS vs. chaining, frontier vs. all) gives us the four algorithms shown in Fig. 8, whose performance spans several orders of magnitude, as shown by the results of Fig. 9, where *AllChSsGen* is a consistently good choice, both (peak) memory and time-wise. Still, the memory required to store $\mathcal{X}_{rch}$ alone is a negligible fraction of the peak requirement (except for the **queen** model, which is pathologically difficult for symbolic methods), leaving hope for improvement, as we see next.

Much lower peak memory requirements can usually be achieved by adopting a *saturation* strategy [13]. Before presenting this approach, we need to introduce the concept of *locality* and a new reduction rule to exploit locality when encoding forward functions of asynchronous systems.

Given $\alpha \in \mathcal{T}$, define the subsets of the state variables $\{v_L, ..., v_1\}$ that can be modified by α as $\mathcal{V}_M(\alpha) = \{v_k : \exists \mathbf{i}, \mathbf{i}' \in \mathcal{X}_{pot}, \mathbf{i}' \in \mathcal{N}_\alpha(\mathbf{i}) \wedge i_k \neq i'_k\}$, and that can disable α as $\mathcal{V}_D(\alpha) = \{v_k : \exists \mathbf{i}, \mathbf{j} \in \mathcal{X}_{pot}, \forall h \neq k, i_h = j_h \wedge \mathcal{N}_\alpha(\mathbf{i}) \neq \emptyset \wedge \mathcal{N}_\alpha(\mathbf{j}) = \emptyset\}$.

If $v_k \notin \mathcal{V}_M(\alpha) \cup \mathcal{V}_D(\alpha)$, we say that α and v_k are *independent*. Most events in *globally-asynchronous locally-synchronous* models are highly *local*; for example, in Petri nets, a transition is independent of any place not connected to it. We let $Top(\alpha) = \max(\mathcal{V}_M(\alpha) \cup \mathcal{V}_D(\alpha))$ and $Bot(\alpha) = \min(\mathcal{V}_M(\alpha) \cup \mathcal{V}_D(\alpha))$ be the highest and the lowest variables dependent on α, respectively, and observe that the *span* of variables $(Top(\alpha), ..., Bot(\alpha))$ is often much smaller than $(v_L, ..., v_1)$.

N	$|\mathcal{X}_{rch}|$	Time				Memory				$\frac{|\mathcal{X}_{rch}|}{mem.}$
		Bf	$AllBf$	Ch	$AllCh$	Bf	$AllBf$	Ch	$AllCh$	mem.
phils										
50	$2.22 \cdot 10^{31}$	4.26	3.52	0.18	0.08	87.81	73.88	9.65	4.98	0.02
100	$4.96 \cdot 10^{62}$	61.01	50.49	1.04	0.34	438.51	371.44	35.18	16.01	0.04
200	$2.46 \cdot 10^{125}$	1550.86	1177.16	5.62	2.31	2795.03	2274.97	138.85	61.30	0.09
robin										
50	$1.26 \cdot 10^{17}$	24.41	34.55	0.43	0.34	172.46	110.83	11.53	9.74	0.10
60	$1.55 \cdot 10^{20}$	51.17	72.41	0.74	0.69	294.42	178.61	17.24	15.70	0.14
70	$1.85 \cdot 10^{23}$	101.45	138.93	1.20	1.14	476.12	278.69	25.01	22.90	0.19
fms										
15	$7.24 \cdot 10^{8}$	9.49	4.12	1.35	0.80	91.11	46.63	23.56	17.68	0.05
20	$8.83 \cdot 10^{9}$	37.13	14.00	4.35	2.26	166.10	79.42	64.00	29.05	0.08
30	$3.43 \cdot 10^{11}$	501.26	94.14	16.41	10.02	497.63	175.90	142.99	77.78	0.19
slot										
20	$2.73 \cdot 10^{20}$	12.81	12.82	12.78	12.81	239.91	239.91	239.91	239.91	0.03
30	$1.03 \cdot 10^{31}$	93.23	92.33	93.18	93.07	1140.41	1140.41	1140.41	1140.41	0.07
40	$4.15 \cdot 10^{41}$	504.23	504.62	490.25	473.10	6272.78	6272.78	6272.78	6272.78	0.13
kanban										
20	$8.05 \cdot 10^{11}$	4.63	4.52	0.92	0.85	89.10	81.12	60.37	53.38	0.07
30	$4.98 \cdot 10^{13}$	28.78	27.45	5.96	5.72	539.73	399.76	160.52	160.45	0.21
40	$9.94 \cdot 10^{14}$	124.92	130.47	28.48	43.45	1530.40	1098.08	527.80	482.77	0.47
leader										
6	$1.89 \cdot 10^{6}$	7.90	15.29	7.86	6.79	73.25	75.66	81.93	57.64	0.32
7	$2.39 \cdot 10^{7}$	37.59	75.16	40.23	35.62	201.83	130.37	254.89	156.12	0.81
8	$3.04 \cdot 10^{8}$	175.88	558.51	200.84	171.32	516.79	201.75	692.89	259.06	1.82
counter										
10	$1.02 \cdot 10^{3}$	0.01	0.04	0.01	0.01	0.71	1.72	0.79	0.67	0.00
15	$3.27 \cdot 10^{4}$	2.29	5.84	1.50	2.38	22.73	5.17	12.14	6.80	0.00
20	$1.04 \cdot 10^{6}$	652.15	447.09	192.11	204.36	795.92	9.33	212.35	15.28	0.00
queen										
10	$3.55 \cdot 10^{4}$	0.68	0.68	0.68	0.68	10.39	10.48	10.40	10.39	1.13
12	$8.56 \cdot 10^{5}$	23.63	23.64	23.62	23.61	220.33	220.54	220.35	220.35	20.77
14	$2.73 \cdot 10^{7}$	1096.51	1097.97	1094.58	1093.75	7305.90	7306.30	7305.93	7305.94	505.73

Fig. 9. Results for four reachability-set generation variants (memory: MB, time: sec)

However, the canonical forms considered so far do not exploit this locality in a symbolic encoding of $\mathcal{N}_\alpha$. We need a more general and flexible canonical form that associates an individual *reduction rule* $R(v_k)$ with each variable v_k:

- If $R(v_k) = F$, variable v_k is *fully-reduced*. No node p associated with v_k can have all children $p[i_k]$, for $i_k \in \mathcal{X}_k$, coincide.
- If $R(v_k) = I$, variable k is *identity-reduced*. Let q associated with v_k be *singular* if it has exactly one edge $q[i_k] \neq \mathbf{0}$; then, no edge $p[i_l]$ can point to q if $i_l = i_k$ or if the edge skips a fully-reduced variable v_h such that $i_k \in \mathcal{X}_h$.
- If $R(v_k) = Q$, variable v_k is *quasi-reduced*. There must be at least one node associated with v_k and no edge can skip v_k.

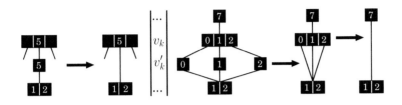

Fig. 10. Advantages of using the identity-reduced rule in the presence of locality

The function $f_p : \mathcal{X}_{pot} \to \mathbb{B}$ encoded by a node p associated with v_k is then

$$f_p(i_L,...,i_1) = \begin{cases} p & \text{if } k=0 \\ f_{p[i_k]}(i_L,...,i_1) & \text{if } k>0 \text{ and } \forall v_k \succ v_h \succ p[i_k].var, \ R(v_h)=I \Rightarrow i_h=i_k \\ 0 & \text{otherwise,} \end{cases}$$

thus, if an edge $p[i_k]$ skips over an identity-reduced variable v_h, the value of i_h must be the same as that of i_k.

This more general reduction is particularly useful when encoding the forward functions of a model with widespread locality. Specifically, when encoding $\mathcal{N}_\alpha$, we still use an interleaved order for the variables, but set $R(v_k') = I$ for all "to", or "primed", variables v_k', while "from", or "unprimed" variables are either all fully-reduced or, alternatively, quasi-reduced if $v_k \in \mathcal{V}_M(\alpha) \cup \mathcal{V}_D(\alpha)$ and fully-reduced otherwise. Fig. 10 illustrates the effect of this choice. On the left, the node associated with v_k' is singular, thus it is eliminated (this corresponds to a Petri net where the firing of α leaves the corresponding place p_k unchanged if p_k contains five tokens). More importantly, the situation on the right considers the common case where α is independent of place p_k. The identity-reduced rule for v_k' means that all nodes associated with v_k' will be singular, thus are eliminated; but then, all nodes associated with v_k, which is fully-reduced, will become redundant, so are eliminated as well. The result is that all edges will simply skip both variables v_k and v_k' in the MDD encoding of $\mathcal{N}_\alpha$.

To fully exploit locality and efficiently build an encoding for the forward function, not only we partition $\mathcal{N}$ as the disjunction $\bigcup_{\alpha \in \mathcal{T}} \mathcal{N}_\alpha$, but we further encode each $\mathcal{N}_\alpha$ as a conjunction. In the best case, $\mathcal{N}_\alpha$ has a conjunctive representation by variable, $\mathcal{N}_\alpha = (\bigcap_{k \in \mathcal{V}_M(\alpha) \cup \mathcal{V}_D(\alpha)} \mathcal{N}_{k,\alpha}) \cap (\bigcap_{k \notin \mathcal{V}_M(\alpha) \cup \mathcal{V}_D(\alpha)} \mathcal{I}_k)$, where the *local* function $\mathcal{N}_{k,\alpha} : \mathcal{X}_k \to 2^{\mathcal{X}_k}$ describes how α depends on v_k and affects v_k', independently of the value of all the other state variables, while $\mathcal{I}_k$ is the identity for v_k, that is, $\mathcal{I}_k(i_k) = \{i_k\}$ for any $i_k \in \mathcal{X}_k$. Along the same lines, a *disjunctive-then-conjunctive* decomposition of $\mathcal{N}$ can be defined for arbitrary models, $\mathcal{N}_\alpha = (\bigcap_{c=1}^{m_\alpha} \mathcal{N}_{c,\alpha}) \cap (\bigcap_{k \notin \mathcal{V}_M(\alpha) \cup \mathcal{V}_D(\alpha)} \mathcal{I}_k)$, where we now have some m_α conjuncts, each one depending on some set of variables $\mathcal{D}_{c,\alpha}$, so that $\bigcup_{c=1}^{m_\alpha} \mathcal{D}_{c,\alpha} = \mathcal{V}_M(\alpha) \cup \mathcal{V}_D(\alpha)$ and $\mathcal{N}_{c,\alpha} : \times_{k \in \mathcal{D}_{c,\alpha}} \mathcal{X}_k \to 2^{\times_{k \in \mathcal{D}_{c,\alpha}} \mathcal{X}_k}$ describes how α is affected and affects the variables in $\mathcal{D}_{c,\alpha}$ as a whole.

As an example, consider the portion of self-modifying Petri net in Fig. 11 (the pseudocode on the right, to be interpreted as an atomic check and concurrent

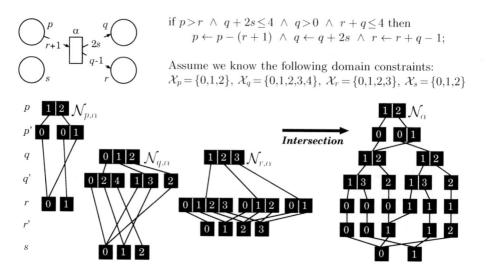

Fig. 11. A transition α in a self-modifying Petri net, its equivalent pseudocode, and the conjunctive decomposition of its forward function $\mathcal{N}_\alpha$

assignment, illustrates the semantic of transition α). The bottom of the figure shows three conjuncts $\mathcal{N}_{p,\alpha}$, $\mathcal{N}_{q,\alpha}$, and $\mathcal{N}_{r,\alpha}$, whose intersection describes the overall enabling conditions and effect of transition α. For example, $\mathcal{N}_{p,\alpha}$ describes how and when p might be updated: p must be greater than r and its value is decreased by $r+1$ if α fires (for clarity, we use the quasi-reduced rule for variables on which a conjunct depends). By decomposing each $\mathcal{N}_\alpha$ in this fashion, we can then build the MDD for each conjunct $\mathcal{N}_{c,\alpha}$ explicitly (as shown in Fig. 11, these conjuncts tend to be small because of locality), and then use symbolic intersection operations to build the MDD encoding the overall $\mathcal{N}_\alpha$, which might instead encode a very large relation. Note that, for this to work efficiently, we need to "play a trick" with the reduction rules: for example, q, q', s, s' and any other variable not explicitly mentioned must be interpreted as fully-reduced in $\mathcal{N}_{p,\alpha}$ prior to performing the intersection with $\mathcal{N}_{q,\alpha}$; however, after performing the intersection, s' must be interpreted as identity-reduced (since s is not affected by α), and any pair of unprimed and primed variables not explicitly mentioned must be interpreted as fully-reduced and identity-reduced, respectively.

We can now describe the *saturation* strategy. We say that a node associated with v_k is *saturated* if it is a fixpoint with respect to all events α such that $Top(\alpha) \leq k$. This implies that all MDD nodes reachable from p are also saturated. The idea is then to saturate the nodes bottom-up, and to saturate any new node prior to inserting it in the unique table:

- Build the L-variable MDD encoding of $\mathcal{X}_{init}$.
- Saturate nodes associated with v_1: fire in them all events α s.t. $Top(\alpha) = 1$.
- Saturate nodes associated with v_2: fire in them all events α s.t. $Top(\alpha) = 2$. If this creates nodes associated with v_1, saturate them immediately.
- ...

---

mdd $Saturate$(variable v_k, mdd p) is   • *quasi-reduced version*

1 if $v_k = v_0$ then return p;
2 if $Cache$ contains entry $\langle Saturate, p : r \rangle$ then return r;
3 foreach $i_k \in \mathcal{X}_k$ do
4      $r_{i_k} \leftarrow Saturate(v_{k-1}, p[i_k])$;   • *first, be sure that the children are saturated*
5 repeat
6   choose $\alpha \in \mathcal{T}$, $i_k, j_k \in \mathcal{X}_k$ s.t. $Top(\alpha) = k$ and $r_{i_k} \neq \mathbf{0}$ and $\mathcal{N}_\alpha[i_k][j_k] \neq \mathbf{0}$;
7      $r_{j_k} \leftarrow Union(r_{j_k}, RelProdSat(v_{k-1}, r_{i_k}, \mathcal{N}_\alpha[i_k][j_k]))$;
8 until $r_0, ..., r_{n_k-1}$ do not change;
9 $r \leftarrow UniqueTableInsert(v_k, r_0, ..., r_{n_k-1})$;
10 enter $\langle Saturate, p : r \rangle$ in $Cache$;
11 return r;

---

mdd $RelProdSat$(variable v_k, mdd q, mdd2 f) is

1 if $v_k = v_0$ then return $q \wedge f$;
2 if $Cache$ contains entry $\langle RelProdSat, q, f : r \rangle$ then return r;
3 foreach $i_k, j_k \in \mathcal{X}_k$ s.t. $q[i_k] \neq \mathbf{0}$ and $f[i_k][j_k] \neq \mathbf{0}$ do
4      $r_{j_k} \leftarrow Union(r_{j_k}, RelProdSat(v_{k-1}, q[i_k], f[i_k][j_k]))$;
5 $r \leftarrow Saturate(v_k, UniqueTableInsert(v_k, r_0, ..., r_{n_k-1}))$;
6 enter $\langle RelProdSat, q, f : r \rangle$ in $Cache$;
7 return r.

Fig. 12. The saturation algorithm to build the reachability set [11]

– Saturate the root associated with v_L: fire in it all events α s.t. $Top(\alpha) = L$. If this creates nodes associated with v_k, $L > k \geq 1$, saturate them immediately.

Fig. 12 shows the pseudocode to implement these steps. With saturation, the traditional idea of a global fixpoint iteration for the overall MDD disappears, and, while markings are not discovered in breadth-first order, the tradeoff is sometimes enormous memory and runtime savings when applied to asynchronous systems. Saturation is not guaranteed to be optimal, but has many advantages: (1) firing α in p benefits from having saturated the nodes below p, thus finds the maximum number of markings under p, (2) once node p associated with v_k is saturated, we never fire an event α with $Top(\alpha) \leq k$ on p or any of the nodes reachable from p, (3) except for the nodes of the MDD describing $\mathcal{X}_{init}$, only saturated nodes are placed in the unique table and the operation cache, and (4) many of these nodes will still be present in the final MDD which, by definition, can only contain saturated nodes.

We observe that, while the notion of a transition is clearly defined for a Petri net level, it is somewhat arbitrary for the corresponding MDDs. Given two transitions α and β with $Top(\alpha) = Top(\beta)$, we could choose to encode $\mathcal{N}_{\alpha,\beta} = \mathcal{N}_\alpha \cup \mathcal{N}_\beta$ with a single MDD instead of two individual MDDs, without affecting (much) the order of node operations performed by saturation. We then consider two extreme cases, *saturation by event*, where each Petri net transition is encoded with a separate MDD, and *saturation by variable*, where we use L MDDs, the kth one encoding $\mathcal{N}_k = \bigcup_{\alpha: Top(\alpha) = v_k} \mathcal{N}_\alpha$ (some $\mathcal{N}_k$ could be empty). The latter requires fewer unions during saturation, but its efficiency depends on the size of

N	$|\mathcal{X}_{rch}|$	$\mathcal{X}_{rch}$ mem.	$\mathcal{N}$ mem.		Peak mem.		Time	
			Event	Variable	Event	Variable	Event	Variable
phils								
200	$2.46 \cdot 10^{125}$	0.09	0.64	0.43	2.05	2.59	0.19	0.20
500	$3.03 \cdot 10^{313}$	0.22	1.60	1.07	4.06	4.43	0.52	0.53
1000	$9.18 \cdot 10^{626}$	0.43	3.20	2.14	6.80	8.34	1.21	1.26
robin								
100	$2.85 \cdot 10^{32}$	0.38	0.13	0.09	7.01	7.00	0.52	0.51
200	$7.23 \cdot 10^{62}$	1.44	0.26	0.18	47.64	47.47	5.19	5.11
500	$3.68 \cdot 10^{153}$	8.75	0.65	0.45	691.14	689.13	102.66	97.37
fms								
30	$3.43 \cdot 10^{11}$	0.19	0.21	0.20	5.49	7.35	11.31	11.56
40	$4.96 \cdot 10^{12}$	0.37	0.35	0.32	7.81	15.61	34.47	35.71
50	$4.08 \cdot 10^{13}$	0.63	0.51	0.48	12.04	26.18	85.30	86.86
slot								
30	$1.03 \cdot 10^{31}$	0.07	0.06	0.04	2.53	1.85	0.17	0.09
50	$1.72 \cdot 10^{52}$	0.20	0.10	0.07	4.22	4.17	0.78	0.35
100	$2.60 \cdot 10^{105}$	0.77	0.19	0.14	6.42	5.75	9.58	2.32
kanban								
10	$1.00 \cdot 10^{9}$	0.01	0.18	0.16	5.19	5.26	0.14	0.14
20	$8.05 \cdot 10^{11}$	0.07	1.22	1.08	44.65	46.13	4.36	4.39
30	$4.98 \cdot 10^{13}$	0.21	3.88	3.42	164.77	160.17	44.81	46.69
leader								
8	$3.04 \cdot 10^{8}$	1.82	0.18	0.09	9.59	9.28	20.26	19.33
9	$3.90 \cdot 10^{9}$	3.75	0.23	0.11	16.36	16.27	66.84	68.43
10	$5.02 \cdot 10^{10}$	7.37	0.29	0.13	29.89	30.48	241.70	231.12
counter								
100	$1.26 \cdot 10^{30}$	0.01	0.51	0.50	0.12	0.12	0.02	0.02
200	$1.60 \cdot 10^{60}$	0.01	2.01	1.99	0.21	0.21	0.11	0.11
300	$2.03 \cdot 10^{90}$	0.02	4.51	4.48	0.29	0.29	0.28	0.31
queen								
12	$8.56 \cdot 10^{5}$	20.77	0.12	0.11	46.69	46.71	2.96	2.69
13	$4.67 \cdot 10^{6}$	99.46	0.16	0.14	218.54	218.57	16.29	14.91
14	$2.73 \cdot 10^{7}$	505.73	0.21	0.19	1112.93	1112.96	95.69	88.12

Fig. 13. Results for saturation by event vs. by variable (memory: MB, time: sec)

the MDD encoding $\mathcal{N}_k$, as compared to that of the various $\mathcal{N}_\alpha$ used to build it. Experimentally, we have found that either approach can work best, depending on the particular model, as shown in Fig. 13. Either one, however, when compared with the results of Fig. 9, demonstrates the effectiveness of the saturation algorithm for reachability-set generation: saturation can scale to much larger values of N because of greatly reduced peak memory and runtime.

3   CTL Model Checking of Petri Nets

The generation of the reachability set for a Petri net is usually just a first step. Often, we want to analyze the behavior of the net, for example verify that certain

$$\sigma \models p \quad \Leftrightarrow \sigma = (\mathbf{s}, \cdots) \text{ and } \mathbf{s} \models p$$
$$\sigma \models \neg q \Leftrightarrow \sigma \not\models q$$
$$\sigma \models q \vee q' \Leftrightarrow \sigma \models q \text{ or } \sigma \models q'$$
$$\sigma \models q \wedge q' \Leftrightarrow \sigma \models q \text{ and } \sigma \models q'$$
$$\sigma \models \mathsf{X}q \quad \Leftrightarrow \sigma_{[1]} \models q$$
$$\sigma \models \mathsf{F}q \quad \Leftrightarrow \exists n \in \mathbb{N}, \sigma_{[n]} \models q$$
$$\sigma \models \mathsf{G}q \quad \Leftrightarrow \forall n \in \mathbb{N}, \sigma_{[n]} \models q$$
$$\sigma \models q \mathsf{U}q' \Leftrightarrow \exists n \in \mathbb{N}, \sigma_{[n]} \models q' \text{ and } \forall m < n, \sigma_{[m]} \models q$$
$$\sigma \models q \mathsf{R}q' \Leftrightarrow \forall m \geq 0, \text{ if } \forall n < m, \sigma_{[n]} \not\models q \text{ then } \sigma_{[m]} \models q'$$

$$\mathbf{s} \models a \quad \Leftrightarrow a \in \mathcal{L}(\mathbf{s})$$
$$\mathbf{s} \models \neg p \Leftrightarrow \mathbf{s} \not\models p$$
$$\mathbf{s} \models p \vee p' \Leftrightarrow \mathbf{s} \models p \text{ or } \mathbf{s} \models p'$$
$$\mathbf{s} \models p \wedge p' \Leftrightarrow \mathbf{s} \models p \text{ and } \mathbf{s} \models p'$$
$$\mathbf{s} \models \mathsf{E}q \quad \Leftrightarrow \exists \sigma = (\mathbf{s}, \cdots), \sigma \models q$$
$$\mathbf{s} \models \mathsf{A}q \quad \Leftrightarrow \forall \sigma = (\mathbf{s}, \cdots), \sigma \models q$$

Fig. 14. CTL semantics [23]

properties are satisfied. In this section, we consider the problem of CTL model checking for Petri nets, including the generation of witnesses or counterexamples and the use of bounded approaches, both of which use more general decision diagrams that can encode integer, not just boolean, functions.

3.1 CTL Model Checking

Temporal logics usually refer to a Kripke structure $(\mathcal{X}_{pot}, \mathcal{X}_{init}, \mathcal{N}, \mathcal{A}, \mathcal{L})$. For Petri nets, we can think of the "$\mathcal{X}_{pot}, \mathcal{X}_{init}, \mathcal{N}$" portion as the potential state space $\mathbb{N}^{|\mathcal{P}|}$, the initial marking(s), and the forward function, while $\mathcal{A}$ is a finite set of *atomic propositions* of interest, such as "place a contains three tokens" or "transition α is enabled", and $\mathcal{L} : \mathcal{X}_{pot} \to 2^{\mathcal{A}}$ is a *labeling function* that specifies which atomic propositions hold in each marking.

We consider the temporal logic CTL (*computation tree logic*) [23], which talks about *state formulas* and *path formulas* using the following syntax:

- If $p \in \mathcal{A}$, p is a state formula.
- If p and p' are state formulas, $\neg p$, $p \vee p'$, and $p \wedge p'$ are state formulas.
- If q is a path formula, $\mathsf{E}q$ and $\mathsf{A}q$ are state formulas.
- If p and p' are state formulas, $\mathsf{X}p$, $\mathsf{F}p$, $\mathsf{G}p$, $p\mathsf{U}p'$, and $p\mathsf{R}p'$ are path formulas.

Fig. 14 illustrates the semantics of a CTL formula, where $\mathbf{s} \models p$ means that state formula p holds in marking $\mathbf{s}$, $\sigma \models q$ means that path formula q holds on path σ, and, given an infinite execution path $\sigma = (\mathbf{s}_0, \mathbf{s}_1, \mathbf{s}_2, \cdots)$ and an integer $n \in \mathbb{N}$, we let $\sigma_{[n]}$ denote the infinite path $(\mathbf{s}_n, \mathbf{s}_{n+1}, \cdots)$.

As we are ultimately interested in whether a certain marking (usually the initial marking) satisfies a given state formula, CTL model-checking can be performed by manipulating just sets of states, not paths, by considering all CTL operators as being formed by the combination of a *path quantifier*, E or A, followed by a *temporal operator*, X, F, G, U, or R. Then, we only need to be able to build the set of markings corresponding to atomic propositions or to the formulas $\mathsf{EX}p$, $\mathsf{E}p\mathsf{U}q$, and $\mathsf{EG}p$, where p and q are themselves atomic propositions or EX, EU, or EG formulas, because of the following equivalences:

$$\mathsf{AX}p = \neg\mathsf{EX}\neg p, \quad \mathsf{EF}p = \mathsf{E}true\mathsf{U}p, \quad \mathsf{AG}p = \neg\mathsf{EF}\neg p, \quad \mathsf{E}p\mathsf{R}q = \neg\mathsf{A}\neg p\mathsf{U}\neg q,$$
$$\mathsf{AF}p = \neg\mathsf{EG}\neg p, \quad \mathsf{A}p\mathsf{U}q = \neg(\mathsf{E}\neg q\mathsf{U}(\neg p \wedge \neg q)) \wedge \neg\mathsf{EG}\neg q, \quad \mathsf{A}p\mathsf{R}q = \neg\mathsf{E}\neg p\mathsf{U}\neg q.$$

3.2   Symbolic CTL Model Checking Algorithms

To compute the set of markings satisfying a CTL formula such as $\mathsf{E}p\mathsf{U}q$, we first compute the sets of markings $\mathcal{X}_p$ and $\mathcal{X}_q$ satisfying the inner formulas p and q, respectively. Fig. 15 shows the explicit algorithms for the EX, EU, and EG operators, on the left, while the their respective symbolic versions are on the right. The symbolic algorithms use $\mathcal{N}^{-1}$, the *backward function*, satisfying $\mathbf{i} \in \mathcal{N}^{-1}(\mathbf{j}) \Leftrightarrow \mathbf{j} \in \mathcal{N}(\mathbf{i})$, to "go backwards". By doing so, they might go through unreachable markings, but this does not lead to incorrect results because, while $\mathcal{N}$ might contain transitions from unreachable to reachable markings, it cannot by definition contain transitions from reachable to unreachable markings. It is remarkable that, while the explicit EG algorithm first discovers all strongly-connected components of $\mathcal{N} \cap \mathcal{X}_p \times \mathcal{X}_p$ (or of its reachable portion), the symbolic algorithm starts with a larger set of markings, (all those in $\mathcal{X}_p$, and *reduces* it, without having to compute the strongly connected components of $\mathcal{N}$.

The symbolic EU and EG algorithms of Fig. 15 proceed in strict breadth-first order. Thus, just as for reachability-set generation, it is natural to attempt to improve them with a saturation-based approach. For EU, we start from $\mathcal{X}_q$ and walk backwards using $\mathcal{N}^{-1}$, while remaining in $\mathcal{X}_p$ at all times. A breadth-first exploration can simply perform an intersection with $\mathcal{X}_p$ at each step, but it is too costly to do this at each lightweight saturation step. We then have two options.

The simplest one is to use *constrained functions* $\mathcal{N}^{-1}_{\alpha,\mathcal{X}_p} = \mathcal{N}^{-1}_\alpha \cap (\mathcal{X}_{pot} \times \mathcal{X}_p)$, i.e., symbolically remove from $\mathcal{N}^{-1}_\alpha$ any backward steps to markings not in $\mathcal{X}_p$. After computing these functions, we can run ordinary saturation, analogous to that for reachability-set generation except that we start from $\mathcal{X}_q$ instead of $\mathcal{X}_{init}$ and we apply $\{\mathcal{N}^{-1}_{\alpha,\mathcal{X}_p} : \alpha \in \mathcal{T}\}$ instead of $\{\mathcal{N}_\alpha : \alpha \in \mathcal{T}\}$. The downside of this approach is a possible decrease in locality, since, if $\mathcal{X}_p$ depends on v_k, i.e., if its fully-reduced encoding has nodes associated with v_k, then $Top(\mathcal{N}^{-1}_{\alpha,\mathcal{X}_p}) \succeq v_k$. In particular, if $\mathcal{X}_p$ depends on v_L, this approach degrades to chaining.

A second approach is instead *constrained saturation*, which uses the original (unconstrained) backward functions $\mathcal{N}^{-1}_\alpha$, but has three, not just two, parameters in its recursive calls: s (a node in the MDD encoding the set of markings being saturated), r (a node in the MDD encoding a backward function), and c (a node in the MDD encoding the constraint $\mathcal{X}_p$), as shown by the pseudocode in Fig. 16. In other words, instead of modifying the backward functions, we constrain the marking exploration *on-the-fly* during the "check-and-fire" steps in saturation, thus we do not reduce locality.

Fig. 17 reports peak memory and runtime experimental results for EU computation. Columns BFS, $ConNSF_{rch}$, and $ConSat_{rch}$ correspond to the traditional symbolic breadth-first algorithm of Fig. 15, the ordinary saturation algorithm employing constrained functions, and the constrained saturation approach of Fig. 16, respectively. In general, saturation does better than BFS, sometimes by a huge factor. Then, among the two saturation approaches, constrained saturation tends to do much better than explicitly constraining the functions and running ordinary saturation. In particular, an advantage of constrained

$ExplicitEX(\mathcal{X}_p, \mathcal{N})$ is	$SymbolicEX(\mathcal{X}_p, \mathcal{N})$ is
1 $\mathcal{Y} \leftarrow \emptyset$;	1 $\mathcal{Y} \leftarrow RelProd(\mathcal{X}_p, \mathcal{N}^{-1})$;
2 while $\mathcal{X}_p \neq \emptyset$ do	2 return $\mathcal{Y}$;
3 remove a marking $\mathbf{j}$ from $\mathcal{X}_p$;	
4 for each $\mathbf{i} \in \mathcal{N}^{-1}(\mathbf{j})$ do	
5 $\mathcal{Y} \leftarrow \mathcal{Y} \cup \{\mathbf{i}\}$;	
6 return $\mathcal{Y}$;	

$ExplicitEU(\mathcal{X}_p, \mathcal{X}_q, \mathcal{N})$ is	$SymbolicEU(\mathcal{X}_p, \mathcal{X}_q, \mathcal{N})$ is
1 $\mathcal{Y} \leftarrow \emptyset$;	1 $\mathcal{Y} \leftarrow \mathcal{X}_q$;
2 for each $\mathbf{i} \in \mathcal{X}_q$ do	2 repeat
3 $\mathcal{Y} \leftarrow \mathcal{Y} \cup \{\mathbf{i}\}$;	3 $\mathcal{O} \leftarrow \mathcal{Y}$;
4 while $\mathcal{X}_q \neq \emptyset$ do	4 $\mathcal{W} \leftarrow RelProd(\mathcal{Y}, \mathcal{N}^{-1})$;
5 remove a marking $\mathbf{j}$ from $\mathcal{X}_q$;	5 $\mathcal{Z} \leftarrow Intersection(\mathcal{W}, \mathcal{X}_p)$;
6 for each $\mathbf{i} \in \mathcal{N}^{-1}(\mathbf{j})$ do	6 $\mathcal{Y} \leftarrow Union(\mathcal{Z}, \mathcal{Y})$;
7 if $\mathbf{i} \notin \mathcal{Y}$ and $\mathbf{i} \in \mathcal{X}_p$ then	7 until $\mathcal{O} = \mathcal{Y}$;
8 $\mathcal{Y} \leftarrow \mathcal{Y} \cup \{\mathbf{i}\}$;	8 return $\mathcal{Y}$;
9 $\mathcal{X}_q \leftarrow \mathcal{X}_q \cup \{\mathbf{i}\}$;	
10 return $\mathcal{Y}$;	

$ExplicitEG(\mathcal{X}_p, \mathcal{N})$ is	$SymbolicEG(\mathcal{X}_p, \mathcal{N})$ is
1 build the set of markings $\mathcal{W}$ in the SCCs in the subgraph of $\mathcal{N}$ induced by $\mathcal{X}_p$;	1 $\mathcal{Y} \leftarrow \mathcal{X}_p$;
2 $\mathcal{Y} \leftarrow \emptyset$;	2 repeat
3 for each $\mathbf{i} \in \mathcal{W}$ do	3 $\mathcal{O} \leftarrow \mathcal{Y}$;
4 $\mathcal{Y} \leftarrow \mathcal{Y} \cup \{\mathbf{i}\}$;	4 $\mathcal{W} \leftarrow RelProd(\mathcal{Y}, \mathcal{N}^{-1})$;
5 while $\mathcal{W} \neq \emptyset$ do	5 $\mathcal{Y} \leftarrow Intersection(\mathcal{Y}, \mathcal{W})$;
6 remove a marking $\mathbf{j}$ from $\mathcal{W}$;	6 until $\mathcal{O} = \mathcal{Y}$;
7 for each $\mathbf{i} \in \mathcal{N}^{-1}(\mathbf{j})$ do	7 return $\mathcal{Y}$;
8 if $\mathbf{i} \notin \mathcal{Y}$ and $\mathbf{i} \in \mathcal{X}_p$ then	
9 $\mathcal{Y} \leftarrow \mathcal{Y} \cup \{\mathbf{i}\}$;	
10 $\mathcal{W} \leftarrow \mathcal{W} \cup \{\mathbf{i}\}$;	
11 return $\mathcal{Y}$;	

Fig. 15. Explicit vs. symbolic CTL model-checking algorithms [11]

saturation is that its lightweight "check-and-fire" approach is not as sensitive to the complexity of the constraint.

Improving the computation of EG using saturation is instead more difficult, since EGp is a *greatest fixpoint*, which means that we initialize a larger set of markings $\mathcal{Y}$ to $\mathcal{X}_p$, then remove from it any marking $\mathbf{i}$ that cannot reach the current set $\mathcal{Y}$ through *any* of the transitions in $\mathcal{T}$. In other words, we cannot eliminate $\mathbf{i}$ from $\mathcal{Y}$ just because $\mathcal{N}_\alpha(\mathbf{i}) \cap \mathcal{Y} = \emptyset$ for a particular α. We then take a completely different approach and build a $2L$-variable MDD encoding the *backward reachability relation*, using constrained saturation, that is, given a set $\mathcal{Y}$ and a marking $\mathbf{i} \in \mathcal{Y}$, we define $\mathbf{j} \in (\mathcal{N}_{\mathcal{Y}, \mathcal{X}_p}^{-1})^+(\mathbf{i})$ iff there exists a *nontrivial* forward path of markings in $\mathcal{X}_p$ from $\mathbf{j}$ to $\mathbf{i}$, where $\mathcal{X}_p$ is the constraint.

To compute the set of markings satisfying EGp, we set $\mathcal{Y}$ to $\mathcal{X}_p$ and observe that, if $\mathbf{j} \in (\mathcal{N}_{\mathcal{X}_p, \mathcal{X}_p}^{-1})^+(\mathbf{i})$, there must exist a marking $\mathbf{i}' \in \mathcal{N}^{-1}(\mathbf{i}) \cap \mathcal{X}_p$ such that

```
mdd  ConsSaturate(mdd c, mdd s)
 1 if InCache(ConsSaturate, c, s, t) then return t;
 2 v_k ← s.var;
 3 t ← NewNode(v_k);
 4 r ← N_k^{-1};
 5 foreach i ∈ X_k s.t. s[i] ≠ 0 do
 6    if c[i] ≠ 0 then t[i] ← ConsSaturate(c[i], s[i]); else t[i] ← s[i];
 7 repeat
 8    foreach i, i' ∈ X_k s.t. r[i][i'] ≠ 0 do
 9       if c[i'] ≠ 0 then
10          u ← ConsRelProd(c[i'], t[i], r[i][i']);
11          t[i'] ← Or(t[i'], u);
12 until t does not change;
13 t ← UniqueTablePut(t);
14 CacheAdd(ConsSaturate, c, s, t);
15 return t;
```

```
mdd  ConsRelProd(mdd c, mdd s, mdd r)
 1 if s = 1 and r = 1 then return 1;
 2 if InCache(ConsRelProd, c, s, r, t) then return t;
 3 v_l ← s.var;
 4 t ← 0;
 5    foreach i, i' ∈ X_l s.t. r[i][i'] ≠ 0 do
 6       if c[i'] ≠ 0 then
 7          u ← ConsRelProd(c[i'], s[i], r[i][i']);
 8          if u ≠ 0 then
 9             if t = 0 then t ← NewNode(v_l);
10             t[i'] ← Or(t[i'], u);
11 t ← ConsSaturate(c, UniqueTablePut(t));
12 CacheAdd(ConsRelProd, c, s, r, t);
13 return t;
```

Fig. 16. The pseudocode for constrained saturation [57]

$\mathbf{j} \in ConsSaturate(\mathcal{X}_p, \{\mathbf{i'}\})$. To build $(\mathcal{N}_{\mathcal{X}_p, \mathcal{X}_p}^{-1})^+$, we apply constrained saturation to the primed variables of the MDD encoding $\mathcal{N}^{-1} \cap (\mathcal{X}_p \times \mathcal{X}_p)$.

Then, $\mathsf{EG}p$ holds in marking $\mathbf{j}$ iff there exists a marking $\mathbf{i} \in \mathcal{X}_p$ that can reach itself through a nontrivial path in $\mathcal{X}_p$, $\mathbf{i} \in (\mathcal{N}_{\mathcal{X}_p, \mathcal{X}_p}^{-1})^+(\mathbf{i})$, and $\mathbf{j}$ can reach $\mathbf{i}$ through a path in $\mathcal{X}_p$, $\mathbf{j} \in (\mathcal{N}_{\mathcal{X}_p, \mathcal{X}_p}^{-1})^+(\mathbf{i})$. To obtain the MDD encoding $\mathsf{EG}p$, we build the $2L$-variable MDD for $(\mathcal{N}_{\mathcal{X}_p, \mathcal{X}_p}^{-1})^+$, then the L-variable MDD for all markings in nontrivial strongly connected components of the restriction of the transition relation to $\mathcal{X}_p$, $\mathcal{X}_{scc} = \{\mathbf{i} : \mathbf{i} \in (\mathcal{N}_{\mathcal{X}_p, \mathcal{X}_p}^{-1})^+(\mathbf{i})\}$, and finally the L-variable MDD for $\mathsf{EG}p$, by computing $RelProd(\mathcal{X}_{scc}, (\mathcal{N}_{\mathcal{X}_p, \mathcal{X}_p}^{-1})^+)$.

Building the reachability relation $(\mathcal{N}_{\mathcal{X}_p, \mathcal{X}_p}^{-1})^+$ is the most expensive step in this approach, but the use of constrained saturation instead of breadth-first iterations greatly improves efficiency. Furthermore, $(\mathcal{N}_{\mathcal{X}_p, \mathcal{X}_p}^{-1})^+$ contains information useful beyond the computation of EG. For example, in EG computation under a fairness constraint $\mathcal{F}$, we seek an infinite execution where some markings in $\mathcal{F}$ appear

N	BFS			$ConsNSF_{rch}$		$ConsSat_{rch}$	
	iter.	time	mem.	time	mem.	time	mem.
phils : $\mathbf{E}(\neg HasL_1 \vee \neg HasR_1)\mathbf{U}(HasL_0 \wedge HasR_0)$							
100	200	7.63	62.06	0.27	10.87	0.01	2.04
500	1000	1843.32	550.01	10.58	186.07	0.09	7.35
1000	–	–	–	73.41	720.98	0.20	13.83
robin : $\mathbf{E}(Pld_1 = 0)\mathbf{U}(Psnd_0 = 1)$							
20	82	0.37	10.52	0.02	1.56	0.00	0.34
100	402	161.46	442.90	1.52	62.29	0.10	8.70
200	–	–	–	796.55	425.72	0.11	51.04
fms : $\mathbf{E}(P_1M_1 > 0)\mathbf{U}(P_1s = P_2s = P_3s = N)$							
10	103	7.11	16.40	0.44	5.35	0.03	2.32
25	–	–	–	410.34	20.73	0.93	8.24
50	–	–	–	–	–	53.29	40.17
slot : $\mathbf{E}(C_0 = 0)\mathbf{U}(C_0 = 1)$							
10	16	0.06	1.94	0.01	1.54	0.00	0.34
20	31	1.46	27.05	0.17	9.39	0.01	1.04
30	46	9.67	129.56	1.50	29.09	0.03	2.20
kanban : $\mathbf{E}(true)\mathbf{U}(out_4 = 0)$							
20	21	0.51	46.13	1.49	46.14	0.04	46.13
30	31	3.75	160.46	16.00	160.47	0.23	160.17
40	41	19.29	378.91	62.67	378.98	0.93	378.91
leader : $\mathbf{E}(pref_1 = 0)\mathbf{U}(status_0 = leader)$							
6	101	12.51	129.39	2.21	16.10	0.78	5.74
7	123	55.63	461.53	23.17	45.78	5.90	8.03
8	145	214.07	1191.79	192.06	119.81	28.23	12.51
counter : $\mathbf{E}(bit_{N-1} = 0)\mathbf{U}(bit_{N-1} = 1)$							
10	513	0.02	1.31	0.00	0.29	0.00	0.04
15	16385	3.01	6.42	0.36	3.42	0.00	0.05
20	524289	394.35	61.62	28.33	7.14	0.00	0.05
queen : $\mathbf{E}(q_0 = 1)\mathbf{U}(q_0 = 0)$							
12	13	11.92	164.95	2.51	185.77	4.40	76.87
13	14	80.83	889.39	18.58	1070.50	44.16	334.36
14	15	531.42	4566.38	–	–	865.23	1677.45

Fig. 17. Results for CTL EU queries (memory: MB, time: sec)

infinitely often. Marking $\mathbf{j}$ satisfies $\mathbf{EG}p$ under fairness constraint $\mathcal{F}$ iff there is a marking $\mathbf{i} \in (\mathcal{N}_{\mathcal{F} \cap \mathcal{X}_p, \mathcal{X}_p}^{-1})^+(\mathbf{i})$ such that $\mathbf{j} \in (\mathcal{N}_{\mathcal{F} \cap \mathcal{X}_p, \mathcal{X}_p}^{-1})^+(\mathbf{i})$. In other words, we simply build the backward reachability relation starting from $\mathcal{F} \cap \mathcal{X}_p$, instead of all of $\mathcal{X}_p$. Experimentally, we found that, while traditional approaches suffer when adding a fairness constraint, our approach may instead become faster, as it performs the same computation, but starting from a reduced set of markings.

A question arising in symbolic CTL model checking is whether to constrain the paths to the reachable markings $\mathcal{X}_{rch}$ during the iterations, since we are usually only interested in reachable markings in the end. This is an issue because backward search can reach unreachable markings from reachable ones but not vice versa, by definition (forward search from a set of reachable markings only finds reachable markings, instead). In other words, there are two reasonable ways to define $\mathcal{X}_p$: as $\mathcal{X}_{p,pot}$ (include in $\mathcal{X}_p$ all potential markings satisfying property p, even if they are not reachable) and as $\mathcal{X}_{p,rch}$ (include in $\mathcal{X}_p$ only the reachable markings satisfying property p), so that $\mathcal{X}_{p,rch} = \mathcal{X}_{p,pot} \cap \mathcal{X}_{rch}$. The latter of course tends to result in (much) smaller sets of markings being manipulated, but it does not follow that the MDD encoding these sets are correspondingly smaller. Indeed, exploration restricted to $\mathcal{X}_{p,pot}$ usually depends on fewer variables, thus may well lead to better saturation behavior.

Fig. 18 reports experimental results for EG computation. Columns *BFS* and *ReachRel* correspond to the traditional symbolic breadth-first algorithm of Fig. 15 and to the approach that builds the reachability relation using constrained saturation, respectively. Obviously, the high cost building *ReachRel* is often overwhelming. However, it should be observed that most of the models we consider are best-case-scenarios for *BFS*, since convergence is achieved immediately (**robin**, **fms**, and **kanban**) or in relatively few iterations; for **counter**, instead, BFS convergence requires $2^N - 1$ iterations and the *ReachRel* saturation approach is obviously enormously superior in runtime.

3.3   Integer-Valued Decision Diagrams

In the following section, we will need to manipulate integer-valued, instead of boolean-valued, functions. Specifically, we will need to encode partial functions from $\mathcal{X}_{pot}$ to $\mathbb{N}$, or, which is the same since it is natural for our purposes to think of "undefined" as being "infinite", total functions from $\mathcal{X}_{pot}$ to $\mathbb{N} \cup \{\infty\}$.

We now introduce two variants of decision diagrams that can do just that. The first one, *(ordered) multi-terminal MDDs* is a fairly obvious extension of ordinary MDDs, where we allow each terminal to correspond to a distinct element of the range of the function to be encoded:

- The *terminal* nodes are distinct elements of a *range* set $\mathcal{X}_0$ and are associated with the range variable v_0, satisfying $v_k \succ v_0$ for any domain variable v_k.

The semantic of this multiway generalization of the MTBDDs introduced by Clarke et al. [22] is still very similar to that of BDDs and MDDs: to evaluate the encoded function on $(i_L, ..., i_1)$, we follow the corresponding path from the root and the reached terminal node, now an element of $\mathcal{X}_0$ instead of just $\mathbf{0}$ or $\mathbf{1}$, is the desired value. Quasi-reduced and fully-reduced (and even identity-reduced) canonical forms can be defined exactly as for BDDs and MDDs.

The second variant *additive edge-valued MDDs*, or EV$^+$MDDs [19], is instead a more substantial departure from the decision diagrams seen so far, as there is a single terminal node carrying no information:

- The only *terminal* node is Ω, associated with variable $\Omega.var = v_0$, satisfying $v_k \succ v_0$ for any domain variable v_k.

N	BFS			ReachRel	
	iter.	time	mem.	time	mem.
phils : EG$\neg(HasL_0 \wedge HasR_0)$					
300	4	0.02	2.78	0.81	8.16
500	4	0.03	4.06	1.60	11.44
1000	4	0.08	7.63	16.91	20.89
robin : EG$(true)$					
20	1	0.00	0.48	0.15	4.16
50	1	0.03	2.58	2.48	36.10
100	1	0.63	14.60	18.96	179.76
fms : EG$(P_1 w P_2 > 0 \wedge P_2 = P_3 = N)$					
8	1	0.00	1.53	27.29	17.92
10	1	0.01	2.18	215.12	31.07
12	1	0.02	2.32	2824.78	59.46
slot : EG$(C_0 = 0)$					
20	781	2.17	6.22	12.23	14.24
25	1227	7.30	11.31	252.18	20.29
30	1771	20.30	20.36	–	–
kanban : EG$(back_2 = N - 1 \vee back_3 = N - 1)$					
10	1	0.00	5.26	3.08	5.29
15	1	0.00	17.43	31.59	17.49
20	1	0.01	46.13	189.99	46.40
leader : EG$(status_0 \neq leader)$					
3	14	0.00	0.64	0.74	7.38
4	18	0.01	1.96	81.29	20.83
5	22	0.05	3.67	–	–
counter : EG$(bit_{N-1} = 0)$					
10	512	0.00	0.24	0.00	0.05
15	16384	0.23	2.46	0.00	0.07
20	524288	17.35	4.74	0.00	0.08
queen : EG$(q_0 = 1)$					
10	10	0.65	16.88	0.58	12.62
11	11	4.34	46.06	4.15	53.42
12	12	37.00	189.22	23.26	244.65

Fig. 18. Results for CTL **EG** queries (memory: MB, time: sec)

while each edge has not only a label but also a value:

- For each $i_k \in \mathcal{X}_k$, a nonterminal node p associated with v_k has an outgoing edge labeled with i_k, pointing to $p[i_k].child$ and having a value $p[i_k].val \in \mathbb{N} \cup \{\infty\}$. We write $p[i_k] = \langle p[i_k].val, p[i_k].child \rangle$ and call such pair an *edge*.

The function $f_p : \mathcal{X}_{pot} \to \mathbb{N} \cup \{\infty\}$ encoded by a node p associated with v_k is

$$f_p(x_L, ..., x_1) = \begin{cases} 0 & \text{if } k = 0, \text{ i.e., } p = \Omega \\ p[i_k].val + f_{p[i_k].child}(x_L, ..., x_1) & \text{if } k > 0, \text{ i.e., } p \neq \Omega. \end{cases}$$

As we mostly operate on edges, we also define the function $f_{\langle \sigma, p \rangle} : \mathcal{X}_{pot} \to \mathbb{N} \cup \{\infty\}$ encoded by edge $\langle \sigma, p \rangle$ as $f_{\langle \sigma, p \rangle} = \sigma + f_p$.

The canonical forms already seen extend to EV$^+$MDDs, once we give proper care to edge values:

1. All nodes are *normalized*: for any nonterminal node p associated with v_k, we must have $p[i_k].val = 0$ for at least one $i_k \in \mathcal{X}_k$. Thus, the minimum of the function encoded by any node is 0, and a function $f : \mathcal{X}_{pot} \to \mathbb{N} \cup \{\infty\}$ is encoded by an edge $\langle \rho, p \rangle$ where $\rho = \min_{\mathbf{i} \in \mathcal{X}_{pot}} \{f(\mathbf{i})\}$.
2. All edges with value ∞ point to Ω: if $p[i_k].val = \infty$ then $p[i_k].child = \Omega$.
3. There are *no duplicates*: if $p.var = q.var = x_k$ and $p[i_k] = q[i_k]$ for all $i_k \in \mathcal{X}_k$, then $p = q$ (now, $p[i_k] = q[i_k]$ means equality for both the identities of the children and the values of the edges).
4. One of the following forms holds
   quasi-reduced form: there is no variable skipping, i.e., if $p.var = v_k$, then $p[i_k].child.var = v_{k-1}$ for any $i_k \in \mathcal{X}_k$, and $k = L$ if p is a root node.
   fully-reduced form: there is maximum variable skipping, i.e., no *redundant* node p exists, with $p[i_k].val = 0$ and $p[i_l].child = q$, for all $i_k \in \mathcal{X}_k$. Thus, a constant function $f = c \in \mathbb{N} \cup \{\infty\}$ is encoded by $\langle c, \Omega \rangle$.

Indeed, while not needed in this survey, we can even associate reduction rules with individual variables, as already discussed for MDDs. If a node q associated with an *identity-reduced* variable v_k is *singular*, i.e., it has one edge $q[i_k]$ with value 0 and all other edges with value ∞, then no edge $p[i_l]$ can point to q if $i_l = i_k$ or if it skips over a fully-reduced variable v_h such that $i_k \in \mathcal{X}_h$. In other words, EV$^+$MDD edges $\langle \infty, \Omega \rangle$ play the same role as MDD edges to the terminal **0**. The next section gives an example of MTMDDs and EV$^+$MDDs.

EV$^+$MDD manipulation algorithms are somewhat more complex than their MDD or MTMDD analogues, as node normalization requires the propagation of numerical values along the edges of the diagram, but they retain the overall recursive flavor seen for other decision diagrams. For example, Fig. 19 shows the pseudocode for the *Minimum* operator, assuming quasi-reduced EV$^+$MDDs. Observe that, when looking up the operation cache in the computation of the minimum of $\langle \alpha, p \rangle$ and $\langle \beta, q \rangle$, we can swap p and q to force a particular order on them (e.g., increasing *node_id*), since *Minimum* is commutative. Furthermore, we can just focus on the difference $\alpha - \beta$, which can be positive, negative, or zero, instead on the actual values of α and β, since $Minimum(\langle 3, p \rangle, \langle 5, q \rangle) = 3 + Minimum(\langle 0, p \rangle, \langle 2, q \rangle)$. As the result is always going to be of the form $\langle \min\{\alpha, \beta\}, r \rangle$, thus $\langle 3, r \rangle$ in our example, the cache only needs to remember the node portion of the result, r.

We conclude this section by stressing a key difference between the original definition of EVBDDs [37] and our EV$^+$MDDs (beyond the facts that EV$^+$MDDs allow a non-binary choice at each nonterminal node and the use of ∞ as an edge value, both of which could be considered as "obvious" extensions). EVBDDs extended BDDs by associating an integer (thus possibly negative) value to each edge, and achieved canonicity by requiring that $p[0].val = 0$, so that a function $f : \mathcal{X}_{pot} \to \mathbb{N}$ is encoded by an edge $\langle \rho, p \rangle$ where $\rho = f(0, ..., 0)$. While this canonical form has smaller memory requirements, as it eliminates the need to explicitly store $p[0].val$, it cannot encode all partial functions, thus is not as

---

edge $Minimum(edge\ \langle\alpha,p\rangle, edge\ \langle\beta,q\rangle)$ • edge is a pair $\langle int,node\rangle$
  1 if $\alpha = \infty$ then return $\langle\beta,q\rangle$;
  2 if $\beta = \infty$ then return $\langle\alpha,p\rangle$;
  3 $v_k \leftarrow p.var$;   • same as q.var
  4 $\mu \leftarrow \min\{\alpha,\beta\}$;
  5 if $p = q$ then return $\langle\mu,p\rangle$;   • includes the case $k = 0$, i.e., $p = q = \Omega$
  6 if $Cache$ contains entry $\langle Minimum, p, q, \alpha - \beta : r\rangle$ then return $\langle\mu,r\rangle$;
  7 $r \leftarrow NewNode(k)$; • create new node associated with v_k with edges set to $\langle\infty,\Omega\rangle$
  8 foreach $i_k \in \mathcal{X}_k$ do
  9    $r[i_k] \leftarrow Minimum(\langle\alpha-\mu+p[i_k].val,p[i_k].child\rangle, \langle\beta-\mu+q[i_k].val,q[i_k].child\rangle)$;
 10 $UniqueTableInsert(r)$;
 11 enter $\langle Minimum, p, q, \alpha - \beta : r\rangle$ in $Cache$;
 12 return $\langle\mu,r\rangle$;

Fig. 19. The *Minimum* operator for quasi-reduced EV$^+$MDDs [19]

general as EV$^+$MDDs. For example, EVBDDs cannot encode the function δ considered in Fig. 21, because $\delta(1,0,0) = \infty$ but $\delta(1,0,1) = 4$, thus there is no way to normalize the node associated with x_1 on the path where $x_3 = 1$ and $x_2 = 0$ in such a way that its 0-edge has value 0.

3.4 Symbolic Computation of CTL Witnesses

A *witness* for an *existential* CTL formula is a finite path $\mathbf{i}^{(0)}$, $\mathbf{i}^{(1)}$, ..., $\mathbf{i}^{(d)}$ of markings in the reachability graph, with $\mathbf{i}^{(0)} \in \mathcal{X}_{init}$, which proves the validity of the formula. For EXa and EFa, assuming a is an atomic proposition, we simply require that a holds in $\mathbf{i}^{(1)}$, or $\mathbf{i}^{(d)}$ for some $d \geq 0$, respectively. For EaUb, a must hold in $\mathbf{i}^{(0)}, \mathbf{i}^{(1)}, ..., \mathbf{i}^{(d-1)}$, and b, also assuming it is an atomic proposition, must hold in $\mathbf{i}^{(d)}$. For EGa, all the markings on the path must satisfy a and, in addition, $\mathbf{i}^{(d)}$ must equal $\mathbf{i}^{(m)}$, for some $m \in \{0, ..., d-1\}$, so that the path contains a cycle. Of course, we cannot provide witnesses to a *universal* CTL formula, but we can disprove it with a *counterexample*, i.e., a witness for its negation.

Witnesses and counterexamples can help us understand and debug a complex model and they are most useful when they are short, thus, ideally, we seek minimal length ones. We then define the *distance function* $\delta : \mathcal{X}_{pot} \to \mathbb{N} \cup \{\infty\}$ as $\delta(\mathbf{i}) = \min\{d : \mathbf{i} \in \mathcal{N}^d(\mathcal{X}_{init})\}$, so that $\delta(\mathbf{i}) = \infty$ iff $\mathbf{i} \notin \mathcal{X}_{rch}$.

We can build δ as a sequence of $d_{max} + 1$ sets encoded as MDDs, where d_{max} is the maximum distance of any marking from $\mathcal{X}_{init}$, using one of the two algorithms shown in Fig. 20. The difference between the two algorithms is that $\mathcal{X}^{[d]}$ contains the markings at distance *exactly* d while $\mathcal{Y}^{[d]}$ contains the markings at distance *up to* d (this is analogous to the "frontier vs. all" approaches to reachability-set generation in Fig. 8). In fact, these algorithms essentially also build the reachability set as a byproduct, since $\mathcal{X}_{rch} = \bigcup_{d=0}^{d_{max}} \mathcal{X}^{[d]} = \mathcal{Y}^{[d_{max}]}$.

Instead of encoding the distance function with a sequence of MDDs, we can encode it more naturally with a single decision diagram having range $\mathbb{N} \cup \{\infty\}$. Fig. 21(a,b) illustrates how the same distance function δ is encoded by five MDDs or a single MTMDD with five terminal nodes (plus terminal ∞, which is

Build $\mathcal{X}^{[d]} = \{\mathbf{i} : \delta(\mathbf{i}) = d\}$, $d = 0, 1, ..., d_{max}$ Build $\mathcal{Y}^{[d]} = \{\mathbf{i} : \delta(\mathbf{i}) \leq d\}$, $d = 0, 1, ..., d_{max}$

$DistanceMddEQ(\mathcal{X}_{init}, \mathcal{N})$ is
1 $d \leftarrow 0$;
2 $\mathcal{X}_{rch} \leftarrow \mathcal{X}_{init}$;
3 $\mathcal{X}^{[0]} \leftarrow \mathcal{X}_{init}$;
4 repeat
5      $\mathcal{X}^{[d+1]} \leftarrow \mathcal{N}(\mathcal{X}^{[d]}) \setminus \mathcal{X}_{rch}$;
6      $d \leftarrow d + 1$;
7      $\mathcal{X}_{rch} \leftarrow \mathcal{X}_{rch} \cup \mathcal{X}^{[d]}$;
8 until $\mathcal{X}^{[d]} = \emptyset$;
9 return $\mathcal{X}^{[0]}, ..., \mathcal{X}^{[d-1]}$;

$DistanceMddLE(\mathcal{X}_{init}, \mathcal{N})$ is
1 $d \leftarrow 0$;
2 $\mathcal{Y}^{[0]} \leftarrow \mathcal{X}_{init}$;
3 repeat
4      $\mathcal{Y}^{[d+1]} \leftarrow \mathcal{N}(\mathcal{Y}^{[d]}) \cup \mathcal{Y}^{[d]}$;
5      $d \leftarrow d + 1$;
6 until $\mathcal{Y}^{[d]} = \mathcal{Y}^{[d-1]}$;
7 return $\mathcal{Y}^{[0]}, ..., \mathcal{Y}^{[d-1]}$;

Fig. 20. Two ways to build a set of MDDs encoding the distance function

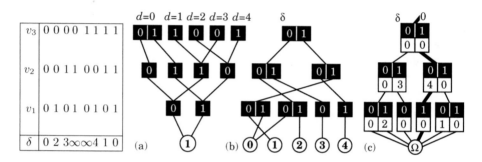

Fig. 21. Encoding the distance function: sequence of MDDs, a MTMDD, an EV$^+$MDD

omitted). However, while MTMDDs are a natural and often useful extension, it is obvious that they can have poor merging toward the bottom of the diagram, just as a sequence of MDDs might have an overall poor merging toward the top. The real problem is that both approaches are explicit in the number of distinct distance values. If the maximum distance d_{max} is very large, these symbolic encodings do not help much: we need edge values, that is, EV$^+$MDDs.

The canonical EV$^+$MDD encoding the distance function δ previously considered is shown in Fig. 21(c), where edges with value ∞ are omitted and the highlighted path describes $\delta(1, 0, 1) = 0 + 0 + 4 + 0 = 4$. While this example does not demonstrate the benefits of EV$^+$MDDs over MTMDDs, one can simply consider the function $f(i_L, ..., i_1) = \sum_{k=1}^{L} i_k \cdot \prod_{l=1}^{k-1} |\mathcal{X}_l|$ to realize that an EV$^+$MDD for this function requires L nonterminal nodes and $\sum_{k=1}^{L} |\mathcal{X}_l|$ edges, an exponential improvement over a canonical MTMDD, which requires $\sum_{k=1}^{L} \prod_{l=2}^{k} |\mathcal{X}_l|$ nonterminal nodes and $\sum_{k=1}^{L} \prod_{l=1}^{k} |\mathcal{X}_l|$ edges.

While storing the distance function using EV$^+$MDDs instead of multiple MDDs or a MTMDD has the potential of improving memory and runtime, much larger improvements are possible if we, again, apply the idea of saturation. First of all, we need to revisit the idea of how the distance function is computed. If we follow a traditional breadth-first thinking, we simply initialize δ to the default

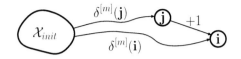

Fig. 22. Computing the distance function as a fixpoint

constant function ∞, then lower its value to 0 for any marking in $\mathcal{X}^{[0]} = \mathcal{X}_{init}$, then lower its value to 1 for any marking reachable from $\mathcal{X}^{[0]}$ in one application of $\mathcal{N}$ and not already in $\mathcal{X}^{[0]}$, then lower its value to 2 for any marking reachable from $\mathcal{X}^{[1]}$ in one application of $\mathcal{N}$ and not already in $\mathcal{X}^{[0]}$ or $\mathcal{X}^{[1]}$, and so on. However, we can also think of the distance function δ as the *fixpoint* of the sequence $(\delta^{[m]} : m \in \mathbb{N})$, initialized with $\delta^{[0]}$ satisfying $\delta^{[0]}(\mathbf{i}) = 0$ if $\mathbf{i} \in \mathcal{X}_{init}$ and ∞ otherwise, and recursively updated by choosing an $\alpha \in \mathcal{T}$ and letting $\delta^{[m+1]}$ satisfy $\delta^{[m+1]}(\mathbf{i}) = \min \left\{ \min_{\mathbf{j} \in \mathcal{N}_\alpha^{-1}(\mathbf{i})} \{1 + \delta^{[m]}(\mathbf{j})\}, \delta^{[m]}(\mathbf{i}) \right\}$, as illustrated in Fig. 22. With this approach, each iteration reduces the value of $\delta^{[m]}(\mathbf{i})$ for at least one marking $\mathbf{i}$, until no more reduction is possible for any $\alpha \in \mathcal{T}$. The value of the distance function for a particular marking $\mathbf{i}$ may be reduced multiple times, as we keep finding new ways to improve our estimate, unlike the traditional *breadth-first* iteration which reduces this value exactly once if $\mathbf{i}$ is reachable: from $\delta^{[m]}(\mathbf{i}) = \infty$, for values of m less than the actual distance d of $\mathbf{i}$, to $\delta^{[m]}(\mathbf{i}) = d$, for values of m greater or equal d.

Fig. 23 shows the memory and time requirements to generate the distance function δ using three approaches: an EV$^+$MDD and saturation (E_s), MDDs and the breadth-first iterations of Fig. 20 on the left, and then either accumulating the distances of the markings $\mathcal{X}^{[d]}$ into a single EV$^+$MDD (E_b), or keeping them as separate MDDs (M_b). Of course, E_s and E_b result in the same final EV$^+$MDD encoding of δ, but they greatly differ in peak memory requirements, thus time. Except for the **queen** model, where all techniques perform approximately the same (and not particularly well compared to an explicit approach, since the decision diagram is quite close to a tree in all cases), the results clearly show the superiority of EV$^+$MDDs over the simpler MDDs for the final encoding of δ. More importantly, the results show the enormous memory and time superiority of saturation over breadth-first search, except for the **queen** model (where E_s is better than E_b but both are somewhat worse than M_b), and the **leader** model (where E_s uses half the memory and twice the time of E_b, but both are worse than M_b, sometimes by up to a factor of two or three, even if their final encoding of δ is over four times better).

Once the distance function has been generated and encoded as an EV$^+$MDD $\langle \rho_*, r_* \rangle$, we can generate a minimal witness for $\mathsf{EF}q$ as shown in Fig. 24, assuming that q_* is the MDD encoding the nonempty set of reachable markings satisfying q. First, we build the EV$^+$MDD $\langle 0, x \rangle$, which is essentially the same as the MDD q^*, except that (1) all its edges have an associated value of 0 unless the MDD edge points to $\mathbf{0}$, in which case the associated value is ∞, and (2) the two MDD terminals $\mathbf{0}$ and $\mathbf{1}$ are merged into the unique EV$^+$MDD terminal Ω. Then, we build the EV$^+$MDD $\langle \mu, m \rangle$ encoding the elementwise maximum of the functions

N	$|\mathcal{X}_{rch}|$	d_{max}	Time			δ mem.		Peak mem.		
			E_s	E_b	M_b	E_s, E_b	M_b	E_s	E_b	M_b
phils										
100	$4.96 \cdot 10^{62}$	200	0.01	1.33	1.13	0.06	4.20	0.25	36.60	24.31
200	$2.46 \cdot 10^{125}$	400	0.02	21.60	20.07	0.11	17.10	0.44	117.14	70.86
500	$3.03 \cdot 10^{313}$	1000	0.05	–	–	0.28	–	0.92	–	–
robin										
50	$1.26 \cdot 10^{17}$	394	0.01	2.04	1.88	0.12	2.78	1.33	34.06	25.06
100	$2.85 \cdot 10^{32}$	794	0.05	33.53	31.76	0.43	16.91	7.36	307.14	257.29
150	$4.81 \cdot 10^{47}$	1194	0.10	174.57	168.34	0.93	50.99	23.20	1206.50	1056.45
fms										
10	$2.53 \cdot 10^{7}$	80	0.02	0.82	0.77	0.03	0.73	0.71	19.89	17.56
15	$7.24 \cdot 10^{8}$	120	0.06	5.49	5.00	0.06	2.24	1.55	57.05	49.23
20	$8.83 \cdot 10^{9}$	160	0.17	24.56	24.08	0.10	5.22	3.24	118.53	102.65
slot										
10	$8.29 \cdot 10^{9}$	114	0.04	0.44	0.39	0.03	0.87	0.53	11.75	8.74
20	$2.73 \cdot 10^{20}$	379	0.34	30.12	28.49	0.17	15.95	3.73	120.93	66.42
30	$1.03 \cdot 10^{31}$	794	1.41	2576.32	2336.05	0.45	92.56	12.50	703.54	388.75
kanban										
20	$8.05 \cdot 10^{11}$	280	0.85	3.26	2.92	0.10	9.32	4.26	75.94	49.57
30	$4.98 \cdot 10^{13}$	420	6.71	28.63	26.99	0.29	43.27	18.65	291.22	176.74
40	$9.94 \cdot 10^{14}$	560	38.84	180.23	162.43	0.66	130.92	43.78	836.24	452.74
leader										
6	$1.89 \cdot 10^{6}$	93	2.64	1.59	1.16	0.85	3.31	13.36	32.12	15.65
7	$2.39 \cdot 10^{7}$	115	16.88	8.63	6.29	2.56	10.79	41.36	96.01	39.08
8	$3.04 \cdot 10^{8}$	139	122.38	69.03	52.72	6.99	31.29	126.79	270.43	91.23
counter										
10	$1.02 \cdot 10^{3}$	$10^{10}-1$	0.00	0.01	0.01	0.00	0.11	0.03	0.70	0.39
20	$1.04 \cdot 10^{6}$	$10^{20}-1$	0.00	400.42	95.13	0.00	112.00	0.04	510.09	183.41
30	$1.07 \cdot 10^{9}$	$10^{30}-1$	0.00	–	–	0.00	–	0.04	–	–
queen										
12	$8.56 \cdot 10^{5}$	12	3.75	3.77	2.77	23.54	20.77	71.84	95.07	63.69
13	$4.67 \cdot 10^{6}$	13	21.57	21.53	16.59	112.61	99.46	340.26	452.85	309.37
14	$2.73 \cdot 10^{7}$	14	127.69	130.78	102.06	572.20	505.74	1737.16	2308.17	1577.99

Fig. 23. Results for distance function computation (memory: MB, time: sec)

encoded by $\langle \rho_*, r_* \rangle$ and $\langle 0, x \rangle$). Note that μ is then the length of one of the minimal witnesses we are seeking. Then, we simply extract from $\langle \mu, m \rangle$ a marking $\mathbf{j}^{(\mu)} = (j_L^{(\mu)}, \ldots, j_1^{(\mu)})$ on a 0-valued path from m to Ω, which is then a reachable marking satisfying q and at the minimum distance μ from $\mathcal{X}_{init}$. Finally, we "walk back" from $\mathbf{j}^{(\mu)}$, finding at each iteration a marking one step closer to $\mathcal{X}_{init}$. We have described this last sequence of steps in an explicit, not symbolic, fashion since its complexity is minimal as long as each $\mathcal{N}^{-1}(\mathbf{j}^{(\nu+1)})$ is small; were this not the case, a symbolic implementation is certainly possible.

marking sequence   *Witness*(*edge* $\langle \rho_*, r_* \rangle$, *mdd* q_*)

1 $\langle 0, x \rangle \leftarrow MddToEvmdd(q_*)$;   • $f_{\langle 0, x \rangle}(\mathbf{i}) = 0$ if $f_{q_*}(\mathbf{i}) = 1$, $f_{\langle 0, x \rangle}(\mathbf{i}) = \infty$ *otherwise*

2 $\langle \mu, m \rangle \leftarrow Maximum(\langle \rho_*, r_* \rangle, \langle 0, x \rangle)$;   • *analogous to the* Minimum *algorithm*

3 choose a marking $\mathbf{j}^{(\mu)}$ on a 0-valued path in $\langle \mu, m \rangle$;

4 for $\nu = \mu - 1$ downto 0 do   • *walk backward a witness of length* μ

5   foreach $\mathbf{i} \in \mathcal{N}^{-1}(\mathbf{j}^{(\nu+1)})$ do

6   if $f_{\langle \rho_*, r_* \rangle}(\mathbf{i}) = \nu$ then   • *there must be at least one such marking* $\mathbf{i}$

7              $\mathbf{j}^{(\nu)} \leftarrow \mathbf{i}$;

8   break;   • *move to the next value of* ν

9 return $(\mathbf{j}^{(0)}, ..., \mathbf{j}^{(\mu)})$;

Fig. 24. Minimal EF witness computation using the distance function [19]

3.5   Bounded Model Checking

When the reachability set is infinite (because some place is unbounded), or even simply when its MDD encoding is unwieldy, even the powerful symbolic methods seen so far fail. *Bounded model checking* has then been proposed as a practical alternative in these cases. Usually implemented through SAT solvers [6], the idea of bounded model checking is in principle independent of their use, as it simply centers around the idea of exploring only a smaller (and certainly finite) portion of the reachability set. Answers to certain CTL queries may still be obtained, as long as no marking can reach an infinite number of states in a single step, which is certainly true for Petri nets, even in the self-modifying case.

As initially proposed, bounded model checking explores only markings whose distance from the initial markings does not exceed a given a bound B. Then, for *safety* queries, we might find a counterexample, or prove that no counterexample exists, or, in the worst case, determine that no incorrect behavior arises within the first B steps (in this last inconclusive case, we might choose to increase B and repeat the analysis). Obviously, B breadth-first iterations starting from $\mathcal{X}_{init}$ can be used to encode the bounded reachability set as a BDD or MDD, but performance tends to be poor compared to SAT-based methods [30,31,42].

One reason for this is that, as we have already observed, the MDD encoding the set of markings reachable in exactly, or up to, d steps is often quite large. Saturation tends to be much better than breadth-first iteration when exploring the entire reachability set but, for bounded exploration, it does not offer an obvious way to limit its exploration to markings within a given distance from $\mathcal{X}_{init}$: ordinary saturation uses an MDD and computes a fixpoint at each node p associated with v_k, stopping only when p encodes all (sub)markings reachable from the (sub)markings it initially encoded, by firing any α with $Top(\alpha) \leq k$.

We then introduced a *bounded saturation* approach that uses an EV$^+$MDD, not simply an MDD, to build a *truncated distance function* δ_{trunc} and bound the amount of exploration on a node p associated with v_k, in one of two ways [56]:

- Ensure that, for any marking $\mathbf{i} \in \mathcal{X}_L \times \cdots \times \mathcal{X}_1$, $\delta_{trunc}(\mathbf{i}) = \delta(\mathbf{i})$ if $\delta(\mathbf{i}) \leq B$ and $\delta_{trunc}(\mathbf{i}) = \infty$ otherwise (*EVMDD-Exact* method).
- Ensure that, for any marking $\mathbf{i} \in \mathcal{X}_L \times \cdots \times \mathcal{X}_1$, $\delta_{trunc}(\mathbf{i}) = \delta(\mathbf{i})$ if $\delta(\mathbf{i}) \leq B$ and $\delta_{trunc}(\mathbf{i}) \geq \delta(\mathbf{i})$ otherwise, while also ensuring that, for any EV$^+$MDD node associated with v_k and any $i_k \in \mathcal{X}_k$, $p[i_k].val \leq B$ or $p[i_k].val = \infty$ (*EVMDD-Approx* method).

While *EVMDD-Exact* finds only and all the markings with distance exactly up to B, *EVMDD-Approx* finds not only all those markings, but also many other markings with distance up to $L \cdot B$. Even with these additional markings being encoded in the EV$^+$MDD, the *EVMDD-Approx* method is sometimes by far the best approach, as shown in Fig. 25, which compares the traditional BFS bounded exploration using MDDs with the two approaches just described. In addition, since *EVMDD-Approx* explores a larger set of markings $\mathcal{X}_{expl}$, it is more likely to find the (un)desired behavior we are looking than its exact alternatives, for a given bound B. Indeed, for the two models where *EVMDD-Approx* performs much worse than breadth-first search, the former ends up exploring the entire state space, i.e., $\mathcal{X}_{expl} = \mathcal{X}_{rch}$ (in this case, of course, ordinary saturation using MDDs would be much more efficient than bounded saturation using EV$^+$MDDs).

4   Further Synergy of Decision Diagrams and Petri Nets

So far, we have considered logical applications of decision diagram technology for the analysis of Petri nets. Even the non-boolean forms of decision diagrams we introduced, MTMDDs and EV$^+$MDDs, have after all been used only to count distances between markings. However, analysis techniques involving numerical computations are often required, especially when working with extensions of the Petri net formalism that take into account timing and probabilistic behavior, and decision diagrams have been successfully employed here as well. We now briefly discuss three such applications where saturation might also be applied, at least on some of the required computation. The last topic of this section, instead of presenting decision diagram algorithms that improve Petri net analysis, illustrates how the help can also "flow the other way", by discussing a heuristic based on the invariants of a Petri net to derive a good order for the variables of the decision diagrams used to study the Petri net itself.

4.1   P-Semiflow Computation

Invariant or semiflow analysis can provide fast (partial) answers to Petri net reachability questions. A *p-semiflow* is a non-negative, non-zero integer solution $\mathbf{w} \in \mathbb{N}^{|\mathcal{P}|}$ to the set of linear flow equations $\mathbf{w}^T \cdot \mathbf{D} = \mathbf{0}$, where $\mathbf{D} = \mathbf{D}^+ - \mathbf{D}^-$ is the *incidence matrix*. If there exists a p-semiflow $\mathbf{w}$ with $w_p > 0$, place p is bounded regardless of the initial marking $\mathbf{i}_{init}$. Indeed, given $\mathbf{i}_{init}$, we can conclude that $i_p \leq (\mathbf{w} \cdot \mathbf{i}_{init})/w_p$ in any reachable marking $\mathbf{i}$. P-semiflows provide necessary, not sufficient, conditions on reachability: we can conclude that a marking $\mathbf{i}$ is not reachable if there is p-semiflow $\mathbf{w}$ such that $\mathbf{w} \cdot \mathbf{i} \neq \mathbf{w} \cdot \mathbf{i}_{init}$.

N	BFS			EVMDD-Exact		EVMDD-Approx		
	$\mathcal{X}_{rch}$	time	mem.	time	mem.	$\mathcal{X}_{rch}$	time	mem.
phils : $B=100$								
100	2.13×10^{59}	0.85	18.52	6.38	14.30	4.96×10^{62}	0.10	1.53
200	1.16×10^{86}	2.63	38.56	22.32	41.10	2.46×10^{125}	0.20	2.60
300	1.18×10^{101}	5.60	89.27	42.54	70.20	1.22×10^{188}	0.31	2.93
robin : $B=N\times2$								
100	1.25×10^{18}	2.44	30.17	2.34	22.04	8.11×10^{20}	0.12	1.70
200	2.65×10^{35}	37.72	250.80	35.06	264.61	7.62×10^{40}	1.05	9.18
300	5.61×10^{52}	192.53	909.86	187.83	1091.43	9.64×10^{60}	3.98	28.09
fms : $B=50$								
10	2.20×10^{7}	0.57	5.63	1.55	9.45	2.53×10^{7}	0.22	1.98
15	1.32×10^{8}	1.93	11.24	28.59	28.52	7.24×10^{8}	0.90	4.27
20	2.06×10^{8}	4.27	19.40	414.29	44.47	8.82×10^{9}	2.55	4.28
slot : $B=30$								
20	1.57×10^{14}	0.10	3.65	7.30	7.49	1.58×10^{20}	0.19	1.14
25	1.93×10^{16}	0.13	4.98	28.17	10.31	2.41×10^{25}	0.26	1.50
30	1.14×10^{18}	0.16	6.12	79.26	12.63	3.69×10^{30}	0.34	2.12
kanban : $B=100$								
11	7.35×10^{8}	1.52	18.77	0.74	6.38	2.43×10^{9}	0.23	6.10
12	1.05×10^{9}	2.51	29.70	1.11	9.30	5.51×10^{9}	0.34	9.13
13	1.42×10^{9}	3.45	25.87	1.57	11.79	1.18×10^{10}	0.53	12.09
leader : $B=50$								
7	7.34×10^{6}	0.94	6.02	90.03	70.55	2.38×10^{7}	18.54	22.33
8	4.73×10^{7}	1.97	6.91	1342.46	204.01	3.04×10^{8}	143.67	72.37
9	3.11×10^{8}	4.15	8.28	–	–	3.87×10^{9}	1853.66	243.89
counter : $B=2^{N/10}$								
100	1.02×10^{3}	0.32	13.39	0.01	0.12	2.04×10^{3}	0.02	0.07
200	1.04×10^{6}	745.80	107.62	3.31	36.96	2.09×10^{6}	0.06	0.11
300	–	–	–	–	–	2.14×10^{9}	0.18	0.14
queen : $B=5$								
13	3.86×10^{4}	0.06	1.18	0.20	2.40	3.86×10^{4}	0.15	1.80
14	6.52×10^{4}	0.07	1.73	0.35	3.58	6.52×10^{4}	0.25	2.97
15	1.05×10^{5}	0.10	2.58	0.58	5.59	1.05×10^{5}	0.42	4.45

Fig. 25. Results for bounded saturation (memory: MB, time: sec)

Explicit p-Semiflow Computation. As any nonnegative integer linear combination of p-semiflows is a p-semiflow, we usually seek the (unique) *generator* $\mathcal{G}$, i.e., the set of *minimal* p-semiflows $\mathbf{w}$ satisfying: (1) $\mathbf{w}$ has a minimal support $Supp(\mathbf{w}) = \{p \in \mathcal{P} : w_p > 0\}$, i.e., no other p-semiflow $\mathbf{w}'$ exists with $Supp(\mathbf{w}') \subset Supp(\mathbf{w})$, and (2) $\mathbf{w}$ is scaled back, i.e., the greatest common divisor of its (non-zero) entries is one.

The standard explicit approach to compute $\mathcal{G}$ is Farka's algorithm [26], which manipulates a matrix $[\mathbf{T}|\mathbf{P}]$ stored as a set $\mathcal{A}$ of integer row vectors of length $m + n$, where m and n are the number of transitions and places, respectively. Initially, $[\mathbf{T}|\mathbf{P}] = [\mathbf{D} \,|\, \mathbf{I}] \in \mathbb{Z}^{n\times m} \times \mathbb{N}^{n\times n}$, where $\mathbf{D}$ is the flow matrix and $\mathbf{I}$ is the

$n \times n$ identity matrix, thus $\mathcal{A}$ contains n rows. Then, we iteratively force zero entries in column j for $j = 1, ..., m$, using the following process:

1. Let $\mathcal{A}_N$ ($\mathcal{A}_P$) be the set of rows with negative (positive) j-entry, respectively.
2. Remove the rows in $\mathcal{A}_N$ or $\mathcal{A}_P$ from $\mathcal{A}$.
3. For each $\mathbf{a}_N \in \mathcal{A}_N$ and $\mathbf{a}_P \in \mathcal{A}_P$, add row $\{(-v/\mathbf{a}_N[j]) \cdot \mathbf{a}_N + (v/\mathbf{a}_P[j]) \cdot \mathbf{a}_P\}$ to $\mathcal{A}$, where v is the minimum common multiple of $-\mathbf{a}_N[j]$ and $\mathbf{a}_P[j]$.

The number of rows may grow quadratically at each step, as we add $|\mathcal{A}_N| \cdot |\mathcal{A}_P|$ rows to $\mathcal{A}$ but only remove $|\mathcal{A}_N| + |\mathcal{A}_P|$ rows from it (the number decreases iff $\mathcal{A}_N$ or $\mathcal{A}_P$ is a singleton). Thus $\mathcal{A}$ can grow exponentially in m in pathological cases. Also, if at the beginning of a step either $\mathcal{A}_N$ or $\mathcal{A}_P$ is empty but not both, no p-semiflows exist.

Once the first m columns of $[\mathbf{T}|\mathbf{P}]$ are all zeros, $\mathbf{P}$, i.e., the rows in $\mathcal{A}$ describe the required p-semiflows, except that some of them may be need to be scaled back and some might not have minimal support. Scaling back $\mathcal{A}$ can be accomplished by dividing each $\mathbf{a} \in \mathcal{A}$ by the GCD of its entries, with time complexity $O(|\mathcal{A}| \cdot n)$. To eliminate non-minimal support rows, instead, we compare the supports of each *pair* of distinct $\mathbf{a}$ and $\mathbf{b}$ in $\mathcal{A}$ and delete $\mathbf{b}$ if its support is a superset of that of $\mathbf{a}$, with time complexity $O(|\mathcal{A}|^2 \cdot n)$. Alternatively, we can minimize $\mathcal{A}$ during Farka's algorithm, so that, before iteration j, $\mathcal{A}$ contains the minimal support p-semiflows ignoring transitions $j, ..., m$, and iteration j adds a row to $\mathcal{A}$ only if it scaled back and its support is not a superset of that of a row already in $\mathcal{A}$; this tends to perform better in practice.

Symbolic p-Semiflow Computation Using Zero-Suppressed MDDs [16].
As described, Farka's algorithm manages a set of rows with elements from $\mathbb{Z}$ (in the first m columns) or $\mathbb{N}$ (in the last n columns). This is similar to managing a set of markings, for which MDDs are ideally suited, with two differences:

- The first m row can have negative entries. We cope by letting MDD nodes have index set $\mathbb{Z}$ instead of $\mathbb{N}$. In either case, the key restriction is the same, only a finite number of indices can be on a path to the terminal node $\mathbf{1}$.
- Many of the entries are zero (and the first m entries of each row will be zero at the end). While this is not a problem for MDDs, it turns out that a new MDD reduction rule (initially proposed for BDDs [55]) improves efficiency. We use *zero-suppressed* MDDs (ZMDDs) [16], where no node p has $p[i_k] = \mathbf{0}$ for all $i_k \neq 0$, and the semantic of an edge $p[i_k] = q$ skipping over variable v_h, is the same as if v_h were quasi-reduced and we inserted a node p' associated with v_h along that edge, with $p'[0] = q$ and $p'[i_h] = \mathbf{0}$ for $i_h \neq 0$, see Fig. 26.

In [16] we described a fully symbolic algorithm for p-semiflow computation that implements Farka's algorithm using an $(m + n)$-variable ZMDD to encode the set of rows $\mathcal{A}$. After the jth iteration, all the rows in $\mathcal{A}$ have zero entries in the first j columns, thus the ZMDD encoding of $\mathcal{A}$ skips those first j variables altogether. Symbolic algorithms were provided to perform the required linear combinations, to eliminate non-minimal support p-semiflows (either periodically or at the end), and to scale back a set of p-semiflows.

$$\mathcal{A} = \{000, 001, 002, 110, 111, 112\}$$

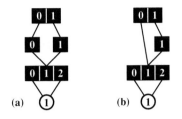

(a)   (b)

Fig. 26. An MDD (a) and a ZMDD (b) encoding the same set $\mathcal{A}$

Experimental results show that our symbolic approach is more efficient than the explicit algorithm implemented in GreatSPN [3] for large enough instances of Petri nets whose generator contains even just a few p-semiflows, while it is of course enormously more efficient when the generator is pathologically large.

While our symbolic algorithms are not expressed as fixpoints, thus do not use saturation, it is conceivable that saturation could be used, especially for the elimination of non-minimal support p-semiflows, to further improve efficiency.

4.2 Integer Timed Petri Nets

Two classic ways to incorporate timed, but not probabilistic, behavior in Petri nets are *timed Petri nets* [58] (the firing time of a transition α is a non-negative real constant) and *time Petri nets* [40] (the firing time lies in a non-negative real interval). In [53], we considered a variant, *integer-timed Petri nets* (ITPNs), where the firing time of a transition is nondeterministically chosen from a finite set of positive integers, and explored two fundamental reachability problems:

- *Timed reachability*: find the set of markings where the Petri net can be at a given finite point θ_f in time.
- *Earliest reachability*: find the first instant of time $\epsilon(\mathbf{i})$ when the Petri net might enter each reachable marking $\mathbf{i}$.

We tackle timed reachability by performing a symbolic simultaneous simulation that manipulates sets of *states* of the form $(\mathbf{i}, \boldsymbol{\tau})$, where $\mathbf{i} \in \mathbb{N}^{|\mathcal{P}|}$ is a marking and $\boldsymbol{\tau} \in (\mathbb{N} \cup \{\infty\})^{|\mathcal{T}|}$ is a vector of *remaining firing times* (RFTs), so that τ_t is the number of time units until t will attempt to fire (∞ if t is disabled in $\mathbf{i}$). We use an MDD on $|\mathcal{P}| + |\mathcal{T}|$ variables to encode the set of states in which the ITPN might be at global time θ, starting with $\theta = 0$. Then, we iteratively:

1. Compute the minimum RFT τ_b for any state encoded by the MDD.
2. Advance θ to the next *breakpoint* $\theta + \tau_b$, and update the MDD by subtracting τ_b from every RFT.
3. Now the MDD contains some *vanishing* states (having one or more RFT equal to zero). Fire all possible *maximally serializable* sets of transitions having zero RFT, until finding all the *tangible* states (having only positive remaining firing times) reachable without further advancing the global time.

When θ reaches the desired final time θ_f, we stop and call a function *Strip* that, given the MDD encoding the states $\mathcal{S}_\theta$ reachable at time θ, computes the MDD encoding just the corresponding markings $\mathcal{X}_\theta = \{\mathbf{i} : \exists \boldsymbol{\tau}, (\mathbf{i}, \boldsymbol{\tau}) \in \mathcal{S}_\theta\}$.

For earliest reachability, we carry out timed reachability, calling *Strip* at every breakpoint, and accumulating the results in an EV$^+$MDD over just the place variables. Initially, the EV$^+$MDD encodes the function $\epsilon(\mathbf{i}) = 0$ if $\mathbf{i}$ is an initial marking, and $\epsilon(\mathbf{i}) = \infty$ otherwise. Then, after stripping the set of markings $\mathcal{X}_\theta$ from the set of states $\mathcal{S}_\theta$ encoded by the MDD at time θ, we transform it into an EV$^+$MDD ϵ_θ evaluating to θ if $\mathbf{i} \in \mathcal{X}_\theta$ and to ∞ otherwise, and we update the EV$^+$MDD so that it encodes the function $\min(\epsilon, \epsilon_\theta)$. In other words, we set the earliest reachability time of any marking in $\mathcal{X}_\theta$ to θ, unless it has already been reached earlier, thus already has a smaller earliest reachability time.

The timed reachability algorithm is guaranteed to halt because θ_f is finite, all firing times are positive integers, and the number of possible firing times for a transitions is finite, However, the earliest reachability algorithm is guaranteed to halt only if the set of reachable markings is finite. Furthermore, the earliest reachability algorithm can be halted only if we accumulate the set of *states* encountered during the timed reachability iterations: failure to increase this set at a breakpoint indicates that no more states can be found; however, accumulating just the reachable markings, or even their earliest reachability function, is not enough, as it is possible to advance to a breakpoint and increase the set of states encountered so far, but not the set of markings.

The results in [53] indicate excellent scalability, showing that problems with very large reachable state spaces can be explored, thanks to the use of symbolic data structures and algorithms. In particular saturation is used in the computation of the tangible states reachable after advancing to a new breakpoint, as this process can be expressed as a fixpoint computation where we need to fire all transitions with a zero RFT in all possible (non-conflicting) sequences. Of course, much of the approach presented is feasible due to the assumption of a discrete set of possible positive integer firing times. Extension to more general firing time assumptions is an interesting challenge that remains to be explored.

4.3   Continuous-Time Markovian Petri Nets

As a last application of decision diagram technology to Petri net analysis, we now consider the generation and numerical solution of Markov models.

Generalized Stochastic Petri Nets (GSPNs) and Their Explicit Solution. GSPNs [1] extend the (untimed) Petri net model by associating a firing time distribution to each transition. Formally, the set of transitions is partitioned into $\mathcal{T}_T$ (*timed*, with an exponentially-distributed firing time) and $\mathcal{T}_V$ (*immediate*, with a constant zero firing time). Immediate transitions have *priority* over timed transitions, thus, a marking $\mathbf{i}$ is either *vanishing*, if $\mathcal{T}(\mathbf{i}) \cap \mathcal{T}_V \neq \emptyset$, which then implies $\mathcal{T}(\mathbf{i}) \subseteq \mathcal{T}_V$ as any timed transition is disabled by definition, or *tangible*, if $\mathcal{T}(\mathbf{i}) \subseteq \mathcal{T}_T$, which includes the case of an absorbing marking, $\mathcal{T}(\mathbf{i}) = \emptyset$.

If marking $\mathbf{i}$ is vanishing, its sojourn time is 0 and the probability that a particular $t \in \mathcal{T}(\mathbf{i})$ fires in $\mathbf{i}$ is $w_t(\mathbf{i})/(\sum_{y \in \mathcal{T}(\mathbf{i})} w_y(\mathbf{i}))$, where $w : \mathcal{T}_V \times \mathbb{N}^{|P|} \to [0, +\infty)$ specifies the marking-dependent firing *weights* (i.e., unnormalized probabilities) of the immediate transitions. If $\mathbf{i}$ is instead tangible, its sojourn time is exponentially distributed with rate $\lambda(\mathbf{i}) = \sum_{y \in \mathcal{T}(\mathbf{i})} \lambda_y(\mathbf{i})$, where $\lambda : \mathcal{T}_T \times \mathbb{N}^{|P|} \to [0, +\infty)$ specifies the marking-dependent firing rates of the timed transitions (of course, the sojourn time is infinite if $\lambda(\mathbf{i}) = 0$, i.e., if $\mathbf{i}$ is absorbing). A *race policy* is employed in this case, thus the probability of $t \in \mathcal{T}(\mathbf{i})$ firing in $\mathbf{i}$ is $\lambda_t(\mathbf{i})/\lambda(\mathbf{i})$.

Except for pathological cases containing *absorbing vanishing loops* [2], a GSPN defines an underlying *continuous-time Markov chain* (CTMC) [10] whose state space is the set of reachable tangible markings of the GSPN, $\mathcal{X}_{tan}$, and whose transition rate matrix $\mathbf{R}$ satisfies $\mathbf{R}[\mathbf{i}, \mathbf{j}] = \sum_{\mathbf{i} \xrightarrow{t} \mathbf{h}} \lambda_t(\mathbf{i}) \cdot \sum_{\sigma \in \mathcal{T}_V^* : \mathbf{h} \xrightarrow{\sigma} \mathbf{j}} Pr\{\mathbf{h} \xrightarrow{\sigma}\}$, where $Pr\{\mathbf{h} \xrightarrow{\sigma}\}$ is the probability of firing the sequence σ of immediate transitions when the marking is $\mathbf{h}$; of course, $\mathbf{i}$ and $\mathbf{j}$ are tangible markings and either $\mathbf{h}$ is vanishing or $\mathbf{h} = \mathbf{j}$, σ is the empty sequence, and we let $Pr\{\mathbf{h} \xrightarrow{\sigma}\} = 1$.

Explicit approaches to GSPN analysis mostly focus on the efficient *elimination* of the vanishing markings, that is, on ways to compute the probability of reaching the *tangible frontier* reachable through immediate firings following a timed firing (although a *preservation* approach that uses as an intermediate step an embedded discrete-time Markov chain with state space including both tangible and vanishing markings has been used as well [18]). Once $\mathbf{R}$ has been obtained, the CTMC can be solved numerically for its steady-state probability (using Gauss-Seidel or Jacobi, possibly with relaxation [50]) or transient probability (using uniformization [29]), after which further measures defined at the net level through *reward measures* can be computed.

We assume that the CTMC is finite and ergodic (all tangible markings are mutually reachable), and focus on steady-state analysis, i.e., computing the probability vector $\boldsymbol{\pi} \in [0, 1]^{|\mathcal{X}_{tan}|}$ solution of $\boldsymbol{\pi} \cdot \mathbf{Q} = \mathbf{0}$, where the *infinitesimal generator* $\mathbf{Q}$ is defined as $\mathbf{Q}[\mathbf{i}, \mathbf{j}] = \mathbf{R}[\mathbf{i}, \mathbf{j}]$ if $\mathbf{i} \neq \mathbf{j}$, and $\mathbf{Q}[\mathbf{i}, \mathbf{i}] = -\sum_{\mathbf{j} \neq \mathbf{i}} \mathbf{R}[\mathbf{i}, \mathbf{j}]$.

Symbolic Encoding of R. As is often the case, the main obstacle to the analysis of GSPNs is the size of the reachability set $\mathcal{X}_{rch}$, or even just of its tangible portion $\mathcal{X}_{tan}$, and of the transition rate matrix $\mathbf{R}$. The symbolic generation of $\mathcal{X}_{rch}$ or $\mathcal{X}_{tan}$ can be performed along the lines of the algorithms of Section 2. However, while the weight and rate information can be ignored during reachability-set generation, the priority of immediate transitions over timed transitions must be taken into account. One way to do so is to build the MDD encoding the set of potential vanishing markings $\mathcal{X}_{potvan}$ (i.e., the union of the enabling conditions of any immediate transition) and restrict the forward function $\mathcal{N}_\alpha$ of any timed transition α to $\mathcal{N}_\alpha \cap (\mathcal{X}_{pot} \setminus \mathcal{X}_{potvan}) \times \mathcal{X}_{pot}$. Indeed, this idea can even be extended to enforce multiple priority levels, not just that of timed vs. immediate transitions [41]. An ordinary saturation approach can then be used to find the reachable markings $\mathcal{X}_{rch}$, from which the set of reachable tangible markings can be obtained as $\mathcal{X}_{tan} = \mathcal{X}_{rch} \setminus \mathcal{X}_{potvan}$.

In many practical models, immediate transitions often have very localized effect. Then, a simpler approach is possible, where a forward function MDD encodes the firing of a timed transition α followed by that of any immediate transition that may become enabled because of the firing of α. For example, consider the **fms** GSPN of Fig. 7, where the firing of transition t_{P1} deposits a token in place P_1wM_1, enabling immediate transition t_{M1} whenever place M_1 is not empty. The forward function $\mathcal{N}_{t_{P1},t_{M1}}$ will then depend on the union of the input and output places for t_{P1}, i.e., P_1 and P_1wM_1, and of t_{M1}, i.e., P_1wM_1, M_1, and P_1M_1. Thanks to our conjunctive encoding of each forward function, the resulting MDD is usually quite manageable. Then, $\mathcal{N}_{t_{P1},t_{M1}}$ can be treated as the forward function of an ordinary timed transition. If this approach is used for all timed transitions that might enable immediate transitions, ordinary saturation can be employed for state-space generation without having to consider priorities, and the resulting algorithm is essentially as efficient as for ordinary Petri nets. This approach is applicable even if a *sequence* of immediate transitions might fire following a timed transition, although in practice it becomes inefficient to build the corresponding forward function if the possible sequences are too complex.

To encode $\mathbf{R}$, real-valued MTBDDs can be employed [36,38], but, as we have already seen, edge-valued approaches are potentially much more efficient. Our EV*MDDs [54], the multiplicative analogue of EV+MDDs, are particularly well suited to generate and store very large transition rate matrices described by GSPNs. In EV*MDDs, all edge values are real values between 0 and 1 (except for the edge pointing to the root, whose value equals the maximum of the function encoded by the EV*MDD), a node must have at least one outgoing edge with value 1, an edge with value 0 must point to Ω, and the function is evaluated by *multiplying* the edge values encountered along the path from the root to Ω.

The EV*MDD encoding $\mathbf{R}$ can be built with an approach analogous to the one used for the forward functions in GSPN state-space generation. We first build the EV*MDD encoding matrix $\mathbf{R}_{\alpha,*}$, corresponding to firing timed transition α (with the appropriate marking-dependent rates) followed by the firing of any sequence of immediate transitions (with the appropriate marking-dependent probabilities). The main difficulty is that the GSPN does not directly specify the firing probabilities of immediate transitions, only their firing weights, which must then be normalized, for example, by encoding the total marking dependent weight in each (vanishing) marking in an EV*MDD, and performing an element-wise division operation on EV*MDDs. $\mathbf{R}$ may be computed as $\sum_{\alpha \in \mathcal{T}_t} \mathbf{R}_{\alpha,*}$, or we might choose to carry on the required numerical solution leaving $\mathbf{R}$ in disjunct form, i.e., as the collection of the EV*MDDs encoding each $\mathbf{R}_{\alpha,*}$.

Unfortunately, the steady-state solution vector rarely has a compact symbolic representation (the MTMDD or EV*MDD encoding $\boldsymbol{\pi}$ is often close to a tree). Thus, the state-of-the-art for an *exact* numerical solution is a *hybrid* approach where the (huge) tangible reachability set $\mathcal{X}_{tan}$ is stored with an MDD and the (correspondingly huge) transition rate matrix $\mathbf{R}$ is stored with an EV*MDD or an MTBDD, but $\boldsymbol{\pi}$ is stored in a full real-valued vector of size $|\mathcal{X}_{tan}|$, where the mapping between tangible markings and their position in this vector, or *indexing* function $\rho : \mathcal{X}_{tan} \to \{0, ..., |\mathcal{X}_{tan}| - 1\}$, can be encoded in an EV+MDD which has the remarkable property of being isomorphic to the MDD encoding $\mathcal{X}_{tan}$ if the index of marking $\mathbf{i}$ is its lexicographic position in $\mathcal{X}_{tan}$ [17].

While this enables the solution of substantially larger CTMC models, since the memory for π is a small fraction of what would be required for an explicit storage of $\mathbf{R}$, it falls short of enabling the analysis of models having similar size as those for which we can answer reachability or CTL queries. In [54], we propose a technique that obviates the need to allocate this full vector, but uses instead memory proportional to the size of the MDD encoding $\mathcal{X}_{tan}$ to store an *approximation* of the solution vector. However, characterizing the quality of the result of this approximation is still an open problem.

In conclusion, saturation helps the analysis of GSPNs when generating the reachability set, and could in principle be used to obtain $\mathbf{R}$ when a fixpoint iteration is required to traverse the sequences of immediate transitions (i.e., if the GSPN gives rise to *transient vanishing loops* [2]) but, at least so far, it has not been employed for the actual numerical solution, even if the traditional solution algorithms are expressed in terms of a fixpoint computation.

4.4   Using Petri Net Invariants to Derive Variable Order Heuristics

We already mentioned that the order of the variables used to encode a particular function with an appropriate form of decision diagrams can affect the resulting size, sometimes exponentially, but finding an optimal variable order is NP-hard [7]. Of course, the problem is even worse in practice, since the fixpoint symbolic algorithms we described manipulate evolving sets of markings, not just a fixed function. Thus, both *static* and *dynamic* heuristics have been proposed, the former to determine a good variable order a priori, the latter to improve the variable order during decision diagram manipulation.

For static orders, a starting point is often to determine groups of two or more variables that should appear "close" in the overall variable order. An obvious example is the relative order of unprimed and primed variables in the representation of the forward function for a transition α; since x'_k is usually a function of x_k (indeed, the two coincide if x_k is independent of α), the size of the MDD encoding $\mathcal{N}_\alpha$ is usually minimized by an interleaved order, and so is the cost of performing a relational product involving $\mathcal{N}_\alpha$. An interleaved order is then almost universally assumed, and the (much harder) remaining problem is that of choosing the order for the L state variables used to encode sets of marking, which then determines the order of the L unprimed-primed state variable pairs used to encode the forward functions.

For this, heuristics such as "inputs to the same logic gate should appear close the output of the logic gate in the variable order" are often employed when verifying digital circuits. Assuming for now that each variable corresponds to a place, the analogous idea for Petri nets is "places connected to a transition should appear close in the variable order", but the problem is more complex since the graph of a Petri net is often cyclic and rather more connected. In [48], we proposed two heuristics to approach this goal in the context of the saturation algorithm for state-space generation: *sum-of-spans* and *sum-of-tops*.

As the name suggests, sum-of-spans aims at finding a variable order that minimizes $SOS = \sum_{\alpha \in \mathcal{E}} Top(\alpha) - Bot(\alpha)$. This tends to "keep together" the input, output, and inhibitor places of each transition. However, since places can be connected to multiple transitions, and vice versa, minimizing SOS is shown to be NP-hard in general. Nevertheless, even just orders that result in small values of SOS tend to perform well (and enormously better than random orders).

Sum-of-tops aims instead at finding a variable order that simply minimizes $SOT = \sum_{\alpha \in \mathcal{E}} Top(\alpha)$. Also this heuristic tends to reduce spans but, in addition, it tends to "push down" the range of variables affected by each transition. When generating the state-space using saturation, which works bottom-up, this means that more transitions can be applied sooner (recall that $\mathcal{N}_\alpha$ is applied to the MDD encoding the currently known set of markings only when we begin saturating nodes associated with $Top(\alpha) = v_k$). Minimizing SOT is also NP-hard but, again, small values of SOT tend to do quite well.

Both sum-of-spans and sum-of-tops, however, are after all quite localized heuristics that fail to take into account the entire structure of the Petri net. Indeed, they do not prioritize the grouping of places connected to a particular transition over those connected to another transition, they simply delegate this choice to the algorithm performing the minimization of SOS or SOT.

In [14], we showed how Petri net invariants can help in a heuristic derivation of static orders. Informally, if places a, b, and c form the support of an invariant $\mathbf{w}_a \cdot \mathbf{i}_a + \mathbf{w}_b \cdot \mathbf{i}_b + \mathbf{w}_c \cdot \mathbf{i}_c = const$, it is good to keep the corresponding variables close to each other in the MDD. While in principle one of the three places can be *eliminated* because its number of tokens can be derived from the other two and the invariant equation, this can decrease locality, which is essential for saturation to work well (and for a compact encoding of the forward functions, regardless of the iteration approach being used). Thus, we showed instead how the bottom two places (in the chosen variable order) should be *merged* into the same variable, resulting in an increased locality and a provably smaller MDD. Ultimately, the goal is a mixed heuristic to minimize both SOS or SOT and the invariant support spans (ISS). While much work remains to be done (e.g., an important question is "What relative weights should be used when minimizing SOS+ISS?", since a net can have exponentially more invariants than transitions), we are starting to gain an understanding of the intuition behind static variable order heuristics.

5   Decision Diagram Implementations and Packages

Over the past two decades, many decision diagram libraries have been developed and many logic, timing, and probabilistic verification tools making use of decision diagram technology have been built. In the following, we mention just a few representative libraries and tools. This list is by no means complete, and new libraries and tools are developed every year.

CUDD (http://vlsi.colorado.edu/~fabio/CUDD/) [49] is by far the most stable and well-known decision diagram library. CUDD implements BDDs, Algebraic Decision Diagrams (similar to MTBDDs), and Zero-suppressed BDDs (the restriction of ZMDDs to boolean domains). Powerful dynamic variable reordering heuristics are provided.

Task	Best suited class of decision diagrams	
State-space generation	MDDs	
CTL model checking	MDDs	for yes/no answers
	EV$^+$MDDs	for witness generation
Bounded model checking	MDDs	if using BFS
	EV$^+$MDDs	if using saturation
P-semiflow computation	ZMDDs	
Timed reachability	MDDs	
Earliest reachability	MDDs and EV$^+$MDDs	
GSPN analysis	MDDs	for state-space generation
	EV$^+$MDDs	for state indexing
	EV*MDDs	for transition rate matrix

Fig. 27. Summary: classes of decision diagrams best suited for various analysis tasks

Meddly (`http://meddly.sourceforge.net/`) [5] is a recent and still very much under development open-source library that implements most (and likely all, eventually) of the classes of decision diagrams discussed in this paper.

NuSMV (`http://nusmv.fbk.eu/`) [21] is an open-source reimplementation of the SMV tool originally developed by McMillan [33]. It uses both decision diagrams and SAT solvers to carry on logic verification. NuSMV is based on CUDD, thus it only uses the classes of decision diagrams supported by it.

GreatSPN (`http://www.di.unito.it/~greatspn/`) [4] is a well known tool for the analysis of GSPNs and related models. Initially developed with explicit analysis techniques in mind, it evolved to include stochastic well-formed nets (SWNs), which tackle state-space growth through symmetry exploitation. More recently, GreatSPN has been enhanced with decision diagram algorithms implemented using Meddly.

PRISM (`http://www.prismmodelchecker.org/`) [35] is an open-source probabilistic model checker. One of its solution engines uses BDDs and MTBDDs for the fully symbolic or hybrid solution of Markovian models.

CADP (`http://www.inrialpes.fr/vasy/cadp.html`) [27] is a tool suite for the design and analysis of communication protocols. Its capabilities include symbolic verification using BDDs.

SMART (`http://www.cs.ucr.edu/~ciardo/SMART/`) [12] is our own tool, developed at the College of William and Mary, University of California at Riverside, and Iowa State University. Initially conceived for explicit analysis of stochastic models, SMART provides now a wide suite of symbolic capabilities. All the results in this paper were obtained using SMART.

6   Conclusion

We have presented a survey of how decision diagram technology, and in particular the saturation algorithm, can be leveraged to greatly improve the size of Petri net models that can be reasonably studied. Fig. 27 summarizes the classes of decision diagrams best suited for the various analysis tasks we discussed.

We believe that this synergy between Petri nets (or similarly structured formalisms) on the one hand and decision diagrams on the other will continue to provide valuable insight into how to advance our ability to analyze increasingly large and complex discrete-state systems.

Acknowledgments. This work was supported in part by the National Science Foundation under Grant CCF-1018057.

References

1. Ajmone Marsan, M., Balbo, G., Conte, G.: A class of generalized stochastic Petri nets for the performance evaluation of multiprocessor systems. ACM Trans. Comp. Syst. 2(2), 93–122 (1984)
2. Ajmone Marsan, M., Balbo, G., Conte, G., Donatelli, S., Franceschinis, G.: Modelling with Generalized Stochastic Petri Nets. John Wiley & Sons (1995)
3. Baarir, S., Beccuti, M., Cerotti, D., De Pierro, M., Donatelli, S., Franceschinis, G.: The GreatSPN tool: recent enhancements. SIGMETRICS Perform. Eval. Rev. 36, 4–9 (2009)
4. Babar, J., Beccuti, M., Donatelli, S., Miner, A.S.: GreatSPN Enhanced with Decision Diagram Data Structures. In: Lilius, J., Penczek, W. (eds.) PETRI NETS 2010. LNCS, vol. 6128, pp. 308–317. Springer, Heidelberg (2010)
5. Babar, J., Miner, A.S.: Meddly: Multi-terminal and Edge-valued Decision Diagram LibrarY. In: Proc. QEST, pp. 195–196. IEEE Computer Society (2010)
6. Biere, A., Cimatti, A., Clarke, E.M., Zhu, Y.: Symbolic Model Checking Without BDDs. In: Cleaveland, W.R. (ed.) TACAS 1999. LNCS, vol. 1579, pp. 193–207. Springer, Heidelberg (1999)
7. Bollig, B., Wegener, I.: Improving the variable ordering of OBDDs is NP-complete. IEEE Trans. Comp. 45(9), 993–1002 (1996)
8. Bryant, R.E.: Graph-based algorithms for boolean function manipulation. IEEE Transactions on Computers 35(8), 677–691 (1986)
9. Burch, J.R., Clarke, E.M., McMillan, K.L., Dill, D.L., Hwang, L.J.: Symbolic model checking: 10^{20} states and beyond. Information and Computation 98, 142–170 (1992)
10. Çinlar, E.: Introduction to Stochastic Processes. Prentice-Hall (1975)
11. Ciardo, G.: Data Representation and Efficient Solution: A Decision Diagram Approach. In: Bernardo, M., Hillston, J. (eds.) SFM 2007. LNCS, vol. 4486, pp. 371–394. Springer, Heidelberg (2007)
12. Ciardo, G., Jones, R.L., Miner, A.S., Siminiceanu, R.: Logical and stochastic modeling with SMART. Perf. Eval. 63, 578–608 (2006)
13. Ciardo, G., Lüttgen, G., Siminiceanu, R.: Saturation: An Efficient Iteration Strategy for Symbolic State Space Generation. In: Margaria, T., Yi, W. (eds.) TACAS 2001. LNCS, vol. 2031, pp. 328–342. Springer, Heidelberg (2001)
14. Ciardo, G., Lüttgen, G., Yu, A.J.: Improving Static Variable Orders Via Invariants. In: Kleijn, J., Yakovlev, A. (eds.) ICATPN 2007. LNCS, vol. 4546, pp. 83–103. Springer, Heidelberg (2007)
15. Ciardo, G., Marmorstein, R., Siminiceanu, R.: The saturation algorithm for symbolic state space exploration. Software Tools for Technology Transfer 8(1), 4–25 (2006)

16. Ciardo, G., Mecham, G., Paviot-Adet, E., Wan, M.: P-semiflow Computation with Decision Diagrams. In: Franceschinis, G., Wolf, K. (eds.) PETRI NETS 2009. LNCS, vol. 5606, pp. 143–162. Springer, Heidelberg (2009)

17. Ciardo, G., Miner, A.S.: A data structure for the efficient Kronecker solution of GSPNs. In: Proc. PNPM, pp. 22–31. IEEE Comp. Soc. Press (1999)

18. Ciardo, G., Muppala, J.K., Trivedi, K.S.: On the solution of GSPN reward models. Perf. Eval. 12(4), 237–253 (1991)

19. Ciardo, G., Siminiceanu, R.: Using Edge-Valued Decision Diagrams for Symbolic Generation of Shortest Paths. In: Aagaard, M.D., O'Leary, J.W. (eds.) FMCAD 2002. LNCS, vol. 2517, pp. 256–273. Springer, Heidelberg (2002)

20. Ciardo, G., Trivedi, K.S.: A decomposition approach for stochastic reward net models. Perf. Eval. 18(1), 37–59 (1993)

21. Cimatti, A., Clarke, E., Giunchiglia, E., Giunchiglia, F., Pistore, M., Roveri, M., Sebastiani, R., Tacchella, A.: NuSMV Version 2: An Open Source Tool for Symbolic Model Checking. In: Brinksma, E., Larsen, K.G. (eds.) CAV 2002. LNCS, vol. 2404, pp. 359–364. Springer, Heidelberg (2002)

22. Clarke, E., Fujita, M., McGeer, P.C., Yang, J.C.-Y., Zhao, X.: Multi-terminal binary decision diagrams: an efficient data structure for matrix representation. In: IWLS 1993 International Workshop on Logic Synthesis (May 1993)

23. Clarke, E.M., Emerson, E.A.: Design and Synthesis of Synchronization Skeletons using Branching Time Temporal Logic. In: Kozen, D. (ed.) Logic of Programs 1981. LNCS, vol. 131, pp. 52–71. Springer, Heidelberg (1982)

24. Clarke, E.M., Wing, J.M., Alur, R., Cleaveland, R., Dill, D., Emerson, A., Garland, S., German, S., Guttag, J., Hall, A., Henzinger, T., Holzmann, G., Jones, C., Kurshan, R., Leveson, N., McMillan, K., Moore, J., Peled, D., Pnueli, A., Rushby, J., Shankar, N., Sifakis, J., Sistla, P., Steffen, B., Wolper, P., Woodcock, J., Zave, P.: Formal methods: state of the art and future directions. ACM Comp. Surv. 28(4), 626–643 (1996)

25. Donatelli, S.: Superposed Generalized Stochastic Petri Nets: Definition and Efficient Solution. In: Valette, R. (ed.) ICATPN 1994. LNCS, vol. 815, pp. 258–277. Springer, Heidelberg (1994)

26. Farkas, J.: Theorie der einfachen ungleichungen. Journal für die reine und andgewandte Mathematik 124, 1–27 (1902)

27. Garavel, H., Lang, F., Mateescu, R., Serwe, W.: Cadp 2010: A Toolbox for the Construction and Analysis of Distributed Processes. In: Abdulla, P.A., Leino, K.R.M. (eds.) TACAS 2011. LNCS, vol. 6605, pp. 372–387. Springer, Heidelberg (2011)

28. Graf, S., Steffen, B., Lüttgen, G.: Compositional minimisation of finite state systems using interface specifications. Journal of Formal Aspects of Computing 8(5), 607–616 (1996)

29. Grassmann, W.K.: Finding transient solutions in Markovian event systems through randomization. In: Numerical Solution of Markov Chains, pp. 357–371. Marcel Dekker, Inc. (1991)

30. Heljanko, K.: Bounded Reachability Checking with Process Semantics. In: Larsen, K.G., Nielsen, M. (eds.) CONCUR 2001. LNCS, vol. 2154, pp. 218–232. Springer, Heidelberg (2001)

31. Heljanko, K., Niemelä, I.: Answer set programming and bounded model checking. In: Answer Set Programming (2001)

32. Itai, A., Rodeh, M.: Symmetry breaking in distributed networks. In: 22th Annual Symp. on Foundations of Computer Science, pp. 150–158. IEEE Comp. Soc. Press (1981)
33. McMillan, K.L.: The SMV system, symbolic model checking - an approach. Technical Report CMU-CS-92-131, Carnegie Mellon University (1992)
34. Kam, T., Villa, T., Brayton, R.K., Sangiovanni-Vincentelli, A.: Multi-valued decision diagrams: theory and applications. Multiple-Valued Logic 4(1-2), 9–62 (1998)
35. Kwiatkowska, M., Norman, G., Parker, D.: PRISM 4.0: Verification of Probabilistic Real-time Systems. In: Gopalakrishnan, G., Qadeer, S. (eds.) CAV 2011. LNCS, vol. 6806, pp. 585–591. Springer, Heidelberg (2011)
36. Kwiatkowska, M.Z., Norman, G., Parker, D.: Probabilistic Symbolic Model Checking with PRISM: A Hybrid Approach. In: Garavel, H., Hatcliff, J. (eds.) TACAS 2003. LNCS, vol. 2619, pp. 52–66. Springer, Heidelberg (2003)
37. Lai, Y.-T., Pedram, M., Vrudhula, B.K.: Formal verification using edge-valued binary decision diagrams. IEEE Trans. Comp. 45, 247–255 (1996)
38. Lampka, K., Siegle, M.: MTBDD-based activity-local state graph generation. In: Proc. PMCCS, pp. 15–18 (September 2003)
39. McMillan, K.L.: Symbolic Model Checking. Kluwer (1993)
40. Merlin, P.M.: A study of the recoverability of computing systems. PhD thesis, Department of Information and Computer Science, University of California, Irvine (1974)
41. Miner, A.S.: Efficient state space generation of GSPNs using decision diagrams. In: Proc. DSN, pp. 637–646 (June 2002)
42. Ogata, S., Tsuchiya, T., Kikuno, T.: SAT-Based Verification of Safe Petri Nets. In: Wang, F. (ed.) ATVA 2004. LNCS, vol. 3299, pp. 79–92. Springer, Heidelberg (2004)
43. Pastor, E., Roig, O., Cortadella, J., Badia, R.M.: Petri Net Analysis using Boolean Manipulation. In: Valette, R. (ed.) ICATPN 1994. LNCS, vol. 815, pp. 416–435. Springer, Heidelberg (1994)
44. Peterson, J.L.: Petri Net Theory and the Modeling of Systems. Prentice-Hall (1981)
45. Petri, C.: Kommunikation mit Automaten. PhD thesis, University of Bonn (1962)
46. Reisig, W.: Elements of Distributed Algorithms (Modeling and Analysis with Petri Nets. Springer, Heidelberg (1998)
47. Roig, O., Cortadella, J., Pastor, E.: Verification of Asynchronous Circuits by BDD-Based Model Checking of Petri Nets. In: DeMichelis, G., Díaz, M. (eds.) ICATPN 1995. LNCS, vol. 935, pp. 374–391. Springer, Heidelberg (1995)
48. Siminiceanu, R., Ciardo, G.: New Metrics for Static Variable Ordering in Decision Diagrams. In: Hermanns, H. (ed.) TACAS 2006. LNCS, vol. 3920, pp. 90–104. Springer, Heidelberg (2006)
49. Somenzi, F.: CUDD: CU Decision Diagram Package, Release 2.4.2, http://vlsi.colorado.edu/~fabio/CUDD/
50. Stewart, W.J.: Introduction to the Numerical Solution of Markov Chains. Princeton University Press (1994)
51. Tilgner, M., Takahashi, Y., Ciardo, G.: SNS 1.0: Synchronized Network Solver. In: 1st Int. Workshop on Manufacturing and Petri Nets, pp. 215–234 (June 1996)
52. Valmari, A.: A Stubborn Attack on the State Explosion Problem. In: Larsen, K.G., Skou, A. (eds.) CAV 1991. LNCS, vol. 575, pp. 156–165. Springer, Heidelberg (1992)
53. Wan, M., Ciardo, G.: Symbolic Reachability Analysis of Integer Timed Petri Nets. In: Nielsen, M., Kučera, A., Miltersen, P.B., Palamidessi, C., Tůma, P., Valencia, F. (eds.) SOFSEM 2009. LNCS, vol. 5404, pp. 595–608. Springer, Heidelberg (2009)

54. Wan, M., Ciardo, G., Miner, A.S.: Approximate steady-state analysis of large Markov models based on the structure of their decision diagram encoding. Perf. Eval. 68, 463–486 (2011)

55. Yoneda, T., Hatori, H., Takahara, A., Minato, S.-I.: BDDs vs. Zero-Suppressed BDDs: For CTL Symbolic Model Checking of Petri Nets. In: Srivas, M., Camilleri, A. (eds.) FMCAD 1996. LNCS, vol. 1166, pp. 435–449. Springer, Heidelberg (1996)

56. Yu, A.J., Ciardo, G., Lüttgen, G.: Decision-diagram-based techniques for bounded reachability checking of asynchronous systems. Software Tools for Technology Transfer 11(2), 117–131 (2009)

57. Zhao, Y., Ciardo, G.: Symbolic CTL Model Checking of Asynchronous Systems using Constrained Saturation. In: Liu, Z., Ravn, A.P. (eds.) ATVA 2009. LNCS, vol. 5799, pp. 368–381. Springer, Heidelberg (2009)

58. Zuberek, W.L.: Timed Petri nets definitions, properties, and applications. Microelectronics and Reliability 31, 627–644 (1991)

Refinement and Asynchronous Composition of Modal Petri Nets

Dorsaf Elhog-Benzina[1], Serge Haddad[1], and Rolf Hennicker[2]

[1] LSV, CNRS & Ecole Normale Supérieure de Cachan
94235 CACHAN, 61 Avenue du Président Wilson, France
{elhog,haddad}@lsv.ens-cachan.fr
[2] Institut für Informatik Universität München
Oettingenstraße 67 D-80538 München, Germany
hennicker@ifi.lmu.de

Abstract. We propose a framework for the specification of infinite state systems based on Petri nets with distinguished *may-* and *must*-transitions (called modalities) which specify the allowed and the required behavior of refinements and hence of implementations. For any modal Petri net, we define its generated modal language specification which abstracts away silent transitions. On this basis we consider refinements of modal Petri nets by relating their generated modal language specifications. We show that this refinement relation is decidable if the underlying modal Petri nets are weakly deterministic. We also show that the membership problem for the class of weakly deterministic modal Petri nets is decidable. As an important application scenario of our approach we consider I/O-Petri nets and their asynchronous composition which typically leads to an infinite state system.

Keywords: Modal language specification and refinement, modal Petri net, weak determinacy, asynchronous composition, infinite state system.

1 Introduction

In component-based software development, *specification* is an important phase in the life cycle of each component. It aims to produce a formal description of the component's desired properties and behavior. A behavior specification can be presented either in terms of transition systems or in terms of logic, which both cannot be directly executed by a machine. Thus an *implementation phase* is required to produce concrete executable programs.

Modal specifications have been introduced in [18] as a formal model for specification and implementation. A modal specification explicitly distinguishes between required transitions and allowed ones. Required transitions, denoted with the modality *must*, are compulsory in all correct implementations while allowed transitions, denoted with the modality *may*, may occur but can also be omitted in an implementation. An implementation is seen as a particular specification in which all transitions are required. Thus modalities support underspecification as well as tight specifications saying that certain activities must be present.

K. Jensen, S. Donatelli, and J. Kleijn (Eds.): ToPNoC V, LNCS 6900, pp. 96–120, 2012.
© Springer-Verlag Berlin Heidelberg 2012

Therefore they provide a flexible tool for system development as decisions can be delayed to later steps of the component's life cycle. Two different modal formalisms have been adopted in the literature, the first one, introduced in [15], is based on transition systems while the second one, introduced in [24], is a language-based model defining *modal language specifications.*

A transformation step from a more abstract specification to a more concrete one is called a *refinement.* It produces a specification that is more precise, i.e. has less possible implementations. Hence the set of implementations of a refinement is included in the set of possible implementations of the original specification. From the practical and from the computational point of view, it is of course an important issue to be able to check refinements, and even better, to decide whether a refinement relation holds. For modal transition systems with finite states and for modal language specifications whose underlying languages are regular, the refinement problem is decidable.

Due to its simplicity and appropriateness to design, this modal approach has led both to industrial case studies, see, e.g., [17], and to theoretical developments in order to integrate timing requirements [6] or probabilistic requirements [8]. However, none of these works deals with infinite state systems or asynchronous composition while in distributed systems such features are indispensable. For instance, (discrete) infinite state systems can easily appear by the asynchronous composition of components, since asynchronous communication introduces a delay between the actions of sending and receiving a message between the communication partners. Indeed the size of every communication channel is potentially unbounded. But also requirement specifications for complex systems may involve infinite state spaces. Thus the motivation of our work was to extend the modal approach to take into account infinite state system specifications and their modal refinement while keeping most of the problems decidable. In particular, our results should be applicable to systems of asynchronoulsy communicating components.

Our Contribution. Petri nets are an appropriate formalism for our needs since they allow for a finite representation of infinite state systems. Automata with queues might be another alternative, but all significant problems (e.g. the reachability problem) are known to be undecidable [7] while they are decidable when considering deterministic Petri nets [21]. In our approach, we consider Petri nets with silent transitions labeled by ϵ. Silent transitions are invisible to the environment and hence are the basis for observational abstraction. This is particularly important to obtain a powerful refinement relation which relies only on observable behaviors. In our approach we define the generated language of a Petri net by abstracting away silent transitions. Then we consider Petri net refinement as inclusion of the generated languages which means that the observable execution traces of a "concrete" (refining) Petri net must be observable execution traces of the "abstract" (refined) Petri net as well. We know from [21] that for languages generated by deterministic Petri nets the language inclusion problem is decidable but also, from [10], that in general the language inclusion problem for Petri nets is undecidable. In the presence of silent transitions we are, unfortunately, very often in a situation where Petri nets have non-deterministic silent choices such that we cannot use the decidability results for the deterministic case. Therefore, we introduce the generalized notion of *weakly deterministic* Petri nets, which are deterministic "up to silent transitions". We show that the following problems are decidable:

1. Decide whether a given Petri net is weakly deterministic.
2. Decide whether a given language $\mathcal{L}(\mathcal{N}')$ generated by a Petri net $\mathcal{N}'$ is included in the language $\mathcal{L}(\mathcal{N})$ generated by a *weakly deterministic* Petri net $\mathcal{N}$.

In the next step, we incorporate modalities in our approach and consider *modal Petri nets* with *may*- and *must*-transitions. For the definition of refinement, we follow again a language-based approach and use modal Petri nets as a device to generate modal language specifications. A subtle aspect of this generation concerns the treatment of silent *may*- and *must*-transitions. Refinement of modal Petri nets is then considered as refinement of their generated modal language specifications in the sense of Raclet *et al.* [25]. In particular, the *must* modality is important here to express that certain activities must be respected by refinements and hence implementations. On the other hand, the language inclusion property following from the *may* modality guarantess, as in the non modal case, that safety properties are preserved by refinements for all observable execution traces. We also extend the notion of weak determinacy to the modal case and show that the following problems, which extend the ones from above to the modal context, are decidable:

3. Decide whether a given modal Petri net is (modally) weakly deterministic.
4. Given two modal language specifications $\mathcal{S}(\mathcal{M}')$ and $\mathcal{S}(\mathcal{M})$ generated by two *weakly deterministic* modal Petri nets $\mathcal{M}'$ and $\mathcal{M}$ respectively, decide whether $\mathcal{S}(\mathcal{M}')$ is a modal language specification refinement of $\mathcal{S}(\mathcal{M})$.

As a particular important application scenario of our approach, we consider asynchronously communicating Petri nets. To realize the communication abilities we distinguish between input, output and internal labels which leads to our notion of a *modal I/O-Petri net*. We define an asynchronous composition operator for such nets where all actions related to communication (i.e. sending and receiving) are represented by internal labels. I/O-Petri nets obtained by asynchronous composition typically exhibit infinite state spaces. When considering refinements, transitions with internal labels should be treated as silent transitions. Therefore, we introduce a hiding operator on I/O-Petri nets which relabels internal labels to the silent label ϵ. Then we can directly apply our techniques and decidability results described above for the treatment of refinements in the context of asynchronously composed I/O-Petri nets. Thus our machinery is particularly useful in typical situations where an infinite abstract requirement specification is implemented by an architecture consisting of asynchronously communicating components. We will illustrate such an application in the context of a cash desk system case study.

Outline of the Paper. We proceed by reviewing in Sect. 2 modal language specifications and their associated notion of refinement. Sect. 3 consists of two parts: In Sect. 3.1 we first recall the notion of a Petri net with silent transitions and then we define its generated language specification by abstracting silent transitions away. We also introduce the notion of weak determinacy and state the first two decision problems from above. In Sect. 3.2 we extend our approach to modal Petri nets. We define the generated modal language specification of a modal Petri net, consider modally weakly determinsitic Petri nets and state the last two decsion problems from above in the context of modalities. In Sect. 4, we focus on asynchronously communicating modal Petri nets over an I/O-alphabet with distinguished input, output, and internal labels. We define the asynchronous composition of modal I/O-Petri nets and adopt them, by hiding of internal labels, to our approch for modal refinement. Then, in Sect. 5, we discuss a case study to illustrate our principles. In Sect. 6 we present the decision algorithms of the four decision problems mentioned above. Sect. 7 concludes this paper and presents some future work perspectives.

2   Modal Language Specifications

Modal specifications were introduced by Larsen and Thomsen in [18] in terms of modal transition systems where transitions are equipped with distinguished *may* (allowed) and *must* (required) modalities. This idea has been adapted by Raclet in his (French) Ph.D. thesis [23] in which he applied it to language specifications where the complexity of decision problems is more tractable than with modal transition systems. Moreover, modal refinement is sound and complete with the language-based formalism while it is non-complete with the transition system based formalism [16]. Therefore we base our considerations on a language approach to modal specifications. Let us first review the underlying definitions of modal language specifications and their refinement as introduced in [24].

Notation. Let E be a set, then $P(E)$ denotes its powerset.

Definition 1 (Modal language specification). *A modal language specification S over an alphabet Σ is a triple $\langle \mathcal{L}, may, must \rangle$ where $\mathcal{L} \subseteq \Sigma^*$ is a prefix-closed language over Σ and $may, must : \mathcal{L} \to P(\Sigma)$ are partial functions. For every trace $u \in \mathcal{L}$,*

- *$a \in may(u)$ means that the action a is allowed after u,*
- *$a \in must(u)$ means that the action a is required after u,*
- *$a \notin may(u)$ means that a is forbidden after u.*

The modal language specification S is consistent *if the following two conditions hold:*
(C1) $\forall\, u \in \mathcal{L}, must(u) \subseteq may(u)$
(C2) $\forall\, u \in \mathcal{L}, may(u) = \{a \in \Sigma \mid u.a \in \mathcal{L}\}$

Observation. If $must(u)$ contains more than one element, this means that any correct implementation must have after the trace u (at least) the choice between all actions in $must(u)$.

Example 1. Let us consider the example of a message producer and a message consumer represented in Fig. 1. The transition with label *in* represents an input received by the producer from the environment, which is followed by the transition with label *m* representing the sending of message *m*. The consumer must be able to perform the transition labeld with *m*, representing the reception of *m*, and then it must be able to "output" *out* to the environment.

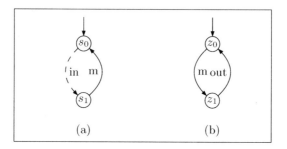

Fig. 1. Modal transition systems for a producer (a) and a consumer (b)

In the producer system, transition $s_0 \xrightarrow{in} s_1$ is allowed but not required (dashed line) while transition $s_1 \xrightarrow{m} s_0$ is required (solid line). In the consumer model all transitions are required. The language associated with the producer is $\mathcal{L} \equiv (in.m)^* + in.(m.in)^*$. The associated modal language specification is then $\langle \mathcal{L}, may, must \rangle$ with:

- $\forall\, u \,\in\, (in.m)^*,\ must(u) = \emptyset \wedge may(u) = \{in\}$
- $\forall\, u \in in.(m.in)^*,\ must(u) = may(u) = \{m\}$

Similarly, the modal language specification associated with the consumer is $\langle (m.out)^* + m.(out.m)^*, may, must \rangle$ with:

- $\forall\, u \,\in\, (m.out)^*,\ must(u) = may(u) = \{m\}$
- $\forall\, u \in m.(out.m)^*,\ must(u) = may(u) = \{out\}$

Modal language specifications can be refined by either removing some allowed events or changing them into required events.

Definition 2 (Modal language specification refinement)
Let $\mathcal{S} \,=\, \langle \mathcal{L}, may, must \rangle$ *and* $\mathcal{S}' = \langle \mathcal{L}', may', must' \rangle$ *be two consistent modal language specifications over the same alphabet* Σ. $\mathcal{S}'$ *is a modal language specification refinement of* $\mathcal{S}$, *denoted by* $\mathcal{S}' \sqsubseteq \mathcal{S}$, *if:*

- $\mathcal{L}' \subseteq \mathcal{L}$,
- for every $u \in \mathcal{L}'$, $must(u) \subseteq must'(u)$, i.e every required action after the trace u in $\mathcal{L}$ is a required action after u in $\mathcal{L}'$.

Modal language specifications support underspecification and thus stepwise refinement but they are not appropriate for the specification of infinite state systems since refinement can not be decided in this case. Moreover, they do not support silent transitions and hence observational abstraction.

3   Modal Petri Nets

Petri nets provide an appropriate tool to specify the behavior of infinite state systems in a finitary way. Therefore we are interested in the following to combine the advantages of Petri nets with the flexibility provided by modalities for the definition of refinements. Of particular interest are Petri nets which support silent transitions. Silent transitions are important to model, e.g., internal alternatives which are invisible to the outside. In the following of this section we will consider such Petri nets and extend them by modalities.

3.1   Petri Nets and Their Generated Languages

In this subsection, we first review basic definitions of Petri net theory and then we develop our first decision problems without taking into account modalities yet.

Definition 3 (Labeled Petri Net). *A* labeled Petri net *over an alphabet* Σ *is a tuple* $\mathcal{N} = (P, T, W^-, W^+, \lambda, m_0)$ *where:*

- *P is a finite set of* places,
- *T is a finite set of* transitions *with $P \cap T = \emptyset$,*
- *W^- (resp. W^+) is a matrix indexed by $P \times T$ with values in $\mathbb{N}$; it is called the* backward (forward) incidence matrix,
- *$\lambda : T \to \Sigma \cup \{\epsilon\}$ is a transition labeling function where ϵ denotes the empty word, and*
- *$m_0 : P \mapsto \mathbb{N}$ is an initial marking.*

A marking *is a mapping* $m : P \mapsto \mathbb{N}$. A transition $t \in T$ is called *silent*, if $\lambda(t) = \epsilon$. The labeling function is extended to sequences of transitions $\sigma = t_1 t_2 ... t_n \in T^*$ where $\lambda(\sigma) = \lambda(t_1)\lambda(t_2)...\lambda(t_n)$. According to this definition $\lambda(\sigma) \in \Sigma^*$, i.e. $\lambda(\sigma)$ represents a sequence of observable actions where silent transitions are abstracted away.

For each $t \in T$, $^\bullet t$ ($t^\bullet$ resp.) denotes the set of *input (output) places* of t. i.e. $^\bullet t = \{p \in P \mid W^-(p,t) > 0\}$ ($t^\bullet = \{p \in P \mid W^+(p,t) > 0\}$ resp.). Likewise for each $p \in P$, $^\bullet p$ ($p^\bullet$) denotes the set of *input (output) transitions* of p i.e. $^\bullet p = \{t \in T \mid W^+(p,t) > 0\}$ ($p^\bullet = \{t \in T \mid W^-(p,t) > 0\}$ resp.). The input (output resp.) vector of a transition t is the column vector of matrix W^- (W^+ resp.) indexed by t.

In the rest of the paper, labeled Petri nets are simply called Petri nets. We have not included final markings in the definition of a Petri net here, because we are interested in potentially infinite system behaviors. We now introduce the notions related to the semantics of a net.

Definition 4 (Firing rule). *Let $\mathcal{N}$ be a Petri net. A transition $t \in T$ is firable from a marking m, denoted by $m[t\rangle$, iff $\forall p \in {}^\bullet t$, $m(p) \geq W^-(p,t)$. The set of firable transitions from a marking m is defined by $firable(m) = \{t \in T \mid m[t\rangle\}$. For a marking m and $t \in firable(m)$, the firing of t from m leads to the marking m', denoted by $m[t\rangle m'$, and defined by $\forall p \in P, m'(p) = m(p) - W^-(p,t) + W^+(p,t)$.*

Definition 5 (Firing sequence). *Let $\mathcal{N}$ be a Petri net with the initial marking m_0. A finite sequence $\sigma \in T^*$ is firable in a marking m and leads to a marking m', also denoted by $m[\sigma\rangle m'$, iff either $\sigma = \epsilon$ or $\sigma = \sigma_1.t$ with $t \in T$ and there exists m_1 such that $m[\sigma_1\rangle m_1$ and $m_1[t\rangle m'$. For a marking m and $\sigma \in T^*$, we write $m[\sigma\rangle$ if σ is firable in m. The set of reachable markings is defined by $Reach(\mathcal{N}, m_0) = \{m \mid \exists \sigma \in T^* such\ that\ m_0[\sigma\rangle m\}$.*

The reachable markings of a Petri net correspond to the reachable states of the modeled system. Since the capacity of places is unlimited, the set of the reachable markings of the Petri nets considered here may be infinite. Thus, Petri nets can model infinite state systems.

The semantics of a net will be given in terms of its generated language. It is important to note that the language generated by a labeled Petri net abstracts from silent transitions and therefore determines the observable execution traces of a net. Technically this is achieved by using the empty word ϵ as a label for silent transitions such that, for each sequence $\sigma \in T^*$ of transitions, $\lambda(\sigma)$ shows only the labels of the observable transitions.

Definition 6 (Petri net language). *Let $\mathcal{N}$ be a labeled Petri net over the alphabet Σ. The language generated by $\mathcal{N}$ is:*

$$\mathcal{L}(\mathcal{N}) = \{u \in \Sigma^* \mid \exists \sigma \in T^* \ and \ m \ such \ that \ \lambda(\sigma) = u \ and \ m_0[\sigma\rangle m\} \ .$$

A particular interesting class of Petri nets are deterministic Petri nets as defined, e.g., in [21]. In our approach, however, we deal with silent transitions which often model non-deterministic choices. For instance, silent transitions with non-deterministic choices will naturally appear in asynchronous compositions considered later on (c.f. Sect. 4) when communication actions are hidden. Therefore, we are interested in a relaxed notion of determinacy which allows us to consider determinism "up to silent moves". This leads to our notion of *weakly deterministic* Petri net. We call a Petri net weakly deterministic if any two firing sequences σ and σ' which produce the same word u can both be extended to produce the same continuations of u. In other words, in a weakly deterministic Petri net, one may fire from a reachable marking two different sequences labelled by the same word but the visible behaviours from the reached markings are the same. So an external observer cannot detect this non-determinism. In this sense our notion of weak deterministic Petri net corresponds to Milner's (weak) determinacy [20] and to the concept of a weakly deterministic transition system described in [11]. The underlying idea is also related to the notion of output-determinacy introduced in [14].

Definition 7 (Weakly Deterministic Petri Net). *Let $\mathcal{N}$ be a labeled Petri net with initial marking m_0 and labeling function $\lambda : T \to \Sigma \cup \{\epsilon\}$. For any marking m, let*

$$may_{mk}(m) = \{a \in \Sigma \mid \exists \sigma \in T^* \text{ such that } \lambda(\sigma) = a \text{ and } m[\sigma\rangle\}$$

be the set of labels that may occur starting from m after a sequence of silent transitions. $\mathcal{N}$ is called weakly deterministic, *if for each $\sigma, \sigma' \in T^*$ with $\lambda(\sigma) = \lambda(\sigma')$ and for markings m and m' with $m_0[\sigma\rangle m$ and $m_0[\sigma'\rangle m'$, we have $may_{mk}(m) = may_{mk}(m')$.*

Weakly deterministic Petri nets will play an important role for deciding refinements. Hence, it is crucial to know whether a given Petri net belongs to the class of weakly deterministic Petri nets. This leads to our first decision problem stated below. Our second decision problem is motivated by the major goal of this work to provide formal support for refinement in system development. Since refinement can be defined by language inclusion, we want to be able to decide this. Unfortunately, it is well-known that the language inclusion problem for Petri nets is undecidable [10]. However, in [21] it has been shown that for languages generated by deterministic Petri nets the language inclusion problem is decidable. Therefore we are interested in a generalization of this result for languages generated by weakly deterministic Petri nets which leads to our second decision problem. Observe that we do not require $\mathcal{N}'$ to be weakly deterministic.

First decision problem. Given a labeled Petri net $\mathcal{N}$, decide whether $\mathcal{N}$ is weakly deterministic.

Second decision problem. Let $\mathcal{L}(\mathcal{N})$ and $\mathcal{L}(\mathcal{N}')$ be two languages on the same alphabet Σ such that $\mathcal{L}(\mathcal{N})$ is generated by a weakly deterministic Petri net $\mathcal{N}$ and $\mathcal{L}(\mathcal{N}')$ is generated by a Petri net $\mathcal{N}'$. Decide whether $\mathcal{L}(\mathcal{N}')$ is included in $\mathcal{L}(\mathcal{N})$.

The descion problems deal with refinements based on an observational abstraction of silent transitions of the underlying Petri nets.

3.2   Modal Petri Nets

In the following we extend our approach by incorporating modalities. For this purpose we introduce, following the ideas of modal transition systems and modal language specifications, modal Petri nets with modalities *may* and *must* on their transitions. Note that we require any *must*-transition to be allowed, i.e. to be a *may*-transition as well.

Definition 8 (Modal Petri net). *A* modal Petri net *$\mathcal{M}$ over an alphabet Σ is a pair $\mathcal{M} = (\mathcal{N}, T_\square)$ where $\mathcal{N} = (P, T, W^-, W^+, \lambda, m_0)$ is a labeled Petri net over Σ and $T_\square \subseteq T$ is a set of* must (required) *transitions. The set of* may (allowed) *transitions is the set of transitions T.*

Example 2. Let us consider the same example of a message producer and a message consumer (see Fig. 2). The producer may receive a message *in* (white transition) but must produce a message *m* (black transition). The consumer must receive a message *m* and then it must produce a message *out*.

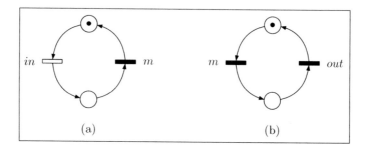

(a)   (b)

Fig. 2. Modal Petri nets for a producer (a) and a consumer (b)

Any modal Petri net $\mathcal{M} = (\mathcal{N}, T_\square)$ gives rise to the construction of a modal language specification (see Def. 1) which extends the language $\mathcal{L}(\mathcal{N})$ by *may* and *must* modalities. Similarly to the construction of $\mathcal{L}(\mathcal{N})$ the definition of the modalities of the generated language specification should take into account abstraction from silent transitions. While for the *may* modality this is rather straightforward, the definition of the *must* modality is rather subtle, since it must take into account silent *must*-transitions which are abstracted away during language generation. For the definition of the *must* modality we introduce the following auxiliary definition which describes, for each marking m, the set $must_{mk}(m)$ of all labels $a \in \Sigma$ which must be produced by firing (from m) some silent *must*-transitions succeeded by a *must*-transition labeled by a. This means that the label a must be producible as the next visible label by some firing sequence of m. Formally, for any marking m, let

$$must_{mk}(m) = \{a \in \Sigma \mid \exists \sigma \in T_\square^*, t \in T_\square \text{ such that } \lambda(\sigma) = \epsilon, \lambda(t) = a \text{ and } m[\sigma t\rangle\}$$

We can now consider for each word $u \in \mathcal{L}(\mathcal{N})$ and for each marking m, reachable by firing a sequence of transitions which produces u and which has no silent transition at the end[1], the set $must_{mk}(m)$. The labels in $must_{mk}(m)$ must be exactly the possible successors of u in the generated modal language specification.

---

[1] We require this to avoid false detection of must transitions starting from intermediate markings which are reachable by silent may transitions.

Definition 9 (Modal Petri Net Language Specification). *Let* $\mathcal{M} = (\mathcal{N}, T_\square)$ *be a modal Petri net over an alphabet* Σ *such that* $\lambda : T \to \Sigma \cup \{\epsilon\}$ *is the labeling function and* m_0 *is the initial marking of* $\mathcal{N}$. $\mathcal{M}$ *generates the* modal language specification $\mathcal{S}(\mathcal{M}) = \langle \mathcal{L}(\mathcal{N}), may, must \rangle$ *where:*

- $\mathcal{L}(\mathcal{N})$ *is the language generated by the Petri net* $\mathcal{N}$,
- $\forall u \in \mathcal{L}(\mathcal{N}), \, may(u) =$
  $\{a \in \Sigma \mid \exists \sigma \in T^* \text{ and } m \text{ such that } \lambda(\sigma) = u, m_0[\sigma\rangle m \text{ and } a \in may_{mk}(m)\}$,
- $\forall u \in \mathcal{L}(\mathcal{N}), x \in \Sigma$,
  - $must(\epsilon) = must_{mk}(m_0)$,
  - $must(ux) = \{a \in \Sigma \mid \exists \sigma \in T^*, t \in T \text{ and } m \text{ such that } \lambda(\sigma) = u, \lambda(t) = x, m_0[\sigma t\rangle m \text{ and } a \in must_{mk}(m)\}$.

Remark 1. Any modal language specification generated by a modal Petri net is consistent. Condition $C1$ is a consequence of the inclusion $must_{mk}(m) \subseteq may_{mk}(m)$ and condition $C2$ is a consequence of the definition of $may_{mk}(m)$.

Example 3. Let us consider the modal Petri net in Fig. 3.

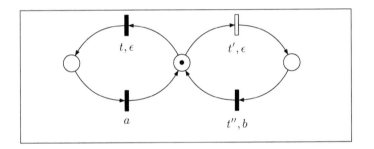

Fig. 3. Modal Petri net with silent transitions

The modal language specification generated by this net consists of the language $\mathcal{L}$ presented by the regular expression $(a^*b^*)^*$ and modalities $may(u) = \{a, b\}$, and $must(u) = \{a\}$ for $u \in \mathcal{L}$. Note that b is not a *must* as it is preceeded by a silent *may*-transition (which can be omitted in a refinement).

The notion of weakly deterministic Petri net can be extended to modal Petri nets by taking into account an additional condition for *must*-transitions. This condition ensures that for any two firing sequences σ and σ' which produce the same word u, the continuations of u produced by firing sequences of *must*-transitions after σ and σ' are the same.

Definition 10 (Weakly Deterministic Modal Petri Net). *Let* $\mathcal{M} = (\mathcal{N}, T_\square)$ *be a modal Petri net over an alphabet* Σ *such that* $\lambda : T \to \Sigma \cup \{\epsilon\}$ *is the labeling function of* $\mathcal{N}$. $\mathcal{M}$ *is (modally) weakly deterministic, if*

1. $\mathcal{N}$ *is weakly deterministic, and*
2. *for each $\sigma, \sigma' \in T^*$ with $\lambda(\sigma) = \lambda(\sigma')$ and for any markings m and m' with $m_0[\sigma\rangle m$ and $m_0[\sigma'\rangle m'$, we have $must_{mk}(m) = must_{mk}(m')$.*

Remark 2. For any weakly deterministic modal Petri net $\mathcal{M} = (\mathcal{N}, T_\Box)$ the definition of the modalities of its generated modal language specification $\mathcal{L}(\mathcal{M}) = \langle \mathcal{L}(\mathcal{N}), may, must \rangle$ can be simplified as follows:

- $\forall u \in \mathcal{L}(\mathcal{N})$, let $\sigma \in T^*$ and let m be a marking such that $\lambda(\sigma) = u$ and $m_0[\sigma\rangle m$, then $may(u) = may_{mk}(m)$.
- $\forall u \in \mathcal{L}(\mathcal{N}), x \in \Sigma$, let $\sigma \in T^*, t \in T$ and let m be a marking such that $\lambda(\sigma) = u, \lambda(t) = x$ and $m_0[\sigma t\rangle m$, then $must(ux) = must_{mk}(m)$. Moreover, $must(\epsilon) = must_{mk}(m_0)$.

Example 4. The Petri net in Fig. 3 (considered without modalities) is not weakly deterministic. Indeed let m_1 be the marking reached by t from m_0. Both markings m_0 and m_1 are reachable by a sequence of silent transitions. However from m_0, the sequence $t't''$ labelled by b is fireable while no sequence labelled by b is fireable from m_1. Hence it is also not modally weakly deterministic.

Let us now consider the modal Petri net in Fig. 4.

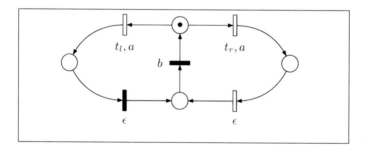

Fig. 4. Non weakly deterministic modal Petri net

Let m_l (m_r resp.) be the marking obtained by firing the transition t_l (t_r resp.). Obviously, both transitions produce the same letter but $must_{mk}(m_l) = \{b\}$ while $must_{mk}(m_r) = \emptyset$ (since the silent transition firable in m_r is only a *may*-transition). Hence the Petri net is not modally weakly deterministic. However, one should note that, if we forget the modalities, then the Petri net in Fig. 4 is weakly deterministic.

The two decision problems of Sect. 3.1 induce the following obvious extensions in the context of modal Petri nets and their generated modal language specifications. Observe that for the refinement problem we require that both nets are weakly deterministic.

> **Third decision problem.** Given a modal Petri net $\mathcal{M}$, decide whether $\mathcal{M}$ is (modally) weakly deterministic.
>
> **Fourth decision problem.** Let $\mathcal{S}(\mathcal{M})$ and $\mathcal{S}(\mathcal{M}')$ be two modal language specifications over the same alphabet Σ such that $\mathcal{S}(\mathcal{M})$ ($\mathcal{S}(\mathcal{M}')$ resp.) is generated by a weakly deterministic modal Petri net $\mathcal{M}$ ($\mathcal{M}$ resp.). Decide whether $\mathcal{S}(\mathcal{M}')$ is a modal language specification refinement of $\mathcal{S}(\mathcal{M})$.

4   Modal I/O-Petri Nets and Asynchronous Composition

A particular application scenario for our approach is given by systems of asynchronously communication components. The characteristic property of this communication style is that communication happens via a potentially unbounded event channel such that the actions of sending (output) and receiving (input) of a message are delayed. In order to model such systems we consider modal Petri nets where the underlying alphabet Σ is partitioned into disjoint sets in, out, and int of input, output and internal labels resp., i.e $\Sigma = in \uplus out \uplus int$. Since $\epsilon \notin \Sigma$, this means that all labels, including the internal ones, are observable. Such alphabets are called *I/O-alphabets* and modal Petri nets over an I/O-alphabet are called *modal I/O-Petri nets*. The discrimination of input, output and internal labels provides a mean to specify the communication abilities of a Petri net and hence provides an appropriate basis for Petri net composition. A syntactic requirement for the composability of two modal I/O-Petri nets is that their labels overlap only on complementary types [2,17], i.e. their underlying alphabets must be composable. Formally, two I/O-alphabets $\Sigma_1 = in_1 \uplus out_1 \uplus int_1$ and $\Sigma_2 = in_2 \uplus out_2 \uplus int_2$ are *composable* if $\Sigma_1 \cap \Sigma_2 = (in_1 \cap out_2) \cup (in_2 \cap out_1)$.[2]

Definition 11 (Alphabet Composition). *Let $\Sigma_1 = in_1 \uplus out_1 \uplus int_1$ and $\Sigma_2 = in_2 \uplus out_2 \uplus int_2$ be two composable I/O-alphabets. The composition of Σ_1 and Σ_2 is the I/O-alphabet $\Sigma_c = in_c \uplus out_c \uplus int_c$ where:*

- $in_c = (in_1 \setminus out_2) \uplus (in_2 \setminus out_1),$
- $out_c = (out_1 \setminus in_2) \uplus (out_2 \setminus in_1),$
- $int_c = \{a^{\triangleright} \mid a \in \Sigma_1 \cap \Sigma_2\} \uplus \{^{\triangleright}a \mid a \in \Sigma_1 \cap \Sigma_2\} \uplus int_1 \uplus int_2.$

The input and output labels of the alphabet composition are the input and output labels of the underlying alphabets which are not used for communication, and hence are "left open". The internal labels of the alphabet composition are obtained from the internal labels of the underlying alphabets and from their shared input/output labels. Since we are interested here in asynchronous communication each shared label a is duplicated to $a^{\triangleright}$ and $^{\triangleright}a$ where the former represents the asynchronous sending of a message and the latter represents the receipt of the message (at some later point in time).

---

[2] Note that for composable alphabets $in_1 \cap in_2 = \emptyset$ and $out_1 \cap out_2 = \emptyset$.

We are now able to define the asynchronous composition of composable modal I/O-Petri nets. We first take the disjoint union of the two nets. Then we add a new place p_a (called channel place) for each shared label a.[3] The shared label a of every output transition t becomes $a^\triangleright$ and such a transition produces a token in p_a. The shared label a of every input transition t becomes $^\triangleright a$ and such a transition consumes a token from p_a. The next definition formalizes this description.

Definition 12 (Asynchronous Composition). *Let $\mathcal{M}_1 = (\mathcal{N}_1, T_{1_\square})$, $\mathcal{N}_1 = (P_1, T_1, W_1^-, W_1^+, \lambda_1, m_{1_0})$ be a modal I/O-Petri net over the I/O-alphabet $\Sigma_1 = in_1 \uplus out_1 \uplus int_1$ and let $\mathcal{M}_2 = (\mathcal{N}_2, T_{2_\square})$, $\mathcal{N}_2 = (P_2, T_2, W_2^-, W_2^+, \lambda_2, m_{2_0})$ be a modal I/O-Petri net over the I/O-alphabet $\Sigma_2 = in_2 \uplus out_2 \uplus int_2$. $\mathcal{M}_1$ and $\mathcal{M}_2$ are composable if $P_1 \cap P_2 = \emptyset$, $T_1 \cap T_2 = \emptyset$ and if Σ_1 and Σ_2 are composable. In this case, their asynchronous composition $\mathcal{M}_c$, also denoted by $\mathcal{M}_1 \otimes_{as} \mathcal{M}_2$, is the modal Petri net over the alphabet composition Σ_c, defined as follows:*

- $P_c = P_1 \uplus P_2 \uplus \{p_a \mid a \in \Sigma_1 \cap \Sigma_2\}$ *(each p_a is a new place)*
- $T_c = T_1 \uplus T_2$ *and* $T_{c,\square} = T_{1_\square} \uplus T_{2_\square}$
- W_c^- *(resp. W_c^+) is the $P_c \times T_c$ backward (forward) incidence matrix defined by:*
  - *for each $p \in P_1 \cup P_2$, $t \in T_c$,*

$$W_c^-(p,t) = \begin{cases} W_1^-(p,t) \text{ if } p \in P_1 \text{ and } t \in T_1 \\ W_2^-(p,t) \text{ if } p \in P_2 \text{ and } t \in T_2 \\ 0 \qquad\qquad otherwise \end{cases}$$

$$W_c^+(p,t) = \begin{cases} W_1^+(p,t) \text{ if } p \in P_1 \text{ and } t \in T_1 \\ W_2^+(p,t) \text{ if } p \in P_2 \text{ and } t \in T_2 \\ 0 \qquad\qquad otherwise \end{cases}$$

  - *for each $p_a \in P_c \setminus \{P_1 \cup P_2\}$ with $a \in \Sigma_1 \cap \Sigma_2$ and for all $\{i,j\} = \{1,2\}$ and each $t \in T_i$ with,*

$$W_c^-(p_a,t) = \begin{cases} 1 \text{ if } a = \lambda_i(t) \in in_i \cap out_j \\ 0 \text{ otherwise} \end{cases}$$

$$W_c^+(p_a,t) = \begin{cases} 1 \text{ if } a = \lambda_i(t) \in in_j \cap out_i \\ 0 \text{ otherwise} \end{cases}$$

- $\lambda_c : T_c \to \Sigma_c$ *is defined, for all $t \in T_c$ and for all $\{i,j\} = \{1,2\}$, by*

$$\lambda_c(t) = \begin{cases} \lambda_i(t) & \text{if } t \in T_i, \ \lambda_i(t) \notin \Sigma_1 \cap \Sigma_2 \\ ^\triangleright\lambda_i(t) & \text{if } t \in T_i, \ \lambda_i(t) \in in_i \cap out_j \\ \lambda_i(t)^\triangleright & \text{if } t \in T_i, \ \lambda_i(t) \in in_j \cap out_i \end{cases}$$

---

[3] Technically, the new places p_a play the same role as interface places in open nets. However, the "openness" of a modal I/O-Petri net is determined by the input/output lables on its transitions rather than by input/output places.

– m_{c_0} is defined, for each place $p \in P_c$, by

$$m_{c_0}(p) = \begin{cases} m_{1_0}(p) & \text{if } p \in P_1 \\ m_{2_0}(p) & \text{if } p \in P_2 \\ 0 & \text{otherwise} \end{cases}$$

Proposition 1. *The asynchronous composition of two weakly deterministic modal I/O-Petri nets is again a weakly deterministic modal I/O-Petri net.*

Proof. (Sketch) We introduce the following notations. Given a word σ over some alphabet A and $A' \subseteq A$, $|\sigma|$ denotes the length of σ, $\sigma_{\lfloor A'}$ denotes the projection of σ on A' and $|\sigma|_{A'}$ is defined by $|\sigma|_{A'} = |\sigma_{\lfloor A'}|$. Given a shared label a, $out(a)$ ($in(a)$ resp.) denotes the set of output (input resp.) transitions with label a. Given a marking m of $\mathcal{M}_c$, $m^{(i)}$ denotes the projection of m on P_i with $i \in \{1, 2\}$.

We start the proof with a key observation. Let $m_0[\sigma\rangle m$ be a firing sequence of $\mathcal{M}_c$. Then:

– For every $i \in \{1, 2\}$, $m_{i_0}[\sigma_{\lfloor T_i}\rangle m^{(i)}$ is a firing sequence of $\mathcal{M}_i$.
– For every shared label a, $m(p_a) = |\sigma|_{out(a)} - |\sigma|_{in(a)}$.

We only prove that $\mathcal{M}_c$ is weakly deterministic. The proof of the other condition is similar.

Let $m_0[\sigma\rangle m[\sigma^* t\rangle m^*$ and $m_0[\sigma'\rangle m'$ be a firing sequence of $\mathcal{M}_c$ with $\lambda_c(\sigma) = \lambda_c(\sigma')$, $\lambda_c(\sigma^*) = \epsilon$ and $\lambda_c(t) \in \Sigma_c$. Due to the equality of labels of σ and σ' (and using the key observation), for every $i \in \{1, 2\}$, $m^{(i)}$ and $m'^{(i)}$ are reached by sequences with same labels and for every shared label a, $m(p_a) = m'(p_a)$.

Assume w.l.o.g. that $t \in T_1$, then by weak determinism of $\mathcal{M}_1$ there is a firing sequence $m'^{(1)}[\sigma_1'^*\rangle$ with $\lambda_1(\sigma_1'^*) = \lambda_1(t)$. If t is not an input transition there is no input transition in $\sigma_1'^*$. So $\sigma_1'^*$ is fireable from m' in $\mathcal{M}_c$ and we are done. Otherwise let $a = \lambda_1(t)$ then (1) $m(p_a)(= m'(p_a)) > 0$ and (2) there is exactly an input transition in $\sigma_1'^*$ and its label is a. So again $\sigma_1'^*$ is fireable from m' in $\mathcal{M}_c$. □

Example 5. Consider the two modal producer and consumer Petri nets of Fig. 2 as I/O-nets where the producer alphabet has the input label in, the output label m and no internal labels while the consumer has the input label m, the output label out and no internal labels as well. Obviously, both nets are composable and their asynchronous composition yields the net shown in Fig. 5. The alphabet of the composed net has the input label in, the output label out and the internal labels $m^{\triangleright}$ and $^{\triangleright}m$. The Petri net composition describes an infinite state system and its generated modal language specification has a language which is no longer regular.

We will now discuss how the results of our theory presented in Sect. 3 can be applied in typical application scenarios involving asynchronous composition. Assume given an abstract requirements specification for a possibly infinite state system given in form of a modal I/O-Petri net $\mathcal{M}$. As an example for $\mathcal{M}$ consider

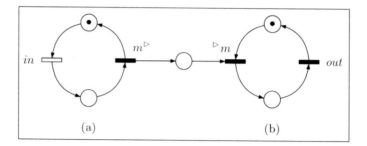

Fig. 5. Composition of the producer and consumer Petri nets

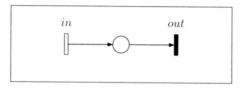

Fig. 6. Requirements specification for an infinite state producer/consumer system

the requirements specification for an infinite state producer/consumer system presented by the modal I/O-Petri net in Fig. 6. The system is infinite since the transition labeled with in can always fire. Such requirements specifications are typically implemented by an architecture which involves several communicating components, presented by modal I/O-Petri nets, say $\mathcal{M}_1$ and $\mathcal{M}_2$. Such components could be, for instance, off-the-shelf components which are now reused for a particular purpose. Then one is interested to check whether the designed architecture, say $\mathcal{M}_c = \mathcal{M}_1 \otimes_{as} \mathcal{M}_2$, obtained by component composition is indeed a correct implementation/refinement of the given requirements specification $\mathcal{M}$. An example architecture for a producer/consumer system is shown by the asynchronous composition of the two Petri nets in Fig. 5. According to our theory in Sect. 3, implementation correctness could mean that the modal language specification $\mathcal{S}(\mathcal{M}_c)$ generated by $\mathcal{M}_c$ is a modal language specification refinement, in the sense of Def. 2, of the modal language specification $\mathcal{S}(\mathcal{M})$ generated by $\mathcal{M}$. Unfortunatley, we can immediately detect that this cannot be the case since the asynchronous composition has additional communication actions represented by internal labels of the form $a^\triangleright$ and $^\triangleright a$ which are not present in the abstract requirements specification. In the example the internal labels are just the labels $m^\triangleright$ and $^\triangleright m$ used for the communication. On the other hand, from the observational point of view internal actions, in particular communication actions, can be abstracted away when considering refinements. In our approach this can be simply achieved by relabeling internal labels, and hence communication labels $a^\triangleright$ and $^\triangleright a$, to ϵ which is formally defined by the following hiding operator:

Definition 13 (Hiding). *Let* $\mathcal{M} = (\mathcal{N}, T_\square)$ *be a modal I/O-Petri net over the I/O-alphabet* $\Sigma = in \uplus out \uplus int$ *with Petri net* $\mathcal{N} = (P, T, W^-, W^+, \lambda, m_0)$. *Let* $\alpha(\Sigma) = in \uplus out \uplus \emptyset$ *and let* $\alpha : \Sigma \cup \{\epsilon\} \to (\Sigma \setminus int) \cup \{\epsilon\}$ *be the relabeling defined by* $\alpha(a) = a$ *if* $a \in in \uplus out$, $\alpha(a) = \epsilon$ *otherwise. Then* hiding *of internal actions from* $\mathcal{M}$ *yields the modal I/O-Petri net* $\alpha(\mathcal{M}) = (\alpha(\mathcal{N}), T_\square)$ *over the I/O-alphabet* $\alpha(\Sigma) = in \uplus out \uplus \emptyset$ *with underlying Petri net* $\alpha(\mathcal{N}) = (P, T, W^-, W^+, \alpha \circ \lambda, m_0)$.

Coming back to the considerations from above we can then express implementation correctness by requiring that the modal language specification $\mathcal{S}(\alpha(\mathcal{M}_c))$ generated by $\alpha(\mathcal{M}_c)$ is a modal language specification refinement of the modal language specification $\mathcal{S}(\mathcal{M})$ generated by $\mathcal{M}$. According to the results of Sect. 6, we can decide this if $\mathcal{M}$ and $\alpha(\mathcal{M}_c)$ belong to the class of weakly deterministic modal Petri nets which again is decidable. Looking to the producer/consumer example the "abstract" Petri net in Fig. 6 is obviously modally weakly deterministic. For the composed Petri nets in Fig. 5 it is not obvious that the hiding operator produces a modally weakly deterministic net but, according to the results of Sect. 6, we can decide it (and get a positive answer). Note, however, that in the case where one of the transitions used for the communication were not a "must" then, after hiding, the Petri net composition would not satisfy the second condition of modal weak determinacy. Finally, we can also decide whether the refinement relation holds in the example between the generated modal language specifications and get also a positive answer.

5   Case Study: Cash Desk Application

In order to illustrate our approach with a more ambitious example we consider a cash desk application (inspired by the case study of a trading system in [26]). First, we provide a requirement specification for the behavior of the cash desk in terms of the modal I/O-Petri net shown in Fig. 7. The net is based on an I/O-alphabet partitioned into sets of input labels and output labels. There are no internal labels in this requirement specification. Here and in the following drawings we write $m?$ to indicate that a label m belongs to the set of input labels; similarly, we write $m!$ if a label m belongs to the set of output labels.

The requirement specification says that a cash desk must be able to read repeatedly an item, represented by the must-transition with input label *item?*, and that afterwards it must be able to print (on the bill) each item's details (output *printItem!*). Since the number of items to be processed is not limited, and since the cash desk can proceed with reading the next item before the details of the previous item have been printed, the system specification involves infinitely many states. On the other hand, the specification determines what must/may be done when a sale is finished. First, when no item is read anymore, it must be possible to finish a sale (input *finishSale?*) and then to print the total sum of the sale (output *printTotal!*). Afterwards the cash desk must be able to accept cash payment (input *cash?*), but it may also be implemented in such a way that one can choose a credit card for the payment. Hence, the transition with input label *creditCard?* is a may-transition. Note that *printItem!* may always

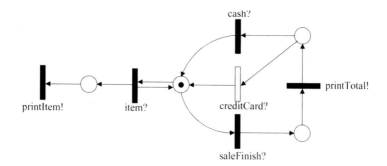

Fig. 7. Requirement specification for a cash desk

interleave with other actions but at most as often as *item?* has occurred before. Hence this is a loose specification. In practice one would expect that *printTotal!* can only occur if the details of all inputed items are indeed printed before, but to specify such a property would need further extensions of the formalism.

We are now going to provide a refinement of the cash desk requirement specification. For this purpose we want to use two components, one representing a graphical user interface of the cash desk (Cash Desk GUI) and another one representing a controller of the cash desk (Cash Desk Controller). The single components with their input and output labels are shown in Fig. 8 and the behavior of each single component is specified by the modal I/O-Petri nets in Fig. 9.

Fig. 8. Components Cash Desk GUI and Cash Desk controller

The specified behavior of the cash desk GUI is straightforward. It is initiated by an input of *newSale?* from the environment and then the GUI must be able to read iteratively items (input *item?*) or to accept a request to finish a sale (input *saleFinish?*). After an item has been read the GUI must immediately forward the details of the item for further processing to the environment (output *itemReady!*). Similarly, if the GUI has received a request to finish a sale it must forward this request to the environment to take over the control (output *finish!*).

The behavior of the cash desk controller specified by the Petri net on the righthand side of Fig. 9 is more subtle. It contains two unconnected parts, the

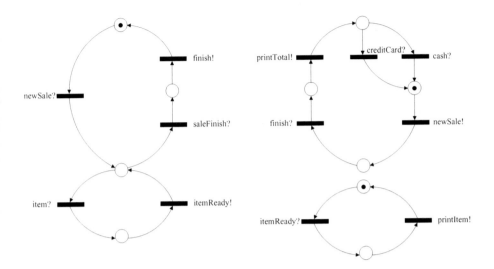

Fig. 9. Modal I/O-Petri nets for Cash Desk GUI (left) and Cash Desk Controller (right)

"upper" part describing a global protocol that a cash desk controller must follow and the "lower" part controlling the printing of items. As a consequence, the cash desk controller is always able to consume items with *itemReady?* and then to print the item with *printItem!*. In particular *printItem!* can interleave everywhere (which, in fact, is also possible in the requirement specification). Of course, this is not a desirable behavior for a concrete implementation of the cash desk controller and it would be better if the cash desk controller could only finish (*finish?*) if there are no more items provided by the environment for *itemReady?*. In a concrete implementation this could be achieved, e.g., by introducing a priority such that the cash desk controller priorizes available inputs for *itemReady?* against available inputs for *finish?*. Such an implementation would be conform to our specification of the cash desk controller, but to specify such a priorization would need further extensions of the formalism.

Finally, we connect the two components which yields the system architecture shown in Fig. 10 whose dynamics is described by the asynchronous composition of the I/O-Petri nets of the single components as shown in Fig. 11.[4]

All Petri nets considered here are modally weakly deterministic, which is decidable by the results of Sect. 6. Moreover, after hiding the communication labels of the form $m^\triangleright$ and $^\triangleright m$ in the asynchronous composition in Fig. 11 (by relabeling them to ϵ), the resulting net is also modally weakly deterministic. Therefore we can also decide, according to Sect. 6, whether the modal language specification generated by the Petri net obtained by hiding the internal communication

---

[4] Remember that in the asynchronous composition of Petri nets the (internal) communication labels are either of the form $m^\triangleright$ (representing the sending of an output to the channel place) or of the form $^\triangleright m$ (representing the reception of an input from the channel place).

Fig. 10. Composition of cash desk GUI and cash desk controller components: static view

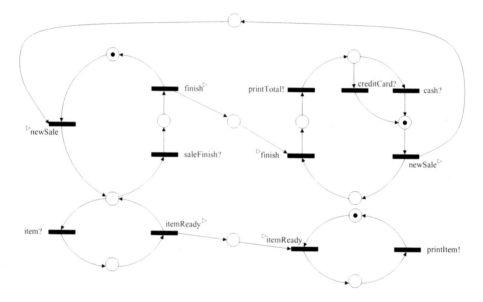

Fig. 11. Asynchronous composition of cash desk GUI and cash desk controller Petri nets

labels from the asynchronous composition in Fig. 11 is a modal refinement of the modal language specification generated by the modal Petri net for the requirement specification in Fig. 7. This is indeed the case but requires a detailed proof.

6   Decision Algorithms

We begin this section by some recalling semi-linear sets and decision procedures in Petri nets.

Let $E \subseteq \mathbb{N}^k$, E is a *linear set* if there exists a finite set of vectors of $\mathbb{N}^k$ $\{v_0, \ldots, v_n\}$ such that $E = \{v_0 + \sum_{1 \leq i \leq n} \lambda_i v_i \mid \forall i \ \lambda_i \in \mathbb{N}\}$. A *semi-linear set* [9] is a finite union of linear sets; a representation of it is given by the family of finite sets of vectors defining the corresponding linear sets. Semi-linear sets are *effectively* closed w.r.t. union, intersection and complementation. This means that one can compute a representation of the union, intersection and complementation starting from a representation of the original semi-linear sets. E is an *upward closed set* if $\forall v \in E \; v' \geq v \Rightarrow v' \in E$. An upward closed set has a finite set of minimal vectors denoted $\min(E)$. An upward closed set is a semi-linear set which has a representation that can be derived from the equation $E = \min(E) + \mathbb{N}^k$ if $\min(E)$ is computable.

Given a Petri net $\mathcal{N}$ and a marking m, the reachability problem consists in deciding whether m is reachable from m_0 in $\mathcal{N}$. This problem is decidable [19]. Furthermore this procedure can be adapted to semi-linear sets when markings are identified to vectors of $\mathbb{N}^{|P|}$. Given a semi-linear set E of markings, in order to decide whether there exists a marking in E which is reachable, we proceed as follows. For any linear set $E' = \{v_0 + \sum_{1 \leq i \leq n} \lambda_i v_i \mid \forall i \; \lambda_i \in \mathbb{N}\}$ associated with E we build a net $\mathcal{N}_{E'}$ by adding transitions $t_1, \ldots, t_n$. Transition t_i has v_i as input vector and the null vector as output vector. Then one checks whether v_0 is reachable in $\mathcal{N}_{E'}$. E is reachable from m_0 iff one of these tests is positive.

In [28] given a Petri net, several procedures have been designed to compute the minimal set of markings of several interesting upward closed sets. In particular, given a transition t, the set of markings m from which there exists a transition sequence σ with $m[\sigma t\rangle$ is effectively computable.

Now we solve the decision problems stated in the previous sections.

Proposition 2. *Let $\mathcal{N}$ be a labeled Petri net, then it is decidable whether $\mathcal{N}$ is weakly deterministic.*

Proof. First we build a net $\mathcal{N}'$ (1) whose places are two copies of places of $\mathcal{N}$, (2) whose firing sequences are pairs of firing sequences in $\mathcal{N}$ with the same label and, (3) whose markings are pairs of the corresponding reached markings in $\mathcal{N}$. Then we define the semilinear sets F_a with $a \in \Sigma$ that characterize the markings of $\mathcal{N}'$ where a firing sequence can produce the label a starting from the first item of the pair while such a sequence does not exist from the second item of the pair. Proceeding in such a way reduces the weak determinism $\mathcal{N}$ to a reachability problem for $\mathcal{N}'$.

Let us detail the proof. $\mathcal{N}'$ is defined as follows.

- Its set of places is the union of two disjoint copies P_1 and P_2 of P.
- There is one transition (t, t') for every t and t' s.t. $\lambda(t) = \lambda(t') \neq \varepsilon$. The input (resp. output) vector of this transition is the one of t with P substituted by P_1 plus the one of t' with P substituted by P_2.
- There are two transitions t_1, t_2 for every t s.t. $\lambda(t) = \varepsilon$. The input (resp. output) vector of t_1 (resp t_2) is the one of t with P substituted by P_1 (resp. P_2).
- The initial marking is m_0 with P substituted by P_1 plus m_0 with P substituted by P_2.

Then for every $a \in \Sigma$, we compute a representation of the set E_a from which, in $\mathcal{N}$ a transition labelled by a is eventually firable after the firing of silent transitions (using results of [28]) and a representation of its complementary set $\overline{E_a}$. Afterwards we compute the representation of the semi-linear set F_a whose projection on P_1 is a vector of E_a with P substituted by P_1 and whose projection on P_2 is a vector of $\overline{E_a}$ with P substituted by P_2. Let $F = \bigcup_{a \in \Sigma} F_a$ then $\mathcal{N}$ is weakly deterministic iff F is not reachable which is decidable. $\qquad \square$

Proposition 3. *Let $\mathcal{N}$ be a weakly deterministic labeled Petri net and $\mathcal{N}'$ be a labeled Petri net then it is decidable whether $\mathcal{L}(\mathcal{N}') \subseteq \mathcal{L}(\mathcal{N})$.*

Proof. W.l.o.g. we assume that P and P' are disjoint. First we build a net $\mathcal{N}''$ (1) whose places are copies of places of $\mathcal{N}$ and $\mathcal{N}'$, (2) whose firing sequences are pairs of firing sequences in $\mathcal{N}$ and $\mathcal{N}'$ with the same label and, (3) whose markings are pairs of the corresponding reached markings in $\mathcal{N}$ and in $\mathcal{N}'$. Then we define the semilinear sets F_a with $a \in \Sigma$ that characterize the markings of $\mathcal{N}''$ where a firing sequence can produce the label a starting from the item of the pair corresponding to $\mathcal{N}'$ while such a sequence does not exist from the item of the pair corresponding to $\mathcal{N}$. Now the key observation is that since $\mathcal{N}$ is weakly deterministic, from any other marking of $\mathcal{N}$ reached by a sequence with the same label there does not exist such a sequence. Thus proceeding in such a way reduces the inclusion $\mathcal{L}(\mathcal{N}') \subseteq \mathcal{L}(\mathcal{N})$ to a reachability problem for $\mathcal{N}''$.

Let us detail the proof. The net $\mathcal{N}''$ is defined as follows.

- Its set of places is the union of P and P'.
- There is one transition (t, t') for every $t \in T$ and $t' \in T'$ s.t. $\lambda(t) = \lambda(t') \neq \varepsilon$. The input (resp. output) vector of this transition is the one of t plus the one of t'.
- Every transition $t \in T \cup T'$ s.t. $\lambda(t) = \varepsilon$ is a transition of $\mathcal{N}''$.
- The initial marking is $m_0 + m_0'$.

Then for every $a \in \Sigma$, we compute a representation of the set $E_{\mathcal{N},a}$ (resp. $E_{\mathcal{N}',a}$) from which in $\mathcal{N}$ a transition labelled by a is eventually firable preceeded only by silent transitions and a representation of its complementary set $\overline{E_{\mathcal{N},a}}$ (resp. $\overline{E_{\mathcal{N}',a}}$). Afterwards we compute the representation of the semi-linear set F_a whose projection on P is a vector of $\overline{E_{\mathcal{N},a}}$ and whose projection on P' is a vector of $E_{\mathcal{N}',a}$. Let $F = \bigcup_{a \in \Sigma} F_a$ then $\mathcal{L}(\mathcal{N}) \subseteq \mathcal{L}'(\mathcal{N}')$ iff F is not reachable. This procedure is sound. Indeed assume that some marking $(m, m') \in F_a$ is reachable in $\mathcal{N}''$ witnessing that after some word w, some firing sequences $\sigma \in \mathcal{N}, \sigma' \in \mathcal{N}'$ s.t. $m_0[\sigma\rangle m$, $m_0'[\sigma'\rangle m'$ and $\lambda(\sigma) = \lambda'(\sigma')$ from m one cannot "observe" a and from m' one can "observe" a. Then due to weak determinism of $\mathcal{N}$ for every m^* s.t. there exists a sequence σ^* with $m_0[\sigma^*\rangle m^*$ and $\lambda(\sigma^*) = \lambda(\sigma)$, m^* is also in $\overline{E_{\mathcal{N},a}}$. $\qquad \square$

Proposition 4. *Let $\mathcal{M}$ be a modal Petri net, then it is decidable whether $\mathcal{M}$ is (modally) weakly deterministic.*

Proof. We first recall the two conditions for weak determinism:

1. $\mathcal{N}$ is weakly deterministic, and
2. for each $\sigma, \sigma' \in T^*$ with $\lambda(\sigma) = \lambda(\sigma')$ and for any markings m and m' with $m_0[\sigma\rangle m$ and $m_0[\sigma'\rangle m'$, we have $must_{mk}(m) = must_{mk}(m')$.

Observe that the first condition for being weakly deterministic is decidable by proposition 2. In order to decide the second condition, we build as in the corresponding proof the net $\mathcal{N}'$. Then we build representations for the following semi-linear sets. G_a is the set of markings m of $\mathcal{N}$ such that from m a transition of $T_\Box$ labelled by a is eventually firable after firing silent transitions of $T_\Box$. Afterwards we compute the representation of the semi-linear set H_a whose projection on P_1 is a vector of G_a with P substituted by P_1 and whose projection on P_2 is a vector of $\overline{G_a}$ with P substituted by P_2. Let $H = \bigcup_{a \in \Sigma} H_a$ then $\mathcal{M}$ fulfills the second condition of weak determinism iff H is not reachable. $\Box$

Proposition 5. *Let $\mathcal{M}, \mathcal{M}'$ be two weakly deterministic modal Petri nets then it is decidable whether the modal specification $\mathcal{S}(\mathcal{M})$ refines $\mathcal{S}(\mathcal{M}')$.*

Proof. We first recall the two conditions for refinement:

1. $\mathcal{L}' \subseteq \mathcal{L}$,
2. for every $u \in \mathcal{L}'$, $must(u) \subseteq must'(u)$, i.e every required action after the trace u in $\mathcal{L}$ is a required action after u in $\mathcal{L}'$.

Observe that the first condition for refinement is decidable by proposition 3. In order to decide the second condition, we build as in the corresponding proof the net $\mathcal{N}''$. Then we build representations for the semi-linear sets G_a (as in the previous proof) and similarly G'_a in the case of $\mathcal{N}'$. Afterwards we compute the representation of the semi-linear set H_a whose projection on P is a vector of G_a and whose projection on P' is a vector of $\overline{G'_a}$. Let $H = \bigcup_{a \in \Sigma} H_a$ then the second condition for refinement holds iff H is not reachable. This procedure is sound. Indeed assume that some marking $(m, m') \in H_a$ is reachable in $\mathcal{N}''$ witnessing that after some word w, some firing sequences $\sigma \in \mathcal{N}, \sigma' \in \mathcal{N}'$ s.t. $m_0[\sigma\rangle m$, $m'_0[\sigma'\rangle m'$ and $\lambda(\sigma) = \lambda'(\sigma') = w$ and from m one can "observe" b by a "must" sequence and from m' one cannot observe a by a must sequence. Then due to (the second condition of) weak determinism of $\mathcal{N}'$ for every m^* s.t. there exists a sequence σ^* with $m'_0[\sigma^*\rangle m^*$ and $\lambda'(\sigma^*) = \lambda'(\sigma')$, m^* is also in $\overline{G'_a}$. $\Box$

7   Conclusion

In the present work, we have introduced modal I/O-Petri nets and we have provided decision procedures to decide whether such Petri nets are weakly deterministic and whether two modal language specifications generated by weakly deterministic modal Petri nets are related by the modal refinement relation. It has been shown that our theory is particularly useful in the context of refinements given by an architecture of asynchronously communicating components.

Our work extends the expressive power of modal transition systems [18,17] and of modal language specifications [23,24] since Petri nets allow to specify with a finite representation the behavior of *infinite* state systems. On the other hand, our work provides also an extension of Petri net theory since we have considered *observational* refinement abstracting silent moves during language generation and we have introduced *modalities* for Petri nets. In particular, the *must* modality is important to express that certain activities must be respected by refinements and hence implementations.

An important role in our approach has been played by the hypothesis of weak determinacy which has two justifications. First, without this hypothesis, the refinement problem is undecidable (but we have not proved it in this paper). Secondly, as nets represent specifications, using weakly deterministic Petri nets limits the class of specifications, but this class is already much more expressive than regular specifications (the standard model). But still weak determinacy is a proper restriction since it does not allow internal decisions if they lead to different observable execution traces. More discussions and examples of weak determinacy in the context of state transition systems without modalities can be found in [11]. In particular, it is shown in [11] that a transition system is weakly deterministic if its minimization w.r.t weak bisimulation leads to a deterministic transition system without silent transitions. From the point of view of complexity, it is well known that reachability of Petri nets has a high theoretical complexity but in practical cases of specifications the empirical complexity is significantly smaller than the theoretical one.

For the application of our theory to asynchronously communicating components we have used a hiding operator which translates communication actions into silent transitions (which then are abstracted for refinement). Since, in general, the hiding operator does not preserve modal weak determinacy, we are interested in the investigation of conditions which ensure this preservation property. This concerns also conditions for single components such that the hiding of communication labels from their composition is automatically modally weakly deterministic. We claim that this is indeed the case if the single components are modally weakly determinsitic and if all transitions concerning communication actions are *must*-transitions. Another direction of future research concerns the study of behavioral compatibility of interacting components on the basis of modal I/O-Petri nets, and the establishment of an interface theory for this framework along the lines of [1,17,5]. This would involve, in particular, compositionality results on the preservation of local refinements by global compositions. Such results are important to achieve independent implementability and thus substitutability of components which may lead to applications of our theory to web service substitutability as considered in [27]. Actually, the refinement notion proposed in [27], called *accordance* there, is conceptually different from ours. In [27], refinement is motivated by requiring preservation of interaction correctness of services with their communication partners. In our approach we do not consider communication partners for the refinement definition, but we compare behaviors of abstract and concrete modal Petri nets (formalized by their generated modal language specifications). Then refinement ensures, first, that all observable execution traces of the concrete net are allowed by the abstract one, hence safety properties are preserved, and secondly, that all required transitions of the abstract net are respected by the concrete one. In modal interface theories [17,5,12] this property has then the *consequence* that certain required interactions are preserved by refinements, much in the spirit of [27].

Acknowledgement. We are very grateful to all reviewers of the submitted version of this paper who have provided detailed reports with many valuable hints and suggestions.

References

1. de Alfaro, L., Henzinger, T.A.: Interface Theories for Component-Based Design. In: Henzinger, T.A., Kirsch, C.M. (eds.) EMSOFT 2001. LNCS, vol. 2211, pp. 148–165. Springer, Heidelberg (2001)
2. de Alfaro, L., Henzinger, T.A.: Interface-based Design. In: NATO Science Series: Mathematics, Physics, and Chemistry, vol. 195, pp. 83–104. Springer, Heidelberg (2005)
3. Antonik, A., Huth, M., Larsen, K.G., Nyman, U., Wasowski, A.: Complexity of Decision Problems for Mixed and Modal Specifications. In: Amadio, R.M. (ed.) FOSSACS 2008. LNCS, vol. 4962, pp. 112–126. Springer, Heidelberg (2008)
4. Antonik, A., Huth, M., Larsen, K.G., Nyman, U., Wasowski, A.: EXPTIME-complete decision problems for mixed and modal specifications. In: Proc. of EXPRESS (July 2008)
5. Bauer, S., Mayer, P., Schroeder, A., Hennicker, R.: On Weak Modal Compatibility, Refinement, and the MIO Workbench. In: Esparza, J., Majumdar, R. (eds.) TACAS 2010. LNCS, vol. 6015, pp. 175–189. Springer, Heidelberg (2010)
6. Bertrand, N., Legay, A., Pinchinat, S., Raclet, J.-B.: A Compositional Approach on Modal Specifications for Timed Systems. In: Breitman, K., Cavalcanti, A. (eds.) ICFEM 2009. LNCS, vol. 5885, pp. 679–697. Springer, Heidelberg (2009)
7. Brand, D., Zafiropulo, P.: On communicating finite-state machines. JACM 30(2), 323–342 (1983)
8. Delahaye, B., Larsen, K.G., Legay, A., Pedersen, M.L., Wasowski, A.: Decision Problems for Interval Markov Chains. In: Dediu, A.-H., Inenaga, S., Martín-Vide, C. (eds.) LATA 2011. LNCS, vol. 6638, pp. 274–285. Springer, Heidelberg (2011)
9. Ginsburg, S., Spanier, E.H.: Semigroups, Presburger formulas and languages. Pacific Journal of Mathematics 16(2), 285–296 (1966)
10. Hack, M.H.T.: Decidability questions for Petri Nets. Ph.D.Thesis. M.I.T (1976)
11. Hennicker, R., Janisch, S., Knapp, A.: On the Observable Behaviour of Composite Components. Electr. Notes Theor. Comput. Sci. 260, 125–153 (2010)
12. Hennicker, R., Knapp, A.: Modal Interface Theories for Communication-Safe Component Assemblies. In: Cerone, A., Pihlajasaari, P. (eds.) ICTAC 2011. LNCS, vol. 6916, pp. 135–153. Springer, Heidelberg (2011)
13. Karp, R.M., Miller, R.E.: Parallel program schemata. JTSS 4, 147–195 (1969)
14. Khomenko, V., Schaefer, M., Vogler, W.: Output-Determinacy and Asynchronous Circuit Synthesis. Fundam. Inf. 88(4), 541–579 (2008)
15. Larsen, K.G.: Modal Specifications. In: Sifakis, J. (ed.) CAV 1989. LNCS, vol. 407, pp. 232–246. Springer, Heidelberg (1990)

16. Larsen, K.G., Nyman, U., Wąsowski, A.: On Modal Refinement and Consistency. In: Caires, L., Vasconcelos, V.T. (eds.) CONCUR 2007. LNCS, vol. 4703, pp. 105–119. Springer, Heidelberg (2007)
17. Larsen, K.G., Nyman, U., Wasowski, A.: Modal I/O Automata for Interface and Product Line Theories. In: De Nicola, R. (ed.) ESOP 2007. LNCS, vol. 4421, pp. 64–79. Springer, Heidelberg (2007)
18. Larsen, K.G., Thomsen, B.: A modal process logic. In: Third Annual IEEE Symposium on Logic in Computer Science LICS, pp. 203–210 (1988)
19. Mayr, E.: An algorithm for the general Petri net reachability problem. In: Proc. 13th Annual ACM Symp. on Theor. of Computing (STOC 1981), pp. 238–246 (1981)
20. Milner, R.: Communication and concurrency. Prentice Hall (1989)
21. Pelz, E.: Closure Properties of Deterministic Petri Net Languages. In: Brandenburg, F.J., Wirsing, M., Vidal-Naquet, G. (eds.) STACS 1987. LNCS, vol. 247, pp. 373–382. Springer, Heidelberg (1987)
22. Peterson, J.L.: Petri net theory and the modeling of systems. Prentice-Hall, Englewood Cliffs (1981)
23. Raclet, J.-B.: Quotient de spécifications pour la réutilisation de composants. PhD Thesis, Ecole doctorale Matisse, Université de Rennes 1, IRISA (December 2007)
24. Raclet, J.-B.: Residual for Component Specifications. In: Proc. of the 4th International Workshop on Formal Aspects of Component Software (FACS 2007), Sophia-Antipolis, France (September 2007)
25. Raclet, J.-B., Badouel, E., Benveniste, A., Caillaud, B., Legay, A., Passerone, R.: Modal Interfaces: Unifying Interface Automata and Modal Specifications. In: Proc. of 9th International Conference on Embedded Software (EMSOFT 2009). ACM, Grenoble (2009)
26. Rausch, A., Reussner, R., Mirandola, R., Nyman, U., Plasil, F.: The Common Component Modeling Example: Comparing Software Component Models. LNCS, vol. 5153. Springer, Heidelberg (2008)
27. Stahl, C., Wolf, K.: Deciding service composition and substitutability using extended operating guidelines. Data Knowl. Eng. 68(9), 819–833 (2009)
28. Valk, R., Jantzen, M.: The Residue of Vector Sets with Applications to Decidability Problems in Petri Nets. In: Rozenberg, G. (ed.) APN 1984. LNCS, vol. 188, pp. 234–258. Springer, Heidelberg (1985)

Computing a Hierarchical Static Order for Decision Diagram-Based Representation from P/T Nets*

Silien Hong[1], Fabrice Kordon[1], Emmanuel Paviot-Adet[2], and Sami Evangelista[3]

[1] Univ. P. & M. Curie, CNRS UMR 7606 – LIP6/MoVe, 4 Place Jussieu, F-75005 Paris
{Silien.Hong,Fabrice.Kordon}@lip6.fr
[2] Univ. Paris Descartes and LIP6/MoVe, 143 Avenue de Versailles, F-75016
Emmanuel.Paviot-Adet@lip6.fr
[3] LIPN, CNRS UMR 7030, Univ. Paris XIII, 99 Avenue J-B. Clément, F-93430 Villetaneuse
Sami.Evangelista@lipn.univ-paris13.fr

Abstract. State space generation suffers from the typical combinatorial explosion problem when dealing with industrial specifications. In particular, memory consumption while storing the state space must be tackled to verify safety properties. Decision Diagrams are a way to tackle this problem. However, their performance strongly rely on the way variables encode a system. Another way to fight combinatorial explosion is to hierarchically encode the state space of a system.

This paper presents how we mix the two techniques via the hierarchization of a precomputed variable order. This way we obtain a *hierarchical static order* for the variables encoding a system. This heuristic was implemented and exhibits good performance.

Keywords: State space generation, Decision Diagrams, Hierarchy.

1 Introduction

Context. Model Checking is getting more and more accepted as a verification technique in the design of critical software such as transportation systems. However, the associated state space generation suffers from the typical combinatorial explosion problem when dealing with industrial specifications. In particular, memory consumption when computing the state space must be tackled to verify safety properties.

Decision Diagrams, such as Binary Decision Diagrams [6], are now widely used as an extremely compact representation technique of state spaces [8]: a state is seen as a vector of values and a state space represented by decision diagrams is a set of such vectors where identical extremities are shared. Performances of decision diagram based techniques are thus strongly related to the way values are ordered to encode a system. Bad performance are observed when the encoding does not exhibit a good sharing factor.

To overcome the problem of shared parts limited to extremities, a hierarchical class of decision diagrams has recently been introduced: Set Decision Diagrams (SDD) [16].

* This work was supported by FEDER Île-de-France/System@tic—free software thanks to the NEOPPOD project.

K. Jensen, S. Donatelli, and J. Kleijn (Eds.): ToPNoC V, LNCS 6900, pp. 121–140, 2012.

Here, values on the arcs may also be sets of vectors of values represented by decision diagrams (and recursively we can have vectors of vectors of... of values), defining a *hierarchical structure*. This way, sub-structures are also shared, the same way the extremities are, allowing more compression. An application to the philosopher problem shows an impressive compression ratio [18].

Problem. Since finding the variable order with the best sharing factor is an NP-complete problem [3], many heuristics have been proposed (see [27] for a survey).

Variable ordering problem can be *static* (the order is computed before the state space enumeration) or *dynamic* (the order is adapted during the state space enumeration). This work focuses on static variable ordering only.

When dealing with hierarchy, the problem is to find a hierarchical structure where sub-structures can be shared. No work has been done, to the best of our knowledge, concerning the definition of heuristics in such a context.

Contribution. This paper proposes ways to order variables in a hierarchical way. To do so, we reuse heuristics for non-hierarchical decision diagrams to hierarchical ones. Our heuristic deals with P/T net because they provide easy ways to exploit their structure.

Experiments and measures show that the hierarchical version of the order performs better than the flat one in most cases.

Structure of the Paper. Section 2 details our objective and refers to some related works. Then, Section 3 introduces the main definitions we use in the paper. Section 4 describes our approach and its performances before some concluding remarks in Section 5.

2   Objectives and Related Work

Context. Historically, Decision Diagrams were first used to encode models for boolean formulæ via Binary Decision Diagrams [6] (BDDs). Therefore, variables have boolean values in this structure.

In BDDs, each variable in a vector is represented by a node and its value labels an arc connecting the node to its successor in the vector as shown in Figure 1(a). A terminal node (terminal for short) is added to the end of the structure. All root nodes are shared, all identical terminal structures are shared and all nodes have distinct labels on their outgoing arcs. These features ensure a canonical representation of the vectors: i.e. no vector can be represented more than once.

Since BDDs has been successfully used in model checking (SMV [15] and VIS [5] model checkers), numerous kinds of decision diagrams have been developed and employed in this domain. Let us cite Interval Decision Diagram – IDDs [29] – where variables values are intervals (used in DSSZ-MC [20], a model checker for P/T nets[1]), Multi-valued Decision Diagram – MDDs [25] – where variables values are integers (used in SMART [13]), Set Decision Diagrams – SDDs [16] – that use integers as variables values and introduce hierarchy (used in the ITS [30] model checker) and sigmaDD [7], an instantiation of SDDs to represent terms in term-writing area. Decision

---

[1] See definition 3.1.

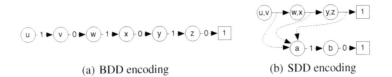

(a) BDD encoding   (b) SDD encoding

Fig. 1. Encoding the initial state of a system with BDD and SDD

diagrams have also been extended to associate values to each vector (MDDs and Algebraic Decision Diagrams [2]). We do not consider such extensions in this work.

Let us now illustrate why hierarchy is a potentially powerful feature. Figure 1 depicts two Decision Diagrams based representation of the boolean formula $u \wedge \bar{v} \wedge w \wedge \bar{x} \wedge y \wedge \bar{z}$. Figure 1(a) is BDD based, while Figure 1(b) is SDD based. Since values of pairs of variables $(u, v), (w, x), (y, z)$ are the same, they can be shared. This is done in Figure 1(b) by adding the sub-structure with variables a and b. This second structure is more compact that the first one. Let us note that the two terminal nodes are not merged to ease readability of the figure, but should be, as it is in memory.

Contribution. To the best of our knowledge, no work has been done to automatically define a hierarchical structure. Such structures are now either defined manually, or directly encoded in higher level formalism such as ITS [30].

Since sub-structures are shared in SDD, we aim at finding parts of the model (in our case P/T nets) that are partially identical thanks to structural analysis. A hierarchical structure is then defined to hierarchically organize these parts.

In this paper, we propose an heuristic reusing an existing variable order to build hierarchical clusters to be encoded using SDD (see Section 4). The existing variable order we use in input of our heuristic can be computed by state of the art algorithms. We observe that, in most cases, hierarchization provides good results.

State of the Art. Heuristics to compute variable order to optimize decision diagrams encoding have been studied in several works [27]. Among them, let us report the two following ones, for which an implementation is available.

FORCE [1] computes the forces acting upon each variable and move them in the corresponding direction. In the context of P/T nets, this corresponds to minimizing the distance between places linked to the same transition. The "average position" of places (e.g. their center of gravity) is recursively computed until stabilization of the algorithm.

The DSSZ-MC model checker for ordinary P/T net, based on Interval Decision Diagrams proposes another heuristic: NAO99 [20]. It exploits the net structure to associate a weight to places and then uses it to compute the variable order.

So far, no heuristic exploiting hierarchical order has been proposed.

3   Preliminary Definitions

This section first recalls the definition of Petri Nets and SDD. Then, it introduces the notions we use to describe our hierarchization algorithm.

3.1 P/T Nets

P/T nets stands for Place/Transition nets (also known as Petri nets). They are one of the numerous models used to describe parallelism.

Definition 1 (P/T nets). *A P/T net is a 4-tuple* $N = \langle P, T, Pre, Post \rangle$ *where:*

- *P is a finite set of places,*
- *T is a finite set of transitions (with $P \cap T = \emptyset$),*
- *$Pre : P \times T \to \mathbb{N}$ (resp. $Post : P \times T \to \mathbb{N}$) is the precondition (resp. postcondition) function.*

A marking M of N is a function associating an integer to each place: $M : P \to \mathbb{N}$. The initial marking is denoted M_0.

The firing of a transition t changes the marking M_1 into a new marking M_2 (denoted $M_1[t > M_2)$:

- *t can be fired iff $\forall p \in P, Pre(p,t) \leq M_1(p)$,*
- *$\forall p \in P, M_2(p) = M_1(p) + Post(p,t) - Pre(p,t)$.*

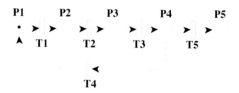

Fig. 2. A simple P/T net

A P/T net is thus a bipartite graph where vertices are places and transitions. Places are depicted by circles (the one of Figure 2 has five places P_1, P_2, P_3, P_4 and P_5), transitions by rectangles (the one of Figure 2 has five transitions T_1, T_2, T_3, T_4 and T_5), and an arc is drawn between a place (resp. transition) and a transition (resp. place) iff the precondition (resp. postcondition) function associates a non null value to the couple. 1 is assumed when no value is associated to arcs in Figure 2). A marking is depicted by black dots in places (in Figure 2 the initial marking of place P_1 is 1).

Note 1 (Successor and predecessor sets). These notations are used later in the paper. The successor set of a place p (resp. transition t) is denoted $p^{\bullet} = \{t \mid Pre(p,t) \geq 1\}$ (resp. $t^{\bullet} = \{t \mid Post(p,t) \geq 1\}$). The predecessor function is defined accordingly: ${}^{\bullet}p = \{t \mid Post(p,t) \geq 1\}$ and ${}^{\bullet}t = \{t \mid Pre(p,t) \geq 1\}$. Those notations are extended to sets of nodes $S \subseteq P \cup T: S^{\bullet} = \bigcup_{s \in S} s^{\bullet}$ and ${}^{\bullet}S = \bigcup_{s \in S} {}^{\bullet}s$.

3.2 Hierarchical Set Decision Diagram [16]

SDDs are data structures representing sets of assignments sequences of the form $\omega_1 \in s_1; \omega_2 \in s_2; \dots; \omega_n \in s_n$ where ω_i are variables and s_i are sets of values. In [16] no variable ordering is assumed, and the same variable can occur several times in an assignment sequence. The terminal (labelled by 1) represents the empty assignment sequence, that terminates any valid sequence. Another terminal labelled by 0 is also used to represent the empty set of assignment sequences that terminates invalid sequences[2]. In the following, *Var* denotes a set of variables, and for any $\omega \in Var$, $Dom(\omega)$ represents the domain of ω which may be infinite.

Definition 2 (Set Decision Diagrams). *Let Σ be the set of SDDs. $\delta \in \Sigma$ is inductively defined by:*

- $\delta \in \{0, 1\}$ *or*
- $\delta = \langle \omega, \pi, \alpha \rangle$ *with:*
  - $\omega \in Var$.
  - *A partition $\pi = s_0 \cup \cdots \cup s_n$ is a finite partition of $Dom(\omega)$, i.e. $\forall i \neq j, s_i \cap s_j = \emptyset, s_i \neq \emptyset$, with n finite.*
  - $\alpha : \pi \to \Sigma$, *such that $\forall i \neq j, \alpha(s_i) \neq \alpha(s_j)$.*

Elements of $Dom(\omega)$ can be integers, real numbers, vectors, etc. These elements can also be sets represented by SDDs, in which case a hierarchical decision diagram structure is obtained.

SDDs are used here to efficiently store P/T nets reachable markings. We need to define a hierarchical structure (see heuristic described in section 4) and automatically encode the *Pre* and *Post* operations.

SDDs also introduce homomorphisms, a "tool box" to manipulate diagrams. Three kinds of homomorphisms are used here: one to access the desired variable in the hierarchy, one to test and decrement the value (*Pre* operation) and the last one to increment the value (*Post* operation). Further description is out of scope. See [16] for more details on homomorphisms.

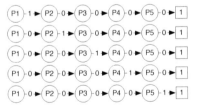

(a) All paths for the state space

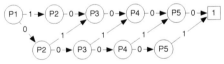

(b) The corresponding SDD without hierarchy

Fig. 3. SDD-based representation of the state space for the P/T net of Figure 2

Let us illustrate the encoding of a P/T net on the example presented in Figure 2. The five states in the reachability graph can be described in the SDD paths shown in Figure 3(a). This leads to the corresponding SDD structure presented in Figure 3(b). This structure does not take advantage of hierarchy.

---

[2] The 0 terminal and paths leading to the 0 terminal are usually not represented in the structure to save memory.

3.3   Hierarchical Static Order

Definition 3 describes the structure used in this work to efficiently encode a P/T net. We compose two techniques: the computation of a static order and the use of hierarchical decision diagrams.

Definition 3 (Hierarchical Static Order). *A hierarchical static order is represented as a list of elements. Each element can be either :*

- *a list of elements $e_1, \ldots, e_n$ denoted $[e_1, \ldots e_n]$,*
- *a place of the encoded P/T net (each place of the net is encoded only once).*

Figure 4 shows the use of a hierarchical static order, $[[P_3, P_4, P_5], [P_1, P_2]]$, to encode the state space for the P/T net of Figure 2. We observe that the sub-structure P_1, P_2 is not shared with the P_4, P_5 one because of the different labelling of the nodes. This problem is tackled in section 3.4.

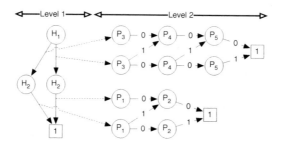

Fig. 4. Final SDD structure with hierarchy

It is also possible to flatten the hierarchy order. This is useful to preserve the precedence relation for each variable and compare the hierarchical static order to its related static order.

Definition 4 (Flattened Hierarchical Static Order). *Let us define a flattened hierarchical static order $f = p_1, p_2, ..., p_n$ with $p_i \in P$. $f = F(h)$ where h is a hierarchical static order. We define F as follows:*

- *$F(h = [h_1, ...h_n]) = [F(h_1), ..., F(h_n)]$, where h_i are the sub-elements of h,*
- *$F(h = [p]) = [p]$ when the element is reduced to a place.*

As an example, the flatten order of $[[P_3, P_4, P_5], [P_1, P_2]]$ is $[P_3, P_4, P_5, P_1, P_2]$.

3.4   Anonymization

Since no hierarchical static order was originally defined for SDDs, variable names were initially associated to SDD nodes. This way, homomorphisms could be defined in such a general structure. In Figure 4, nodes P_4 and P_5 are not shared with P_1 and P_2 because of their different labeling. We thus propose to remove it. Thus the encoding without labelling is said to be *anonymized*.

This labeling information is redundant when a hierarchical static order is defined because the path followed in the structure is sufficient to retrieve the variable name associated to each node.

Definition 5 (Anonymous SDD). *An* anonymous SDD *is defined over a set Var reduced to a unique variable:* $|Var| = 1$.

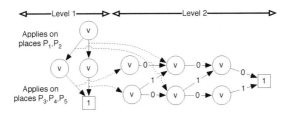

Fig. 5. Final SDD structure with hierarchy and anonymization

Figure 5 illustrates the advantages of anonymization on the SDD structure presented in Figure 4. Since nodes in the second level have similar structures, homomorphisms must be aware of the path followed at the first level: e.g. if the second level is considered as a value of the root node of the first level, then nodes are implicitly labelled $P1$ and $P2$, otherwise, they are labelled $P3$, $P4$ and $P5$. The final hierarchical SDD contains 9 nodes instead of 13 in Figure 4.

Remark. In this specific example, let us notice that the flattened SDD encoding in Figure 3(b) holds as many nodes as in the hierarchical one of Figure 5. This is a side effect due to the small size of an understandable example. Benchmarks provided later in this paper show the benefits of hierarchy for large models.

4   Hierarchization of Computed Flat Static Orders

As presented in Section 3.3, we must increase the number of identical modules to increase the sharing via hierarchy and anonymization. A first approach is to define the hierarchy when modeling the system. In [30], a new type of formalism (ITS for Instantiable Transition Systems) allows such a hierarchical modeling with an appropriate relation to SDD. This relation allows an efficient encoding when the model has symmetries. As an example, the state space for the philosopher model with $2^{20.000}$ philosophers could be encoded. However, this technique assumes that the system designer is able to build this "well formed" hierarchy.

To automate the building of a hierarchical structure, we could have used symmetries as defined in [9] for colored net and [28] for P/T net. But this would lead to a restrictive application of the technique. For instance the model in Figure 2 does not exhibit any symmetry for set of places $[P_4, P_5]$ and $[P_1, P_2]$ but Figure 5 shows that the projection of the state spaces of these sets are the same.

So, we propose to split an already computed "flat" variable static order into modules. Then, a hierarchical structure is defined on top of these modules. This approach allows to adapt all the previously proposed heuristics to compute static variable orders. It also allows us to validate the gain we can obtain from the hierarchy. It is, however, a bit rough since no clue is given on modules similarity. We thus call this heuristic: *N-Cut-Naive Hierarchy*.

4.1   Algorithm

The main idea of this heuristic is to create a hierarchy of decision diagrams representing portions of markings that are similar ones to the others, thus increasing the sharing of elements. We exploit the hierarchical static order together with the anonymization mechanism (introduced in section 3.4).

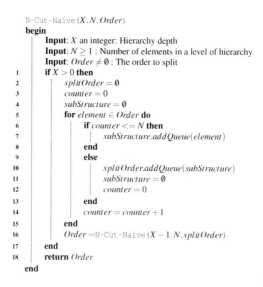

Fig. 6. Algorithm of the N-Cut-Naive Hierarchy heuristic

Our heuristic is presented in Figure 6. It requires in input: *i)* a precomputed flat order (*Order*), *ii)* the maximum number of elements in a module (*N*) and *iii)* the height of the hierarchical structure (*X*).

To give an intuition of the way our algorithm behaves, let us assume the following input order:

$$[P_1, P_2, P_3, P_4, P_5, P_6, P_7, P_8, P_9, P_{10}, P_{11}, P_{12}]$$

where P_i are variables encoding places of a P/T Net. We split the initial flat order into modules of size *n* specified by the user. When the number of modules is large enough, the list of modules is recursively split to add an extra-level to the hierarchical structure.

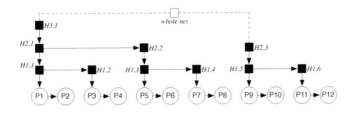

Fig. 7. Computed Static Hierarchical Order with $X = 3$ and $N = 2$

Figure 7 depicts the obtained hierarchical structure when $N = 2$. Here, three levels are needed $H_{1,x}$, $H_{2,x}$ and $H_{3,x}$.

The size of the module is a critical parameter: it is obvious that if we construct two modules by randomly choosing an identical number of places, the sharing factor between the two modules usually decreases when the parameter N grows. We have the same kind of effect with parameter X.

In the representation of Figure 7, sub-structures $H_{1,1}$ and $H_{1,2}$ can be represented by a single SDD if P_1, P_2 valuations are *identical* to P_3, P_4 ones. At the next level, the condition is more difficult to satisfy since a single representation for $H_{2,1}$ and $H_{2,2}$ requires that $H_{1,1}, H_{1,2}$ are identical to $H_{1,3}, H_{1,4}$ (*e.g.* the valuations of P_1, P_2, P_3, P_4 is identical to P_5, P_6, P_7, P_8).

Let us note that this computed static order hierarchy represents a sharing potential that is only possible when sub-structures are identical. This is where the structure of the P/T net introduces constraints. All hierarchical structures do not systematically exhibit a good sharing factor but we statistically observe that, for small values of X, the algorithm provides good results.

We have empirically computed (see experiment 1 in section 4.2) that, for $N = 2$ and $X = \lceil log_N(|P|) \rceil$, the sharing factor is close to the optimal one.

4.2   Performance Analysis

This section evaluates the performance of the N-Cut-Naive Hierarchy heuristic compared to given flat orders. Evaluation is done for state space generation. Experiments are performed using a tool developed within the NEOPPOD project to verify safety properties: PNXDD [21]. Performances are computed on an 2.80GHz Intel Hyperthreaded Xeon computer with 14Gbyte of memory.

Models. We have selected three types of models to assess our contribution:

- *"Colored" model* that are P/T nets derived from colored models by unfolding[3]. In this category, we can use the size of color domains as a parameter to increase the size of the obtained models.

---

[3] Here, unfolding means the expansion of a colored net into its corresponding P/T places as presented in [23]. It suppresses all 0-bounded places and the transitions pre and post-conditions of such places.

Table 1. Presentation of the models selected for our benchmark

Model	scaling parameter	Places	Transitions	Description
Colored Models				
Philosopher [17]	300 500 800 2,000 4,000	1,200 2,000 3,200 8,000 16,000	1,500 2,500 4,000 10,000 20,000	Classical multi-process synchronization problem. The scaling parameter corresponds to the number of philosophers around the table.
Peterson [26]	2 3 4 5	30 102 244 480	30 126 332 690	Concurrent programming algorithm for mutual exclusion. The scaling parameter corresponds to the number of processes to be synchronized.
Token Ring [11]	5 10 100 200 500	40 80 800 1,600 4,000	40 80 800 1,600 4,000	Classical local network protocol communication. The scaling parameter corresponds to the number of processes involved in the ring.
K-bounded Models				
FMS [14]	10 to 30	22	20	Model of a Flexible Manufacturing System. The scaling parameter changes the initial number of tokens in several places of the model.
Kanban [13]	50 to 3,000	16	16	Kanban system modeling. The scaling parameter changes the number of tokens in several places of the model.
Cases Studies Models				
Neoppod [10]	2 3 4 5 6	49 120 229 382 585	30 118 330 753 1,498	Broadcast Consensus Protocol in a distributed database system when the set of masters nodes in the system are electing the primary master. The scaling parameter corresponds to the number of master nodes.
PolyOrb [22]	2 3 4 5 6	222 297 372 447 522	962 1,444 1,925 2,414 2,902	Models the core of a middleware that manages parallelism between a set of threads to be operated. We use a configuration with 4 event sources, and an query FIFO with 4 slots. The scaling parameter corresponds to the number of threads that are really activated in the middleware.
MAPK [19]	8 to 80	22	30	Bio-chimical modeling. The scaling parameter changes the number of tokens in several places of the model.

- *K-Bounded models*[4] for which the number of initial tokens is the scaling parameter.
- *Cases studies models* that are extracted from projects involving industrial problems and are thus larger. Neoppod and PolyORB are not fully colored since they contain some uncolored places that have an effect on the unfolding into P/T. MAPK is purely K-bounded. These models have a more complex structure from which extraction of patterns is more difficult.

The two first types of benchmarks correspond to typical combinatorial explosion situations to be handled in state space generation. The third one shows more "realistic" situations from an industrial point of view.

Table 1 summarizes for each model: its origin, what it is modeling, the meaning of its scaling parameter, and its size (number of places and transitions) according to the scaling parameters (the number of instance corresponds either to the cardinality of a color domain or to the number of tokens in the place modeling the initial state of an actor).

---

[4] Let us note K-Bounded models where $K > 1$ and K is the maximal number of tokens for each place in any reachable marking.

Evaluation Procedure. Evaluation is performed on each model and for various scaling parameters using the following procedure:

1. produce a flat order using external ways (e.g. from the state of the art),
2. apply our heuristic to generate a hierarchical static order,
3. generate the state space using the flat order as well as the hierarchical static one (PNXDD is able to import a given precomputed order, flat or hierarchical) and compare them,

To compare the generated state spaces, we consider the following parameters:

- the number of nodes in the final SDD diagram and the total number of nodes used during the computation of the state space (peak[5]), for the studied hierarchical order and its associated flattened version,
- CPU time in seconds used for computation,
- memory used for computation in Mbytes. This involves the nodes used while computing the state space, as well as the operation caches used to speed up SDD operations [4].

Experiments. Three experiments have been elaborated. Experiment 1 aims at studying the impact of the hierarchical structure height (parameter X in function N-Cut-Naive). To do so, we use an existing flat static order *Order* computed using NOA99. We apply function N-Cut-Naive$(X,N,Order)$ to build a hierarchical order before evaluating the memory required to store the state space. This experience shows that if we use $N = 2$ and $X = \lceil log_N(|P|) \rceil$ we are usually close to the optimal values for X and N by studying the obtained performance with different values of N (in $\{2,5\}$) and X (in $\{0,5\}$[6] except for Philosopher (300) where a wider range is used because of the large number of places). Performances strongly depend on the initial flat order.

Experiment 2 uses the values of N and X validated in experiment 1. Here the objective is to show that hierarchy allows us to study more complex models than the flat version does. We compare here the performance obtained using NOA99 and FORCE heuristics (in a flat and hierarchical version) for models with larger instances than in experiment 1.

In experiment 3, we check the general behavior of hierarchization to be sure that there is no side-effect due to the selected heuristics (FORCE and NOA99). To do so, we select two models from the "case study" group: Neoppod (mostly colored) and MAPK (strictly K-bounded) to check the behavior of our heuristic on 500 randomly generated flat static orders.

4.3 Experiment 1: Effects of Parameters X and N

This experiment aims at studying the impact of the hierarchical structure height in order to find an appropriate value to be used in our heuristic.

---

[5] Once a node is created, it is never destroyed in this implementation. So the term *peak* refers here to the total number of nodes used for the computation.
[6] When $X = 0$, the hierarchical order becomes a flat one.

Results. They are displayed in Figure 8 that shows the evolution of memory consumption according to values of X and N (each value of N is a curve, and X values are shown in abscissa). The table in Figure 8(i) summarizes memory consumption in the best case, the worst case, and for the pair $\langle X, N \rangle$ when $X = \lceil log_N(|P|) \rceil$ and $N = 2$ (later referred to as the "computed solution").

Conclusions. Almost all curves for a fixed N (variation of X) have the same shape: for a given value of N, performance start to be better while X increases. However, after a while, performance decreases when X continues to increase (performance loss is important in most examples). An explanation could be that adding a hierarchical level is only of interest when many modules are shared in its immediate sub-level. This is unlikely the case when the number of modules in this sub-level is not great enough (when splitting the flat order, we are not sure to obtain identical modules). This is why we decided to use the following formula $X = \lceil log_N(|P|) \rceil$.

Table in Figure 8(i) shows that in most cases, our automatic computation of X for $N = 2$ (value selected in our heuristic) provides performances that are reasonably close to the best solution.

4.4   Experiment 2: Gain with Respect to Existing Flat Orders Heuristics

The aim is to compare our N-Cut-Naive Hierarchy heuristic performance to the ones of the two flat static orders we introduced in section 2: FORCE [1] and NOA99 [20] (respectively noted F and N in Tables 2 to 4). We compare the state space generated for the benchmark models. For each scaling parameter, we measure:

- The total SDD nodes once the state space is produced,
- The peak SDD nodes when producing the state space,
- Computation time in seconds,
- The peak of memory consumption (in Mbytes).

In the tables, MOF means that the experiment could not be computed due to the lack of Memory (> 10 Go). SOF means that execution reached a Stack OverFlow (we used the default Unix stack size on our machine) and TOF that we reached a Time OverFlow (3 days).

There are three sets of data: measures on flat orders, measures on the hierarchization of the associated flat order and finally, the gain we measure from the flat order to the hierarchy one.

Results. Measures are shown in Table 2 for colored models, in Table 3 for K-bounded ones, and in Table 4 for case studies models. It is of interest to see that, over the types of model, our heuristic behaves differently.

We can observe on Table 2 that for colored models, we get good results. Our heuristic save memory up to 80% for the Neoppod and Peterson models. It even allows the computation of the state space when the flat orders fail for the philosopher and token ring models. We also observe a good scalability parameter: in all cases, increasing of the color cardinalities means an increase of the gain we observe.

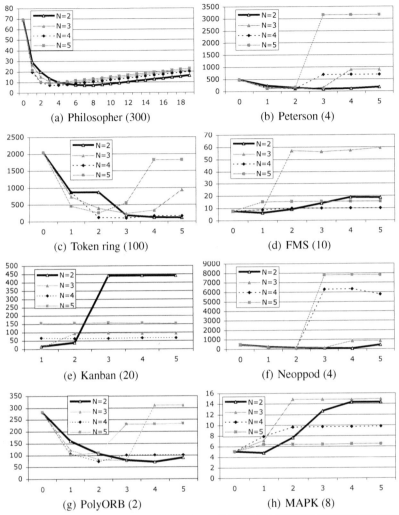

(a) Philosopher (300)

(b) Peterson (4)

(c) Token ring (100)

(d) FMS (10)

(e) Kanban (20)

(f) Neoppod (4)

(g) PolyORB (2)

(h) MAPK (8)

Model	Best Solution			Computed Solution			Worst Solution			Loss with respect to Best Solution	Gain with respect to Worst Solution
	N	X	memory (MB)	N	X	memory (MB)	N	X	memory (MB)		
Philosopher 300	4	4	7.17	2	4	10.04	–	0	69.3	-40%	85%
Peterson 4	2	3	98.31	2	3	98.10	4	5	3167	0%	97%
Token Ring 100	4	3	105.88	2	4	121.30	–	0	2048.5	-14.5%	94%
FMS 10	2	1	6.43	2	1	6.43	3	3	56.3	0%	67.8%
Kanban 20	3	1	7.90	2	1	18.00	2	5	443.00	-56%	98%
Neoppod 4	2	4	77.03	2	3	114.50	4	5	7821	-48.5%	99%
PolyORB 2	2	4	72.00	2	5	89.00	5	3	311.00	-19%	71%
MAPK 8	2	1	4.81	2	1	4.81	3	5	15	0%	89.1%

(i) Comparison of best and worst solutions to one computed by our heuristic

Fig. 8. Analysis of the impact of the X and N parameters on the N-Cut-Naive Hierarchy heuristic (vertical scale shows memory usage in Mbyte). Abscissa of figure 8(e) starts with $X = 1$ because execution was too fast to capture memory for $X = 0$.

Table 2. Results of experiment 2 on colored models. Time is expressed in seconds.

Number of Instances	State Space Size	Flat	Flat order performance				Hierarchical order performance				Gain (in %)			
			Final	Peak	Time	MB	Final	Peak	Time	MB	Final	Peak	Time	Mem
Philosopher's diner														
300	1.4×10^{143}	F	7,216	33,449	7.9	39.22	813	9,787	0.5	13,1	89	71	94	67
		N	7,769	42,106	8.9	69.30	430	4,350	0.5	13.11	94	90	93	81
500	3.6×10^{238}	F	12,061	55,992	20.5	80.12	1,219	14,802	0.9	18,2	90	74	96	77
		N	12,969	70,306	22.2	151.61	390	3,810	1.0	12.29	97	95	95	92
800	4.0×10^{381}	F	19,275	89,722	77.3	260.39	1,492	18,432	1.9	27,6	92	79	98	89
		N	20,769	112,606	79.4	260.52	577	5,883	2.6	20.03	97	95	97	92
2000	1.7×10^{954}	F	SOF	SOF	SOF	SOF	2,459	30,786	8,9	63,6	∞	∞	∞	∞
		N	SOF	SOF	SOF	SOF	724	7,415	25.6	45.42	∞	∞	∞	∞
4000	3.0×10^{1908}	F	SOF	SOF	SOF	SOF	SOF	SOF	SOF	SOF	–	–	–	–
		N	SOF	SOF	SOF	SOF	1,349	14,287	96.5	125,3	∞	∞	∞	∞
Peterson algorithm														
2	158	F	188	1,085	0.06	4.25	78	415	0.01	3.98	59	62	72	6
		N	135	777	0.04	4.10	66	357	0.01	3.93	51	54	62	4
3	20,754	F	3,767	41,395	2.8	24.54	769	10,857	0.4	11.26	80	74	84	54
		N	4,441	62,317	3.9	28.19	756	10,837	0.2	9.54	83	83	93	66
4	3.4×10^{6}	F	81,095	1.3×10^{6}	482.1	897.81	10,719	344,170	37.7	241.5	87	74	92	73
		N	72,578	996,414	265.8	483.53	9,291	262,144	13.8	98.31	87	74	95	80
Token Ring protocol														
5	53,856	F	246	3,424	0.1	5.08	96	1,889	0.03	3.95	61	45	83	22
		N	230	2,882	0.1	4.86	75	1,549	0.02	3.86	67	46	82	21
10	8.3×10^{9}	F	997	17,263	0.9	10.19	281	10,198	0.1	6.67	72	41	82	35
		N	809	16,708	0.9	9.62	200	9,523	0.1	6.45	75	43	84	33
100	2.6×10^{105}	F	93,534	8.4×10^{6}	2,712	2.367	5,954	3.5×10^{6}	178.1	636.8	94	59	93	73
		N	71099	5.9×10^{6}	1671.62	2048	2,613	538,470	23.7	123.4	96	91	99	94
200	8.3×10^{211}	F	MOF	MOF	MOF	MOF	14,623	2.4×10^{7}	2,114	4,961	∞	∞	∞	∞
		N	MOF	MOF	MOF	MOF	5,150	4.1×10^{6}	206.2	657	∞	∞	∞	∞
500	5.0×10^{531}	F	MOF	MOF	MOF	MOF	MOF	MOF	MOF	MOF	–	–	–	–
		N	MOF	MOF	MOF	MOF	31,473	5.7×10^{7}	3,140	8,860	∞	∞	∞	∞

Table 3. Results of experiment 2 on K-bounded models. Time is expressed in seconds.

Number of Instances	State Space Size	Flat	Flat order performance				Hierarchical order performance				Gain (in %)			
			Final	Peak	Time	MB	Final	Peak	Time	MB	Final	Peak	Time	Mem
Flexible Modeling System (FMS)														
10	2.5×10^{9}	F	338	4,325	0.21	5.14	257	5,075	0.14	5.42	24	-17	33	-6
		N	1,256	13,578	0.61	7.85	684	9,144	0.17	6.45	46	33	72	18
20	6.0×10^{12}	F	848	16,480	0.7	8.88	697	23,455	1.1	11.98	18	-42	-41	-35
		N	4,391	64,728	2.7	22.43	2,354	47,784	1.4	19.13	46	26	47	15
50	4.2×10^{17}	F	3,578	129,745	5.7	45.75	3,217	238,347	39.1	103.47	10	-84	-575	-126
		N	25,196	488,059	27	134.93	13,364	432,297	105	266.55	47	11	-292	-98
Kanban														
50	1.0×10^{16}	F	3,216	30.770	0.86	0.0	4,235	144,373	148	423	-31	-369	-17109	−∞
		N	53,791	1.0×10^{7}	1,170	3,009	8,060	4.3×10^{6}	397	955	85	57	34	68
100	1.7×10^{19}	F	11,416	111,570	2.84	30.91	15,960	873,517	26,484	2,246	-39	-682	-9×10^{5}	-7166
		N	MOF	MOF	MOF	MOF	MOF	MOF	MOF	MOF	-	-	-	-
2,000	2.9×10^{33}	F	4.0×10^{6}	3.3×10^{7}	48,243	6,971	MOF	MOF	MOF	MOF	-	-	-	-
		N	MOF	MOF	MOF	MOF	MOF	MOF	MOF	MOF	-	-	-	-
3,000	-	F	MOF	MOF	MOF	MOF	MOF	MOF	MOF	MOF	-	-	-	-
		N	MOF	MOF	MOF	MOF	MOF	MOF	MOF	MOF	-	-	-	-

As shown in Table 3, results are not that good for K-bounded models: the peak size remains reasonable, but the memory consumption increases faster with the hierarchical version than with the flat one. This is due to the cache size that, in our experiments is

Table 4. Results of experiment 2 on case studies models. Time is expressed in seconds.

number of Instances	State Space Size	Flat	Flat order performance				Hierarchical order performance				Gain (in %)			
			Final	Peak	Time	MB	Final	Peak	Time	MB	Final	Peak	Time	Mem
Mitogen Activated Protein Kinase (MAPK)														
8	6.1×10^6	F	452	4,018	0.28	5.1	256	4,819	0.14	5.2	43	-20	51	-3
		N	498	5,705	0.28	5.1	336	5,628	0.35	5.4	33	1	-23	-7
20	8.8×10^{10}	F	2,812	29,332	1.9	13.1	1,177	43,856	0.4	20.6	58	-50	78	-57
		N	3,082	52,264	2.8	18.5	1,992	69,661	3.6	23.9	35	-33	-27	-30
80	5.6×10^{18}	F	94,582	962,902	112.5	310.0	10,719	344,170	37.7	241.5	89	64	67	22
		N	96,462	2.4×10^6	290	651.4	-	-	-	-	-	-	-	-
NEOPPOD Consensus protocol														
2	194	F	202	679	0.024	4.1	80	217	0.007	3.42	60	68	71	17
		N	463	1,688	0.024	4.5	154	558	0.011	3.57	67	67	55	21
3	90,861	F	5,956	48,269	0.86	19.0	1,126	12,491	0.15	8.2	81	74	82	57
		N	3,820	23,974	0.76	12.2	709	4,838	0.10	6.7	81	80	87	45
4	9.7×10^8	F	84,398	1.0×10^6	62.6	338.8	11,728	178,921	5.0	70.83	86	82	92	79
		N	155,759	1.3×10^6	186.1	490.3	19,875	217,536	0.007	114.2	87	83	99	77
PolyOrb														
2	1.6×10^6	F	223,243	3.1×10^6	580.8	1,316	27,548	491,803	29.3	352	88	84	95	73
		N	78,785	451,494	98.7	273	10,050	127,791	6.2	81	87	72	94	70
3	2.8×10^7	F	593,363	1.2×10^7	4,708	2,851	78,067	2.1×10^6	188.7	692	87	83	96	76
		N	280,068	2.5×10^6	948.8	1,513	33,526	524,288	64.3	358	88	79	93	76
4	2.1×10^8	F	1.2×10^6	3.1×10^7	8,310	5,765	146,589	4.2×10^6	528.7	1,780	87	86	94	69
		N	666,886	8.4×10^6	217,173	2,457	84,126	2.1×10^6	326.0	1,451	87	75	99	41
5	1.4×10^9	F	TOF	TOF	TOF	TOF	143,903	1.1×10^7	2,361.6	3,045	∞	∞	∞	∞
		N	TOF	TOF	TOF	TOF	87,875	4.2×10^6	1,045.1	2,216	∞	∞	∞	∞
6	9.2×10^9	F	TOF	TOF	TOF	TOF	288,649	2.2×10^7	15,757	6,144	∞	∞	∞	∞
		N	TOF	TOF	TOF	TOF	140,565	1.5×10^7	19,474	4,865	∞	∞	∞	∞
7	-	F	TOF	TOF	TOF	TOF	MOF	MOF	MOF	MOF	-	-	-	-
		N	TOF	TOF	TOF	TOF	TOF	TOF	TOF	TOF	-	-	-	-

never cleaned. Other experimentations with different cleaning policies did not lead to better results.

In the FMS model, marking complexity increases slower than in MAPK. However, we can observe that increasing the initial marking decreases performance.

Table 4 shows that our heuristic scales up quite well for large models but still remains less efficient for purely K-bounded models (MAPK). It is of interest to observe that, for PolyORB that contains some K-bounded places, performances of our algorithms are still good: the flat orders we used fail for PolyORB 5 while the hierarchical one fails for 7

The MAPK model also reveals very different behavior of our algorithm when we elaborate the hierarchy from NOA99 or FORCE flat orders.

Conclusions. It is obvious from this experiment that the N-Cut-Naive Hierarchy heuristic is of interest for large P/T net models, like the ones obtained by unfolding of colored nets (or mostly colored nets). The increase of color classes cardinality generates numerous P/T places, thus increasing the probability to find identical parts that can be shared. This is why this approach scales up well.

However, our heuristic is less adapted for K-bounded models such as FMS, Kanban and MAPK. Our diagnostic is threefold:

– First, they are small (22 places or less) and thus, the probability to have identical part of SDD is practically null.

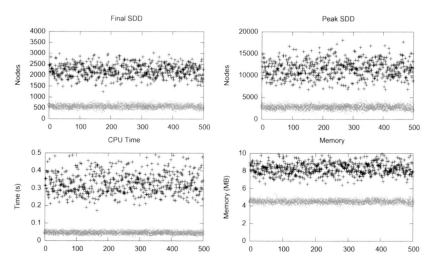

(a) Measures for the 500 experiments

Measure	Flat			Hierarchicalized			Success Rate	Lowest Gain	Highest Gain
	Min	Avg	Max	Min	Avg	Max			
Final SDD	1 254	2 211	3 027	348	581	790	100%	72%	75%
Peak SDD	6 790	11 556	18 113	1 552	2 830	4 640	100%	64%	85%
Time (s)	0.17	0.32	0.56	0.03	0.05	0.07	100%	78%	90%
Memory (Mbytes)	6.4	8.28	10.33	3.97	4.54	5.19	100%	36%	54%

(b) Summary of data

Fig. 9. Experiment on random orders and associated hierarchization for Neoppod (2)

- Second, since the models do not grow in number of places but only involve more tokens, the SDD structure remains the same (with no more sharing probability). The gain from the structure remains fixed while, when initial marking increases, the complexity due to the generated markings still increases (this effect is contradictory to the previous one).
- Third, an in-depth analysis of the SDD structure shows that, if the SDD size grows in depth (longer sequences and hierarchies) for colored models, complexity increases in width for K-bounded models. In this configuration, exploration of values during the union and intersection operations grows quadratically with the width of the SDD[7].

4.5   Experiment 3: Interest for Hierarchical Encoding

The objective is to check if no side-effect comes from the selected flat order heuristics. To do so, we proceed to an analysis of performances against random flat orders. We apply these orders on two cases studies models: Neoppod 2 (mostly colored) and MAPK 8 (K-bounded).

---

[7] This ruins the saturation [12] mechanism we aim to activate with our encoding.

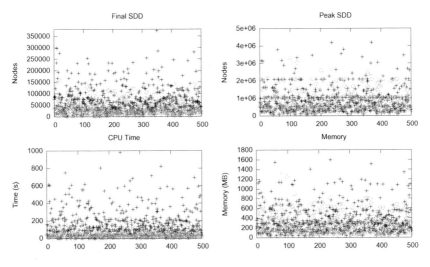

(a) Measures for the 500 experiments

Measure	Flat			Hierarchicalized			Success Rate	Lowest Result	Highest result
	Min	Avg	Max	Min	Avg	Max			
Final SDD	2 845	71 255	373 639	1 513	36 182	200 176	100%	29%	71%
Peak SDD	84 240	932 657	4 194 300	72 305	795 300	3 292 390	65%	-173%	71%
Time (s)	4.40	164.63	980.54	1.42	49.73	233.83	99%	-38%	93%
Memory (Mbytes)	34.89	362.69	1598.36	26.12	250.31	1251.59	91%	-122%	79%

(b) Summary of data

Fig. 10. Experiment on random orders and associated hierarchization for MAPK (8)

Results. They are displayed on Figures 9 (for Neoppod 2) and 10 (for MAPK 8). Each figure contains four charts showing, for each of the 500 executions: *i)* as "+" dots, the value for the selected random flat static order and *ii)* as "○" dots, the value we get when the N-Cut-Naive Hierarchy heuristics is processed on this order for $N = 2$. Four values are measured:

- The number of SDD nodes,
- The peak of SDD nodes,
- Time computation in seconds,
- The peak of memory consumption in Mbytes.

For each figure, a table summarizes results and shows the success rate of the N-Cut-Naive Hierarchy heuristic (*i.e.* the hierarchical order is better than the flat one). The lowest and highest gains between the flat static order and the hierarchical one are also shown on this table.

Conclusions. Once again, we observe different results for the Colored and K-bounded models. For Neoppod, there is always a clear separation between the two measures, showing that, in all cases, our heuristic provides better results (see summary in Table 9(b)):

- more than 72% gain for the final number of SDD,
- more than 64% gain for the SDD peak,
- more than 78% gain for CPU,
- more than 36% gain for memory.

These are good results since the proposed flat orders are usually not efficient.

For MAPK, results are not as good as for the other model. The hierarchical static order is not always better than the flat ones. However, except for the peak, hierarchization often generates a better results (91% hits for memory consumption). This is consistent with the second experience. However, we note in Table 10(b) that we sometimes get good results (for example, up to 79% memory gain).

4.6 Discussion

From these experiments we can conclude that our heuristic is good for large P/T nets and of less interest when the size of the state space depends on the number of tokens only (*e.g.* K-bounded models).

The last experiment also showed that our heuristic does not rely on any flat static order. It can thus be plugged to any existing heuristic providing a flat order.

However, this heuristic suffers from its blindness: it does not consider the structure of the P/T net and thus may discard parts of the structure that could have been shared efficiently.

5 Conclusion

In this paper, we propose a hierarchical way to encode a state space using decision diagrams (Hierarchical Set Decision Diagrams – SDD [16]) to cope with combinatorial explosion of state space generation. To the best of our knowledge no work has been done to automatically define a hierarchical static order with decision diagrams.

We present the N-Cut-Naive heuristics. It starts from an existing flat order and builds a hierarchical order suitable for large P/T net models.

Benefits of the proposed algorithm are:

- State space generation consumes less memory than the one needed when using flat orders, thus allowing to process larger specifications.
- the CPU time required to hierarchize a flat order is negligible compared to the state space generation.

Experiments show excellent gains when the complexity comes from the structure of the specification (*e.g.* large models). However, this is not the case for smaller specifications with a large state space due to numerous tokens hold in places. This is illustrated with two characteristics of our benchmark models: P/T nets unfolded from Colored nets (large models) and K-bounded P/T nets (large markings).

Nevertheless, one can think that when modeling complex systems, both types of complexity are present in the specification: thus, our approach should provide benefits for model checking of most P/T nets. This is confirmed by our results on some "case studies" models that do not exclusively belong to one class (*i.e.* Neoppod and PolyORB models).

Future Work. The problems detected for K-bounded models comes from the presence of strongly communicating places (this is very true in the MAKP specification). A future study would be to mix IDD and SDD (allowing intervals to label some arcs of hierarchical diagram). However, such a study needs a more detailed static analysis of the structure of the model. In that domain, more flexible classes of decision diagrams such as the poly-DD [24] might offer better solutions.

Another extension of this work concerns the elaboration of an algorithm that directly computes a hierarchical order. Once again, the use of structural analysis such as P-invariants, deadlocks, or traps in the model is needed to provide the computation modules leading to a better sharing in the state space and thus, to a better compression ratio.

Thanks. The authors thank the anonymous reviewers for their useful comments on the paper.

References

1. Aloul, F.A., Markov, I.L., Sakallah, K.A.: FORCE: a fast and easy-to-implement variable-ordering heuristic. In: ACM Great Lakes Symposium on VLSI, pp. 116–119. ACM (2003)
2. Bahar, R., Frohm, E., Gaona, C., Hachtel, G., Macii, E., Pardo, A., Somenzi, F.: Algebric decision diagrams and their applications. Formal Methods in System Design 10, 171–206 (1997)
3. Bollig, B., Wegener, I.: Improving the variable ordering of obdds is np-complete. IEEE Transactions on Computers 45(9), 993–1002 (1996)
4. Brace, K.S., Rudell, R.L., Bryant, R.E.: Efficient implementation of a BDD package. In: 27th Annual ACM IEEE Design Automation Conference, pp. 40–45. ACM (1991)
5. Brayton, R., Hachtel, G., Sangiovanni-Vincentelli, A., Somenzi, F., Aziz, A., Cheng, S., Edwards, S., Khatri, S., Kukimoto, Y., Pardo, A., Qadeer, S., Ranjan, R., Sarwary, S., Staple, T., Swamy, G., Villa, T.: Vis: A System for Verification and Synthesis. In: Alur, R., Henzinger, T.A. (eds.) CAV 1996. LNCS, vol. 1102, pp. 428–432. Springer, Heidelberg (1996)
6. Bryant, R.: Graph-based algorithms for boolean function manipulation C-35(8), 677–691 (1986)
7. Buchs, D., Hostettler, S.: Sigma decision diagrams. In: Corradini, A. (ed.) TERMGRAPH 2009: Premiliminary Proceedings of the 5th International Workshop on Computing with Terms and Graphs, number TR-09-05, Università di Pisa, pp. 18–32 (2009)
8. Burch, J.R., Clarke, E.M., McMillan, K.L., Dill, D.L., Hwang, L.J.: Symbolic Model Checking: 10^{20} States and Beyond. In: 5th Annual IEEE Symposium on Logic in Computer Science, pp. 428–439 (1990)
9. Chiola, G., Dutheillet, C., Franceschinis, G., Haddad, S.: Stochastic well-formed colored nets and symmetric modeling applications. IEEE Transactions on Computers 42(11), 1343–1360 (1993)
10. Choppy, C., Dedova, A., Evangelista, S., Hong, S., Klai, K., Petrucci, L.: The NEO Protocol for Large-Scale Distributed Database Systems: Modelling and Initial Verification. In: Lilius, J., Penczek, W. (eds.) PETRI NETS 2010. LNCS, vol. 6128, pp. 145–164. Springer, Heidelberg (2010)
11. Ciardo, G., Lüttgen, G., Miner, A.S.: Exploiting interleaving semantics in symbolic state-space generation. Formal Methods in System Design 31(1), 63–100 (2007)

12. Ciardo, G., Lüttgen, G., Siminiceanu, R.: Saturation: An Efficient Iteration Strategy for Symbolic State Space Generation. In: Margaria, T., Yi, W. (eds.) TACAS 2001. LNCS, vol. 2031, pp. 328–342. Springer, Heidelberg (2001)
13. Ciardo, G., Miner, A.S.: Smart: Simulation and markovian analyzer for reliability and timing, p. 60. IEEE Computer Society, Los Alamitos (1996)
14. Ciardo, G., Trivedi, K.: A decomposition approach for stochastic reward net models. Perf. Eval. 18, 37–59 (1993)
15. Cimatti, A., Clarke, E., Giunchiglia, F., Roveri, M.: NUSMV: A New Symbolic Model Verifier. In: Halbwachs, N., Peled, D.A. (eds.) CAV 1999. LNCS, vol. 1633, pp. 495–499. Springer, Heidelberg (1999)
16. Couvreur, J.-M., Thierry-Mieg, Y.: Hierarchical Decision Diagrams to Exploit Model Structure. In: Wang, F. (ed.) FORTE 2005. LNCS, vol. 3731, pp. 443–457. Springer, Heidelberg (2005)
17. Dijkstra, E.W.: Hierarchical ordering of sequential processes. Acta Informaticae 1, 115–138 (1971)
18. Hamez, A., Thierry-Mieg, Y., Kordon, F.: Building efficient model checkers using hierarchical set decision diagrams and automatic saturation. Fundamenta Informaticae 94(3-4), 413–437 (2009)
19. Heiner, M., Gilbert, D., Donaldson, R.: Petri Nets for Systems and Synthetic Biology. In: Bernardo, M., Degano, P., Tennenholtz, M. (eds.) SFM 2008. LNCS, vol. 5016, pp. 215–264. Springer, Heidelberg (2008)
20. Heiner, M., Schwarick, M., Tovchigrechko, A.: DSSZ-MC - A Tool for Symbolic Analysis of Extended Petri Nets. In: Franceschinis, G., Wolf, K. (eds.) PETRI NETS 2009. LNCS, vol. 5606, pp. 323–332. Springer, Heidelberg (2009)
21. Hong, S., Paviot-Adet, E., Kordon, F.: PNXDD model checkers (2010), https://srcdev.lip6.fr/trac/research/NEOPPOD/wiki
22. Hugues, J., Thierry-Mieg, Y., Kordon, F., Pautet, L., Baarir, S., Vergnaud, T.: On the Formal Verification of Middleware Behavioral Properties. In: 9th International Workshop on Formal Methods for Industrial Critical Systems (FMICS 2004), pp. 139–157. Elsevier (2004)
23. Kordon, F., Linard, A., Paviot-Adet, E.: Optimized Colored Nets Unfolding. In: Najm, E., Pradat-Peyre, J.-F., Donzeau-Gouge, V.V. (eds.) FORTE 2006. LNCS, vol. 4229, pp. 339–355. Springer, Heidelberg (2006)
24. Linard, A., Paviot-Adet, E., Kordon, F., Buchs, D., Charron, S.: polyDD: Towards a Framework Generalizing Decision Diagrams. In: 10th International Conference on Application of Concurrency to System Design (ACSD 2010), Braga, Portugal, pp. 124–133. IEEE Computer Society (2010)
25. Miner, A.S., Ciardo, G.: Efficient Reachability Set Generation and Storage using Decision Diagrams. In: Donatelli, S., Kleijn, J. (eds.) ICATPN 1999. LNCS, vol. 1639, pp. 6–25. Springer, Heidelberg (1999)
26. Peterson, G.L.: Myths about the mutual exclusion problem. Information Processing Letters 12(3), 115–116 (1981)
27. Rice, M., Kulhari, S.: A survey of static variable ordering heuristics for efficient BDD/MDD construction. Technical report, UC Riverside (2008)
28. Schmidt, K.: How to Calculate Symmetries of Petri Nets. Acta Informaticae 36(7), 545–590 (2000)
29. Strehl, K., Thiele, L.: Symbolic model checking of process networks using interval diagram techniques. In: ICCAD 1998: Proceedings of the 1998 IEEE/ACM International Conference on Computer-Aided Design, pp. 686–692. ACM, New York (1998)
30. Thierry-Mieg, Y., Poitrenaud, D., Hamez, A., Kordon, F.: Hierarchical Set Decision Diagrams and Regular Models. In: Kowalewski, S., Philippou, A. (eds.) TACAS 2009. LNCS, vol. 5505, pp. 1–15. Springer, Heidelberg (2009)

Bounded Model Checking
for Parametric Timed Automata*

Michał Knapik[1] and Wojciech Penczek[1,2]

[1] Institute of Computer Science, Polish Academy of Sciences,
J.K. Ordona 21, 01-237 Warszawa, Poland
Michal.Knapik@ipipan.waw.pl
[2] Institute of Informatics, University of Natural Sciences and Humanities,
3 Maja 54, 08-110 Siedlce, Poland
penczek@ipipan.waw.pl

Abstract. This paper shows how bounded model checking can be applied to parameter synthesis for parametric timed automata with continuous time. While it is known that the general problem is undecidable even for reachability, we show how to synthesize a part of the set of all the parameter valuations under which the given property holds in a model. The results form a full theory which can be easily applied to parametric verification of a wide range of temporal formulae – we present such an implementation for the existential part of CTL_{-X}.

1 Introduction and Related Work

The growing abundance of complex systems in real world, and their presence in critical areas fuels the research in formal specification and analysis. One of the established methods in systems verification is model checking, where the system is abstracted into an algebraic model (e.g. various versions of Kripke structures, Petri nets, timed automata), and then processed with respect to the given property (usually a formula of modal or temporal logic). Classical methods have their limits however – the model is supposed to be a complete abstraction of system behaviour, with all the timing constraints explicitly specified. This situation has several drawbacks, e.g. the need to perform a batch of tests to confirm the proper system design (or find errors) is often impossible to fulfill due to the high complexity of the problem. Introducing parameters into models changes the task of *property verification* to task of *parameter synthesis*, meaning that parametric model checking tool produces the set of parameter valuations under which the given property holds instead of simple *holds/does not hold* answer. Unfortunately, the problem of parameter synthesis is shown to be undecidable for some of widely used parametric models, e.g. parametric timed automata [3,11] and bounded parametric time Petri nets [23].

Many of model checking tools acquired new capabilities of parametric verification, e.g. UPPAAL-PMC [16] – the parametric extension of UPPAAL, LPMC

---

* Partly supported by the Polish Ministry of Science and Higher Education.

[20] – extending PMC. Some of the tools were built from scratch with parametric model checking in mind, e.g. TREX [5] and MOBY/DC [10]. A parametric analysis is also possible with HyTech by means of hybrid automata [15,1,13].

Both UPPAAL-PMC and TREX deal with verification of properties in parametric timed automata by employing Constrained Parametric Difference Bound Matrices (PDBMS) which are basically tuples (C, D), where C is a set of constraints on parameter values, and D is a set of constraints on clocks. These constraints are updated and simplified (brought to the canonical form) during the analysis of the state-space of a given automaton, where the process is exhaustive and may not stop. UPPAAL-PMC allows for verification of parametric reachability for models containing linear constraints, TREX additionally enables for verification of some types of liveness and allows for products of parameters in constraints.

HyTech allows for the verification of properties specified in Integrator Computation Tree Logic over linear hybrid automata. Linear hybrid automata are a subclass of hybrid automata with linearity restrictions on continuous activities and discrete transitions. HyTech explores the state-space of a given automaton by applying partition refinement or forward reachability. Similarly, LPMC applies partition refinement techniques for the parametric verification of models specified in a certain extension of a timed automata class – namely eXtended Timed Graphs (XTG). In this case the property specification logic is a variant of TCTL.

MOBY/DC accepts parametric phase automata as its model description language. Nonparametric phase automata contain phases (local states) which may be joined by arcs, and equipped with clocks. The values of mentioned clocks can be constrained by extended reals (with infinity allowed), or (in the case of parametric phase automata) linear constraints. MOBY/DC applies compositional model checking techniques to solve the problem of verification of the properties specified in Duration Calculus – an interval-based logic. As the problem is undecidable, MOBY/DC attempts to overapproximate the correct solution set, which additionally guarantees the termination of the procedure.

Another, very interesting approach is given in the recently developed IMITATOR II tool [4]; given both the parametric timed automaton and the initial parameter valuation, IMITATOR II synthesizes a set of parameter constraints. Substituting the parameters with a valuation satisfying these constraints is guaranteed to produce the timed automaton which is *time-abstract* equivalent to the one obtained from substituting the parameters with the initial valuation.

Due to undecidability issues, many of the algorithms implemented in the above tools need not stop and may be very resource consuming.

In this paper we present a new approach to parametric model checking, based on the observation that while we are not able to synthesize the *full* set of parameter constraints in general, there is no fundamental rule which forbids us from obtaining a *part* of this set, which may be perceived as obtaining an underapproximation of the set of solutions, as opposed to the MOBY/DC's overapproximation. In Section 2 we introduce the parametric region graph – an extension of the region graph used in the theory of the timed automata [2] and show (in Section 3) how the computation tree of a model can be unwinded up to some finite depth in order to apply bounded model checking (BMC) techniques [6]. The techniques of unwinding of a parametric region graph are similar to the PDBM transformations introduced in [16].

To the best knowledge of the authors, this is the first application of BMC to parametric timed automata and seems to be a quite promising direction of research. Firstly due to the unique BMC advantage, which allows for the verification of properties over a limited part of the model. Secondly due to the fact that it is quite easy to present the extension of our approach to the existential parts of many modal and temporal logics. In fact we describe how Parametric BMC can be implemented for the existential subset of the CTL_{-X} logic in Section 3, including the analysis of a simplified parametric model of the 4-phase handshake protocol.

2   Theory of Parametric Timed Automata

In this paper we use two kinds of variables, namely *parameters* $P = \{p_1, \ldots, p_m\}$ and *clocks* $X = \{x_0, \ldots, x_n\}$. Let $\mathbb{Z}$ denote the set of integer numbers. An expression of the form $\sum_{i=1}^{m} t_i \cdot p_i + t_0$, where $t_i \in \mathbb{Z}$ is called a *linear expression*. A *simple guard* is an expression of the form $x_i - x_j \prec e$, where $i \neq j$, $\prec \in \{\leq, <\}$ and e is a linear expression. A conjunction of simple guards is called a *guard* and the set of all guards is denoted by G. We valuate the clocks in nonnegative reals, and parameters in naturals (including 0) that is $v : P \to \mathbb{N}$ is a *parameter valuation* and $\omega : X \to \mathbb{R}_{\geq 0}$ is a *clock valuation* (both v and ω can be thought of as points in, respectively, $\mathbb{N}^m$ and $\mathbb{R}_{\geq 0}^n$). Additionally, following [16] we assume that for each clock valuation ω we have that $\omega(x_0) = 0$ – the "false clock" x_0 is fixed on 0 for convenience only, for uniform presentation of guards. By $e[v]$ we denote the value obtained by substituting the parameters in a linear expression e according to parameter valuation v. We denote $\omega \models_v x_i - x_j \prec e$ iff $\omega(x_i) - \omega(x_j) \prec e[v]$ holds, and naturally extend this notion to guards. We also need a notion of *reset* that is a set of expressions of the form $x_i := b_i$ where $b_i \in \mathbb{N}$, and $0 < i \leq n$. The set of all resets is denoted by R, and the action of resetting a clock valuation ω by reset $r \in R$ is defined as following: $\omega[r]$ is a clock valuation such that $\omega[r](x_i) = b_i$ if $x_i := b_i \in r$, and $\omega[r](x_i) = \omega(x_i)$ otherwise. If $\delta \in \mathbb{R}$ and ω is a clock valuation, then $\omega + \delta$ is a clock valuation such that $(\omega + \delta)(x_i) = \omega(x_i) + \delta$ for all $0 < i \leq n$, and $\omega(x_0) = 0$. An *initial clock valuation* ω_0 is the valuation satisfying $\omega_0(x_i) = 0$ for all $x_i \in X$.

We also adopt a convenient notation from [16], where the $\leq$ symbol is treated as *true* and the $<$ symbol is treated as *false*. The propositional formulae built from symbols $\leq$ and $<$ are evaluated in the standard way. As to give an example, $\leq \Rightarrow <$ evaluates to $<$, $< \Rightarrow \leq$ evaluates to $\leq$, and $\neg(\leq \vee <)$ evaluates to $<$.

2.1 Parametric Timed Automata

Let us recall some notions from the theory of the parametric timed automata. The (non-parametric) timed automata [2] are state-transition graphs augmented with a finite number of clocks, and clock constraints guarding the transitions between states. Their parametric version [3] allows for using parameters (other than clocks) in the guard expressions – which may be perceived as creating the general template for system behaviour under more abstract timed constraints.

Definition 1. *A tuple* $\mathcal{A} = \langle Q, q_0, A, X, P, \rightarrow, I \rangle$, *where:*

- Q *is a set of* locations,
- $q_0 \in Q$ *is the* initial location,
- A *is a set of* actions,
- X *and* P *are, respectively, sets of clocks and parameters,*
- $I : Q \rightarrow G$ *is an* invariant *function,*
- $\rightarrow \subseteq Q \times A \times G \times R \times Q$ *is a* transition relation,

is called a parametric timed automaton *(PTA). All the above sets are finite. We abbreviate* (q, a, g, r, q') *as* $q \xrightarrow{a,g,r} q'$.

Definition 2. *A tuple* $LTS = \langle S, s_0, \rightarrow \rangle$, *where* S *is a set of states,* $s_0 \in S$ *is an initial state, and* $\rightarrow \subseteq S \times Act \times S$ *is a (labelled) transition relation is called* labelled transition system *over a set of labels* Act. *A (finite) sequence of states* $s^1, s^2, s^3 \ldots$ *($s^1, s^2, s^3, \ldots, s^n$, resp.) such that for all* $1 \leq i$ *($1 \leq i < n$, resp.) we have* $s^i \in S$, *and* $(s^i, act^i, s^{i+1}) \in \rightarrow$ *for some* $act^i \in Act$ *is called a* (finite, resp.) run *in* LTS.

The semantics of PTA is presented below in the form of a labelled transition system.

Definition 3 (Concrete semantics). *Let* $\mathcal{A} = \langle Q, q_0, A, X, P, \rightarrow, I \rangle$ *be a parametric timed automaton, and* υ *be a parameter valuation. The labelled transition system of* $\mathcal{A}$ *under* υ *is defined as a tuple* $[\mathcal{A}]_\upsilon = \langle S, s_0, \xrightarrow{d} \rangle$, *where:*

- $S = \{(q, \omega) \mid q \in Q, \text{ and } \omega \text{ is a clock valuation such that } \omega \models_\upsilon I(q)\}$,
- $s_0 = (q_0, \omega_0)$ *(we assume that* $\omega_0 \models_\upsilon I(q_0)$*),*
- *let* $(q, \omega), (q', \omega') \in S$. *The transition relation* $\xrightarrow{d}$ *is defined as follows:*
  - *if* $d \in \mathbb{R}_{\geq 0}$, *then* $(q, \omega) \xrightarrow{d} (q', \omega')$ *iff* $q = q'$ *and* $\omega' = \omega + d$,
  - *if* $d \in A$, *then* $(q, \omega) \xrightarrow{d} (q', \omega')$ *iff* $q \xrightarrow{a,g,r} q'$, *and* $\omega \models_\upsilon g$, *and* $\omega' = \omega[r]$.

The elements of S *are called the* concrete states *of* $\mathcal{A}_\upsilon$.

Example 1. Consider the following example of a parametric timed automaton. The example automaton can stay in the initial state s_0 for at most p time units. After that either the transition from s_0 to itself or from s_0 to s_1 has to be traversed. Note that we can always move along the transition from s_0 to s_0 as this arc lacks any guard expression, but such a movement results in resetting of

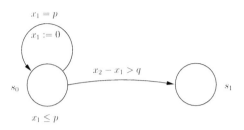

x_1 to 0. The clock x_2 progresses continuously without resets, and it is easy to notice that $x_2 - x_1 = r_{count} \times p$, where r_{count} is a number of times the clock x_1 was subject to a reset. Taking the guard between s_0 and s_1 into account, we easily obtain that the state s_1 is reachable from s_0 iff $r_{count} > \frac{q}{p}$. As the number of possible resets of the clock x_1 is not limited, we obtain that state s_1 is reachable for any choice of p, q, with $p \neq 0$.

The automaton obtained by substituting the parameters in the guards and the invariants of $\mathcal{A}$ by the appropriate values of the parameter valuation v is denoted by $\mathcal{A}_v$. The concrete semantics of $\mathcal{A}_v$ is defined as $[\mathcal{A}_v] = [\mathcal{A}]_v$. Notice that $\mathcal{A}_v$ is a timed automaton and $[\mathcal{A}_v]$ is its concrete semantics [2].

Our definition of the parametric timed automata slightly differs from the one presented in [16], namely, we do not allow for non-negative reals as parameter values. As it was shown in [3], the choice of the parameter valuation codomain does not change the fact that the emptiness problem is undecidable. We explain the origin of this restriction in the following subsection.

2.2   Parametric Region Graph

In the non-parametric timed automata theory, the *region graph* [2] is used to represent the concrete state space in a uniform and finite way. The finiteness of the resulting structure is a result of the presence of both the *bounded* and *unbounded* regions. Intuitively, the bounded regions are convex bounded sets in the space of clock valuations, while the unbounded regions are convex and unbounded. The second ones are defined using the maximal values of clock constraints – this is not possible in the general case of parametric timed automata (see however the optimization techniques in [16]), therefore in this paper we consider only the bounded regions. We divide the space of all the clock valuations into the set of *regions* using the following equivalence relation.

Definition 4. *Let ω, ω' be valuations of clocks $X = \{x_0, \ldots, x_n\}$. Then $\omega \approx \omega'$ iff the following conditions hold:*

- *$\lfloor \omega(x_i) \rfloor = \lfloor \omega'(x_i) \rfloor$ for all $1 \leq i \leq n$,*
- *and $frac(\omega(x_i)) < frac(\omega(x_j)) \iff frac(\omega'(x_i)) < frac(\omega'(x_j))$ for all $i \neq j, 1 \leq i, j \leq n$,*
- *and $frac(\omega(x_i)) = 0 \iff frac(\omega'(x_i)) = 0$ for all $1 \leq i \leq n$,*

where $frac(\omega(x_i))$ denotes the fractional part of $\omega(x_i)$. The equivalence classes of $\approx$ are called (detailed) regions.

For technical reasons it is convenient to describe the regions as sets of valuatons satisfying certain guard expressions.

Lemma 1. Let $X = \{x_0, \ldots, x_n\}$ be a set of clocks, and let Z be a region of valuations. There exists a guard $g_Z = \bigwedge_{i,j \in \{0,\ldots,n\}, i \neq j} x_i - x_j \prec_{ij} b_{ij}$, such that $\prec_{ij} \in \{\leq, <\}$ and $b_{ij} \in \mathbb{Z}$ satisfying:

$$Z = \{\omega \mid \omega \models g_Z\}.$$

Proof. We need to specify the values of b_{ij} together with the accompanying relation $\prec_{ij}$. Let $Z = [\omega]_{\approx}$ (the following considerations are valid for any choice of ω from Z).

- If $frac(\omega(x_i)) = 0$, $frac(\omega(x_j)) = 0$, let $\prec_{ij} = \leq$ and $b_{ij} = \lfloor \omega(x_i) \rfloor - \lfloor \omega(x_j) \rfloor$,
- if $frac(\omega(x_i)) \neq 0$, $frac(\omega(x_j)) = 0$, let $\prec_{ij} = <$ and $b_{ij} = \lceil \omega(x_i) \rceil - \lfloor \omega(x_j) \rfloor$,
- if $frac(\omega(x_i)) = 0$, $frac(\omega(x_j)) \neq 0$, let $\prec_{ij} = <$ and $b_{ij} = \lfloor \omega(x_i) \rfloor - \lfloor \omega(x_j) \rfloor$,
- for $frac(\omega(x_i)) \neq 0$, $frac(\omega(x_j)) \neq 0$:
  - if $frac(\omega(x_i)) = frac(\omega(x_j))$, let $\prec_{ij} = \leq$, $b_{ij} = \lfloor \omega(x_i) \rfloor - \lfloor \omega(x_j) \rfloor$,
  - if $frac(\omega(x_i)) < frac(\omega(x_j))$, put $\prec_{ij} = <$, $b_{ij} = \lfloor \omega(x_i) \rfloor - \lfloor \omega(x_j) \rfloor$,
  - if $frac(\omega(x_i)) > frac(\omega(x_j))$, let $\prec_{ij} = <$, $b_{ij} = \lceil \omega(x_i) \rceil - \lfloor \omega(x_j) \rfloor$.

It is easy to see that if $\omega \approx \omega'$, then for any guard g we have $\omega \models g$ iff $\omega' \models g$. Therefore, as g_Z was constructed in such a way that $\omega \models g_Z$, we have also $\omega' \models g_Z$ for all $\omega' \in Z$.

If $\omega' \models g_Z$, then satisfaction of the guards of form $x_i - x_0 \prec_{i0} b_{i0}$ and $x_0 - x_i \prec_{0i} b_{0i}$ (recall that x_0 is fixed) guarantees that $\lfloor \omega'(x_j) \rfloor = \lfloor \omega(x_j) \rfloor$ for all $x_j \in X$. Similarly, $\omega'(x_i)$ has nonzero fractional value iff $frac(\omega(x_i)) \neq 0$, as $\omega'(x_i) \in (\lfloor \omega(x_i) \rfloor, \lceil \omega(x_i) \rceil)$, provided that $frac(\omega(x_i)) \neq 0$. Let us assume that $0 < frac(\omega(x_i))$ and $frac(\omega(x_i)) < frac(\omega(x_j))$, then from $\omega(x_i) - \omega(x_j) < \lfloor \omega(x_i) \rfloor - \lfloor \omega(x_j) \rfloor$ we have $\omega'(x_i) - \omega'(x_j) < \lfloor \omega'(x_i) \rfloor - \lfloor \omega'(x_j) \rfloor$. Therefore $\omega'(x_i) - \lfloor \omega'(x_i) \rfloor < \omega'(x_j) - \lfloor \omega'(x_j) \rfloor$, thus $frac(\omega'(x_i)) < frac(\omega'(x_j))$.   □

The guard constructed in the proof of the above lemma is called the *characteristic guard* of Z. In the above proof we used the fact that if one representative of an equivalence class satisfies a guard g, then so do all the remaining members. This is not true if we allow nonnegative reals as parameter values – for example it is easy to see that only some of representatives of class $[(0, 0.3)]$ satisfy $x_1 - x_0 < p$ under parameter valuation v such that $v(p) = 0.5$.

Definition 5. Let $\mathcal{A} = \langle Q, q_0, A, X, P, \rightarrow, I \rangle$ be a parametric timed automaton, $X = \{x_0, \ldots, x_n\}$, and $P = \{p_1, \ldots, p_m\}$. We introduce a relation in the set of all the pairs (Z, C), where Z is a region, and $C \subseteq \mathbb{N}^m$ is a subset of the set of all the valuations of parameters (treated as natural vectors). Let $s = x_i - x_j \prec e$ be a simple guard, and $g_Z = \bigwedge_{i,j \in \{0,\ldots,n\}, i \neq j} x_i - x_j \prec_{ij} b_{ij}$ the characteristic guard of region Z. Then we define:

$$(Z, C) \overset{s}{\rightsquigarrow} (Z', C') \text{ iff } Z = Z' \text{ and } C' = C \cap \{v \mid b_{ij}(\prec_{ij} \Rightarrow \prec)e[v]\}.$$

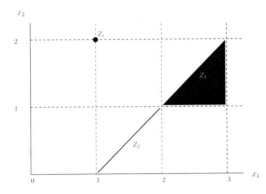

Fig. 1. Three example regions: Z_1, Z_2, Z_3 and their (simplified) characteristic guards:
$g_{Z_1} = (x_1 = 1) \wedge (x_2 = 2)$,
$g_{Z_2} = (1 < x_1 < 2) \wedge (0 < x_2 < 1) \wedge (x_1 - x_2 \leq 1) \wedge (x_2 - x_1 \leq -1)$,
$g_{Z_3} = (2 < x_1 < 3) \wedge (1 < x_2 < 2) \wedge (x_2 - x_1 < -1)$

If g be a guard and s is a simple guard, then we have:

$$(Z, C) \overset{g \wedge s}{\rightsquigarrow} (Z', C') \text{ iff for some } (Z'', C'') \text{ we have } (Z, C) \overset{g}{\rightsquigarrow} (Z'', C'')$$

$$\text{and } (Z'', C'') \overset{s}{\rightsquigarrow} (Z', C').$$

There is a natural intuition behind the above definition – if $(Z, C) \overset{g}{\rightsquigarrow} (Z', C')$ then (Z', C') contains all the pairs $(\omega, \upsilon) \in Z \times C$ such that $\omega \models_\upsilon g$. Such an operation is a counterpart for guard addition from [16], notice however that we do not need a burden of a costly canonicalization. Below, we state some basic properties of the $\overset{g}{\rightsquigarrow}$ relation.

Lemma 2. *Let $(Z, C) \overset{g}{\rightsquigarrow} (Z', C')$, where g is a guard. Then, the following conditions hold:*

1. if $(\omega, \upsilon) \in (Z, C)$ and $\omega \models_\upsilon g$, then $(\omega, \upsilon) \in (Z', C')$,
2. if $(\omega, \upsilon) \in (Z', C')$, then $\omega \models_\upsilon g$.

Proof. Let us start with the first part of the lemma. Let us assume that $\omega \models_\upsilon g$. By induction on the structure of g we prove that $\upsilon \in C'$.

The base case is when $g = x_i - x_j \prec e$ (g is a simple guard). Let us assume that g_Z contains a simple guard of the form $x_i - x_j \leq b_{ij}$ where $b_{ij} \in \mathbb{Z}$. Notice that in this case the characteristic guard contains also a simple guard of the form $x_j - x_i \leq -b_{ij}$, therefore $b_{ij} = \omega'(x_i) - \omega'(x_j)$ for each $\omega' \in Z$. As $\omega \models_\upsilon g$, then $b_{ij} = \omega'(x_i) - \omega'(x_j) \prec e[\upsilon]$. Therefore $b_{ij} \prec e[\upsilon]$, which in this case means that $b_{ij}(\prec_{ij} \Rightarrow \prec) e[\upsilon]$. Now let us assume that g_Z contains a simple guard of the form $x_i - x_j < b_{ij}$. In this case, for each $\omega' \in Z$ there exists $\delta \in (0, 1)$ such that $\omega'(x_i) - \omega'(x_j) = (b_{ij} - 1) + \delta$. Let us notice that $e[\upsilon] \in \mathbb{Z}$, therefore from $(b_{ij} - 1) + \delta = \omega'(x_i) - \omega'(x_j) \prec e[\upsilon]$ we obtain $b_{ij} \leq e[\upsilon]$. As $\prec_{ij} \Rightarrow \prec$ evaluates to $\leq$, the second inequality means that in this case $b_{ij}(\prec_{ij} \Rightarrow \prec) e[\upsilon]$ holds.

For the induction step, notice that if $(Z, C) \overset{g' \wedge s}{\rightsquigarrow} (Z', C')$ (g' is a guard, and s a simple guard), then there exists (Z'', C'') such that $(Z, C) \overset{g'}{\rightsquigarrow} (Z'', C'')$ and $(Z'', C'') \overset{s}{\rightsquigarrow} (Z', C')$. From the inductive assumption we obtain that as $\omega \models_v g' \wedge s$ implies $\omega \models_v g'$, then $v \in C''$. Similarly, as $(\omega, v) \in (Z'', C'')$ and $\omega \models_v s$, we have $v \in C'$.

The proof of the second part of the lemma is also by induction on the structure of g. Assume that $g = x_i - x_j \prec e$ and g_Z contains a simple guard of form $x_i - x_j \prec_{ij} b_{ij}$. If $(Z, C) \overset{g}{\rightsquigarrow} (Z', C')$, then $C' = C \cap \{v \mid b_{ij}(\prec_{ij} \Rightarrow \prec)e[v]\}$. As $\omega(x_i) - \omega(x_j) \prec_{ij} b_{ij}$ and $b_{ij}(\prec_{ij} \Rightarrow \prec)e[v]$ then $\omega(x_i) - \omega(x_j)(\prec_{ij} \wedge(\prec_{ij} \Rightarrow \prec))e[v]$. Therefore we have $\omega(x_i) - \omega(x_j) \prec e[v]$, thus $\omega \models_v g$.

For the induction step, let us notice that if $(Z, C) \overset{g' \wedge s}{\rightsquigarrow} (Z', C')$, then there exists (Z'', C'') such that $(Z, C) \overset{g'}{\rightsquigarrow} (Z'', C'')$ and $(Z'', C'') \overset{s}{\rightsquigarrow} (Z', C')$. If $(\omega, v) \in (Z', C')$ then by the inductive assumption $\omega \models_v s$ holds. As $C' \subseteq C'' \subseteq C$, then $v \in C''$ and $(\omega, v) \in (Z'', C'')$. Therefore, from the inductive assumption we obtain $\omega \models_v g'$ and, finally, $\omega \models_v g' \wedge s$. □

From the above lemma we immediately obtain the following corollary.

Corollary 1. *Let Z be a region, and C a subset of the set of all the parameter valuations. Then the following conditions hold:*

1. *if $(Z, C) \overset{g}{\rightsquigarrow} (Z', C')$, then $Z' = Z$ and $C' = C \cap \{(\omega, v) \mid \omega \models_v g\}$,*
2. *if $\omega \in Z$, $v \in C$, and $\omega \models_v g$, then $(Z, C) \overset{g}{\rightsquigarrow} (Z', C')$ for some Z', C' such that $(\omega, v) \in Z' \times C'$.*

Note that from the above it follows that if $(Z_1, C_1) \overset{g_1}{\rightsquigarrow} (Z_2, C_2) \overset{g_2}{\rightsquigarrow} (Z_3, C_3) \overset{g_3}{\rightsquigarrow} \ldots$ then $C_1 \supseteq C_2 \supseteq C_3 \supseteq \ldots$ ($\{C_i\}_{i \in \mathbb{N}}$ form a descending chain).

In order to develop our theory further, we need to define two additional operations on regions.

Definition 6. *Let $Z = [\omega]_\approx$ be a region, and $r \in R$ be a reset. Then, resetting of Z by r is defined as $Z[r] = [\omega[r]]_\approx$.*

Clearly, resetting of a region does not depend on the choice of a representative.

Definition 7. *Let Z and Z' be two different regions. Region Z' is called the time successor of Z (denoted by $\tau(Z)$) iff for all $\omega \in Z$ there exists $\delta \in \mathbb{R}$ such that $\omega + \delta \in Z'$ and $\omega + \delta' \in Z \cup Z'$ for all $\delta' \leq \delta$.*

Now, we are in the position to present the notion of the *parametric region graph*, being an extension of the *region graph* used in the theory of the timed automata [2]. The main idea is to augment regions with sets of parameter valuations under which the given concrete state (its equivalence class) is reachable from the initial state, and to mimic the transitions in the concrete semantics by their counterparts in the parametric region graph.

Definition 8. *Let* $\mathcal{A} = \langle Q, q_0, A, X, P, \rightarrow, I \rangle$ *be a parametric timed automaton. Define the* parametric region graph *of* $\mathcal{A}$ *as the tuple* $PREG(\mathcal{A}) = \langle S, s_0, \overset{d}{\rightarrow} \rangle$ *where:*

- $S = \{(q, Z, C) \mid q \in Q, Z \text{ is a region}, C \subseteq \mathbb{N}^m \text{ and } \forall_{v \in C} \exists_{w \in Z} \ w \models_v I(q)\}$,
- $s_0 = (q_0, Z_0, C_0)$ *where* $Z_0 = [w_0]_\approx$ *and* $C_0 = \{v \mid w_0 \models_v I(q_0)\}$,
- $(q, Z, C) \overset{d}{\rightarrow} (q', Z', C')$ *is defined as follows:*
  - *if* $d = \tau$ *(time transition), then* $q = q'$, $Z' = \tau(Z)$, *and* C' *is such that* $(Z', C) \overset{I(q)}{\rightsquigarrow} (Z', C')$,
  - *if* $d \in A$ *(action transition), then there exists a transition* $q \overset{d,g,r}{\rightarrow} q'$ *in* $\mathcal{A}$ *and* C'' *such that* $(Z, C) \overset{g}{\rightsquigarrow} (Z, C'')$ *and* $(Z[r], C'') \overset{I(q')}{\rightsquigarrow} (Z', C')$.

Additionally, we call nodes of type $(q, Z, \emptyset)$ dead, *and assume that they have no outgoing transitions.*

Notice that in the above definition we could replace $\exists$ with $\forall$, due to the fact that for any guard g, a fixed parameter valuation v, and clock valuations ω, ω' such that $\omega \approx \omega'$, we have $\omega \models_v g$ iff $\omega' \models_v g$.

Both the concrete semantics of (parametric) timed automata, and (parametric) region graphs are defined as labelled transition systems.

Lemma 3. *Let* A *be a parametric timed automaton, and* $\rho = s_0, s_1, \ldots s_n$ *a finite run in* $PREG(\mathcal{A})$, *where* $s_i = (q_i, Z_i, C_i)$, *and* $C_n \neq \emptyset$. *For any* $(\omega, v) \in Z_n \times C_n$ *there exists a finite run* $\mu = t_0, t_1, \ldots t_n$ *in* $\mathcal{A}_v$, *such that* $t_i = (q_i, \omega_i)$, $\omega_i \in Z_i$ *for* $i \in \{0, \ldots, n\}$, *and* $\omega_n = \omega$.

Proof. The base case of $n = 0$ is straightforward as from the definition of $PREG(\mathcal{A})$ we have $\omega \models_v I(q_0)$ for any $(\omega, v) \in Z_0 \times C_0$.

Recall that $C_n \subseteq C_{n-1}$. If $s_{n-1} \overset{d}{\rightarrow} s_n$ is a time transition (with $d = \tau$), then $\tau(Z_{n-1}) = Z_n$. Therefore, for each $\omega_n \in Z_n$ there exist $\omega_{n-1} \in Z_{n-1}$, and $l \in \mathbb{R}$, such that $\omega_n = \omega_{n-1} + l$. We conclude the case by noticing that $(\omega_{n-1}, v) \in Z_{n-1} \times C_{n-1}$, $\omega_n \models_v I(q_n)$, and using the inductive assumption.

Now, if $s_{n-1} \overset{d}{\rightarrow} s_n$ is an action transition ($d \in A$), then there exists a transition $q_{n-1} \overset{d,g,r}{\rightarrow} q_n$ in $\mathcal{A}$, and a subset C' of $\mathbb{N}^m$, such that $(Z_{n-1}, C_{n-1}) \overset{g}{\rightsquigarrow} (Z_{n-1}, C')$, and $(Z_{n-1}[r], C') \overset{I(q_n)}{\rightsquigarrow} (Z_{n-1}[r], C_n)$. Therefore, for each $\omega_n \in Z_n$ we have $\omega_n \models_v I(q_n)$, and there exists $\omega_{n-1} \in Z_{n-1}$ such that $\omega_n = \omega_{n-1}[r]$, $\omega_{n-1} \models_v I(q_{n-1})$, and $\omega_{n-1} \models_v g$ (notice that $v \in C_n \cap C' \cap C_{n-1}$). We conclude the case by assuming $t_{n-1} = (q_{n-1}, \omega_{n-1})$, $t_n = (q_n, \omega_n)$ and using the inductive assumption. $\square$

Notice that the definition of the transition relation in $PREG(\mathcal{A})$ implies that in ρ_n we have $C_{i+1} \subseteq C_i$ for all $0 \leq i < n$. In particular $C_n \subseteq C_i$ for all $0 \leq i \leq n$.

The next example shows the reason for which we restrict ourselves to finite runs in the above lemma.

Example 2. Consider the following simple parametric timed automaton:

$x_1 - x_0 < p$

The below infinite run in $PREG(\mathcal{A})$ does not have a counterpart in $\mathcal{A}_v$ due to the fact that p is unbounded.

$$(q, [(0,0)], \{p \mid p \geq 1\}) \xrightarrow{\tau} (q, [(0,0.1)], \{p \mid p \geq 1\}) \xrightarrow{\tau}$$

$$(q, [(0,1)], \{p \mid p \geq 2\}) \xrightarrow{\tau} (q, [(0,1.1)], \{p \mid p \geq 2\}) \xrightarrow{\tau} \dots$$

Consider a transition $(q, Z, C) \xrightarrow{d} (q', Z', C')$ in $PREG(\mathcal{A})$. Notice that if $\omega \in Z$, $v \in C'$, then $(q, \omega) \xrightarrow{d'} (q', \omega')$ in $[\mathcal{A}_v]$, where $d' = d$ if d is an action, and d' is some real number if $d = \tau$. From this observation and Lemma 3 we obtain the following corollary.

Corollary 2. *Let $\rho = s_0, s_1, \dots$ be an infinite run in $PREG(\mathcal{A})$, such that $s_i = (q_i, Z_i, C_i)$ for some Z_i, C_i, and let $v \in C_i$ for all $i \geq 0$. Then, there exists an infinite run $\mu = t_0, t_1, \dots$ in the concrete semantics of $\mathcal{A}_v$ such that $t_i = (q_i, \omega_i)$, and $\omega_i \in Z_i$ for all $i \geq 0$.*

The counterpart of Lemma 3 holds without the restriction on the finiteness of runs. Note that we allow for several consecutive time transitions in a run, therefore we can restrict our considerations to runs where each time transition corresponds to a movement from a region to its time successor.

Lemma 4. *Let $\mathcal{A}$ be a parametric timed automaton, v be a parameter valuation, and $\mu = t_0, t_1, \dots t_n \dots$ be an infinite (finite) run in $\mathcal{A}_v$, where $t_i = (q_i, \omega_i)$, and such that if $t_i \xrightarrow{d} t_{i+1}$ is a time transition, then $[\omega_{i+1}] = \tau([\omega_i])$. Then, there exists an infinite (finite, resp.) run $\rho = s_0, s_1, \dots s_n \dots$ in $PREG(\mathcal{A})$ such that $s_i = (q_i, Z_i, C_i)$, and $(\omega_i, v) \in Z_i \times C_i$ for each $i \geq 0$ ($0 \leq i \leq n$, resp.).*

Proof. Let us start with the finite run case, and let $Z_i = [\omega_i]$. The base case is straightforward: just assume $C_0 = \{u \mid \omega_0 \models_u I(q_0)\}$ and notice that $v \in C_0$.

Assume that we have already constructed a finite run $\rho_n = s_0, s_1, \dots s_{n-1}$.

If $t_{n-1} \xrightarrow{d} t_n$ is a time transition, then $\tau(Z_{n-1}) = Z_n$, $\omega_n \in Z_n$, $v \in C_{n-1}$, and $\omega_n \models_v I(q_n)$. Therefore, from Corollary 1 we obtain that there exists C' such that $(Z_n, C_{n-1}) \overset{I(q_n)}{\rightsquigarrow} (Z_n, C')$, $v \in C'$, and conclude the case by placing $C_n = C'$, and the inductive assumption.

If $t_{n-1} \xrightarrow{d} t_n$ is an action transition, then there exists a transition in $\mathcal{A}$ such that for some guard g and reset r we have $q_{n-1} \xrightarrow{d,g,r} q_n$. Notice that as $(\omega_{n-1}, v) \in Z_{n-1} \times C_{n-1}$, $\omega_{n-1} \models_v g$, $\omega_{n-1}[r] = \omega_n$, and $\omega_n \models_v I(q_n)$, from Corollary 1 we have that there exist sets C', C'' satisfying $(Z_{n-1}, C_{n-1}) \overset{g}{\rightsquigarrow} (Z_{n-1}, C')$, $v \in C'$, and $(Z_{n-1}, C') \overset{I(q_n)}{\rightsquigarrow} (Z_n, C'')$. We conclude the case by assuming $C_n = C''$.

Let $\mu = t_0, t_1, \ldots$ be an infinite run in $\mathcal{A}_v$. We have already shown that for each finite prefix $\mu_n = t_0, t_1, \ldots t_n$ we can construct its counterpart $\rho_n = s_0^n, s_1^n, \ldots s_n^n$ in $PREG(\mathcal{A})$, where $s_n^i = (q_i, Z_i, C_i^n)$. Notice that $C_i^n = C_i^{n+1}$, so the infinite sequence $\rho = s_0, s_1, \ldots$, where $s_i = (q_i, Z_i, C_i^i)$ is a valid infinite run in $PREG(\mathcal{A})$ satisfying $(\omega_i, v) \in Z_i \times C_i^i$ for all $i \geq 0$.   □

The following definition formalizes the connection between parametric region graphs and region graphs. In what follows, by a subgraph of $PREG(\mathcal{A}) = \langle S, s_0, \overset{d}{\rightarrow} \rangle$ we mean a tuple $\langle S', s_0, \overset{d}{\rightarrow} \rangle$, where S' is a subset of S with $s_0 \in S'$, and $\overset{d}{\rightarrow}$ is the restriction of $\overset{d}{\rightarrow}$ to S'.

Definition 9. *Let $\mathcal{A}$ be a parametric timed automaton, v be a parameter valuation, and B be a subgraph of $PREG(\mathcal{A})$. By $proj(B, v)$ we define a subgraph of B whose states are tuples (q, Z, C) such that $v \in C$.*

Observe that $proj(PREG(\mathcal{A}), v)$ is in fact isomorphic with the region graph of $\mathcal{A}_v$ by a forgetful functor removing C from the each tuple (q, Z, C).

3   Bounded Model Checking for ECTL$_{-X}$

The central idea of bounded model checking is to unfold the computation tree of a considered model up to some depth, and then perform the analysis of such a finite structure [6]. Such an approach limits us to the verification (and in our case to a parameter synthesis) of existential properties. Bounded model checking seems to be especially effective in searching for counterexamples, i.e., in proving that some undesirable property holds in a model. This allows for a detection of serious design flaws of concurrent and reactive systems.

A non-parametric model checking tool verifies a model (system specification) against a given property (usually in the form of a temporal logic formula), producing the answer of the simple *holds/does not hold* type. Its parametric counterpart is supposed to work slightly differently – having a parametric model we expect the answer in the form of a set of parameter values under which a given property is satisfied. The automated synthesis of a complete set of the desired parameter valuations is not possible in the case of timed automata due to general undecidability of the problem, however obtaining a part of this set still seems to be a worthy goal. Our approach allows for an incremental synthesis of parameters, i.e., if the valuations obtained by analysis of a part of a computation tree are not sufficient, then the tree can be unfolded up to a greater depth for a further analysis. Combined with an expert supervision, the synthesized parameter valuations can give rise to hypotheses specifying the whole space of the desired parameters.

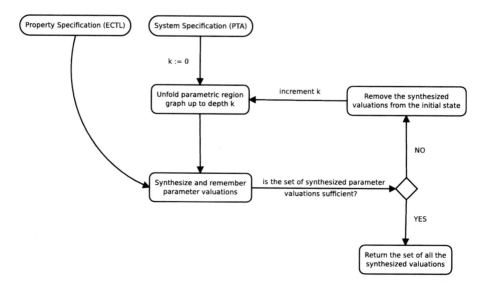

Fig. 2. Parametric Bounded Model Checking schema

We propose the general flow of the property verification/parameter synthesis as shown in Fig. 2.

Bounded model checking is often used in exposing design errors. Let us assume that a property ϕ expresses that a system behaves incorrectly. It should be noted that the set of parameter valuations synthesized for ϕ when dealing with unwindings of the parametric region graph up to the depth k is precisely the set of valuations under which the said unwanted behaviour can be observed in k or less (time / action) steps.

One of the approaches in the current applications of bounded model checking to the verification of system properties is to encode a limited part of the computation tree together with a property in question as a propositional formula [9,19]. The result can be checked using an efficient SAT-solver. In our case, each of the elements of the parametric region graph consists of a state, a region, and constraints on parameters. In [25] the authors show how to perform the verification of the existential fragment of TCTL for timed automata by means of a discretization of the region graph. It seems that this approach can be applied to our case as well, where the constraints on parameters can be encoded using a separate set of propositional variables. The manipulations of these constraints needed to perform the unwinding of the parametric region graph can be limited to a simple check of non-emptiness of their set of solutions (i.e., checking if the node is not dead). In view of [18,21] this can probably be effectively achieved.

3.1   From Parametric Region Graph to Concrete Semantics

The $PREG(\mathcal{A})$ structure is infinite. In order to represent infinite runs in a finite substructure we need a notion of *loop*.

Definition 10. *Let* $\rho_n = s_0, s_1, \ldots s_n$ *be a finite run in* $PREG(\mathcal{A})$, *and* $s_i \xrightarrow{d} s_{i+1}$ *for all* $0 \leq i < n$. *If* $s_n = (q_n, Z_n, C_n)$ *and there exists* $s_i = (q_i, Z_i, C_i)$, *where* $0 \leq i < n$ *such that* $s_n \xrightarrow{d} s_i$ *and* $q_n = q_i$, $Z_n = Z_i$, *then* ρ_n *is called a loop.*

Let $\rho_n = s_0, s_1, \ldots s_n$ be a loop in $PREG(\mathcal{A})$, such that $s_i = (q_i, Z_i, C_i)$, and $(q_n, Z_n) = (q_j, Z_j)$ for some $j < n$. We can create an infinite run $\hat{\rho} = \hat{s_0}, \hat{s_1}, \ldots$ by unwinding the ρ_n loop as follows:

$$\hat{s_i} = \begin{cases} (q_i, Z_i, C_n) & \text{for } i < n \\ (q_{j+(n-i)mod(n-j)}, Z_{j+(n-i)mod(n-j)}, C_n) & \text{for } i \geq n. \end{cases}$$

The idea of the above construction is based on the observation that $C_n \subseteq C_i$ for all $0 \leq i \leq n$ and the fact that the transitions in $PREG(\mathcal{A})$ are defined in terms of g_Z and guards only. Applying Corollary 2 to such an unwinding we obtain the following corollary.

Corollary 3. *Let* $\rho = s_0, s_1, \ldots, s_n$ *be a loop in* $PREG(\mathcal{A})$, *where* $s_i = (q_i, Z_i, C_i)$, *and let* $v \in C_n$ *be a parameter valuation. There exists an infinite run* $\mu_t = t_0, t_1, \ldots$ *in the concrete semantics of* $\mathcal{A}_v$, *where* $t_i = (\hat{q_i}, \omega_i)$, $\omega_i \in Z_i$ *for* $i < n$, $\omega_i \in Z_{j+(n-i)mod(n-j)}$ *for* $i \geq n$, *and:*

$$\hat{q_i} = \begin{cases} q_i & \text{for } i < n \\ q_{j+(n-i)mod(n-j)} & \text{for } i \geq n. \end{cases}$$

3.2   Parametric Bounded Model Checking for ECTL$_{-X}$

The presented method can be applied to the verification of a variety of properties. As the example, in this subsection we present the application of the introduced theory to the verification of the properties specified in the existential part of Computation Tree Logic (CTL$_{-X}$) without the *next* operator [12] – namely ECTL$_{-X}$. Intuitively, CTL$_{-X}$ uses a branching time model, where many possible paths in the future exist. The whole CTL$_{-X}$ contains both the universal ("for all the possible paths") and existential modalities ("there exists a path in the future") while ECTL$_{-X}$ contains only the existential ones – see [19] for more thorough treatment.

Definition 11 (CTL$_{-X}$ and ECTL$_{-X}$ syntax). *Let* $\mathcal{PV}$ *be a set of propositions containing the* true *symbol, and* $p \in \mathcal{PV}$. *The set of well-formed* CTL$_{-X}$ *formulae is given by the following grammar:*

$$\Phi ::= p \mid \neg\Phi \mid \Phi \vee \Phi \mid \Phi \wedge \Phi \mid EG\Phi \mid E\Phi U\Phi.$$

The existential subset of CTL$_{-X}$, *i.e.,* ECTL$_{-X}$ *is defined as the restriction of* CTL$_{-X}$ *such that the negation can be applied to the propositions only.*

Additionally we use the derived modalities: $EF\alpha \overset{def}{=} E(trueU\alpha)$, $AF\alpha \overset{def}{=} \neg EG\neg\alpha$, $AG\alpha \overset{def}{=} \neg EF\neg\alpha$. Each modality of CTL$_{-X}$ has an intuitive meaning. The path quantifier A stands for "on every path" and E means "there exists a path". The modality G stands for "in all the states", F means "in some state", and U has a meaning of "until".

We augment a given parametric timed automaton $\mathcal{A} = \langle Q, q_0, A, X, P, \rightarrow, I \rangle$ with a labelling function $\mathcal{L} : Q \rightarrow 2^{\mathcal{PV}}$. Let us present an interpretation of ECTL$_{-X}$ formulae for a parametric region graph.

Definition 12 (ECTL$_{-X}$ semantics for parametric region graph). *Let $\mathcal{A} = \langle Q, q_0, A, X, P, \rightarrow, I \rangle$ be a parametric timed automaton, $\mathbb{L} : Q \rightarrow 2^{\mathcal{PV}}$ be a labelling function, and B be a subgraph of parametric region graph of $\mathcal{A}$, such that (q_0, Z_0, C_0'), where $C_0' \subseteq C_0$, is a state of B. Let s be a state of B, $p \in \mathcal{PV}$, and α, β be ECTL$_{-X}$ formulae. We treat B as a model for ECTL$_{-X}$ formulae, defining the $\models$ relation as follows.*

1. *$B, (q, Z, C) \models p$ iff $p \in \mathcal{L}(q)$,*
2. *$B, s \models \neg p$ iff $B, s \not\models p$,*
3. *$B, s \models \alpha \vee \beta$ iff $B, s \models \alpha$ or $B, s \models \beta$,*
4. *$B, s \models \alpha \wedge \beta$ iff $B, s \models \alpha$ and $B, s \models \beta$,*
5. *$B, s \models E\alpha U\beta$ iff there exists a run $\rho_n = s_0, s_1, \ldots$, where $s_0 = s$, s_i are states of B for $i \geq 0$, $B, s_j \models \beta$ for some $j \geq 0$, and $B, s_i \models \alpha$ for all $i < j$,*
6. *$B, s \models EG\alpha$ iff there exists a run $\rho_n = s_0, s_1, \ldots$, such that $s_0 = s$, and $B, s_i \models \alpha$ for all $i \geq 0$.*

We abbreviate $B, (q_0, Z_0, C_0) \models \alpha$ as $B \models \alpha$.

The counterpart of the above definition for the timed automaton $\mathcal{A}_v = \langle S, s_0, \xrightarrow{d} \rangle$ obtained from the parametric timed automaton $\mathcal{A}$ under the parameter valuation v is similar – except for that it is defined over the concrete semantics ($s \in S$). Therefore, the only difference is in the first clause which takes the following form:

1. *$\mathcal{A}_v, (q, \omega) \models p$ iff $p \in \mathcal{L}(q)$*

As previously, we abbreviate $\mathcal{A}_v, (q_0, \omega_0) \models \alpha$ as $\mathcal{A}_v \models \alpha$.

In order to apply bounded model checking to the verification of temporal properties in $PREG(\mathcal{A})$ we need to specify the version of the above semantics for finite subgraphs of $PREG(\mathcal{A})$. The only difference concerns the clauses 4 and 5, which take now the following form:

5. *$B, s \models E\alpha U\beta$ iff there exists a finite run $\rho_n = s_0, s_1, \ldots s_n$, where $s_0 = s$, s_i are states of B for $0 \leq i \leq n$, $B, s_j \models \beta$ for some $0 \leq j \leq n$, and $B, s_i \models \beta$ for all $i < j$,*
6. *$B, s \models EG\alpha$ iff there exists a loop $\rho_n = s_0, s_1, \ldots, s_n$, such that $s_0 = s$, and $B, s_i \models \alpha$ for all $0 \leq i \leq n$.*

Recall that the timed automaton $\mathcal{A}_v$ is *strongly non-zeno* (see [24]) iff for each sequence of states $q_1, \ldots, q_n$ such that $q_i \xrightarrow{a_i, g_i, r_i} q_{i+1}$ for all $0 \leq i < n$, and $q_n \xrightarrow{a_n, g_n, r_n} q_1$ (we call such a sequence a *structural loop*) there exists a clock x satisfying the following conditions:

- for some $1 \leq i \leq n$ the x clock is reset in step i (i.e. $x := 0 \in r_i$),
- there exists $1 \leq j \leq n$ such that for any clock valuation ω if $\omega \models_v g_j$, then $\omega(x) \geq 1$.

If an automaton is strongly non-zeno, then in each loop at least one unit of time elapses ([24]). Notice that checking if the automaton is strongly non-zeno does not require any representation of its state space.

Theorem 1. *Let $\mathcal{A}$ be a parametric timed automaton, B be a finite subgraph of $PREG(A)$ containing state (q_0, Z_0, C_0'), where $C_0' \subseteq C_0$, and let $C_{min} = \bigcap \{ C \mid (q, Z, C)$ is a node of $B \}$. If C_{min} is nonempty, and $\mathcal{A}_v$ is strongly non-zeno for each $v \in C_{min}$, then for each formula $\alpha \in \mathrm{ECTL}_{-\mathrm{X}}$ if $B \models \alpha$, then $\mathcal{A}_v \models \alpha$ for all $v \in C_{min}$.*

Proof. Let $v \in C_{min}$ be a parameter valuation. Denote by $\hat{B}$ a (possibly infinite) subgraph of $PREG(\mathcal{A})$ created in two steps:

- firstly, by adding to B the new states created by unwinding each loop along the lines presented above – obtaining B',
- secondly, by replacing all the states (q, Z, C) in B' by (q, Z, C_{min}) – obtaining $\hat{B}$.

It is easy to see that $B \models \alpha$ iff $\hat{B} \models \alpha$. Recall that $proj(\hat{B}, v)$ is isomorphic to some subgraph of the region graph of $\mathcal{A}_v$. As satisfiability of the $\mathrm{ECTL}_{-\mathrm{X}}$ formulae in a subgraph of the region graph implies satisfiability in the region graph, and satisfiability in the region graph is equivalent to satisfiability in the concrete model (see [24], Lemma 7.1) we obtain the thesis of the theorem.   □

If we substitute a single finite run of length k for B, then C_{min} is precisely the set of parameter substitutions under which the run observes the validity of the property in question. Typically, we want to compute such sets of parameter valuations for all the possible runs of a given depth. Therefore, in order to obtain the set of valuations for which the given property holds for the unwindings of the computation tree of depth k, the above theorem needs to be applied separately to each of the finite runs of length k. The sum of all the resulting sets of the constraints is a full characterisation of the sought set of parameter valuations. Notice, however, that in practice it suffices to take sets of parameter valuations synthesized at the end of each run (due to the fact that sets of valuations present in the nodes of a run form a descending chain).

It should be noted that the region graph also preserves the properties expressed in $TCTL$ and $CTL*_{-\mathrm{X}}$ ([24]), therefore the above treatment of $\mathrm{ECTL}_{-\mathrm{X}}$ can be extended to the existential parts of the mentioned logics.

3.3   Example – Four Phase Handshake Protocol

In this section we perform a first step in a parametric analysis of a simplified version of four phase handshake protocol. The protocol is extensively used in practice and widely studied, having both the software and hardware implementations [7,14]. The considered system consists of two communicating entities – the Producer and the Consumer. The Producer creates data packages and sends them to the Consumer. Both the components communicate using two shared boolean variables, that is: **req** (request) governed by the Producer and used to signal the Consumer that the data is prepared and ready to be read, and **ack** (acknowledge) governed by the Consumer and used to signal the Producer that the data has been read successfully and the Consumer is ready. The initial value of both the variables is *false*.

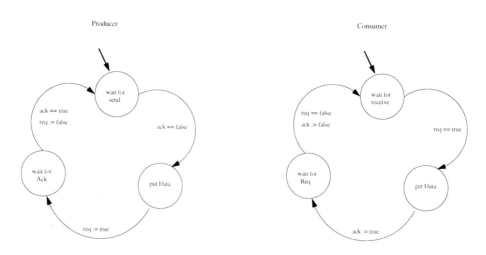

Fig. 3. 4–phase handshake protocol

The running system goes through the following sequence of signals (req, ack):

$$(false, false) \rightarrow (true, false) \rightarrow (true, true) \rightarrow (false, true) \rightarrow (false, false).$$

As we have no tool for an automated analysis at our disposal yet, we analyze the simplified version of the system behaviour. We introduce two parameters, omitting the signal propagation time, namely: $minIO$, and $maxIO$ being, respectively, the lower and the upper bound on read/write time.

The *IdleSender* function guards the time that the Producer is allowed to be idle after putting data into some shared transmission vehicle (e.g. a bus). Let us put $IdleSender() := maxIO - minIO$ and unwind the parametric region graph of Figure 4 (we omit the dummy clock x_0).

Notice that the above graph contains a loop, introduced by the sequence of actions: $\tau, \tau, putData, readData, return$. This loop can be unwinded as presented in Subsection 4.1 into an infinite path in the parametric region graph, and into loops in concrete semantics of non-parametric timed automata with $minIO = 0$, and $maxIO$ instantiated by any value greater than 1.

The graph of Figure 5, treated as a subgraph of the parametric region graph of Figure 4 allows us to observe that in the considered system the property

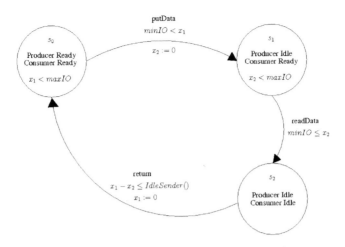

Fig. 4. 4–phase handshake protocol, behaviour diagram

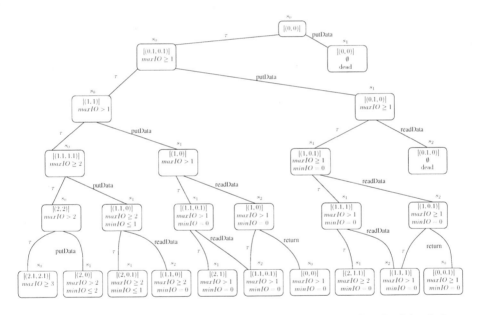

Fig. 5. The 4–phase handshake protocol, Parametric Region Graph of depth 5

$EGEF(ProducerIdle \wedge ConsumerReady)$ holds for $minIO = 0$, and $maxIO > 1$, with the previously mentioned loop as a witness. The intuition behind the considered formula is that the Producer will put data into the transmission infinitely often in the running system.

Of course, this is only the first, hand-made, step of synthesis of the parameter valuations under which the considered property is satisfied. The complete analysis of non-simplified versions with more parameters and components has to wait until we develop the planned tool.

It should be pointed out that the process of synthesis may be either fully- or semi-automatic. In the first case, the user provides together with a model and a property to verify an additional criterion for measurement of quality of the proposed solution. The process of a model unwinding and a constraint synthesis carries until the proposed valuations fall into the accepted range. Note that "exclude trivial solutions" is a valid criterion, if well formulated. In the case of a semi-automatic process, the user is presented with parts of the solutions set until he or she decides that the obtained results are sufficient.

4   Future Work

The theory presented in this paper is to be implemented in the Verics model checker [17]. First, however, several difficulties need to be overcome. Bounded model checking can be performed by means of a translation of the unwinding of a model up to a finite depth (together with the property in question) to the propositional formula, which can then be checked for satisfiability with a SAT-checker. In order to implement our method in this way we should be able to efficiently encode and manipulate linear constraints on parameters as well as states and transitions in a model. We also consider another approach, where Reduced Binary Ordered Decision Diagrams (ROBDD) [8] are used to represent a parametric state-space and the constraints on the parameters.

There is a growing evidence [20,22] of a success of model checking in the verification of safety critical industrial applications. Moreover, the idea of a parameter synthesis for a complex model or protocol seems to be promising in the analysis and the design of real-world systems. Finally, as this method is quite general, we expect that it may be applied to many known temporal, modal, and epistemic logics.

References

1. Ábrahám, E., Herbstritt, M., Becker, B., Steffen, M.: Bounded model checking with parametric data structures. Electr. Notes Theor. Comput. Sci. 174(3), 3–16 (2007)
2. Alur, R., Dill, D.: A theory of timed automata. Theoretical Computer Science 126(2), 183–235 (1994)
3. Alur, R., Henzinger, T., Vardi, M.: Parametric real-time reasoning. In: Proc. of the 25th Ann. Symp. on Theory of Computing (STOC 1993), pp. 592–601. ACM (1993)
4. André, E., Chatain, T., Encrenaz, E., Fribourg, L.: An inverse method for parametric timed automata. International Journal of Foundations of Computer Science 20(5), 819–836 (2009)
5. Annichini, A., Bouajjani, A., Sighireanu, M.: TREX: A Tool for Reachability Analysis of Complex Systems. In: Berry, G., Comon, H., Finkel, A. (eds.) CAV 2001. LNCS, vol. 2102, pp. 368–372. Springer, Heidelberg (2001)
6. Biere, A., Cimatti, A., Clarke, E., Strichman, O., Zhu, Y.: Bounded model checking. Advances in Computers 58, 118–149 (2003)

7. Blunno, I., Cortadella, J., Kondratyev, A., Lavagno, L., Lwin, K., Sotiriou, C.P.: Handshake protocols for de-synchronization. In: Proc. of 10th International Symposium on Advanced Research in Asynchronous Circuits and Systems (ASYNC 2004), pp. 149–158 (2004)
8. Bryant, R.: Graph-based algorithms for boolean function manipulation. IEEE Trans. on Computers 35(8), 677–691 (1986)
9. Clarke, E., Biere, A., Raimi, R., Zhu, Y.: Bounded model checking using satisfiability solving. Formal Methods in System Design 19(1), 7–34 (2001)
10. Dierks, H., Tapken, J.: Moby/DC - A Tool for Model-Checking Parametric Real-Time Specifications. In: Garavel, H., Hatcliff, J. (eds.) TACAS 2003. LNCS, vol. 2619, pp. 271–277. Springer, Heidelberg (2003)
11. Doyen, L.: Robust parametric reachability for timed automata. Inf. Process. Lett. 102, 208–213 (2007)
12. Emerson, E.A., Clarke, E.: Using branching-time temporal logic to synthesize synchronization skeletons. Science of Computer Programming 2(3), 241–266 (1982)
13. Frehse, G., Jha, S.K., Krogh, B.H.: A Counterexample-Guided Approach to Parameter Synthesis for Linear Hybrid Automata. In: Egerstedt, M., Mishra, B. (eds.) HSCC 2008. LNCS, vol. 4981, pp. 187–200. Springer, Heidelberg (2008)
14. Furber, S.B., Day, P.: Four-phase micropipeline latch control circuits. IEEE Trans. Very Large Scale Integr. Syst. 4, 247–253 (1996)
15. Henzinger, T., Ho, P., Wong-Toi, H.: HyTech: A Model Checker for Hybrid Systems. In: Grumberg, O. (ed.) CAV 1997. LNCS, vol. 1254, pp. 460–463. Springer, Heidelberg (1997)
16. Hune, T., Romijn, J., Stoelinga, M., Vaandrager, F.: Linear parametric model checking of timed automata. J. Log. Algebr. Program 52-53, 183–220 (2002)
17. Kacprzak, M., Nabiałek, W., Niewiadomski, A., Penczek, W., Półrola, A., Szreter, M., Woźna, B., Zbrzezny, A.: VerICS 2008 - a model checker for time Petri nets and high-level languages. In: Proc. of Int. Workshop on Petri Nets and Software Engineering (PNSE 2009), pp. 119–132. University of Hamburg (2009)
18. Li, R., Zhou, D., Du, D.: Satisfiability and integer programming as complementary tools. In: Proc. of the 2004 Asia and South Pacific Design Automation Conference, ASP-DAC 2004, pp. 879–882. IEEE Press, Piscataway (2004)
19. Penczek, W., Woźna, B., Zbrzezny, A.: Bounded model checking for the universal fragment of CTL. Fundamenta Informaticae 51(1-2), 135–156 (2002)
20. Spelberg, R.L., De Rooij, R.C.H., Toetenel, W.J.: Application of parametric model checking - the root contention protocol using LPMC. In: Proc. of the 7th ASCI Conference, Beekbergen, The Netherlands, pp. 73–85 (Febuary 2000)
21. Srebrny, M., Stepień, L.: SAT as a programming environment for linear algebra. Fundamenta Informaticae 102, 115–127 (2010)
22. Stoelinga, M.: Fun with firewire: A comparative study of formal verification methods applied to the IEEE 1394 root contention protocol. Formal Asp. Comput. 14(3), 328–337 (2003)
23. Traonouez, L.-M., Lime, D., Roux, O.H.: Parametric Model Checking of Time Petri Nets with Stopwatches using the State-Class Graph. In: Cassez, F., Jard, C. (eds.) FORMATS 2008. LNCS, vol. 5215, pp. 280–294. Springer, Heidelberg (2008)
24. Tripakis, S., Yovine, S.: Analysis of timed systems using time-abstracting bisimulations. Formal Methods in System Design 18(1), 25–68 (2001)
25. Woźna, B., Zbrzezny, A.: Bounded model checking for the existential fragment of TCTL_G and diagonal timed automata. Fundamenta Informaticae 79(1-2), 229–256 (2007)

Synthesis Problem for Petri Nets with Localities

Maciej Koutny and Marta Pietkiewicz-Koutny

School of Computing Science
Newcastle University
Newcastle upon Tyne, NE1 7RU
United Kingdom
{maciej.koutny,marta.koutny}@newcastle.ac.uk

Abstract. There is a growing need to introduce and develop computational models capable of faithfully modelling systems whose behaviour combines synchrony with asynchrony in a variety of complicated ways. Examples of such real-life systems can be found from VLSI hardware to systems of cells within which biochemical reactions happen in synchronised pulses. One way of capturing the resulting intricate behaviours is to use Petri nets with localities partitioning transitions into disjoint groups within which execution is synchronous and maximally concurrent. In this paper, we generalise this type of nets by allowing each transition to belong to several localities. Moreover, we define this extension in a generic way for all classes of nets defined by net-types.

The semantics of nets with overlapping localities can be defined in different ways, and we here discuss four fundamental interpretations, each of which turns out to be an instance of the general model of nets with policies. Thanks to this fact, it is possible to automatically synthesise nets with localities from behavioural specifications given in terms of finite transition systems. We end the paper outlining some initial ideas concerning net synthesis when the association of transitions to localities is not given and has to be determined by the synthesis algorithm.

Keywords: theory of concurrency, Petri net, locality, analysis and synthesis, step sequence semantics, conflict, theory of regions, transition system, step firing policy, net-type.

1 Introduction

In the formal modelling of computational systems there is a growing need to faithfully capture real-life systems exhibiting behaviour which can be described as 'globally asynchronous locally (maximally) synchronous' (GALS). Examples can be found in hardware design, where a VLSI chip may contain multiple clocks responsible for synchronising different subsets of gates [5], and in biologically inspired membrane systems representing cells within which biochemical reactions happen in synchronised pulses [15]. To capture such systems in a formal manner, [8] introduced *Place/Transition-nets with localities* (PTL-nets), where

K. Jensen, S. Donatelli, and J. Kleijn (Eds.): ToPNoC V, LNCS 6900, pp. 160–180, 2012.

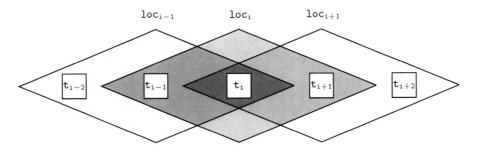

Fig. 1. Transitions with multiple overlapping localities

each locality identifies a distinct set of transitions which must be executed synchronously, i.e., in a maximally concurrent manner (akin to *local maximal concurrency*).

The modelling power of PTL-nets (even after enhancing them with inhibitor and activator arcs in [7]) was constrained by the fact that each transition belonged to a unique locality, and therefore localities were all *non-overlapping*. In this paper, we drop this restriction aiming at a net model which we feel could provide a greater scope for faithful (or direct) modelling features implied by the complex nature of, for example, modern VLSI systems or biological systems. The paper deals with theoretical underpinnings of such an approach.

To explain the basic idea behind nets with *overlapping localities*, let us consider transitions $t_0, t_1, \ldots, t_{n-1}$ arranged in a circular manner, i.e., t_i is adjacent to $t_{(i+n-1) \bmod n}$ and $t_{(i+1) \bmod n}$ which are transitions forming its 'neighbourhood'. Figure 1 shows the overlapping of the localities

$$\mathtt{loc}_{i-1} = \{t_{i-2}, t_{i-1}, t_i\} \quad \mathtt{loc}_i = \{t_{i-1}, t_i, t_{i+1}\} \quad \mathtt{loc}_{i+1} = \{t_i, t_{i+1}, t_{i+2}\}$$

to which a transition t_i belongs (note that in the diagrams localities are depicted as shaded diamonds encompassing the transitions they contain). Each of the transitions belongs to some subsystem which is left unspecified apart from the fact that, in the initial marking, all the t_i's are concurrently enabled.

One can consider at least two different interpretations of the meaning of the localities as in Figure 1 from the point of view of transitions' executability.

1ST INTERPRETATION: *The execution is triggered by the stimulation of localities, and at each stimulated locality one executes as many (enabled) transitions as possible.*

For example, the following would be examples of legal steps:

$\{t_2, t_3, t_4\}$	$\mathtt{loc}_3$ stimulated
$\{t_2, t_3, t_4, t_5, t_8, t_9, t_{10}\}$	$\mathtt{loc}_3$, $\mathtt{loc}_4$ and $\mathtt{loc}_9$ stimulated

and $\{t_3\}$ would be example of an illegal step. According to the first interpretation, a transition can be forced to fire if at least one of its localities has been stimulated. This changes in the second interpretation when this happens only if all of its localities have been stimulated.

2ND INTERPRETATION: *To be executed, transition t_i needs all the localities it belongs to be stimulated.*

For example, the following would be examples of legal steps:

$$\{t_3\} \qquad \qquad loc_2, loc_3 \text{ and } loc_4 \text{ stimulated}$$
$$\{t_0, t_1, \ldots, t_{n-1}\} \qquad loc_0, loc_1, \ldots, loc_{n-1} \text{ stimulated}$$

and $\{t_2, t_4\}$ would be example of an illegal step. The above will be two out of the four fundamental interpretations of nets with overlapping localities which we will introduce and investigate in this paper. It is not our intention in this paper to make a judgement as to which of these four interpretations is more useful or reasonable. Instead, our aim is to investigate and compare their key properties, in particular, those relating to the net synthesis problem.

In this paper, rather than introducing overlapping localities for PT-nets or their standard extensions, we will move straight to the general case of τ-nets [2] which encapsulate a majority of Petri net classes for which the synthesis problem has been investigated and solved. In fact, the task of defining τ-nets with (potentially) overlapping localities is straightforward, as the resulting model of *τ-nets with localities* turns out to be an instance of the general framework of τ-nets with *policies* introduced in [4].

After introducing the new model of nets, we turn our attention to their automatic synthesis from behavioural specifications given in terms of step transition systems. Since τ-nets with localities are an instance of a more general scheme treated in [4], we directly import synthesis results presented there which are based on the regions of a transition system studied in other contexts, in particular, in [1,2,3,6,9,10,13,14,16].

The results in [4] assume that policies are given which, in our case, means that we know exactly the localities associated with all the net transitions. This may be difficult to guarantee in practice, and we end the paper outlining some initial ideas concerning net synthesis when this is not the case.

The paper is organised in the following way. In the next section, in order to make the paper self-contained, we recall the notions and results relating to the general theory of the synthesis of nets with policies. After that, we define four semantic interpretations of nets with overlapping localities, and prove that in each case the resulting model defines nets with policies. We also discuss and compare some basic properties of the new policies, in particular, we formulate a main result concerning the synthesis of nets with overlapping localities. In the last section, we outline some initial ideas concerning the synthesis problem when not only the net, but also the localities need to be constructed. The appendix presents proofs of results omitted from the main body of the paper.

2 Preliminaries

In this section, we recall some basic notions concerning general Petri nets, policies and the synthesis problem as presented in [4].

Abelian Monoids and Multisets. An *abelian monoid* is a set S with a commutative and associative binary (composition) operation $+$ on S, and a neutral element $\mathbf{0}$. The monoid element resulting from composing n copies of $s \in S$ will be denoted by $n \cdot s$, and so $\mathbf{0} = 0 \cdot s$ and $s = 1 \cdot s$. As we will see, weighted arcs between places and transitions in PT-nets can be expressed using the abelian monoid $\mathbb{S}_{PT}$ which is the product $\mathbb{N} \times \mathbb{N}$ with the pointwise arithmetic addition operation and $\mathbf{0} = (0, 0)$.

Steps of Transitions. Potential *steps* of a Petri net with transition set T can be captured by the free abelian monoid $\langle T \rangle$ generated by T. Note that $\langle T \rangle$ can be seen as the set of all the multisets over T; for example, $aaab = \{a, a, a, b\}$. We will use $\alpha, \beta, \gamma, \ldots$ to range over the elements of $\langle T \rangle$. Moreover, for all $t \in T$ and $\alpha \in \langle T \rangle$, we will use $\alpha(t)$ to denote the multiplicity of t in α.

The sum of two multisets, α and β, will be denoted by $\alpha + \beta$, and a singleton multiset $\{t\}$ simply by t. We will then write $t \in \alpha$ whenever $\alpha(t) > 0$, and use $supp(\alpha)$ to denote the set of all $t \in \alpha$. We denote $\alpha \leq \beta$ whenever $\alpha(t) \leq \beta(t)$ for all $t \in T$ (and $\alpha < \beta$ if $\alpha \leq \beta$ and $\alpha \neq \beta$). Whenever $\alpha = \beta + \gamma$, we denote the multiset γ by $\alpha - \beta$. For $X \subseteq \langle T \rangle$, we denote by $\max_{\leq}(X)$ the set of all $\leq$-maximal elements of X.

Transition Systems. A *transition system* over an abelian monoid S is a triple (Q, S, δ) such that Q is a set of *states*, and $\delta : Q \times S \to Q$ a partial *transition function*[1] satisfying $\delta(q, \mathbf{0}) = q$ for all $q \in Q$. An *initialised* transition system $\mathcal{T} \stackrel{\text{df}}{=} (Q, S, \delta, q_0)$ has in addition an *initial* state $q_0 \in Q$ from which every other state is *reachable*. For every state q of a (non-initialised or initialised) transition system TS, $enbld_{TS}(q) \stackrel{\text{df}}{=} \{s \in S \mid \delta(q, s) \text{ is defined}\}$.

Initialised transition systems $\mathcal{T}$ over free abelian monoids — called *step transition systems* — will represent concurrent behaviours of Petri nets. Non-initialised transition systems τ over arbitrary abelian monoids — called *net-types* — will provide ways to define various classes of nets. Throughout the paper, we will assume that:

- T is a <u>fixed</u> finite set (of net transitions);
- $\mathcal{T} = (Q, S, \delta, q_0)$ is a <u>fixed</u> step transition system over $S = \langle T \rangle$.
- $\tau = (\mathbb{Q}, \mathbb{S}, \Delta)$ is a <u>fixed</u> net-type over an abelian monoid $\mathbb{S}$.

Assumption 1. *In this paper, we will assume that τ is sub-step closed which means that, for every state $q \in \mathbb{Q}$, if $\alpha + \beta \in enbld_\tau(q)$ then also $\alpha \in enbld_\tau(q)$.*

The above assumption will imply that sub-steps of *resource enabled steps* (i.e., steps enabled by the standard token game) are also resource enabled which is a condition usually satisfied in practice.

Petri Nets Defined by Net-Types. The net-type $\tau = (\mathbb{Q}, \mathbb{S}, \Delta)$ may be conveniently used as a parameter in the definition of a class of nets, called τ-*nets*. The net-type specifies the values (markings) that can be stored within

---

[1] Transition functions and net transitions are unrelated notions.

net places ($\mathbb{Q}$), the operations and tests (inscriptions on the arcs) that a net transition may perform on these values ($\mathbb{S}$), and the enabling condition and the newly generated values for steps of transitions (Δ).

Definition 1 (τ-net). *A τ-net is a bi-partite graph (P, T, F), where P and T are respectively disjoint sets of places and transitions, and $F : (P \times T) \to \mathbb{S}$ is a (generalised) flow mapping. A* marking *of the τ-net is a map $M : P \to \mathbb{Q}$. A τ-net system $\mathcal{N}$ is a τ-net with an initial marking M_0.*

In what follows, for each place $p \in P$ and step $\alpha \in \langle T \rangle$ we will denote the cumulative flow between α and p by $F(p, \alpha) = \sum_{t \in T} \alpha(t) \cdot F(p, t)$.

Definition 2 (step semantics). *Given a τ-net system $\mathcal{N} = (P, T, F, M_0)$, a step $\alpha \in \langle T \rangle$ is (resource)* enabled *at a marking M if, for every place $p \in P$:*

$$F(p, \alpha) \in enbld_\tau(M(p)) \,.$$

We denote this by $\alpha \in enbld_\mathcal{N}(M)$. The firing *of such a step produces the marking M' such that $M'(p) = \Delta(M(p), F(p, \alpha))$, for every place $p \in P$. We denote the fact that α is enabled at M and its firing leads to M' by $M[\alpha\rangle M'$, and then define the* concurrent reachability graph $CRG(\mathcal{N})$ *of $\mathcal{N}$ as the step transition system formed by firing inductively from M_0 all possible (resource) enabled steps of $\mathcal{N}$.*

Note that a step α is resource enabled at a marking M in a τ-net system if for every place p there is an $F(p, \alpha)$-labelled arc outgoing from the node $M(p)$ in τ, and the firing of such a step leads to the new marking M', where $M'(p)$ is simply the target node of such an arc in τ.

PT-Nets are τ-Nets. A *PT-net* is a triple $N = (P, T, W)$, where P and T are disjoint sets of places and transitions, and $W : (P \times T) \cup (T \times P) \to \mathbb{N}$ specifies directed edges with integer weights. Its markings are mappings $M : P \to \mathbb{N}$, and a *PT-net system* is N together with an initial marking M_0, as illustrated in Figure 2(a). Figure 2(b) shows the concurrent reachability graph of the PT-net system in Figure 2(a).

As we will shortly see, it is possible to render PT-nets as τ-nets. Crucially, one can encode the PT-net system's arc weights, $W(p, t)$ and $W(t, p)$, by setting $F(p, t) = (W(p, t), W(t, p)) \in \mathbb{S}_{PT}$. The resulting change of notation, for the net from Figure 2(a), is represented graphically in Figure 2(c). Notice that, in particular, $F(\mathsf{q}, \mathsf{b}) = (0, 0)$ means that q and b in Figure 2(a) are disconnected. The markings are represented so that the lack of tokens is indicated by *0*, one token by *1*, two tokens by *2*, etc.

To show that a PT-net can indeed be seen as a τ-net, we define a suitable (infinite) net-type, $\tau_{PT} = (\mathbb{N}, \mathbb{S}_{PT}, \Delta_{PT})$ over $\mathbb{S}_{PT}$, a fragment of which is shown in Figure 2(d). In general, for every $n \in \mathbb{N}$ and $(in, out) \in \mathbb{S}_{PT}$, $(in, out) \in enbld_{\tau_{PT}}(n) \Leftrightarrow in \le n$. Moreover, in such a case $\Delta_{PT}(n, (in, out)) = n - in + out$. Then, in order to transform a PT-net into an equivalent τ_{PT}-net, all one needs

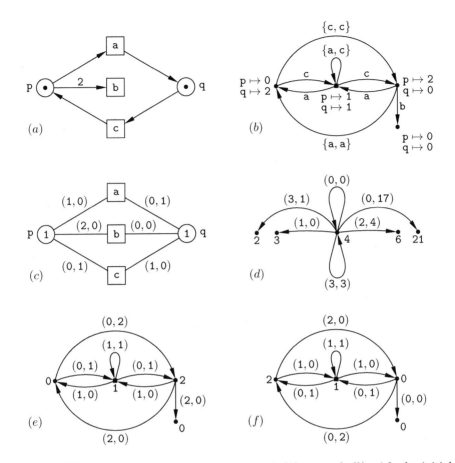

Fig. 2. A PT-net system (a); its concurrent reachability graph (b) with the initial state represented by a small square and the trivial 0-labelled arcs being omitted; and its rendering as a τ_{PT}-net system (c). A fragment of the net-type τ_{PT} is shown in (d). In (e) and (f) we re-trace in (b) the behaviour of places p and q, respectively, in terms of the net-type τ_{PT}.

to do is to insert integers, representing the number of tokens, in each place and set $F(p,t) = (W(p,t), W(t,p))$, for all places p and transitions t, as already mentioned. In other words, $F(p,t) = (in, out)$ means that in is the weight of the arc from p to t, and out the weight of the arc in the opposite direction, see Figure $2(a,c)$.

Although we talked about a single transition t, the graph of τ_{PT} provides equally accurate information about the enabling and firing of a step of transitions α. Indeed, all one needs to do is calculate

$$(in, out) = F(p, \alpha) = (W(p, \alpha), W(\alpha, p)) .$$

For the net in Figure $2(a)$, we obtain $F(\mathsf{p}, \{\mathsf{a},\mathsf{c}\}) = (1,0) + (0,1) = (1,1)$ and $F(\mathsf{q}, \{\mathsf{a},\mathsf{c}\}) = (0,1) + (1,0) = (1,1)$ which, together with $\Delta_{PT}(1, (1,1)) = 1$, means that: (i) the net in Figure 2(a) enables the step $\{a, c\}$ at the initial marking; and (ii) its firing results in the same marking.

Any evolution of a PT-net system can be 're-traced' from the point of view of an individual place. Consider again the PT-net system in Figure 2(a) and its concurrent reachability graph in Figure 2(b). For the latter, let us consider the local markings of the place p as well as the 'connections' which effected the changes of those local markings. We can do this by labelling each state with the corresponding marking of p, and each arc with the cumulative arc weights between p and the step α labelling that arc, i.e., $F(p, \alpha)$. The result is shown in Figure 2(e).

The graph in Figure 2(e) can be 're-discovered' in the graph of the net-type τ_{PT}. This can be achieved by mapping any node labelled n in the former graph to the node n in the latter, and then all the arcs in the former graph are instances of arcs in the latter. We call the graph in Figure 2(e) a τ_{PT}-labelling of the graph in Figure 2(b). Clearly, we may repeat the same procedure for the place q, obtaining another τ_{PT}-labelling depicted in Figure 2(f).

τ-Nets with Policies. Step firing policies are means of controlling and constraining the huge number of execution paths resulting from the highly concurrent nature of many computing systems.

Let $\mathcal{X}_\tau$ be the family of all sets of steps enabled at some reachable marking M of some τ-net $\mathcal{N}$ with the set of transitions T.

Definition 3 (bounded step firing policy). *A bounded step firing policy for τ-nets over $\langle T \rangle$ is given by a control disabled steps mapping* $cds : 2^{\langle T \rangle} \to 2^{\langle T \rangle \setminus \{0\}}$ *such that, for all $X \subseteq \langle T \rangle$, the following hold:*

1. *If X is infinite then $cds(X) = \varnothing$.*
2. *If X is finite then, for every $Y \subseteq X$:*
   (a) $cds(X) \subseteq X$;
   (b) $cds(Y) \subseteq cds(X)$; and
   (c) $X \in \mathcal{X}_\tau$ and $X \setminus cds(X) \subseteq Y$ imply $cds(X) \cap Y \subseteq cds(Y)$.

Intuitively, Definition 3(2.c) captures a kind of monotonicity in control disabling resource enabled steps. If control disabling a step in X is due to the (resource) enabling of some steps included in X, then if these disabling steps are also present in Y, any $\alpha \in Y$ which is control disabled in X will also be control disabled in Y.

Step firing policies constrain the behaviour of nets by blocking some of the resource enabled steps.

Definition 4 (τ-net system with policy). *A τ-net system with policy is a tuple $\mathcal{NP} \stackrel{\mathrm{df}}{=} (P, T, F, M_0, cds)$ such that $\mathcal{N} = (P, T, F, M_0)$ is a τ-net system and cds is a bounded step firing policy for τ-nets over $\langle T \rangle$.*

The notions of marking and execution of enabled steps in $\mathcal{NP}$ are inherited from $\mathcal{N}$. Moreover, the resource enabled and control enabled steps of $\mathcal{NP}$ at a marking M are given, respectively, by:

$$enbld_{\mathcal{NP}}(M) \overset{\text{df}}{=} enbld_{\mathcal{N}}(M)$$
$$Enbld_{\mathcal{NP}}(M) \overset{\text{df}}{=} enbld_{\mathcal{N}}(M) \setminus cds(enbld_{\mathcal{N}}(M)).$$

We will denote by $CRG(\mathcal{NP})$ the step transition system with the initial state M_0 formed by firing inductively from M_0 all possible control enabled steps of $\mathcal{NP}$, and call it the concurrent reachability graph of $\mathcal{NP}$.

Step firing policies can often be defined by pre-orders on step sequences. More precisely a bounded step firing policy given by $cds : 2^{\langle T \rangle} \to 2^{\langle T \rangle \setminus \{\mathbf{0}\}}$ is pre-order based if there is a pre-order $\preceq$ on $\langle T \rangle$ such that, for all finite $X \subseteq \langle T \rangle$,

$$cds(X) = \{\alpha \in X \mid \alpha \neq \varnothing \wedge \exists \beta \in X : \alpha \prec \beta\} .$$

In such a case we denote cds by $cds_{\preceq}$. For example, the maximally concurrent execution semantics of a PT-net can be captured by the bounded step firing policy $cds_{\max}$ such that, for every non-empty set of steps X, $cds_{\max}(X) \overset{\text{df}}{=} \{\alpha \in X \mid \alpha \neq \varnothing \wedge \alpha \notin \max_{\leq}(X)\}$. Such a policy is in fact pre-order based (it suffices to take $\preceq$ to be sub-multiset order $\leq$).

Synthesis of τ-Net Systems with Policies. In this paper, by solving a synthesis problem we mean finding a procedure for building a net of a certain class with a given concurrent reachability graph, as follows.

SYNTHESIS PROBLEM
   Let $\mathcal{T}$ be a given finite step transition system, τ a net-type, and cds a control disabled steps mapping for τ-nets over $\langle T \rangle$. Provide necessary and sufficient conditions for $\mathcal{T}$ to be realised by some τ-net system with policy $\mathcal{NP} = (P, T, F, M_0, cds)$ (i.e., $\mathcal{T} \cong CRG(\mathcal{NP})$ where $\cong$ is transition system isomorphism preserving the initial states and transition labels).

The solution of the synthesis problem we seek is based on the idea of a region of a transition system.

Definition 5 (τ-region). A τ-region of $\mathcal{T}$ is a pair of mappings

$$(\sigma : Q \to \mathbb{Q} , \ \eta : \langle T \rangle \to \mathbb{S})$$

such that η is a morphism of monoids and, for all $q \in Q$ and $\alpha \in enbld_{\mathcal{T}}(q)$:

$$\eta(\alpha) \in enbld_{\tau}(\sigma(q)) \quad and \quad \Delta(\sigma(q), \eta(\alpha)) = \sigma(\delta(q, \alpha)) .$$

For every state q of Q, we denote by $enbld_{\mathcal{T},\tau}(q)$ the set of all steps α such that $\eta(\alpha) \in enbld_{\tau}(\sigma(q))$, for all τ-regions (σ, η) of $\mathcal{T}$.

Intuitively, for PT-net systems, τ_{PT}-regions correspond to the τ_{PT}-labellings of the concurrent reachability graph like those depicted in Figure 2(e, f). We then obtain a general net synthesis result [4].

Theorem 1. $\mathcal{T}$ *can be realised by a τ-net system with a (bounded step firing) policy cds iff the following two regional axioms are satisfied:*

AXIOM I: STATE SEPARATION

For any pair of states $q \neq r$ of $\mathcal{T}$, there is a τ-region (σ, η) of $\mathcal{T}$ such that $\sigma(q) \neq \sigma(r)$.

AXIOM II: FORWARD CLOSURE WITH POLICIES

For every state q of $\mathcal{T}$, $enbld_\mathcal{T}(q) = enbld_{\mathcal{T},\tau}(q) \setminus cds(enbld_{\mathcal{T},\tau}(q))$.   □

A net solution to the synthesis problem is obtained if one can compute a <u>finite</u> set $\mathcal{WR}$ of τ-regions of $\mathcal{T}$ *witnessing* the satisfaction of all instances of AXIOMS I and II [6]. A suitable τ-net system with policy cds, $\mathcal{NP}_{\mathcal{WR}} = (P, T, F, M_0, cds)$, can be then constructed with $P = \mathcal{WR}$ and, for any place $p = (\sigma, \eta)$ in P and every $t \in T$, $F(p,t) = \eta(t)$ and $M_0(p) = \sigma(q_0)$ (recall that q_0 is the initial state of $\mathcal{T}$, and $T \subseteq \langle T \rangle$).

3   Nets with General Localities

We will now introduce a general class of Petri nets with localities, and then introduce four fundamental ways of interpreting the semantics of such nets based on specific kinds of *cds* mappings.

A *locality set* for the transition set T is any finite family $\mathcal{L}$ of non-empty sets of transitions — called *localities* — covering T, i.e., $\bigcup \mathcal{L} = T$. Below we will denote by $\mathcal{L}_t$ the set of all localities to which a given transition t belongs. Moreover, $\mathcal{L}_\alpha \overset{\text{df}}{=} \bigcup_{t \in \alpha} \mathcal{L}_t$ is the set of localities involved in a step α. Note that if we additionally assume that the sets in $\mathcal{L}$ are disjoint, then we obtain the model of transition localities considered in [9,10,11].

Policies Based on Localities. We consider four policy mappings based on localities, $cds_\mathcal{L}^{✠}$, where $✠ \in \{\exists, \forall, \exists \subseteq, \forall \subseteq\}$. Each of these four is a mapping $cds_\mathcal{L}^{✠} : 2^{\langle T \rangle} \to 2^{\langle T \rangle \setminus \{\mathbf{0}\}}$ such that, for every infinite set of steps $X \subseteq \langle T \rangle$, we have $cds_\mathcal{L}^{✠}(X) = \varnothing$, and for every finite set of steps $X \subseteq \langle T \rangle$:

$$cds_\mathcal{L}^{\exists}(X) \overset{\text{df}}{=} \{\alpha \in X \mid \exists v \in \alpha \; \exists \ell oc \in \mathcal{L}_v \; \exists \alpha + t \in X : t \in \ell oc\}$$
$$cds_\mathcal{L}^{\exists \subseteq}(X) \overset{\text{df}}{=} \{\alpha \in X \mid \exists v \in \alpha \; \exists \ell oc \in \mathcal{L}_v \; \exists \alpha + t \in X : t \in \ell oc \wedge \mathcal{L}_t \subseteq \mathcal{L}_\alpha\}$$
$$cds_\mathcal{L}^{\forall}(X) \overset{\text{df}}{=} \{\alpha \in X \mid \exists v \in \alpha \; \forall \ell oc \in \mathcal{L}_v \; \exists \alpha + t \in X : t \in \ell oc\} \tag{1}$$
$$cds_\mathcal{L}^{\forall \subseteq}(X) \overset{\text{df}}{=} \{\alpha \in X \mid \exists v \in \alpha \; \forall \ell oc \in \mathcal{L}_v \; \exists \alpha + t \in X : t \in \ell oc \wedge \mathcal{L}_t \subseteq \mathcal{L}_\alpha\}$$

Consider, for example, a PT-net with two localities, $\mathbf{loc_1} = \{\mathsf{a}, \mathsf{b}\}$ and $\mathbf{loc_2} = \{\mathsf{b}, \mathsf{c}\}$, depicted in Figure 3(a). In its initial marking, the set X of resource enabled steps is:

$$\mathsf{X} = \{\varnothing, \{\mathsf{a}\}, \{\mathsf{b}\}, \{\mathsf{c}\}, \{\mathsf{a}, \mathsf{b}\}, \{\mathsf{a}, \mathsf{c}\}, \{\mathsf{b}, \mathsf{c}\}, \{\mathsf{a}, \mathsf{b}, \mathsf{c}\}\} \; .$$

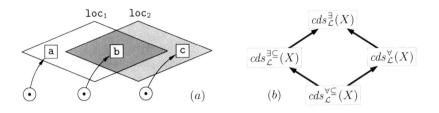

Fig. 3. Comparing different policies based on localities (a), and relationships between different policy mappings (b)

Thus, according to the definitions of the four policy mappings, we have:

$$
\begin{aligned}
cds_{\mathcal{L}}^{\exists}(\mathbf{X}) &= \{\{a\}, \{b\}, \{c\}, \{a,b\}, \{a,c\}, \{b,c\}\} \\
cds_{\mathcal{L}}^{\exists\subseteq}(\mathbf{X}) &= \{\{b\}, \{a,b\}, \{a,c\}, \{b,c\}\} \\
cds_{\mathcal{L}}^{\forall}(\mathbf{X}) &= \{\{a\}, \{b\}, \{c\}, \{a,c\}\} \\
cds_{\mathcal{L}}^{\forall\subseteq}(\mathbf{X}) &= \{\{b\}, \{a,c\}\} \, .
\end{aligned}
\tag{2}
$$

Our main result is that the *cds* mappings we have just introduced give rise to bounded step firing policies.

Theorem 2. $cds_{\mathcal{L}}^{\maltese}$ *is a bounded step firing policy, for each* $\maltese \in \{\exists, \forall, \exists\subseteq, \forall\subseteq\}$.

As to the direct relationships between the policy mappings based on localities, Figure 3(b) shows an inclusion diagram with arrows indicating set inclusions which hold in all cases. No other arrows (i.e., set inclusions) can be added as can be seen by inspecting the PT-net with localities depicted in Figure 3(a) and the sets returned by each of the four policy mappings shown in (2). Hence, in general, the four *cds* mappings induce *different* control policies for nets with localities.

In the papers [9,10,11], localities $\mathcal{L}$ formed a partition of T. In such a case, the four policy mappings collapse to:

$$
cds_{\mathcal{L}}(X) \stackrel{\mathrm{df}}{=} \{\alpha \in X \mid \exists v \in \alpha \; \exists \alpha + t \in X : \; \ell oc_t = \ell oc_v\}
$$

where, for every transition u, ℓoc_u denotes the unique locality belonging to $\mathcal{L}_u$. Thus all four policies introduced in this paper are conservative extensions of that investigated previously.

It is interesting to observe that in the (previously considered) case of non-overlapping localities, $cds_{\mathcal{L}}$ can be defined through a pre-order on steps. This is no longer the case for the general locality mappings. In the proof of Theorem 2 we established that both $cds_{\mathcal{L}}^{\exists}$ and $cds_{\mathcal{L}}^{\exists\subseteq}$ are pre-order based policies. This, however, does not extend to the remaining two mappings, as we show next.

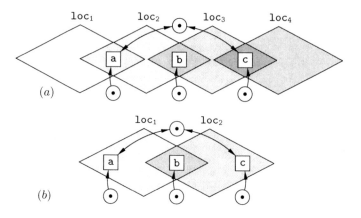

Fig. 4. $cds_{\mathcal{L}}^{\forall}$ and $cds_{\mathcal{L}}^{\forall \subseteq}$ are not pre-order based policies

Proposition 1. $cds_{\mathcal{L}}^{\forall}$ and $cds_{\mathcal{L}}^{\forall \subseteq}$ are not pre-order based policies.

Proof. To show the result in the first case, let us assume that $cds_{\mathcal{L}}^{\forall}$ for the PT-net system with localities in Figure 4(a) can be captured by a suitable pre-order $\preceq$ on steps. In the initial marking M_0, the resource enabled steps are: $\{a\}$, $\{b\}$, $\{c\}$, $\{a, b\}$ and $\{b, c\}$. Since one of them, $\{b\}$, is not control enabled there must be a resource enabled step α such that $\{b\} \preceq \alpha$. As the net is symmetric w.r.t. transitions a and c, we can suppose w.l.o.g. that $\{b\} \preceq \{a, b\}$ or $\{b\} \preceq \{a\}$ holds. We then consider the marking M obtained by firing the control enabled step $\{c\}$, i.e., $M_0[\{c\}\rangle M$. At such a marking, the steps $\{a\}$, $\{b\}$ and $\{a, b\}$ are both resource enabled and control enabled. But this contradicts the assumption that $\{b\} \preceq \{a, b\}$ or $\{b\} \preceq \{a\}$ holds.

The result can also be shown for $cds_{\mathcal{L}}^{\forall \subseteq}$ by taking the PT-net system with localities in Figure 4(b) and applying exactly the same reasoning as above. $\square$

Net Systems with General Localities. For each $✠ \in \{\exists, \forall, \exists \subseteq, \forall \subseteq\}$, we will call a τ-net system with the bounded step firing policy $cds_{\mathcal{L}}^{✠}$ a $\tau_{\mathcal{L}}^{✠}$-net system. Moreover, we will call $\mathcal{T}$ a $\tau_{\mathcal{L}}^{✠}$-transition system if AXIOM I and AXIOM II are satisfied for $\mathcal{T}$ with the policy $cds = cds_{\mathcal{L}}^{✠}$. Below, for $✠ \in \{\exists, \forall, \exists \subseteq, \forall \subseteq\}$, we denote:

$$Enbld_{\mathcal{NP}}^{✠}(M) \stackrel{\text{df}}{=} enbld_{\mathcal{NP}}(M) \setminus cds_{\mathcal{L}}^{✠}(enbld_{\mathcal{NP}}(M)) . \tag{3}$$

The above equation defines the set of control enabled steps at a given marking M of a $\tau_{\mathcal{L}}^{✠}$-net system $\mathcal{NP}$.

For $\tau_{\mathcal{L}}^{\exists}$-net system, the control enabled steps at a given marking are those which cannot be extended within any of their localities any further as resource enabled steps. Looking at the example from Figure 3(a), we can see that this policy is very restrictive, leaving the step $\{a, b, c\}$ as the only non-empty step control enabled at the initial marking. The second policy, defined by the policy mapping $cds_{\mathcal{L}}^{\exists \subseteq}$, is less restrictive. It takes into consideration, when extending a resource enabled step, not only localities of this step, but as well the new ones that might be introduced when the step is extended. This time control enabled steps are not only the steps that are 'maximal' within their existing localities, but as well those which can be extended to other resource enabled steps only at the cost of introducing some new localities. This allows, in the example of Figure 3(a), steps $\{a\}$ and $\{c\}$ to join the set of control enabled steps at the initial marking. Although they both can be extended to resource enabled steps, $\{a, b\}$ and $\{b, c\}$, respectively, the extension has a new locality (loc_2 in the first case, and loc_1 in the second). So, this policy treats steps $\{a\}$ and $\{c\}$ as 'maximal' within the sets of their existing localities.

The third policy, defined by the policy mapping $cds_{\mathcal{L}}^{\vee}$, is looking only at the possibility of extending resource enabled steps within their existing localities (no matter whether the extension brings new localities or not), and this time the requirement for being a control enabled step is less demanding. Any resource enabled step that is already 'maximal' within at least one locality per step's transition is considered control enabled. So, $\{a\}$ and $\{c\}$ are not control enabled under this policy. They can be extended to bigger resource enabled steps, $\{a, b\}$ and $\{b, c\}$, respectively. However, $\{a, b\}$ and $\{b, c\}$, that were excluded by the previous policy, are control enabled under this policy, as the first one is 'maximal' within locality loc_1 (for both a and b) and the second one within locality loc_2 (for both b and c).

The last policy, defined by the policy mapping $cds_{\mathcal{L}}^{\vee\subseteq}$, is the least restrictive and considers a step to be control enabled if it is 'maximal' within at least one locality per step's transition, or if any extension would introduce some new localities. These permissive conditions mean that only $\{b\}$ and $\{a, c\}$ fail to satisfy them as both can be extended to resource enabled steps $\{a, b\}$ or $\{b, c\}$ (in the case of $\{b\}$), and $\{a, b, c\}$ (in the case of $\{a, c\}$) within their existing localities.

Synthesis of Nets with Localities

We obtain an immediate solution of the synthesis problem for all proposed policies based on possibly overlapping localities.

Theorem 3. *For each* $\maltese \in \{\exists, \forall, \exists \subseteq, \forall \subseteq\}$, *a finite step transition system* $\mathcal{T}$ *can be realised by a* $\tau_{\mathcal{L}}^{\maltese}$*-net system iff* $\mathcal{T}$ *is a* $\tau_{\mathcal{L}}^{\maltese}$*-transition system.*

Proof. Follows from Theorems 1 and 2.   □

As to the effective construction of synthesised net, it has been demonstrated in [9,10,11] that this can be easily done for non-overlapping localities in the case of PT-nets and EN-systems with localities (and with or without inhibitor and read arcs). Similar argument can be applied also in the general setting of overlapping localities and τ-nets corresponding to PT-nets and EN-systems with localities. We omit fairly straightforward details.

4 Saturated Localities

In this section, we will look closely at the relationship between control enabled steps and the degree of activation exhibited by different localities involved.

Given a step α which is resource enabled at some marking M of a net with localities $\mathcal{NP}$, a locality $\ell oc \in \mathcal{L}_\alpha$ is *globally saturated* if

$$\alpha + u \notin enbld_{\mathcal{NP}}(M) ,$$

for every transition $u \in \ell oc$. We denote this by $\ell oc \in gsatloc_M(\alpha)$. Similarly, we say that a locality $\ell oc \in \mathcal{L}_\alpha$ is *locally saturated* if

$$\mathcal{L}_u \subseteq \mathcal{L}_\alpha \implies \alpha + u \notin enbld_{\mathcal{NP}}(M) ,$$

for every transition $u \in \ell oc$. We denote this by $\ell oc \in lsatloc_M(\alpha)$. Consider, for example, the net in Figure 4(a) in the initial marking M_0. Then we have:

$$gsatloc_{M_0}(\{\mathsf{a},\mathsf{b}\}) = \{\mathtt{loc}_1, \mathtt{loc}_2, \mathtt{loc}_3\}$$
$$gsatloc_{M_0}(\{\mathsf{a}\}) \quad = \{\mathtt{loc}_1\}$$
$$gsatloc_{M_0}(\{\mathsf{b}\}) \quad = \varnothing .$$

Intuitively, globally saturated localities of a step α are those which have been 'fully active' during the execution of α. They made α control enabled or contributed to its control enabledness. The relationship between control enabledness and global saturation of localities is given by the following result.

Proposition 2. *Let M be a marking of a $\tau_\mathcal{L}^\vee$-net ($\tau_\mathcal{L}^\exists$-net) system $\mathcal{NP}$ such that the set $enbld_{\mathcal{NP}}(M)$ is finite. Then*

(a) $Enbld_{\mathcal{NP}}^\vee(M) = \{\alpha \in enbld_{\mathcal{NP}}(M) \mid supp(\alpha) \subseteq \bigcup gsatloc_M(\alpha)\}$.
(b) $Enbld_{\mathcal{NP}}^\exists(M) = \{\alpha \in enbld_{\mathcal{NP}}(M) \mid \mathcal{L}_\alpha = gsatloc_M(\alpha)\}$.

Locally saturated localities of a step α are the localities that cannot 'contribute' any more transitions to the extension of the step α (as a resource enabled step) without introducing localities that are not present in α. For the net in Figure 4(a), in the initial marking M_0, we have:

$$lsatloc_{M_0}(\{\mathsf{a},\mathsf{b}\}) = \{\mathtt{loc}_1, \mathtt{loc}_2, \mathtt{loc}_3\}$$
$$lsatloc_{M_0}(\{\mathsf{a}\}) \quad = \{\mathtt{loc}_1, \mathtt{loc}_2\}$$
$$lsatloc_{M_0}(\{\mathsf{b}\}) \quad = \{\mathtt{loc}_2, \mathtt{loc}_3\} .$$

The difference between locally saturated localities and globally saturated localities is most visible in the case of 'small' steps. Some of their localities can be locally saturated, but not yet globally saturated (see the steps $\{\mathsf{a}\}$ and $\{\mathsf{b}\}$ considered above).

The relationship between control enabledness and local saturation of localities is clarified by the next result.

Proposition 3. *Let M be a marking of a $\tau_{\mathcal{L}}^{\forall\subseteq}$-net ($\tau_{\mathcal{L}}^{\exists\subseteq}$-net) system $\mathcal{NP}$ such that the set $enbld_{\mathcal{NP}}(M)$ is finite. Then*

(a) $Enbld_{\mathcal{NP}}^{\forall\subseteq}(M) = \{\alpha \in enbld_{\mathcal{NP}}(M) \mid supp(\alpha) \subseteq \bigcup lsatloc_M(\alpha)\}.$
(b) $Enbld_{\mathcal{NP}}^{\exists\subseteq}(M) = \{\alpha \in enbld_{\mathcal{NP}}(M) \mid \mathcal{L}_\alpha = lsatloc_M(\alpha)\}.$

Consider now the net discussed in the introduction together with its initial marking M_0. It can be checked that:

$$
\begin{aligned}
gsatloc_{M_0}(\{t_2, t_3, t_4\}) &= \{loc_3\} \\
gsatloc_{M_0}(\{t_2, t_3, t_4, t_5, t_8, t_9, t_{10}\}) &= \{loc_3, loc_4, loc_9\} \\
gsatloc_{M_0}(\{t_3\}) &= \varnothing \qquad\qquad (*) \\
lsatloc_{M_0}(\{t_3\}) &= \{loc_2, loc_3, loc_4\} \quad (**)\\
lsatloc_{M_0}(\{t_0, t_1, \ldots, t_{n-1}\}) &= \{loc_0, loc_1, \ldots, loc_{n-1}\} \\
lsatloc_{M_0}(\{t_2, t_4\}) &= \{loc_1, loc_2, loc_4, loc_5\}\,.
\end{aligned}
$$

Hence the first interpretation of the overlapping localities in Figure 1 conforms to the rules of $\tau_{\mathcal{L}}^{\forall}$-net systems (but not $\tau_{\mathcal{L}}^{\exists\subseteq}$-net systems, on account of $(**)$), and the second interpretation conforms to the rules of $\tau_{\mathcal{L}}^{\exists\subseteq}$-net systems (but not $\tau_{\mathcal{L}}^{\forall}$-net systems, on account of $(*)$).

5   Towards Synthesis with Unknown Localities

The synthesis result presented in the previous section, Theorem 3, has been obtained assuming that the locality set $\mathcal{L}$ was given. However, localities might be (partially) unknown, and part of the outcome of a successful synthesis procedure would be a suitable or, in the terminology used below, *good* locality set. Clearly, as there are only finitely many different locality sets, the synthesis procedure could simply enumerate them and check each one in turn using Theorem 3. This, however, would be impractical as the number of locality sets is double exponential in the number of transitions. We will now present our initial findings concerning possible reductions of the number of potentially good locality sets. It is worth noting that, in general, for a given τ-net there can be different locality sets yielding the same reachability graph. The example in Figure 5 shows that this holds for all the locality based policies considered in this paper as it is based on disjoint localities.

In what follows, we assume that $\mathcal{T}$ is *finite*. We also assume that we have checked that, for every state q of $\mathcal{T}$, the set of steps $enbld_{\mathcal{T},\tau}(q)$ is finite; otherwise $\mathcal{T}$ could not be isomorphic to the concurrent reachability graph of any τ-net with localities (see AXIOM II and Theorem 3). For a set Y and a finite set of sets $\mathcal{Z} = \{Z_1, \ldots, Z_k\}$ we denote by $Y \sqcap \mathcal{Z}$ the set of all non-empty intersections of Y and the Z_i's, i.e., the set $\{Y \cap Z_i \mid i \le k \wedge Y \cap Z_i \ne \varnothing\}$.

In the rest of this section, for every state q of the step transition system $\mathcal{T}$, and any two locality sets, $\mathcal{L}$ and $\mathcal{L}'$:

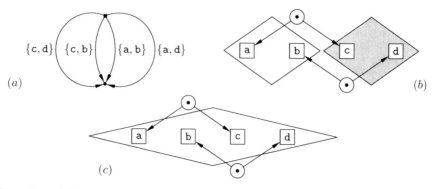

Fig. 5. Two different sets of localities, (b) and (c), for a PT-net system giving rise to the same concurrent reachability graph (a)

- $allSteps_q$ is the set of all steps labelling arcs outgoing from q.
- T_q is the set of all net transitions occurring in the steps of $allSteps_q$.
- $clusters_q^{\mathcal{L}}$ is the set of (locality) *clusters* at q, defined as $T_q \cap \mathcal{L}$.
- $\mathcal{L}$ and $\mathcal{L}'$ are *node-consistent* if $clusters_q^{\mathcal{L}} = clusters_q^{\mathcal{L}'}$, for every state q of the transition system $\mathcal{T}$.

Note that the clusters are all the non-empty projections of the localities onto the transitions fired at an individual state.

A major result concerning locality sets is that they are equally suitable for being good locality sets whenever they induce the same clusters in each node of the step transition system.

Theorem 4. *Let $\mathcal{L}^0$ and $\mathcal{L}^1$ be two node-consistent locality sets. Then $\mathcal{T}$ is $\tau_{\mathcal{L}^0}^{\maltese}$-transition system iff $\mathcal{T}$ is $\tau_{\mathcal{L}^1}^{\maltese}$-transition system, for every $\maltese \in \{\exists, \forall, \exists \subseteq, \forall \subseteq\}$.*

The above theorem implies that a good locality set can be arbitrarily modified to yield another good locality set as long as both are node-consistent (there is no need to re-check the two axioms involved in Theorem 3). This should facilitate searching for an optimal good locality set starting from some initial choice (for example, one might prefer to have as few localities per transition as possible, or as many transitions per locality as possible, or as few localities as possible, etc).

Theorem 4 leads to another important observation, namely that in order to be a good locality set, all that matters are the projections of the localities onto transition sets enabled at the states of the transition system $\mathcal{T}$. As a consequence, the construction of a good locality set can be turned into modular process, in the following way.

First, for each state q and $\maltese \in \{\exists, \forall, \exists \subseteq, \forall \subseteq\}$, we identify possible cluster-sets $ClSets_q^{\maltese}$ of transitions in T_q induced by hypothetical good locality sets. Each such cluster-set $clSet = \{C_1, \ldots, C_k\} \in ClSets_q^{\maltese}$ is a cover of T_q and:

$$enbld_{\mathcal{T}}^{\maltese}(q) = enbld_{\mathcal{T},\tau}(q) \setminus cds_{clSet}^{\maltese}(enbld_{\mathcal{T},\tau}(q))$$

where we have the following (below $clSet_t \stackrel{\text{df}}{=} \{C_i \in clSet \mid t \in C_i\}$ and $clSet_\alpha \stackrel{\text{df}}{=} \{C_i \in clSet \mid \exists t \in \alpha : t \in C_i\}$):

$$cds^{\exists}_{clSet}(X) \stackrel{\text{df}}{=} \{\alpha \in X \mid \exists C_i \in clSet_\alpha \; \exists \alpha + t \in X : t \in C_i\}$$
$$cds^{\exists\subseteq}_{clSet}(X) \stackrel{\text{df}}{=} \{\alpha \in X \mid \exists C_i \in clSet_\alpha \; \exists \alpha + t \in X : t \in C_i \wedge clSet_t \subseteq clSet_\alpha\}$$
$$cds^{\forall}_{clSet}(X) \stackrel{\text{df}}{=} \{\alpha \in X \mid \exists v \in \alpha \; \forall C_i \in clSet_v \; \exists \alpha + t \in X : t \in C_i\}$$
$$cds^{\forall\subseteq}_{clSet}(X) \stackrel{\text{df}}{=} \{\alpha \in X \mid \exists v \in \alpha \; \forall C_i \in clSet_v \; \exists \alpha + t \in X : t \in C_i \wedge clSet_t \subseteq clSet_\alpha\}.$$

We can then select different cluster-sets (one per each state of the step transition system) and check whether combining them together yields a good locality set. Such a procedure was used in [11] to construct 'canonical' locality sets for the case of non-overlapping localities (and the combining of cluster-sets was based on the operation of transitive closure). This effort can be reduced by observing that some cluster-sets cannot be combined to yield a good locality set. A simple check is provided by the following result.

Proposition 4. *Let q and q' be two states of the transition system $\mathcal{T}$ and $\maltese \in \{\exists, \forall, \exists\subseteq, \forall\subseteq\}$. Moreover, let $clSet \in ClSets^{\maltese}_q$ and $clSet' \in ClSets^{\maltese}_{q'}$ be cluster-sets such that $T_q \cap clSet' \neq T_{q'} \cap clSet$. Then there is no locality set $\mathcal{L}$ which is good w.r.t. $\maltese$ as well as satisfying $T_q \cap \mathcal{L} = clSet$ and $T_{q'} \cap \mathcal{L} = clSet'$.*

It is, in general, difficult to estimate how many combinations of cluster-sets one needs to consider or how many of these yield good locality sets. One can, however, obtain important insights if one looks for solutions in a specific class of nets, or if the locality set is partially known or constrained (for example, if two specific transitions cannot share a locality).

6 Concluding Remarks

In this paper, we introduced four different semantics of nets based on transition localities. In the future research, we plan to work on an efficient synthesis procedure of PT-nets with localities with unknown locality sets. The problem has been investigated in [11] for non-overlapping localities, and some initial results have been obtained in [12] for the case of $cds^{\forall}_{\mathcal{L}}$.

Acknowledgement. We would like to thank Piotr Chrzastowski-Wachtel for his suggestion to investigate nets with overlapping localities. We are indebted to the reviewers of both [12] and this paper for their detailed and helpful comments; in particular, for a suggestion which has led to the introduction of two policies, $cds^{\exists}_{\mathcal{L}}$ and $cds^{\exists\subseteq}_{\mathcal{L}}$, as well as identifying mistakes in the treatment of some of the results. This research was supported by EPSRC VERDAD project, and NSFC Grants 60910004 and 2010CB328102.

References

1. Badouel, E., Bernardinello, L., Darondeau, P.: The Synthesis Problem for Elementary Net Systems is NP-complete. Theoretical Computer Science 186, 107–134 (1997)
2. Badouel, E., Darondeau, P.: Theory of Regions. In: Reisig, W., Rozenberg, G. (eds.) APN 1998. LNCS, vol. 1491, pp. 529–586. Springer, Heidelberg (1998)
3. Bernardinello, L.: Synthesis of Net Systems. In: Marsan, M.A. (ed.) ICATPN 1993. LNCS, vol. 691, pp. 89–105. Springer, Heidelberg (1993)
4. Darondeau, P., Koutny, M., Pietkiewicz-Koutny, M., Yakovlev, A.: Synthesis of Nets with Step Firing Policies. Fundamenta Informaticae 94, 275–303 (2009)
5. Dasgupta, S., Potop-Butucaru, D., Caillaud, B., Yakovlev, A.: Moving from Weakly Endochronous Systems to Delay-Insensitive Circuits. Electronic Notes in Theoretical Computer Science 146, 81–103 (2006)
6. Desel, J., Reisig, W.: The Synthesis Problem of Petri Nets. Acta Informatica 33, 297–315 (1996)
7. Kleijn, J., Koutny, M.: Processes of Membrane systems with Promoters and Inhibitors. Theoretical Computer Science 404, 112–126 (2008)
8. Kleijn, H.C.M., Koutny, M., Rozenberg, G.: Towards a Petri Net Semantics for Membrane Systems. In: Freund, R., Paun, G., Rozenberg, G., Salomaa, A. (eds.) WMC 2005. LNCS, vol. 3850, pp. 292–309. Springer, Heidelberg (2006)
9. Koutny, M., Pietkiewicz-Koutny, M.: Transition Systems of Elementary Net Systems with Localities. In: Baier, C., Hermanns, H. (eds.) CONCUR 2006. LNCS, vol. 4137, pp. 173–187. Springer, Heidelberg (2006)
10. Koutny, M., Pietkiewicz-Koutny, M.: Synthesis of Elementary Net Systems with Context Arcs and Localities. Fundamenta Informaticae 88, 307–328 (2008)
11. Koutny, M., Pietkiewicz-Koutny, M.: Synthesis of Petri Nets with Localities. Scientific Annals of Computer Science 19, 1–23 (2009)
12. Koutny, M., Pietkiewicz-Koutny, M.: Synthesis of General Petri Nets with Localities. In: Desel, J., Yakovlev, A. (eds.) Application of Region Theory (ART), pp. 15–28. IEEE (2010)
13. Mukund, M.: Petri Nets and Step Transition Systems. International Journal of Foundations of Computer Science 3, 443–478 (1992)
14. Nielsen, M., Rozenberg, G., Thiagarajan, P.S.: Elementary transition systems. Theoretical Compututer Science 96, 3–33 (1992)
15. Păun, G.: Membrane Computing, An Introduction. Springer, Heidelberg (2002)
16. Pietkiewicz-Koutny, M.: The Synthesis Problem for Elementary Net Systems with Inhibitor Arcs. Fundamenta Informaticae 40, 251–283 (1999)

Appendix

Proof of Theorem 2

We first show that $cds_{\mathcal{L}}^{\exists}$ is a pre-order based bounded step firing policy.

In what follows, we denote $\gamma <^1 \gamma'$ if there is a transition t such that $\gamma' = \gamma + t$. For all steps α and β, we define $\alpha \preceq_{\mathcal{L}}^{\exists} \beta$ if $\alpha = \beta$ or if $\alpha < \beta$ and there are steps $\alpha = \alpha_1 <^1 \ldots <^1 \alpha_k = \beta$ such that, for all $1 \le i < k$, $\mathcal{L}_{\alpha_i} \cap \mathcal{L}_{\alpha_{i+1}-\alpha_i} \ne \varnothing$. Clearly, $\preceq_{\mathcal{L}}^{\exists}$ is both transitive and reflexive, and so it is a pre-order.

We therefore have, for every finite set of steps X:

$$cds_{\preceq_{\mathcal{L}}^{\exists}}(X) = \{\alpha \in X \mid \alpha \ne \varnothing \wedge \exists \beta \in X : \alpha \prec_{\mathcal{L}}^{\exists} \beta\}$$
$$= \{\alpha \in X \mid \alpha \ne \varnothing \wedge \exists \beta \in X : \alpha < \beta \wedge \exists \alpha = \alpha_1 <^1 \ldots <^1 \alpha_k = \beta$$
$$\forall 1 \le i < k : \mathcal{L}_{\alpha_i} \cap \mathcal{L}_{\alpha_{i+1}-\alpha_i} \ne \varnothing\} \, .$$

What we need to show is that:

$$\alpha \in cds_{\preceq_{\mathcal{L}}^{\exists}}(X) \Longleftrightarrow \alpha \in \{\alpha \in X \mid \exists v \in \alpha \, \exists loc \in \mathcal{L}_v \, \exists \alpha + t \in X : t \in loc\} \, .$$

($\Longleftarrow$) Suppose that $v \in \alpha$, $loc \in \mathcal{L}_v$ and $\alpha + t \in X$ are such that $t \in loc$. Since $v \in \alpha$, we have $\alpha \ne \varnothing$. We can take $\alpha_1 = \alpha$ and $\alpha_2 = \beta = \alpha + t \in X$. Then $\mathcal{L}_\alpha \cap \mathcal{L}_{\beta-\alpha} \ne \varnothing$ because $\beta - \alpha = t$ and $t \in loc$ and $loc \in \mathcal{L}_\alpha$ (as $v \in \alpha$ and $loc \in \mathcal{L}_v$).

($\Longrightarrow$) Suppose that $\alpha, \beta \in X$ and $\alpha = \alpha_1 <^1 \ldots <^1 \alpha_k = \beta$ are such that $\mathcal{L}_{\alpha_i} \cap \mathcal{L}_{\alpha_{i+1}-\alpha_i} \ne \varnothing$, for $1 \le i < k$. Hence there is t such that $\alpha_2 = \alpha_1 + t$ and $\mathcal{L}_{\alpha_1} \cap \mathcal{L}_{\alpha_2-\alpha_1} \ne \varnothing$. This means that there is $v \in \alpha$ ($\alpha \ne \varnothing$)such that $\mathcal{L}_v \cap \mathcal{L}_t \ne \varnothing$. So, there are $v \in \alpha$ and $loc \in \mathcal{L}_v$ such that $t \in loc$. All we still need to show is that $\alpha + t \in X$ which follows from $\alpha + t \le \beta \in X$ and Assumption 1.

Next, we show that $cds_{\mathcal{L}}^{\exists \subseteq}$ is also a pre-order based bounded step firing policy. For all steps α and β, we define $\alpha \preceq_{\mathcal{L}}^{\exists \subseteq} \beta$ if $\alpha \preceq_{\mathcal{L}}^{\exists} \beta$ and $\mathcal{L}_\alpha = \mathcal{L}_\beta$. Clearly, $\preceq_{\mathcal{L}}^{\exists \subseteq}$ is both transitive and reflexive as $\preceq_{\mathcal{L}}^{\exists}$ is.

We therefore have, for every finite set of steps X:

$$cds_{\preceq_{\mathcal{L}}^{\exists \subseteq}}(X) = \{\alpha \in X \mid \alpha \ne \varnothing \wedge \exists \beta \in X : \alpha \prec_{\mathcal{L}}^{\exists \subseteq} \beta\}$$
$$= \{\alpha \in X \mid \alpha \ne \varnothing \wedge \exists \beta \in X : \alpha \prec_{\mathcal{L}}^{\exists} \beta \wedge \mathcal{L}_\alpha = \mathcal{L}_\beta\} \, .$$

We need to show that:

$$\alpha \in cds_{\preceq_{\mathcal{L}}^{\exists \subseteq}}(X) \Longleftrightarrow$$
$$\alpha \in \{\alpha \in X \mid \exists v \in \alpha \, \exists loc \in \mathcal{L}_v \, \exists \alpha + t \in X : t \in loc \wedge \mathcal{L}_t \subseteq \mathcal{L}_\alpha\} \, .$$

The proof is similar to that for $\preceq_{\mathcal{L}}^{\exists}$.

To show that $cds_{\mathcal{L}}^{\forall}$ is a bounded step firing policy, we need to prove that if $X \in \mathcal{X}_\tau$ is finite and $Y \subseteq X$ and $X \setminus cds_{\mathcal{L}}^{\forall}(X) \subseteq Y$ and $\alpha \in cds_{\mathcal{L}}^{\forall}(X) \cap Y$, then $\alpha \in cds_{\mathcal{L}}^{\forall}(Y)$. Before proceeding with the proof, we note that in the proofs of the key Theorems 4.1 and 4.3 of [4] from which Theorem 1 in this paper is derived, the set Y appearing in Definition 3(2) is always taken to be of the form $enbld_{T,\tau}(q)$. Hence, due to Assumption 1, we can assume in Definition 3(2) that Y is sub-step closed.

We first observe that $\max_{\leq}(X) \cap cds_{\mathcal{L}}^{\forall}(X) = \varnothing$ and so we have $\max_{\leq}(X) \subseteq X \setminus cds_{\mathcal{L}}^{\forall}(X) \subseteq Y$. Then we observe that since X is finite and $\alpha \in cds_{\mathcal{L}}^{\forall}(X)$, there is a transition $v \in \alpha$ such that for all $\ell oc \in \mathcal{L}_v$ there exists $\alpha + \beta \in \max_{\leq}(X) \subseteq Y$ with $\ell oc \in \mathcal{L}_\beta$. Since, as we explained above, the set Y may be assumed to be sub-step closed, there exists $t \in \beta$ such that $\alpha + t \in Y$ and $\ell oc \in \mathcal{L}_t$ ($t \in \ell oc$). This and the fact that Y is finite (as $Y \subseteq X$) means that we have $\alpha \in cds_{\mathcal{L}}^{\forall}(Y)$.

Finally, we show that $cds_{\mathcal{L}}^{\forall \subseteq}$ is also a bounded step firing policy. We need to show that if $X \in X_\tau$ is finite and $Y \subseteq X$ and $X \setminus cds_{\mathcal{L}}^{\forall \subseteq} \subseteq Y$ and $\alpha \in cds_{\mathcal{L}}^{\forall \subseteq}(X) \cap Y$, then $\alpha \in cds_{\mathcal{L}}^{\forall \subseteq}(Y)$.

We first observe that $\max_{<}(X) \cap cds_{\mathcal{L}}^{\forall \subseteq}(X) = \varnothing$ and so we have $\max_{<}(X) \subseteq X \setminus cds_{\mathcal{L}}^{\forall \subseteq}(X) \subseteq Y$. Then we observe that since X is finite and $\alpha \in cds_{\mathcal{L}}^{\forall \subseteq}(X)$, there is a transition $v \in \alpha$ such that, for all $\ell oc \in \mathcal{L}_v$, there exists $\alpha + t \leq \alpha + \beta \in \max_{<}(X) \subseteq Y$ with $\ell oc \in \mathcal{L}_t$ and $\mathcal{L}_t \subseteq \mathcal{L}_\alpha$. This and the fact that Y is finite (as $Y \subseteq X$) means that we have $\alpha \in cds_{\mathcal{L}}^{\forall \subseteq}(Y)$.

Proof of Proposition 2

To show (a) we observe that the following holds.

$\alpha \in \{\alpha \in enbld_{\mathcal{NP}}(M) \mid supp(\alpha) \subseteq \bigcup gsatloc_M(\alpha)\}$ $\Leftrightarrow$

$\alpha \in enbld_{\mathcal{NP}}(M) \wedge \forall v \in \alpha \; \exists \ell oc \in gsatloc_M(\alpha) : v \in \ell oc$ $\Leftrightarrow$

$\alpha \in enbld_{\mathcal{NP}}(M) \wedge \forall v \in \alpha \; \exists \ell oc \in gsatloc_M(\alpha) : \ell oc \in \mathcal{L}_v$ $\Leftrightarrow$

$\alpha \in enbld_{\mathcal{NP}}(M) \wedge \forall v \in \alpha \; \exists \ell oc \in \mathcal{L}_v : \ell oc \in gsatloc_M(\alpha)$ $\Leftrightarrow$ (def. $gsatloc_M(\alpha)$)

$\alpha \in enbld_{\mathcal{NP}}(M) \wedge \forall v \in \alpha \; \exists \ell oc \in \mathcal{L}_v \forall t \in \ell oc : \alpha + t \notin enbld_{\mathcal{NP}}(M)$ $\Leftrightarrow$

$\alpha \in enbld_{\mathcal{NP}}(M) \wedge \forall v \in \alpha \; \exists \ell oc \in \mathcal{L}_v \forall \alpha + t \in enbld_{\mathcal{NP}}(M) :$
$\qquad\qquad\qquad\qquad\qquad\qquad t \notin \ell oc$ $\Leftrightarrow$ (by (1) and (3))

$\alpha \in Enbld_{\mathcal{NP}}^{\forall}(M)$.

Then, to show (b), we proceed as follows.

$\alpha \in \{\alpha \in enbld_{\mathcal{NP}}(M) \mid \mathcal{L}_\alpha = gsatloc_M(\alpha)\}$ $\Leftrightarrow$

$\alpha \in enbld_{\mathcal{NP}}(M) \wedge \forall \ell oc \in \mathcal{L}_\alpha \; \forall t \in \ell oc : \alpha + t \notin enbld_{\mathcal{NP}}(M)$ $\Leftrightarrow$

$\alpha \in enbld_{\mathcal{NP}}(M) \wedge \forall \ell oc \in \mathcal{L}_\alpha \; \forall \alpha + t \in enbld_{\mathcal{NP}}(M) : t \notin \ell oc \Leftrightarrow$ (by (1) and (3))

$\alpha \in Enbld_{\mathcal{NP}}^{\exists}(M)$.

Proof of Proposition 3

To show (a) we observe that the following holds.

$$\alpha \in \{\alpha \in enbld_{\mathcal{NP}}(M) \mid supp(\alpha) \subseteq \bigcup lsatloc_M(\alpha)\} \qquad \Leftrightarrow$$

$$\alpha \in enbld_{\mathcal{NP}}(M) \wedge \forall v \in \alpha\; \exists loc \in lsatloc_M(\alpha) : v \in \ell oc \qquad \Leftrightarrow$$

$$\alpha \in enbld_{\mathcal{NP}}(M) \wedge \forall v \in \alpha\; \exists loc \in lsatloc_M(\alpha) : \ell oc \in \mathcal{L}_v \qquad \Leftrightarrow$$

$$\alpha \in enbld_{\mathcal{NP}}(M) \wedge \forall v \in \alpha\; \exists loc \in \mathcal{L}_v : \ell oc \in lsatloc_M(\alpha) \quad \Leftrightarrow \; (\text{def. } lsatloc_M(\alpha))$$

$$\alpha \in enbld_{\mathcal{NP}}(M) \wedge \forall v \in \alpha\; \exists loc \in \mathcal{L}_v \forall t \in \ell oc :$$
$$\mathcal{L}_t \subseteq \mathcal{L}_\alpha \Rightarrow \alpha + t \notin enbld_{\mathcal{NP}}(M) \qquad \Leftrightarrow$$

$$\alpha \in enbld_{\mathcal{NP}}(M) \wedge \forall v \in \alpha\; \exists loc \in \mathcal{L}_v \forall t \in \ell oc :$$
$$\neg(\mathcal{L}_t \subseteq \mathcal{L}_\alpha \wedge \alpha + t \in enbld_{\mathcal{NP}}(M)) \qquad \Leftrightarrow$$

$$\alpha \in enbld_{\mathcal{NP}}(M) \wedge \forall v \in \alpha\; \exists loc \in \mathcal{L}_v \forall t \in \ell oc :$$
$$\mathcal{L}_t \setminus \mathcal{L}_\alpha \neq \varnothing \vee \alpha + t \notin enbld_{\mathcal{NP}}(M) \qquad \Leftrightarrow$$

$$\alpha \in enbld_{\mathcal{NP}}(M) \wedge \forall v \in \alpha\; \exists loc \in \mathcal{L}_v \forall t :$$
$$t \in \ell oc \Rightarrow (\mathcal{L}_t \setminus \mathcal{L}_\alpha \neq \varnothing \vee \alpha + t \notin enbld_{\mathcal{NP}}(M)) \Leftrightarrow$$

$$\alpha \in enbld_{\mathcal{NP}}(M) \wedge \forall v \in \alpha\; \exists loc \in \mathcal{L}_v \forall t :$$
$$t \notin \ell oc \vee \mathcal{L}_t \setminus \mathcal{L}_\alpha \neq \varnothing \vee \alpha + t \notin enbld_{\mathcal{NP}}(M) \qquad \Leftrightarrow$$

$$\alpha \in enbld_{\mathcal{NP}}(M) \wedge \forall v \in \alpha\; \exists loc \in \mathcal{L}_v \forall t :$$
$$\alpha + t \in enbld_{\mathcal{NP}}(M) \Rightarrow (t \notin \ell oc \vee \mathcal{L}_t \setminus \mathcal{L}_\alpha \neq \varnothing) \Leftrightarrow$$

$$\alpha \in enbld_{\mathcal{NP}}(M) \wedge \forall v \in \alpha\; \exists loc \in \mathcal{L}_v \forall \alpha + t \in enbld_{\mathcal{NP}}(M) :$$
$$t \notin \ell oc \vee \mathcal{L}_t \setminus \mathcal{L}_\alpha \neq \varnothing \qquad \Leftrightarrow \; (\text{by (1) and (3)})$$

$$\alpha \in Enbld_{\mathcal{NP}}^{\forall\subseteq}(M) .$$

Then, to show (b), we proceed as follows.

$$\alpha \in \{\alpha \in enbld_{\mathcal{NP}}(M) \mid \mathcal{L}_\alpha = lsatloc_M(\alpha)\} \qquad \Leftrightarrow$$

$$\alpha \in enbld_{\mathcal{NP}}(M) \wedge \forall loc \in \mathcal{L}_\alpha\; \forall t \in \ell oc : \mathcal{L}_t \subseteq \mathcal{L}_\alpha \Rightarrow \alpha + t \notin enbld_{\mathcal{NP}}(M) \Leftrightarrow$$

$$\alpha \in enbld_{\mathcal{NP}}(M) \wedge \forall loc \in \mathcal{L}_\alpha\; \forall \alpha + t \in enbld_{\mathcal{NP}}(M) :$$
$$t \notin \ell oc \vee \mathcal{L}_t \nsubseteq \mathcal{L}_\alpha \quad \Leftrightarrow \; (\text{by (1) and (3)})$$

$$\alpha \in Enbld_{\mathcal{NP}}^{\exists\subseteq}(M) .$$

Proof of Theorem 4

Suppose that $\mathcal{T}$ is $\tau_{\mathcal{L}^0}^{\maltese}$-transition system. First we notice that AXIOM I does not depend on the locality set. For AXIOM II and $\mathcal{L}^1$ it suffices to show that, for each state q of $\mathcal{T}$:

$$cds_{\mathcal{L}^0}^{\maltese}(enbld_{\mathcal{T},\tau}(q)) = cds_{\mathcal{L}^1}^{\maltese}(enbld_{\mathcal{T},\tau}(q)) . \qquad (4)$$

We observe that since the maximal steps in $enbld_{\mathcal{T},\tau}(q)$ never belong to the set $cds_{\mathcal{L}^0}^{\maltese}(enbld_{\mathcal{T},\tau}(q))$ and AXIOM II holds for $\mathcal{L}^0$ we have:

$$\forall \alpha \in enbld_{\mathcal{T},\tau}(q)\; \forall u \in \alpha : u \in T_q . \qquad (5)$$

We now take $i \in \{0,1\}$ and consider four cases.

Case 1: $\alpha \in cds_{\mathcal{L}^i}^{\exists\subseteq}(enbld_{\mathcal{T},\tau}(q))$. Then $\alpha \in enbld_{\mathcal{T},\tau}(q)$ and there are $v \in \alpha$, $\ell oc \in \mathcal{L}_v^i$ and $\alpha + t \in enbld_{\mathcal{T},\tau}(q)$ such that $t \in \ell oc$ and $\mathcal{L}_t^i \subseteq \mathcal{L}_\alpha^i$. Hence, by (5), we have that $v, t \in T_q$ and $v, t \in C \in clusters_q^{\mathcal{L}^i}$, where $C = T_q \cap \ell oc$. By the node-consistency of $\mathcal{L}^i$ and $\mathcal{L}^{1-i}$ we obtain that there is $\ell oc' \in \mathcal{L}^{1-i}$ such that $C = T_q \cap \ell oc'$. Hence $\ell oc' \in \mathcal{L}_v^{1-i}$ and $t \in \ell oc'$.

Now suppose that $\mathcal{L}_t^{1-i} \not\subseteq \mathcal{L}_\alpha^{1-i}$, and so there is $\ell oc'' \in \mathcal{L}_t^{1-i} \setminus \mathcal{L}_\alpha^{1-i}$. Then, there exists $C' \in clusters_q^{\mathcal{L}^{1-i}}$, where $C' = T_q \cap \ell oc''$. By the node-consistency of $\mathcal{L}^i$ and $\mathcal{L}^{1-i}$ there is $\ell oc''' \in \mathcal{L}^i$ such that $T_q \cap \ell oc''' = C'$. So $\ell oc''' \in \mathcal{L}_t^i$. Since, by (5), all $u \in \alpha$ are such that $u \in T_q$, and $\ell oc'' \notin \mathcal{L}_\alpha^{1-i}$, we have $\ell oc''' \notin \mathcal{L}_\alpha^i$. Hence $\ell oc''' \in \mathcal{L}_t^i \setminus \mathcal{L}_\alpha^i$, producing a contradiction with $\mathcal{L}_t^i \subseteq \mathcal{L}_\alpha^i$.

As a result, $\alpha \in cds_{\mathcal{L}^{1-i}}^{\exists\subseteq}(enbld_{\mathcal{T},\tau}(q))$.

Case 2: $\alpha \in cds_{\mathcal{L}^i}^{\exists}(enbld_{\mathcal{T},\tau}(q))$. We proceed as in Case 1, ignoring the parts concerned with $\mathcal{L}_t^i \subseteq \mathcal{L}_\alpha^i$ and $\mathcal{L}_t^i \subseteq \mathcal{L}_\alpha^{1-i}$.

Case 3: $\alpha \in cds_{\mathcal{L}^i}^{\forall\subseteq}(enbld_{\mathcal{T},\tau}(q))$. Then $\alpha \in enbld_{\mathcal{T},\tau}(q)$ and there is $v \in \alpha$ such that for all $\ell oc \in \mathcal{L}_v^i$ there is $\alpha + t \in enbld_{\mathcal{T},\tau}(q)$ satisfying $t \in \ell oc$ and $\mathcal{L}_t^i \subseteq \mathcal{L}_\alpha^i$.

Let us now consider any $\ell oc' \in \mathcal{L}_v^{1-i}$ and take $C = T_q \cap \ell oc'$. By (5), we have $v \in C$ and so, by the node-consistency of $\mathcal{L}^i$ and $\mathcal{L}^{1-i}$, there is $\ell oc \in \mathcal{L}_v^i$ with $C = T_q \cap \ell oc$. We know that there is $\alpha + t \in enbld_{\mathcal{T},\tau}(q)$ satisfying $t \in \ell oc$ and $\mathcal{L}_t^i \subseteq \mathcal{L}_\alpha^i$ (and also, by (5), $t \in T_q$). Hence $t \in C$. We thus have $t \in \ell oc'$.

Now suppose that $\mathcal{L}_t^{1-i} \not\subseteq \mathcal{L}_\alpha^{1-i}$, and so there is $\ell oc'' \in \mathcal{L}_t^{1-i} \setminus \mathcal{L}_\alpha^{1-i}$. Then, there exists $C' \in clusters_q^{\mathcal{L}^{1-i}}$, where $C' = T_q \cap \ell oc''$. By the node-consistency of $\mathcal{L}^i$ and $\mathcal{L}^{1-i}$ there is $\ell oc''' \in \mathcal{L}^i$ such that $T_q \cap \ell oc''' = C'$. So $\ell oc''' \in \mathcal{L}_t^i$. Since, by (5), all $u \in \alpha$ are such that $u \in T_q$, and $\ell oc'' \notin \mathcal{L}_\alpha^{1-i}$, we have $\ell oc''' \notin \mathcal{L}_\alpha^i$. Hence $\ell oc''' \in \mathcal{L}_t^i \setminus \mathcal{L}_\alpha^i$, producing a contradiction with $\mathcal{L}_t^i \subseteq \mathcal{L}_\alpha^i$.

As a result, $\alpha \in cds_{\mathcal{L}^{1-i}}^{\forall\subseteq}(enbld_{\mathcal{T},\tau}(q))$.

Case 4: $\alpha \in cds_{\mathcal{L}^i}^{\forall}(enbld_{\mathcal{T},\tau}(q))$. We proceed as in Case 3, ignoring the parts concerned with $\mathcal{L}_t^i \subseteq \mathcal{L}_\alpha^i$ and $\mathcal{L}_t^{1-i} \subseteq \mathcal{L}_\alpha^{1-i}$.

A Petri Net Perspective on the Resource Allocation Problem in Software Engineering[*]

Juan-Pablo López-Grao[1] and José-Manuel Colom[2]

[1] Dpt. of Computer Science and Systems Engineering (DIIS)
[2] Aragon Institute of Engineering Research (I3A)
University of Zaragoza, Spain
{jpablo,jm}@unizar.es

Abstract. Resource Allocation Systems (RAS) were intensively studied in the last years for Flexible Manufacturing Systems (FMS). The success of this research stems from the identification of subclasses of Petri Nets that correspond to an RAS abstraction of these systems. In this paper we take a parallel road to that travelled through for FMS, but for the case of software applications. These applications present concurrency, and deadlocks can happen due to the allocation of shared resources. We reveal that the existing subclasses of Petri Nets used to study this kind of deadlock problems are insufficient, even for very simple software systems. We propose a new subclass of Petri Nets that generalizes the previously known RAS subclasses and we present a taxonomy of anomalies that can be found in the context of software systems.

1 Introduction

Among the most recurrent patterns in a wide range of engineering disciplines, the competition for shared resources among concurrent processes takes a prominent position. The perspective of discrete event systems theory proves appropriate and powerful as a framework in which solutions are provided to the so-called Resource Allocation Problem (RAP) [14]. Systems of this kind are often called Resource Allocation Systems (RAS) [3,15].

RAS are usually conceptualized around two distinct entities, processes and resources, thanks to a prior abstraction process which is inherent in the discipline. RAP refers to satisfying successfully the requests for resources made by the processes, ensuring that no process ever falls in a deadlock. A set of processes is deadlocked when they indefinitely wait for resources that are already held by other processes of the same set [2].

We focus on Sequential RAS with serially reusable resources [19]. Therefore, a process can increase or decrease the quantity of free resources during its execution. Still, resources are used conservatively.

Although other models of concurrency have also been considered [8], Petri nets [17] have arguably taken a leading role in the family of formal models

---

[*] This work has been partially supported by the European Community's 7th Framework Programme under Project DISC (Grant Agreement n. INFSO-ICT-224498).

K. Jensen, S. Donatelli, and J. Kleijn (Eds.): ToPNoC V, LNCS 6900, pp. 181–200, 2012.
© Springer-Verlag Berlin Heidelberg 2012

used for dealing with RAP [4,6]. One of the strengths of this approach is the smooth mapping between the main entities of RAS and the basic elements of Petri nets. A resource type can be modelled using a place; its instances are modelled with tokens. Meanwhile, sequential processes are modelled with tokens progressing through state machines. Arcs from resource places to transitions (from transitions to resource places) represent the acquisition (release) of some resources by a process. Petri nets thus provide a natural formal framework for the analysis of RAS, besides benefiting from the goods of compositionality.

This fact is well recognized in the domain of Flexible Manufacturing Systems (FMS), where Petri net models for RAS have widely succeeded since the work of Ezpeleta et al. was introduced [4]. This is based upon two solid pillars: 1) the definition of a rich syntax from a physical point of view, which enables the natural expression of a wide disparity of plant configurations; and 2) the contribution of sound scientific results which let us characterize deadlocks from the model structure, as well as provide a well-defined methodology to automatically correct them in the real system.

Nowadays, there exists a plethora of Petri net models for modelling RAS in the context of FMS, which often overcome syntactic limitations of the S^3PR class [4]. S^4PR nets [22,18] generalize the earlier, while allowing multiple simultaneous resource allocations per process. S^*PR nets [7] extend the expressive power of the processes to that of state machines. Other classes such as NS-RAP [6], ERCN-merged nets [23] or PNR nets [13] extend the capabilities of S^3PR/S^4PR models beyond Sequential RAS by way of lot splitting or merging operations.

Most analysis and control techniques in the literature are based on a structural element which characterizes deadlocks in many RAS models: the so-called *bad siphon*. A bad siphon is a siphon which is not the support of a p-semiflow. If bad siphons become (sufficiently) emptied, their output transitions die since the resource places of the siphon cannot regain tokens anymore, thus revealing the *deadly embrace*. Control techniques thus rely on the insertion of monitor places [12] which limit the leakage of tokens from the bad siphons.

Although there exist obvious resemblances between RAP in FMS and that of parallel or concurrent software, previous attempts to bring these well-known RAS techniques into the field of software engineering have been, to the best of our knowledge, either too limiting or unsuccessful. In this work, we analyze why the net classes and results introduced in the context of FMS can fail when brought to the field of concurrent programming.

Section 2 presents a motivating example and discusses the elements that an RAS net model should desirably feature in order to successfully explore RAP within the software engineering discipline. Taking into account those considerations, Sect. 3 introduces a new Petri net class, called PC^2R. Section 4 relates the new class to those defined in our previous works and forewarn us about new behavioural phenomena. Some of these anomalies highlight the fact that previous theoretical results in the context of FMS are insufficient in the new framework. Section 5 summarizes the results of the paper. Finally, some useful definitions and basic concepts of Petri nets are provided as reference in appendix A.

2   The RAS View of a Software Application

Example 1 presents a humorous variation of Dijkstra's classic problem of the dining philosophers which adopts the beautiful writing by Hoare at [11].

Example 1. The postmodern dining philosophers. "Five philosophers spend their lives thinking and eating. The philosophers share a common dining room where there is a circular table surrounded by five chairs, each belonging to one philosopher. A microwave oven is also available. In the center of the table there is a large bowl of spaghetti which is frequently refilled (so it cannot be emptied), and the table is laid with five forks. On feeling hungry, a philosopher enters the dining room, sits in his own chair, and picks up the fork on the left of his place. Then he touches the bowl to feel its temperature. If he feels the spaghetti got too cold, he leaves his fork and takes the bowl to the microwave. Once it is warm enough, he comes back to the table, sits on his chair and leaves the bowl on the table after recovering his left fork. Unfortunately, the spaghetti is so tangled that he needs to pick up and use the fork on his right as well. If he can do this before the bowl gets cold again, he serves himself and starts eating. When he has finished, he puts down both forks and leaves the room."

According to the classic RAS nomenclature, each philosopher is a sequential process, and the five forks plus the bowl are serially reusable resources which are shared among the five processes. From a software perspective, each philosopher can be a process or a thread executed concurrently.

Algorithm 1 introduces the code for each philosopher. Notationally, we modelled the acquisition / release of resources by way of the wait() / signal() operations, respectively. Both of them have been generalized for the acquisition of multiple resources (separated by commas when invoking the function). Finally, the trywait() operation is a non-blocking wait operation. If every resource is available at the time trywait() is invoked, then it acquires them and returns TRUE. Otherwise, trywait() will return FALSE without acquiring any resource. For the sake of simplicity, it is assumed that the conditions with two or more literals are evaluated atomically.

Figure 1 depicts the net for Algorithm 1, with $i = 1$, after abstracting the relevant information from an RAS perspective. Figure 2 renders the composition of the five philosopher nets via fusion of the common shared resources. Note that if we remove the dashed arcs from Fig. 2, then we can see five disjoint strongly connected state machines plus six isolated places.

Each state machine represents the control flow for a philosopher. Every state machine is composed of seven states (places). Tokens in a state machine represent concurrent processes/threads which share the same control flow. At the initial state, every philosopher is thinking (outside the room), i.e. the unique token in each machine is located at the so-called *idle place*. In general, the idle place can be seen as a mechanism which limits the number of concurrent *active threads*. Here, at most one philosopher of type i can be inside the room, for each $i \in \{1, ..., 5\}$.

The six isolated places are called *resource places*. A resource place represents a resource type, and the number of tokens in it represents the quantity of free instances of that resource type. In this case, every resource place is monomarked. Thus, at the initial state there is one fork of type i, for every $i \in \{1, ..., 5\}$, plus one bowl of spaghetti (modelled by the resource place at the centre of the figure).

Finally, the dashed arcs represent the acquisition or release of resources by the active threads when they change their execution state. Every time a transition fires, the total amount of resources available is altered. Please note, however, that moving one isolated token of a state machine (by firing its transitions) until the token reaches back the idle state, leaves the resource places marking unaltered. Thus, the resource usage is conservative.

Algorithm 1 – Code for Philosopher i (where $i \in \{1, 2, 3, 4, 5\}$)

```
var
      fork: array [1..5] of semaphores;    // shared resources
      bowl: semaphore;                      // shared resource
begin
   do while (1)
      THINK;
      Enter the room;
(T1)  wait(fork[i]);                (T6)

      do while (not(trywait(bowl, fork[i mod 5 +1]))
               or the spaghetti is cold)
(T2)     if (trywait(bowl)
               and the spaghetti is cold) then
(T3)        signal(fork[i]);
            Go to the microwave;
            Heat up spaghetti;
            Go back to table;
(T4)        wait(fork[i]);
(T5)        signal(bowl);
         end if;
      loop;
      Serve spaghetti;
(T7)  signal(bowl);
      EAT;
(T8)  signal(fork[i], fork[i mod 5 +1]);
      Leave the room;
   loop;
```

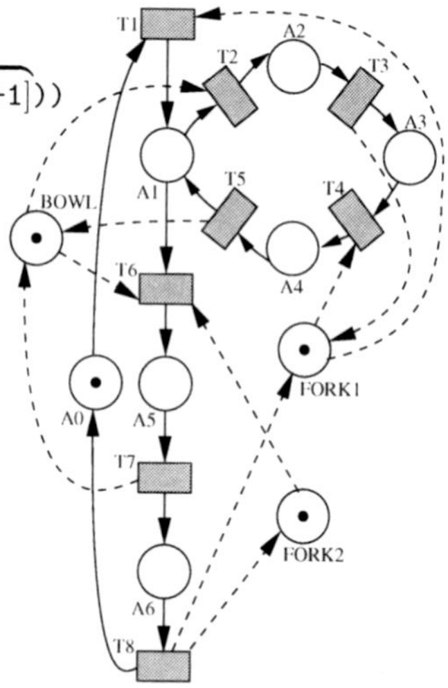

Fig. 1. Philosopher 1

At this point, we discuss some capabilities that an RAS model should have so as to support the modelling of concurrent programs.

State machines without internal cycles are rather versatile for modelling sequential processes in the context of FMS. The sucess of the S^3PR and S^4PR classes, in which every circuit in the state machines traverses the idle place, proves this. Nevertheless, this is clearly too constraining even for very simple software systems. Considering Böhm and Jacopini's theorem [10], however,

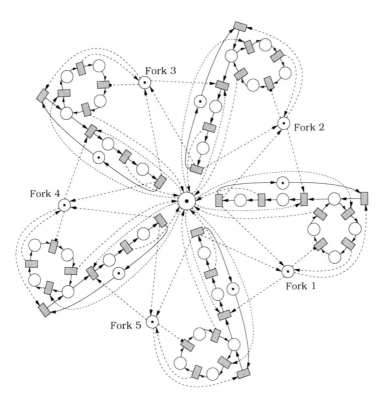

Fig. 2. The dining philosophers are thinking. Arcs from/to P_R are dashed for clarity.

we can assume that every non-structured sequential program can be refactored into a structured one using `while-do` loops. Meanwhile, calls to procedures and functions can be substituted by inlining techniques. Let us also remind that `fork/join` operations can also be unfolded into isolated concurrent sequential processes, as evidenced in [6]. As a result, we can restrict process models to state machines in which decisions and iterations (in the form of `while-do` loops) are supported, but not necessarily every kind of unstructured branch.

Another significant difference between FMS and software systems from an RAS perspective is that resources in the latter are not necessarily physical (e.g., a file) but can also be logical (e.g., a semaphore). This has strong implications in the degree of freedom in allocating those resources: we return to this issue later.

In this domain, a resource is an object that is shared among concurrent processes/threads and must be used in mutual exclusion. Since the number of resources is limited, the processes compete for the resource and use it in a non-preemptive way. This particular allocation scheme can be imposed by the resources' own access primitives, which may be blocking. Otherwise, the resource can be protected by a binary semaphore/mutex/lock (if there is only one instance of that resource type) or by a counting semaphore (multiple instances). Note that this kind of resources can be of varied nature (e.g., shared memory locations, storage space, database table rows) but the required synchronization scheme is inherently similar.

On the other hand, it is well-known that semaphores used in that context can also be seen as non-preemptive resources which are used in a conservative way. For example, a counting semaphore that limits the number of connections to a database can be interpreted in that way from an RAS point of view. Here processes wait for the semaphore when attempting to establish a database connection, and release it when they decide to close the aforementioned connection.

However, semaphores also perform a relevant role as an interprocess signaling facility, which can also be a source of deadlocks. In this work, our goal is the study of RAP, so this mode of use is out of scope. We propose fixing deadlock problems due to resource allocation issues firstly, and later apply other techniques for amending those due to message passing.

Due to their versatility, semaphore primitives are interesting for studying how resources can be allocated by a process/thread. For instance, XSI semaphores (also known as System V semaphores) have a multiple wait primitive (semop with sem_op<0). An example of multiple resource allocation appears in Algorithm 1. Besides, an XSI semaphore can be decremented atomically in more than one unit. Both POSIX semaphores (through sem_trywait) and XSI semaphores (through semop with sem_op<0 and sem_flag=IPC_NOWAIT) have a non-blocking wait primitive. Again, Algorithm 1 could serve as an example. Finally, XSI semaphores also feature inhibition mechanisms (through semop with sem_op=0), i.e. processes can wait for a zero value of the semaphore.

As we suggested earlier, the fact that resources in software engineering do not always have a physical counterpart is a peculiar characteristic with consequences. In this context, processes do not only consume resources but also can *create* them. A process will destroy the newly created resources before its termination. For instance, a process can create a shared memory variable (or a service!) which can be allocated to other processes/threads. Hence the resource allocation scheme is no longer *first-acquire-later-release*, but it can be the other way round too. Still, all the resources are used conservatively by the processes (either by a create-destroy sequence or by a wait-release sequence). As a side effect, and perhaps counterintuitively, there may not be free resources during the system startup (as they still must be created), yet the system is live.

Summing up, for successfully modelling RAS in the context of software engineering, a Petri net model should at least fulfill the following requirements:

1. The control flow of the processes should be represented by state machines with support for decisions (if-then-else blocks) and nested internal cycles (while-do blocks).
2. There can be several resource types and multiple instances of each one.
3. State machines can have multiple tokens (representing concurrent threads).
4. Processes/threads use resources in a conservative way.
5. Acquisition/release arcs can have non-ordinary weights (e.g., a semaphore value can be atomically incremented/decremented in more than one unit).
6. Atomic multiple acquisition/release operations must be allowed.

7. Processes can have decisions dependent of the allocation state of resources (due to the non-blocking wait primitives, as in Fig. 2).

8. Processes can lend resources. As a side effect, there could exist processes that depend on resources which must be created/lent by other processes.

3   PC²R Nets

In this section, we present a new Petri net class, which fulfills the list of abstract requirements enunciated in Sect. 2: the class of Processes Competing for Conservative Resources (PC²R). This class generalizes other subclasses of the S^nPR family while respecting the design philosophy on these. Hence, previous results are still valid in the new framework. However, PC²R nets can deal with more complex scenarios which were not yet addressed from the domain of S^nPR nets.

It should be remarked that no S^nPR net class fulfills all requirements presented at the end of Sect. 2. Although Requirements 2–6 are satisfied by the S^4PR class, requirement 1 is only verified by the S^*PR class, and fulfillment of Requirement 8 has never been addressed before, justifying the next definition.

Definition 1 presents a subclass of state machines used for modelling the control flow of the processes in isolation. Iterations are allowed, as well as decisions within internal cycles, in such a way that the control flow of structured programs can be fully supported, in fulfillment of Requirement 1.

Definition 1. *An iterative state machine* $\mathcal{N} = \langle \{p_k\} \cup P_1 \cup P_2, T, C \rangle$ *is a strongly connected state machine such that: (i) P_1, P_2 and $\{p_k\}$ are disjoint sets, (ii) $P_1 \neq \emptyset$, (iii) The subnet generated by $\{p_k\} \cup P_1, {}^\bullet P_1 \cup P_1{}^\bullet$ is a strongly connected state machine in which every cycle contains p_k, and (iv) If $P_2 \neq \emptyset$, the subnet generated by $\{p_k\} \cup P_2, {}^\bullet P_2 \cup P_2{}^\bullet$ is an iterative state machine.*

As Fig. 3 shows, P_1 contains the set of places of an outermost iteration block, while P_2 is the set of places of the rest of the state machine (the inner structure, which may contain multiple loops within). The place p_0 represents the place "p_k" that we choose after removing every iteration block. In the net of Fig. 1, if we remove the resource places $FORK1$, $FORK2$ and $BOWL$, we obtain an iterative state machine, with $P_1 = \{A2, A3, A4\}$, $P_2 = \{A0, A5, A6\}$ and $p_k = A1$.

PC²R nets are modular models composed by iterative state machines and shared resources. Two PC²R nets can be composed into a new PC²R model via

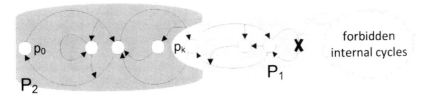

Fig. 3. Schematic diagram of an iterative state machine

fusion of the common resources. Note that a PC^2R net can simply be one process modelled by an iterative state machine along with the set of resources it uses.

The class supports iterative processes, multiple resource acquisitions, non-blocking wait operations and resource lending. Inhibition mechanisms are not natively supported (although some cases can still be modelled with PC^2R nets).

Definition 2. *Let $I_{\mathcal{N}}$ be a finite set of indices. A PC^2R net is a connected generalized self-loop free P/T net $\mathcal{N} = \langle P, T, C \rangle$ where:*

1. $P = P_0 \cup P_S \cup P_R$ *is a partition such that: (a)* [idle places] $P_0 = \{p_{0_1}, ..., p_{0_{|I_{\mathcal{N}}|}}\}$; *(b)* [process places] $P_S = P_1 \cup ... \cup P_{|I_{\mathcal{N}}|}$, *where $\forall i \in I_{\mathcal{N}}: P_i \neq \emptyset$ and $\forall i, j \in I_{\mathcal{N}}: i \neq j, P_i \cap P_j = \emptyset$; (c)* [resource places] $P_R = \{r_1, ..., r_n\}, n > 0$.
2. $T = T_1 \cup ... \cup T_{|I_{\mathcal{N}}|}$, *where $\forall i \in I_{\mathcal{N}}, T_i \neq \emptyset$, and $\forall i, j \in I_{\mathcal{N}}, i \neq j, T_i \cap T_j = \emptyset$.*
3. *For all $i \in I_{\mathcal{N}}$ the subnet generated by $\{p_{0_i}\} \cup P_i, T_i$ is an iterative state machine.*
4. *For each $r \in P_R$, there exists a unique minimal p-semiflow associated to r, $Y_r \in \mathbb{N}^{|P|}$, fulfilling: $\{r\} = \|Y_r\| \cap P_R, (P_0 \cup P_S) \cap \|Y_r\| \neq \emptyset$, and $Y_r[r] = 1$.*
5. $P_S \subseteq \bigcup_{r \in P_R} (\|Y_r\| \setminus \{r\})$.

In fulfillment of Requirement 8, the support of the Y_r p-semiflows (point 4 of Definition 2) may include P_0: this is new with respect to S^4PR nets. Such a resource place r is called a *lender* resource place. If r is a lender, then there exists a process which creates (*lends*) instances of r. As a consequence, there might exist additional minimal p-semiflows containing more than one resource place. This is also new and will be discussed in subsection 4.1.

The next definition generalizes the notion of acceptable initial marking introduced for the S^4PR class. In software systems all processes/threads are initially inactive and start from the same point (the `begin` statement). Hence, all of the corresponding tokens are in the idle place at the initial marking (the process places being therefore empty).

Definition 3. *Let $\mathcal{N} = \langle P_0 \cup P_S \cup P_R, T, C \rangle$ be a PC^2R. An initial marking m_0 is acceptable for $\mathcal{N}$ iff $\|m_0\| \setminus P_R = P_0$, and $\forall p \in P_S, r \in P_R : Y_r^T \cdot m_0 \geq Y_r[p]$.*

Note that lender resource places may be empty for an acceptable initial marking. Figure 2 shows a PC^2R net with an acceptable initial marking which does not belong to the S^4PR class.

4 Properties of PC^2R Nets: Pitfalls and Fallacies

4.1 Hierarchy of Classes and P-Semiflows

Definition 4. *Previous classes of the S^nPR family are defined as follows:*

- *An S^5PR [16] is a PC^2R where $\forall r \in P_R: \|Y_r\| \cap P_0 = \emptyset$.*
- *An S^4PR [22] is an S^5PR where $\forall i \in I_{\mathcal{N}}$ the subnet generated by $\{p_{0_i}\} \cup P_i, T_i$ is a strongly connected state machine in which every cycle contains p_{0_i} (i.e., a iterative state machine with no internal cycles).*

- An S^3PR [4] is an S^4PR where $\forall p \in P_S$: $|^{\bullet\bullet}p \cap P_R| = 1$, $(^{\bullet\bullet}p \cap P_R = p^{\bullet\bullet} \cap P_R)$.
- An L-S^3PR [5] is an S^3PR where $\forall p \in P_S$: $|^\bullet p| = |p^\bullet| = 1$.

Property 1. $L\text{-}S^3PR \subseteq S^3PR \subseteq S^4PR \subseteq S^5PR \subseteq PC^2R$.

The preceding property is straightforward from Definition 4. It is worth noting that Definition 3 collapses with the definition of acceptable initial markings respectively provided for those subclasses [4,5,22].

Besides, there exists another class for Sequential RAS, called SPQR [16], which does not strictly contain or is contained by the PC^2R class. Yet, there exist transformation rules to travel between PC^2Rs and Structurally Bounded (SB) SPQRs. Note that, by construction, PC^2R nets are conservative, and hence SB, but this is not true for SPQRs. The SPQR class is interesting from an analytical point of view thanks to its syntactic simplicity, as discussed in subsection 4.4.

One perspective for inspecting the differences between the subclasses of PC^2R is that of the form and number of minimal p-semiflows. All subclasses are conservative by definition. Let Y_{S_i} denote the unique minimal p-semiflow induced by the iterative state machine generated by restricting $\mathcal{N}$ to $\langle \{p_{0_i}\} \cup P_i, T_i \rangle$.

Lemma 1. *Let $\mathcal{N} = \langle P, T, C \rangle$ be a PC^2R. A basis of the left annuller space of the incidence matrix C contains $|P_R| + |I_{\mathcal{N}}|$ vectors.*

Proof. For every $r \in P_R$, let $Y_r^- = Y_r - \sum_{i \in I_{\mathcal{N}}} Y_r[p_{0_i}] \cdot Y_{S_i}$. The set of vectors $A = \{Y_{S_i} \mid i \in I_{\mathcal{N}}\} \cup \{Y_r^- \mid r \in P_R\}$ contains $|P_R| + |I_{\mathcal{N}}|$ vectors and they are linearly independent, because for each $p \in P_R \cup P_0$ there exists one and only one distinct vector $y \in A$ such that $y[p] = 1$ and $\forall y' \in A$, $y' \neq y$, $y'[p] = 0$. Moreover, A is a basis because there is no other vector linearly independent with the vectors of A. We prove by contradiction this last statement. Let us suppose that there exists y being a left annuller of C and y cannot be generated from vectors of A. Construct the vector $y' = y - \sum_{i \in I_{\mathcal{N}}} y[p_{0_i}] \cdot Y_{S_i} - \sum_{r \in P_R} y[r] \cdot Y_r^-$. Obviously, y' is a left annuller of $\mathcal{N}$ because so are the vectors of A and y, but $\|y'\| \subseteq P_S$, and this is not possible because there is no left annullers of the iterative state machines without their idle places.   □

Now let B be a matrix of dimensions $(|P_R| + |I_{\mathcal{N}}|) \times |P|$ of integers such that the rows of B are the set of vectors A defined in the previous proof.

Lemma 2. *If $\mathcal{N}$ is an S^5PR, B is a non-negative canonical basis of p-semiflows.*

Proof. By reordering columns in B so that the first ones correspond to $P_R \cup P_0$, and subsequently reordering the rows of B, we obtain a matrix of the form $[I|B']$, where I is the identity matrix of dimension $|P_R| + |I_{\mathcal{N}}|$, and B' is a matrix of dimensions $(|P_R| + |I_{\mathcal{N}}|) \times |P_S|$ of non-negative integers, since in S^5PR nets, $\forall r \in P_R$, $Y_r[P_0] = \mathbf{0}$ and $Y_r^- = Y_r$.   □

Corollary 1. *If $\mathcal{N}$ is an S^3PR, then every row in B belongs to $\{0,1\}^{|P|}$.*

However, nets belonging to the S^4PR class may have non-binary minimal p-semiflows. Furthermore, PC^2R nets feature a new kind of minimal p-semiflows:

Lemma 3. *If $\mathcal{N}$ is a PC^2R but not an S^5PR, there exists at least one minimal p-semiflow whose support contains more than one resource place.*

Proof. Since $\mathcal{N}$ is not an S^5PR, there exists $r \in P_R$, $i \in I_{\mathcal{N}}$ such that $p_{0_i} \in \|Y_r\|$. In that case, there exists at least one $p \in P_{S_i}$ such that $p \notin \|Y_r\|$ (otherwise, $Y_r - Y_{S_i} \geq \mathbf{0}$ and Y_r is not minimal). Let A be the minimal set of minimal p-semiflows, $\{Y_u \mid u \in P_R\}$, that are essential to cover every $p \in P_{S_i}$ such that $Y_r[p] = 0$. This means that $Y_u \in A$ iff $\exists p \in P_{S_i}$, $Y_r[p] = 0$, $Y_u[p] \neq 0$ and $\forall Y_v \in A$, $Y_v \neq Y_u : Y_v[p] = 0$. By Definition 2.5, this set A exists. We construct $Y'_r = Y_r + \sum_{Y_u \in A} Y_u$, that obviously contains, at least, the p-semiflow Y_{S_i}. Therefore, $Y_r^- = Y'_r - k \cdot Y_{S_i}$, $k = \min_{p \in \|Y_{S_i}\|} \{Y'_r[p]\}$, is a p-semiflow by construction, and $Y_r^-[P_R] = Y'_r[P_R]$. In the same way, we detract other Y_{S_j} that can be contained in Y_r^-.

Y_r^- is minimal. By contradiction. Let us suppose that Y_r^- contains Y_v. The resource v must be either r or a resource for which its minimal p-semiflow Y_v is in A. If v is r then $Y_v[r] = Y_r^-[r]$, and $(Y_r^- - Y_v)[p_{0_i}] < 0$. Therefore, we reach a contradiction. If v holds $Y_v \in A$ then $Y_v[v] = Y_r^-[v]$ because the weight $Y_r^-[u]$ is not modified by the previous operations. And $(Y_r^- - Y_v)[p] < 0$ for some $p \in P_{S_i}$ for which Y_v becomes essential in the set A, since $Y_r^-[p] \leq Y_v[p] - k$. $\square$

In other words, the above result reveals that the set of minimal p-semiflows contains strictly a basis of the left annuller space of the incidence matrix C.

4.2   Liveness Characterization and Siphons

Traditionally, empty or insufficiently marked siphons have been a fruitful structural element for characterizing non-live RAS. The more general the net class, however, the more complex the siphon-based characterization is. The following results can be easily obtained from previously published works. The originality here is to point out the strict conditions that the siphons must fulfill.

Theorem 1. *Let $\langle \mathcal{N}, m_0 \rangle$ be a marked S^3PR with an acceptable initial marking. $\langle \mathcal{N}, m_0 \rangle$ is non-live iff $\exists m \in RS(\mathcal{N}, m_0)$ and a <u>minimal</u> siphon D: $m[D] = \mathbf{0}$.*

Proof. In [4] it is proved that $\langle \mathcal{N}, m_0 \rangle$ is non-live iff $\exists m \in RS(\mathcal{N}, m_0)$ and an empty siphon D at m, i.e. $m[D] = \mathbf{0}$. Hence, the sufficient part is straightforward. Now suppose that the empty siphon D is not minimal. Then there must exist a minimal siphon $D' \subset D$. Since $m[D'] = \mathbf{0}$, an empty minimal siphon exists. $\square$

For instance, the marked S^3PR in Fig. 4 is non-live with $K_0 = K_1 = 1$, $K_3 = 2$. From this acceptable initial marking, the marking $(A4 + B4 + R2 + 2 \cdot R3)$ can be reached by firing σ, where $\sigma = \langle TB1, TA1, TB2, TA2, TB3, TA3, TB4, TA4 \rangle$. This firing sequence empties the siphon $\{A1, B1, A5, B5, R1, R4\}$.

However, this characterization is sufficient, but not necessary, in general, for S^4PR nets. Hence, the concept of *empty siphon* had to be generalized. Given a marking m in an S^4PR net, a transition t is said to be *m-process-enabled* (*m-process-disabled*) iff it has (not) one marked input process place, and *m-resource-enabled* (*m-resource-disabled*) iff its input resource places have (not) enough tokens to fire it, i.e., $m[P_R, t] \geq Pre[P_R, t]$ ($m[P_R, t] \not\geq Pre[P_R, t]$).

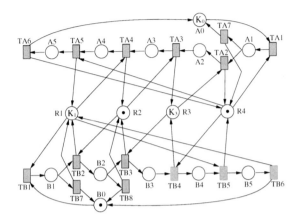

Fig. 4. An S^3PR which is non-live iff $(K_0 \geq K_1, K_3 \geq 2) \vee (K_0 \cdot K_1 \cdot K_3 = 0)$

Theorem 2. *[22] Let $\langle \mathcal{N}, m_0 \rangle$ be a marked S^4PR with an acceptable initial marking. $\langle \mathcal{N}, m_0 \rangle$ is non-live iff $\exists m \in RS(\mathcal{N}, m_0)$ and a siphon D such that: i) There exists at least one m-process-enabled transition; ii) Every m-process-enabled transition is m-resource-disabled by resource places in D; iii) Process places in D are empty at m.*

Such a siphon D is said to be insufficiently marked at m. In Theorems 1 and 2, the siphon captures the concept of circular wait, revealing it from the underlying net structure. In contrast to the S^3PR class, it is worth noting the following fact about *minimal* siphons in S^4PR nets, which emerges because of their minimal p-semiflows not being strictly binary.

Property 2. *There exist non-live S^4PR nets with an acceptable initial marking for which every siphon characterizing the non-liveness is non-minimal, i.e. minimal siphons are insufficient to characterize non-liveness.*

Proof. The net in Fig. 5 is non-live, but there is no minimal siphon containing both resource places $R1$ and $R2$. Note that the siphon $D = \{R1, R2, A3, B2\}$ becomes insufficiently marked at m, where $m = A1 + B1 + R1 + R2$, but it contains the minimal siphon $D' = \{R2, A3, B2\}$. D' is not insufficiently marked for any reachable marking. It is also worth noting that no siphon is ever emptied. □

Thus we must take care of non-minimal siphons for dealing with deadlocks in systems more complex than S^3PR. On the other hand, we have noticed that insufficiently marked siphons (even considering those non-minimal) are not enough for characterizing liveness for more complex systems such as S^5PR models. This means that siphon-based control techniques for RAS do not work in general for concurrent software, even in the 'good' case in which every wait-like operation precedes its complementary signal-like operation.

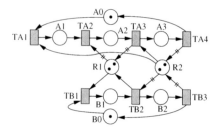

Fig. 5. A non-live S^4PR with no minimal siphon becoming insufficiently marked

Property 3. *There exists an S^5PR with an acceptable initial marking $\langle \mathcal{N}, m_0 \rangle$ which is non-live but insufficiently marked siphons do not characterize non-liveness (dead markings).*

Proof. The net in Fig. 6 models a special case of Example 1 with only two philosophers. This system is non-live, while there exist three bad siphons, which are $D_1 = \{A2, A3, A4, A5, A6, B2, B4, B5, B6, FORK2, BOWL\}$, $D_2 = \{A2, A4, A5, A6, B2, B3, B4, B5, B6, FORK1, BOWL\}$ and $D_3 = \{A2, A4, A5, A6, B2, B4, B5, B6, FORK1, FORK2, BOWL\}$. Besides, every transition in the set $\Omega = \{TA2, TA3, TA4, TA5, TB2, TB3, TB4, TB5\}$ is an output transition of D_1, D_2 and D_3. After firing $m_0[TA1\,TB1\rangle$, the state $A1 + B1 + BOWL$ is reached. This marking belongs to a livelock with other six markings. The reader can check that there exists a firable transition in Ω for every marking in the livelock, and in any case there is no insufficiently marked siphons. □

Revisiting Example 1 and its associated Algorithm 1, it is not difficult to see that, if every philosopher enters the room, sits down and picks up the fork on the left of himself, the philosophers will be trapped in a livelock. Every philosopher can eventually take the bowl of spaghetti and heat it up in the microwave. This pattern can be repeated infinitely often, but it is completely useless, since no philosopher will ever be able to have dinner.

4.3   Deadlock-Freeness, Liveness, Reversibility and Livelocks

In general, livelocks with dead transitions are not a new phenomenon in the context of Petri net models for RAS. Figure 7 shows that, even for L-S^3PR nets, deadlock freeness does not imply liveness.

Property 4. *There exists a marked L-S^3PR with an acceptable initial marking such that it is deadlock-free but not live.*

This net system has no deadlock but two reachable livelocks: (i) $\{(A0 + B2 + C0 + D1 + R1), (A1 + B2 + C0 + D1)\}$, and (ii) $\{(A0 + B1 + C0 + D2 + R3), (A0 + B1 + C1 + D2)\}$. Nevertheless, these livelocks are captured by insufficiently marked siphons. Unfortunately, this no longer holds for some kind of livelocks in S^5PR or more complex systems. Indeed, PC^2R nets feature some complex properties which complicate the finding of a liveness characterization.

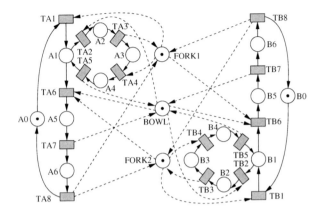

Fig. 6. Two postmodern dining philosophers

Property 5. *There exists an S^3PR such that liveness is not monotonic, neither with respect to the marking of the idle/process places, nor that of the resource places, i.e., liveness is not always preserved when those are increased.*

Proof. With respect to P_R: The system in Fig. 4 is live with $K_0 = K_1 = K_3 = 1$ and non-live with $K_0 = K_1 = 1$, $K_3 = 2$ (however, it becomes live again if we increase enough the marking of $R1$, $R2$ and $R4$; so as to make every resource place an implicit place).

With respect to P_0: The system in Fig. 4 is live with $K_0 = 1$, $K_1 = K_3 = 2$ and non-live with $K_0 = K_1 = K_3 = 2$. □

Note that liveness is monotonic for every net belonging to the L-S³PR class [9] with respect to the resource places. But, from S³PR nets upwards, there is a discontinuity zone between the point where the resource places are empty enough so that every transition is dead (also held for lower markings), and the point where every resource place is implicit (liveness is preserved if their marking is increased). Markings within these bounds fluctuate between liveness and non-liveness. The location of those points also depends on the marking of the idle/process places: the more tokens in them, the farther the saturation point.

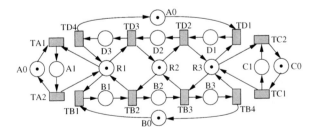

Fig. 7. A non-live L-S³PR which is deadlock-free

Nevertheless, an interesting property of S^4PR nets is that liveness equals reversibility. This, along with the fact that the idle place does not belong to any p-semiflow Y_r, is a powerful feature. If every token in a process net can be moved to the idle place, then the net is not dead (yet).

Theorem 3. *Let $\langle \mathcal{N}, m_0 \rangle$ be an S^4PR with an acceptable initial marking. $\langle \mathcal{N}, m_0 \rangle$ is live iff m_0 is a home state (i.e., the system is reversible).*

Proof. $\Rightarrow$) Let us suppose that m_0 is not a home state, i.e. $\exists m' \in RS(\mathcal{N}, m_0)$ such that $m_0 \notin RS(\mathcal{N}, m')$. Let $m \in RS(\mathcal{N}, m')$ obtained by moving forward all the active processes (firing transitions $T \setminus P_0{}^\bullet$) until no process enabled transition can be fired. Since $m_0 \notin RS(\mathcal{N}, m')$, $m \neq m_0$, and the set of m-process-enabled transitions is non-empty, and each one of these transitions is m-resource-disabled. Hence, by Theorem 2, $\langle \mathcal{N}, m_0 \rangle$ is non-live.

$\Leftarrow$) Let m be a reachable marking from m_0, $m \in RS(\mathcal{N}, m_0)$, and t a transition of the net. We prove that there exists a successor marking of m, m', from which t is firable. Since m_0 is a home state, there exists a firable sequence from m such that $m[\sigma\rangle m_0$. Taking into account that for acceptable initial markings in S^4PR, every t-semiflow can be fired in isolation from the initial marking [21], then there exists a sequence X whose characteristic vector $\overline{X}$ is equal to the t-semiflow containing t (this t-semiflow exists because the net is consistent). Let $X = \sigma' t \sigma''$ be a decomposition of the firing sequence X to point out the first firing of t. Therefore $\sigma\sigma'$ is firable leading to a marking m' from which t is firable. Because m and t have been selected without constraints, the net is live.   □

However, Theorem 3 is false in general for S^5PR nets. In fact, the directedness property [1] does not even hold. This implies that an S^5PR may not have a home state, even being live.

Property 6. *There exists an S^5PR with an acceptable initial marking $\langle \mathcal{N}, m_0 \rangle$ such that the system is live but there is no home state.*

Proof. The net system in Fig. 8 has no home state in spite of being live. Due to the large size of the net, complete state space enumeration has been omitted, but a sketch of its reachability graph is included.   □

Having said that, S^5PR nets still retain an interesting property: its minimal t-semiflows are eventually realizable from an acceptable initial marking.

Theorem 4. *Let $\langle \mathcal{N}, m_0 \rangle$ be an S^5PR with an acceptable initial marking. For every (minimal) t-semiflow x, there exists a reachable marking $m \in RS(\mathcal{N}, m_0)$ such that x is realizable from m, i.e. $\exists \sigma$ such that $m[\sigma\rangle$, $\overline{\sigma} = x$.*

Proof. This can be easily proven from Definitions 2 and 3. As in S^4PR nets [21], an acceptable initial marking m_0 guarantees the executability from m_0 of every minimal t-semiflow (elementary circuit) whose corresponding t-component contains an idle place. Once the token is carried to the entry place p of an internal cycle, the number of available resources guarantees the executability of every minimal t-semiflow such that its t-component contains p. Following an inductive reasoning, every (minimal) t-semiflow is eventually realizable from m_0.   □

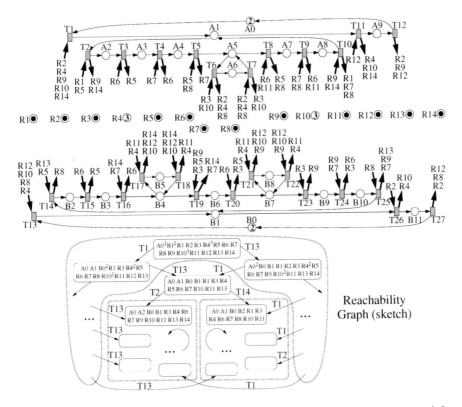

Fig. 8. A live S^5PR which has no home state. The arcs from/to P_R are omitted for clarity. Instead, the set of input and output resource places are listed next to each transition. The net is ordinary. Below, a sketch of its reachability graph.

However, for PC^2R nets there may not exist minimal t-semiflows being eventually realizable; even for live systems.

Property 7. *There exists a PC^2R with an acceptable initial marking $\langle \mathcal{N}, m_0 \rangle$ such that the system is live and there exists a minimal t-semiflow x such that $\forall m \in RS(\mathcal{N}, m_0)$, $\nexists\sigma$ such that $m[\sigma\rangle$ and $\bar{\sigma} = x$, i.e. x is realizable from m.*

Proof. The reader can check that the net system in Fig. 9 has no home state in spite of being live. Depending on which transition we fire first (either $T1$ or $T8$) we fall in a different livelock. Besides, for every reachable marking, there is no minimal t-semiflow such that it is realizable, i.e. firable in isolation. Instead, both state machines need each other to progress from the very beginning. Again, state space enumeration has been omitted for the sake of concision.   □

4.4   Relation with the SPQR Class

Finally, we feel it is worth bringing to attention that in [16] we introduced a new class of Petri net models for RAS, called SPQR (Systems of Processes

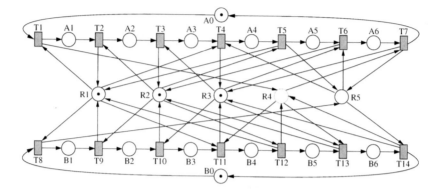

Fig. 9. A marked PC²R for which no minimal t-semiflow is ever realizable

Quarreling over Resources). SPQR nets feature an appealing syntactic simplicity and expressive power though they are very challenging from an analytical point of view. They can be roughly described as RAS nets in which the process subnets are acyclic and the processes can lend resources in any possible (conservative) manner. Every PC²R can be transformed into a Structurally Bounded SPQR net (SB SPQR net). Note that SB SPQRs are conservative since they are consistent by construction, and consistency plus structurally boundedness implies conservativeness [20].

We believe that the transformation of PC²R nets into SB SPQR can be useful to understand the above phenomena from a structural point of view. Intuitively speaking, the concept of *lender resource* seems a simple yet powerful instrument which still remains to be fully explored. Still, SB SPQRs can present very complex behaviour [16].

The transformation rule is based on the idea of converting every `while-do` block into an acyclic process which is activated by a lender resource place. This lender place gets marked once the thread reaches the while-do block. The token is removed at the exit of the iteration. This transformation must be applied from the innermost loops outwards. Figure 10 depicts the transformation rule. The rule preserves the language accepted by the net (and thus liveness) since it

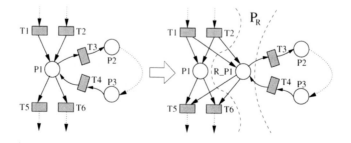

Fig. 10. Transforming PC²Rs into SB SPQRs: From iterative to acyclic processes

basically consists in the addition of a implicit place (place $P1$ in the right hand net of Fig. 10, since R_P1 can be seen as a renaming of $P1$ in the left hand net).

Figure 11 illustrates the transformation of the PC^2R in Fig. 6 into the corresponding SB SPQR.

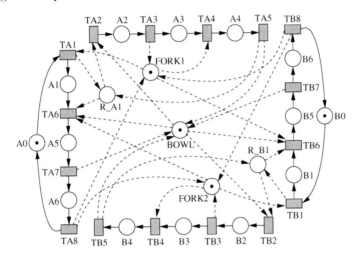

Fig. 11. From PC^2R to SB SPQR: Two postmodern dining philosophers

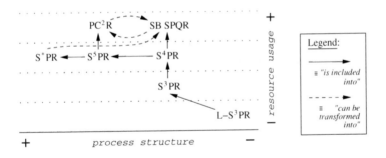

Fig. 12. Inclusion relations between Petri net classes for RAS

Out of curiosity, the concept of *acceptable initial marking* has not been defined for the SPQR class, since it was conceived as an instrumental model class with no physical meaning. On the other hand, the concept of acceptable initial marking does have a physical meaning in the context of PC^2R nets modelling real-world systems in software engineering. As a lateral effect, the transformation of a SB SPQR $\langle \mathcal{N}, m_0 \rangle$ into a marked PC^2R $\langle \mathcal{N}', m_0' \rangle$ may not produce a net system with an acceptable initial marking m_0', even when $m_0[P_S] = \mathbf{0}$.

Figure 12 introduces the inclusion relations between a variety of Petri net classes for Sequential RAS.

5   Conclusion and Future Work

Although there exist a variety of Petri net classes for RAS, many of these definition efforts have been directed to obtain powerful theoretical results for the analysis and synthesis of this kind of systems. Nevertheless, we believe that the process of abstraction is a central issue in order to have useful models from a real-world point of view, and therefore requires careful attention. In this work, we have followed that path and constructed a requirements list for obtaining an interesting Petri net subclass of RAS models applied to the software engineering domain. Considering that list, we defined the class of PC^{2}R nets, which fulfills those requirements while respecting the design philosophy on the RAS view of systems. We also introduced some useful transformation and class relations so as to locate the new class among the myriad of previous models. Finally we proved that the problem of liveness in the new context is non-trivial and presented some cases of bad behaviour which will be subject of subsequent work.

A   Petri Nets: Basic Definitions

A *place/transition net* (P/T net) is a 3-tuple $\mathcal{N} = \langle P, T, W \rangle$, where W is a total function $W : (P \times T) \cup (T \times P) \to \mathbb{N}$, being P, T non empty, finite and disjoint sets. Elements belonging to the sets P and T are called respectively *places* and *transitions*.

The *preset* (*poset*) or set of input (output) nodes of a node $x \in P \cup T$ is denoted by $^\bullet x$ ($x^\bullet$), where $^\bullet x = \{y \in P \cup T \mid W(y, x) \neq 0\}$ ($x^\bullet = \{y \in P \cup T \mid W(x, y) \neq 0\}$). The preset (poset) of a set of nodes $X \subseteq P \cup T$ is denoted by $^\bullet X$ ($X^\bullet$), where $^\bullet X = \{y \mid y \in {}^\bullet x, x \in X\}$ ($X^\bullet = \{y \mid y \in x^\bullet, x \in X\}$)

An *ordinary P/T net* is a net with unitary arc weights (i.e., $W : (P \times T) \cup (T \times P) \to \{0, 1\}$). Otherwise, the P/T net is called *generalized*. A *state machine* is an ordinary net such that for every $t \in T$, $|^\bullet t| = |t^\bullet| = 1$. An *acyclic state machine* is an ordinary net such that for every $t \in T$, $|^\bullet t|, |t^\bullet| \leq 1$, and there is no circuit in it.

A *self-loop place* $p \in P$ is a place such that $p \in p^{\bullet\bullet}$. A *self-loop free P/T net* is a net with no self-loop places that can be also defined by the 3-tuple $\mathcal{N} = \langle P, T, C \rangle$, where C is called the *incidence matrix*, $C[p, t] = W(p, t) - W(t, p)$.

A *p-flow* is a vector $Y \in \mathbb{Z}^{|P|}$, $Y \neq \mathbf{0}$, which is a left annuler of the incidence matrix, $Y \cdot C = \mathbf{0}$. The support of a p-flow is denoted $\|Y\|$. A *p-semiflow* is a non-negative p-flow. The P/T net $\mathcal{N}$ is *conservative* iff every place is covered by a p-semiflow. A *minimal p-semiflow* is a p-semiflow such that the g.c.d of its non-null components is one and its support $\|Y\|$ is not an strict superset of the support of another p-semiflow.

A set of places $D \subseteq P$ is a *siphon* iff every place $p \in {}^\bullet D$ satisfies $p \in D^\bullet$. The support of a p-semiflow is a siphon but the opposite does not hold in general.

Let $\mathcal{N} = \langle P, T, W \rangle$ be a P/T net, and let $P' \subseteq P$ and $T' \subseteq T$, where $P', T' \neq \emptyset$. The P/T net $\mathcal{N}' = \langle P', T', W' \rangle$ is the subnet generated by P', T' iff $W'(x, y) \Leftrightarrow W(x, y)$, for every pair of nodes $x, y \in P' \cup T'$.

A *marking* m of a P/T net $\mathcal{N}$ is a vector $\mathbb{N}^{|P|}$, assigning a finite number of *tokens* $m[p]$ to every place $p \in P$. The *support* of a marking, $\|m\|$, is the set of places which are marked in m, i.e. $\|m\| = \{p \in P \mid m[p] \neq 0\}$. We define a *marked P/T net* (also P/T net system) as the pair $\langle \mathcal{N}, m_0 \rangle$, where $\mathcal{N}$ is a P/T net, and m_0 is a marking for $\mathcal{N}$, also called *initial marking*. $\mathcal{N}$ is said to be the structure of the system, while m_0 represents the system state.

Let $\langle \mathcal{N}, m_0 \rangle$ be a marked P/T net. A transition $t \in T$ is *enabled* (also *firable*) iff $\forall p \in {}^\bullet t \; : \; m_0[p] \geq W(p,t)$, which is denoted by $m_0[t\rangle$. The *firing* of an enabled transition $t \in T$ changes the system state to $\langle \mathcal{N}, m_1 \rangle$, where $\forall p \in P \; : \; m_1[p] = m_0[p] + C[p,t]$, and is denoted by $m_0[t\rangle m_1$. A *firing sequence* σ from $\langle \mathcal{N}, m_0 \rangle$ is a non-empty sequence of transitions $\sigma = t_1 t_2 \ldots t_k$ such that $m_0[t_1\rangle m_1[t_2\rangle \ldots m_{k-1}[t_k\rangle m_k$. The firing of σ is denoted by $m_0[\sigma\rangle m_k$. The *language* of $\langle \mathcal{N}, m_0 \rangle$, $\mathcal{L}(\mathcal{N}, m_0)$, is the set of firing sequences from $\langle \mathcal{N}, m_0 \rangle$. A marking m is *reachable* from $\langle \mathcal{N}, m_0 \rangle$ iff there exists a firing sequence σ such that $m_0[\sigma\rangle m$. The *reachability set* $RS(\mathcal{N}, m_0)$ is the set of reachable markings, i.e. $RS(\mathcal{N}, m_0) = \{m \mid \exists \sigma \; : \; m_0[\sigma\rangle m\}$. A place $p \in P$ is a *sequential implicit place* in $\langle \mathcal{N}, m_0 \rangle$ (or, simply, *implicit*) iff $\mathcal{L}(\mathcal{N}, m_0) = \mathcal{L}(\mathcal{N}', m_0')$, where $\langle \mathcal{N}', m_0' \rangle$ is the net system resulting from removing the place p from the original net.

A transition $t \in T$ is *live* iff for every reachable marking $m \in RS(\mathcal{N}, m_0)$, $\exists m' \in RS(\mathcal{N}, m)$ such that $m'[t\rangle$. The system $\langle \mathcal{N}, m_0 \rangle$ is *live* iff every transition is live. Otherwise, $\langle \mathcal{N}, m_0 \rangle$ is *non-live*. A transition $t \in T$ is *dead* iff there is no reachable marking $m \in RS(\mathcal{N}, m_0)$ such that $m[t\rangle$. The system $\langle \mathcal{N}, m_0 \rangle$ is a *total deadlock* iff every transition is dead, i.e. no transition is firable. A *home state* m_k is a marking such that it is reachable from every reachable marking, i.e. $\forall m \in RS(\mathcal{N}, m_0) \; : \; m_k \in RS(\mathcal{N}, m)$. The net system $\langle \mathcal{N}, m_0 \rangle$ is *reversible* iff m_0 is a home state. A non-empty set of markings is a *livelock* of $\langle \mathcal{N}, m_0 \rangle$ iff for every $m \in M : RS(\mathcal{N}, m) = M$ and $m_0 \notin M$.

References

1. Best, E., Voss, K.: Free Choice Systems Have Home States. Acta Informatica 21, 89–100 (1984)
2. Coffman, E.-G., Elphick, M., Shoshani, A.: System Deadlocks. ACM Computing Surveys 3(2), 67–78 (1971)
3. Colom, J.-M.: The Resource Allocation Problem in Flexible Manufacturing Systems. In: van der Aalst, W.M.P., Best, E. (eds.) ICATPN 2003. LNCS, vol. 2679, pp. 23–35. Springer, Heidelberg (2003)
4. Ezpeleta, J., Colom, J.M., Martínez, J.: A Petri Net Based Deadlock Prevention Policy for Flexible Manufacturing Systems. IEEE Transactions on Robotics and Automation 11(2), 173–184 (1995)
5. Ezpeleta, J., García-Valles, F., Colom, J.M.: A Class of Well Structured Petri Nets for Flexible Manufacturing Systems. In: Desel, J., Silva, M. (eds.) ICATPN 1998. LNCS, vol. 1420, pp. 64–83. Springer, Heidelberg (1998)
6. Ezpeleta, J., Recalde, L.: A Deadlock Avoidance Approach for Non-Sequential Resource Allocation Systems. IEEE Transactions on Systems, Man and Cybernetics. Part–A: Systems and Humans 34(1) (2004)

7. Ezpeleta, J., Tricas, F., García-Vallés, F., Colom, J.M.: A Banker's Solution for Deadlock Avoidance in FMS with Flexible Routing and Multiresource States. IEEE Transactions on Robotics and Automation 18(4), 621–625 (2002)
8. Fanti, M.P., Maione, B., Mascolo, S., Turchiano, B.: Event-based Feedback Control for Deadlock Avoidance in Flexible Production Systems. IEEE Transactions on Robotics and Automation 13(3), 347–363 (1997)
9. García-Vallés, F.: Contributions to the Structural and Symbolic Analysis of Place/Transition Nets with Applications to Flexible Manufacturing Systems and Asynchronous Circuits. Ph.D. thesis. University of Zaragoza, Zaragoza (April 1999)
10. Harel, D.: On Folk Theorems. Communications of the ACM 23(7), 379–389 (1980)
11. Hoare, C.A.R.: Communicating Sequential Processes. Communications of the ACM 21(8), 666–677 (1978)
12. Hu, H.S., Zhou, M.C., Li, Z.W.: Liveness Enforcing Supervision of Video Streaming Systems Using Non-Sequential Petri Nets. IEEE Transactions on Multimedia 11(8), 1446–1456 (2009)
13. Jeng, M.D., Xie, X.L., Peng, M.Y.: Process Nets with Resources for Manufacturing Modeling and their Analysis. IEEE Transactions on Robotics 18(6), 875–889 (2002)
14. Lautenbach, K., Thiagarajan, P.S.: Analysis of a Resource Allocation Problem Using Petri Nets. In: Syre, J.C. (ed.) Proc. of the 1st European Conf. on Parallel and Distributed Processing, Cepadues Editions, Toulouse, pp. 260–266 (1979)
15. Li, Z.W., Zhou, M.C.: Deadlock Resolution in Automated Manufacturing Systems: A Novel Petri Net Approach. Springer, New York (2009)
16. López-Grao, J.P., Colom, J.M.: Lender Processes Competing for Shared Resources: Beyond the S^4PR Paradigm. In: Proc. of the 2006 Int. Conf. on Systems, Man and Cybernetics, pp. 3052–3059. IEEE (2006)
17. Murata, T.: Petri Nets: Properties, Analysis and Applications. Proceedings of the IEEE 77(4), 541–580 (1989)
18. Park, J., Reveliotis, S.A.: Deadlock Avoidance in Sequential Resource Allocation Systems with Multiple Resource Acquisitions and Flexible Routings. IEEE Transactions on Automatic Control 46(10), 1572–1583 (2001)
19. Reveliotis, S.A., Lawley, M.A., Ferreira, P.M.: Polynomial Complexity Deadlock Avoidance Policies for Sequential Resource Allocation Systems. IEEE Transactions on Automatic Control 42(10), 1344–1357 (1997)
20. Silva, M.: Introducing Petri Nets. In: Di Cesare, F., Harhalakis, G., Proth, J.M., Silva, M., Vernadat, F. (eds.) Practice of Petri Nets in Manufacturing, pp. 1–62. Chapman and Hall (1993)
21. Tricas, F.: Deadlock Analysis, Prevention and Avoidance in Sequential Resource Allocation Systems. Ph.D. thesis. University of Zaragoza, Zaragoza (May 2003)
22. Tricas, F., García-Valles, F., Colom, J.M., Ezpeleta, J.: A Petri Net Structure-Based Deadlock Prevention Solution for Sequential Resource Allocation Systems. In: Proc. of the 2005 Int. Conf. on Robotics and Automation (ICRA), pp. 272–278. IEEE, Barcelona (2005)
23. Xie, X., Jeng, M.D.: ERCN-Merged Nets and their Analysis Using Siphons. IEEE Transactions on Robotics and Automation 29(4), 692–703 (1999)

Nets-Within-Nets Paradigm and Grid Computing*

Marco Mascheroni and Fabio Farina

Dipartimento di Informatica, Sistemistica e Comunicazione
Università degli Studi di Milano Bicocca
Viale Sarca, 336, I-20126 Milano, Italy
{mascheroni,farina}@disco.unimib.it

Abstract. Grid is one of the most effective new paradigms in large scale distributed computing. Only recently Petri nets have been adopted as a formal modeling framework for describing some features related to Grid infrastructures: mostly related to the description of large-scale dynamic workflows. In this paper we describe a Grid tool for High Energy Physics data analysis, and we show how modeling its architecture with nets-within-nets has led us to identify and solve a number of defects affecting the current implementation.

Keywords: Grid, Petri nets, nets-within-nets, hypernet, validation.

1 Introduction

In the last decade the grid computing [12,11] approach to parallel and distributed computing has defined a new path to enable high performance data- and through-put intensive applications. Grid infrastructures expose computational and storage resources provided by different computing centers as uniform families of services that can be coordinated to create large scale e-Science workflows [23].

Grand-challenge experiments, like those related to High Energy Physics, life science, and environmental science adopted the grid as the underlying paradigm for implementing analysis software. In this paper, we will consider a grid distributed data analysis tool developed to serve the community of the Compact Muon Solenoid (CMS) [24] experiment at the CERN Large Hadron Collider (LHC) [25]. A specific software tool has been developed to analyze physics data over the grid, so that the users are protected from the architectural complexities of the distributed infrastructure itself. This application, called CMS Remote Analysis Builder (CRAB) [8] is released as open source software and has been adopted by the physics community since 2005. Even though the code quality is being continuously improved thanks to code analyzers (e.g., a python version lint [10]), the overall architecture has never been validated with formal tools like Petri nets.

This work investigates the possibility of using hierarchical Petri net models to design grid distributed systems. We chose to model a localized but important use

---

* Partially supported by MIUR (Italian Ministry of Education, University and Scientific Research).

K. Jensen, S. Donatelli, and J. Kleijn (Eds.): ToPNoC V, LNCS 6900, pp. 201–220, 2012.

case of the CRAB tool: the submission use case. The question we try to answer is if the nets-within-nets paradigm, where the tokens of a Petri net can be Petri nets themselves, is suitable for modeling grid distributed systems. The RENEW tool [19] has been chosen as modeling platform, as it is the only nets-within-nets tool that is mature enough to describe a real system like CRAB. In particular, the features of RENEW used to model the system are such that the obtained model is very similar to a hypernet [2]. This is a class of high level Petri nets which implements the nets-within-nets paradigm using a dynamic hierarchy, and a bounded state space [3]. As detailed in Section 4, this approach allowed us to isolate some problems in the CRAB implementation. Our approach does not cover analysis yet: modeling and systematic simulations are the two means used to unveil these problems.

In the literature, high level Petri nets have been applied to different contexts related to grid computing technologies. Most of the works in this field focus on the usage of Petri nets as a tool for workflows specification and execution [1,15,13]. A different application of Petri nets to grid is reported in [5]. Here the resources exposed by the distributed computing infrastructure are modeled directly with the aim of validating both properties like the soundness and the fairness of their sharing for a process mining workflow. As far as we know, high-level Petri nets, and in particular hierarchical nets, have been applied neither to the grid infrastructure, nor to the study of a classical grid application pattern like the distributed data analysis. Only very recent works [7,22] have followed similar approaches focusing on distributed databases and storage systems.

The remainder of the paper is organized as follows: Section 2 introduces the basic notion of nets-within-nets we refer to, and the RENEW tool. Section 3 describes the grid architecture we are considering, while in Section 4 the modeling of the system and the bugs found thanks to the formal approach are presented. A discussion of the modeling choices used in our approach is made in Section 5. Finally, some conclusions are reported in Section 6.

2   The Nets-Within-Nets Paradigm and RENEW

According to the nets-within-nets paradigm, the tokens of a Petri net can be structured as Petri nets themselves. This idea is due to Valk (see [26]), who defined and studied the class of *Elementary Object Nets (EOS)* in [27]. Later on, properties of EOS were studied in [17], and other classes of high level Petri nets which uses the nets-within-nets paradigm were defined, like for example [14,2,16,28,20].

In all these models a system is usually modeled as a collection of nets. One net is designated as the *system net*, the top level of the net hierarchy. All other nets are assigned to an *initial place*, a place in which they reside initially. This distribution of nets induces a hierarchy. The system evolves by moving tokens from place to place through the firing of autonomous transitions, or by synchro-nizing transitions between nets at different levels. The hierarchical structure of the model is usually static, but in some models there can be interactions be-tween nets at different levels in the hierarchy which can dynamically change the hierarchy itself. For example, in hypernets a net N can be moved from a place belonging to a net A, to a place belonging to a distinct net B. The interaction between nets A and B is only possible if they are close in the hierarchy.

The RENEW software tool [19], a Java-based high-level Petri net simulator that provides a flexible modelling approach based on Reference nets [18], allows the use of this paradigm to model real systems. RENEW is not only a nets-within-nets editor and simulator: it allows the use of high level net concepts like arc inscriptions, transition guards, and coloured tokens. However, we only use a subset of the features of RENEW. In particular, we choose to model the system with a hypernet-like model [2] (we will discuss in section 5 why the system is not a proper hypernet). The system is modeled as a collection of *net instances*. Tokens are *references* to net instances. Therefore it is possible that a net has more than one reference (token) in the system which refer to it. Arc inscriptions contain single variables. When a transition is fired tokens are bound to these variables. Transition inscriptions may contain channel names, used by two or more nets when they need to synchronize. An *uplink* is used when a net wants to synchronize with the net above it in the hierarchy, a *downlink* is used when a net wants to synchronize with one of the reference tokens it contains. When two transitions *synchronize* then they are executed as an atomic transition. The references which are bound to input arcs variables of both the transitions are handled in a single atomic firing step.

From a syntactical point of view the RENEW constructs we used in our model are the following:

- A net instance is created by a transition inscription of the form *var : new netname*, which means that the variable *var* will be assigned a new net instance of type *netname*.
- An *uplink* is specified as a transition inscription *:channelname (expr)*. It provides a name for the channel and a variable which is used for *vertical* communication between nets.
- A *downlink* has the form *netvar :channelname (expr)* where *netvar* is an expression that must evaluate to a net reference.

To fire a transition that has a downlink, there must be an input arc labelled with a proper variable name (*netvar* for the previous downlink example), and this variable must evaluate to a net instance. The referenced net instance must provide an uplink with the same name,and it must be possible to bind the variables suitably so that the channel expressions evaluate to the same values on both sides. The parameter is bound to a variable present in one of the input arcs of the up(down)-link, and then it is bound to the parameter in the corresponding down(up)-link. Then the transitions can fire simultaneously.

For example, if we want to fire transition *exchangeANet* of Figure 1(a) which has two downlinks *c1:ch(net)* and *c2:ch(net)* then the instances bound to variables *c1* and *c2* must be net instances. Moreover, these instances must provide two transitions which have a suitable uplink. Finally, it must be possible to bind the channel parameter *net*.

The exchange of (structured) tokens between nets, is possible by means of parameters. Figure 1 shows an example. The only transition enabled at the beginning is *create* (Figure 1(a)), which creates an empty *child1* net, and a *child2* net (Figure 1(b), and Figure 1(c) respectively). The difference between using the parenthesis or not using the parenthesis in creating a new net is that, if you use them, then the transition that is being fired must synchronize on the channel *new()* in the child net. Therefore, transition *create* in the system net synchronizes with transition *create* in the child1 net, which creates the *ANet* net. Afterwards, transitions *exchangeNet, moveANet, receiveANet* can fire, moving *ANet* to *child2*.

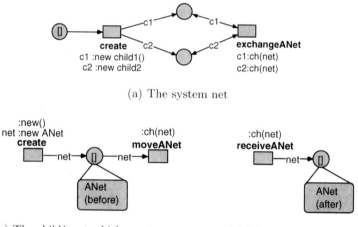

(a) The system net

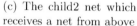

(b) The child1 net which creates a net of type *ANet* and sends it upward

(c) The child2 net which receives a net from above

Fig. 1. A simple example

Let us notice that in our model the exchange of tokens between the two children nets, *child1* and *child2*, is made under the supervision of the system net. This means that the *system net* in some way observes the token exchange between its children.

3   The Application Context: Grid Distributed Analysis

The CMS experiment at CERN produces about two Petabytes of data to be stored every year, and a comparable amount of simulated data is generated. Data needs to be accessed for the whole lifetime of the experiment. They are accessed for analysis by a worldwide community of about 3000 collaborators, coming from 183 institutes and spread over 38 countries all around the world.

The CMS computing model uses the infrastructure provided by the Worldwide LHC Computing grid (WLCG) Project [6] through the supporting projects EGEE, OSG and Nordugrid. Grid analysis in CMS is data driven. A prerequisite is that data are already distributed to remote computing centers and published in the CMS data catalogue. Users discover available datasets by querying the CMS data catalogue. Parallelization is provided by splitting the analysis of large data samples into several jobs. The output data produced by the analyses are typically copied to the storage of a site and registered in the experiment specific catalogue. Small output data files are returned to the user. In the CMS experiment, the CRAB tool set has been developed in order to enable physicists to perform distributed analysis over the grid. The role of CRAB is to allow the user to run over distributed datasets the very same analysis she/he ran locally, and collect the results. CRAB interacts with the distributed environment and the CMS services, hiding as much of the complexity of the system as possible. CMS community members use CRAB as a front-end, which provides a thin client, and an analysis server, which does most of the work in terms of automation and recovery, with respect to the direct interactions with the grid. The analysis server enables full workflow automation among different grid middlewares and the CMS data and workload management systems. Indeed, the main reasons behind the development for the analysis server are:

- automating as much as possible the whole analysis workflow;
- reducing the unnecessary human load, moving all possible actions to server side, keeping a thin and light client as the user interface;
- automating as much as possible the interactions with the grid, performing submission, resubmission, error handling, output retrieval, post-mortem operations;
- allowing better job distribution and management;
- implementing advanced use cases for important analysis workflows

The server architecture adopts a modular software approach. The Analysis Server comprises of a set of independent components (purely reactive agents) implemented as daemons and communicating asynchronously through a shared messaging service, supporting the publish & subscribe communication paradigm. Most of the components are themselves implemented as multi-threaded systems, to allow a multi-user scalable system, and to avoid bottlenecks. The task analyses are handled during their lifetime by the server through different families of components: there are components devoted to monitoring the grid status of individual jobs in a task, other groups of agents coordinate to manage the output retrieval and the recovery of the failed jobs by scheduling their resubmission automatically. A large part of the agent pool handles the submission chain of user tasks to the grid, as this use case is the most complex, involving the orchestration and the synchronization of the grid services. Because of the Analysis Server internal architecture, made of independent agents communicating through the asynchronous exchange of structured objects, we decided to model the system using high-level Petri nets. In particular, its hierarchical structure makes the use of hierarchical formalisms very appealing. We decided to model and study the grid submission chain because it is the use case that involves most of the components of the architecture. Other uses cases, like the tracking of the computation and the retrieval of the produced output are designed to involve single dedicated components. For these reason their modeling would provide a limited knowledge about how the components in the system interact. In fact, the aim of this study is to check that the agents in the system behave correctly with respect to the submission workflow specified in the computing model provided by the CMS computing coordinators. We decided to consider the system both at the component and task and job levels, organized in hierarchical way. In general, a task is organized as a collection of jobs and most of the components handle tasks, altering the status of their the jobs with a single action. On the other hand, the component that actually submits jobs to the grid does a splitting of a task into sets of jobs: the handling of homogeneous simpler objects let the grid middleware apply optimizations (e.g., the automatic creation of DAGs of jobs with common data dependencies). In addition, this mid-scale point of view represents a good compromise between the effects perceived by the final users and the large number of technical details that a complete representation of the grid would require.

4   Modeling the Submission Use-Case

In this Section we describe in detail the process of submitting jobs to the Grid through the CRAB Analysis Server. For each component of the system involved in the submission process its net representation is discussed. In addition, the bugs that have been discovered thanks to the net models are presented with the solutions that the actual code has adopted in order to solve the issues. The CRAB analysis suite was modeled using nets in a hierarchical fashion. Figure 2 shows the nets used to model the system. A vertical line with multiplicity n, indicates the presence of n nets in the higher one (e.g.: the CRABClient net contains from 1 to N Task nets); a horizontal dashed line indicates that the linked nets contain references to the same net. For example, CRABClient and TaskRegister nets can both contain references to the same task. In our modeling we consider one client for the purpose of simplicity. Additional clients would increase the number of task and job nets, however, as there are no direct interactions among jobs of distinct tasks, the description of the submission flow does not change with respect to the number of these nets. The discussed functionalities and use cases still hold when a larger number of clients is considered, as the client-server model assumes no direct interactions among the clients. In addition, for the use case that will be discussed, the server code separates the execution process of every task by instantiating new instances of its threads (called workers).

The OverallSystem net, which is the system net, contains three nets which respectively model the behavior of the client who is using the CRAB server (*CRABClient net*), the TaskRegister component which is a thread running on the CRAB server (*TaskRegister net*), and the CRABServerWorker which is also a thread running on the server (*CRABServerWorker net*). *Tasks* are the objects a client creates, and deals with. They are composed of *jobs*, the single units of work that need to be performed. The TaskRegister component is responsible for registering tasks, i.e. creating some data structures on server disks, checking if

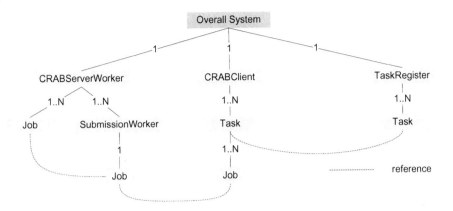

Fig. 2. The Nets hierarchy for the CRAB suite

each task has all the inputs it needs to be executed, and checking if the Grid can access the proper security credentials to execute it. The CRABServerWorker component continuously receives jobs, schedules them for execution on the Grid infrastructure, and creates a SubmissionWorker thread which monitors the life-cycle of each job on the Grid. It is relevant to observe that CRABServerWorker handle tasks as a whole (its transitions has to keep track of the job nets that compose the task), while the SubmissionWorker submits the job to the grid mid-dleware and alters the job net (a finite state automata) so that the changes of the status are reported to the users of the CRAB client. The clients interact with the server, and can initiate some operations like: submitting jobs, killing them if needed, and asking for the results.

All these nets will be discussed in detail in the following subsections.

4.1 OverallSystem

The OverallSystem net is the system net and it is shown in Figure 3.

In the initial marking, which is the rectangular token in the precondition of *begin*, the only enabled transition is *begin* itself. This transition creates three structured tokens of type *CRABServerWorker, CRABClient, and TaskRegister* respectively. These are the three main component of the CRAB tool as shown in Figure 2, and *begin* is used to start the behavior only once. The other three transitions model communication operation made by these components. They transfer/copy references from one net to another one. For example, transition *crab -submit(first)* models the fact that a user can submit one task to the server. This task is handled by the TaskRegister component. As a matter of fact a copy of a task reference is sent by the CRABClient component to the TaskRegister component.

The other modules which constitute the system are discussed in the next Sections.

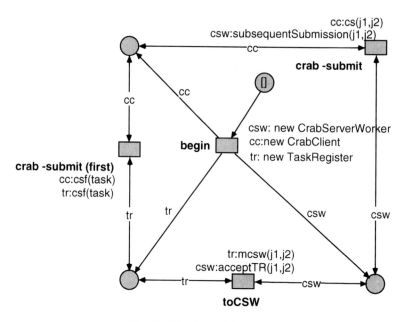

Fig. 3. The OverallSystem net

4.2   CRABClient, Tasks, and Jobs

The first component we are going to discuss is the CRAB client, which is modeled with the net in Figure 4. This component is what enables all the action sequences that the users can do on their Grid analyses.

The first thing a client does is to create a new task on the client machine. The typical usage pairs a unique task with a CRAB analysis session. We can assume that the *tasksPool* can contain a finite number of tokens: a typical analysis task involves hundreds of jobs, and produces several GBs of results. For these reasons users tend to work on no more than three tasks at the time. Similarly to the number of jobs in a task, this assumption does not affects the model of the system itself as the tasks owned by distinct users do not communicate directly. After the task has been locally created on the client machine, the client can perform a submit operation, which is of course the most important one as it starts the submission chain. The first time a task is submitted to the server, it is also registered by the TaskRegister component. Subsequent submits are handled directly by the CRABServerWorker component. This kind of action denotes of jobs in the same task: users usually submit few jobs in a task to check their input configuration are correct, then submit the remainig jobs of a task in a single step. In our model the difference between the two types of submits is modeled as two different transitions. In particular **c**rab -s*ubmit(fi̇rst)* transition has an uplink (*:csf(task)*), which means that it must be synchronized with the upper level. As a result the task reference is copied to the TaskRegister component by the Overall System net. After creation, the main operations a user can do

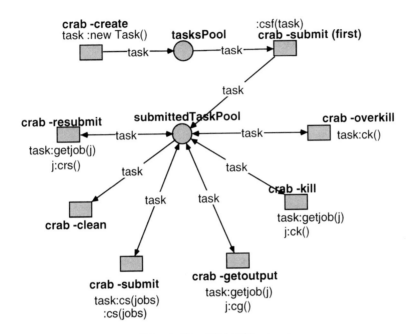

Fig. 4. The CRABClient net

are submit, resubmit, kill, getoutput, and clean. All these operations require an interaction with the server, but since we have focused on the submission use case, these interactions have not been explicitly modeled. For example the *getOutput* command is modeled as an interaction between the client and the job by means of two inscriptions. Handling all the possible interactions between the actors involved in the system would have resulted in a very big model, making it impossible to describe in this paper.

A task, see Figure 5, is a bag of jobs (the system allows to collect up to 4000 jobs into a singe task) and it is a representation that CRAB uses to perform collective actions on the Grid processes. Places *notRegistered, registering, registered* of the Task net contain information about the state of a task itself. These places control the enabledness of transitions *crab -submitFirst*, and *taskRegistered*, which are respectively called by the CRABClient when a job is submitted, and by the TaskRegister component when the task has been successfully registered after a *submit first* operation. The submit transition is called when a CRABClient performs a *submit subsequent* action. In our model both *taskRegistered*, and *submit* transitions send upward two jobs through a synchronous channel, and make the job move to the submission request state.

The net representing the state of Grid jobs and their allowed actions is depicted in Figure 6. The job net has been modeled combining the finite state machine reported in the CRAB official documentation with the information extracted directly from the portion of code devoted to the Grid job state handling. Several transitions of this net contain uplinks, and therefore have to be

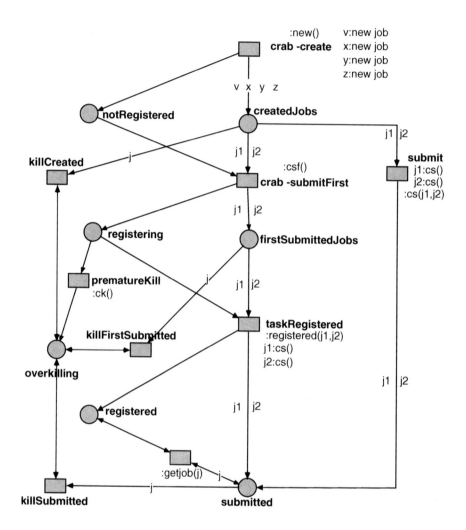

Fig. 5. The Task net. Only four jobs are considered in order to exemplify the relation with the job net.

synchronized with some net. Transitions with a *:crs()* uplink (CRAB Resubmit) are transition enabled only if the job is in a state where a resubmit is possible, and are synchronized with the *crab -resubmit* transition of the CRABClient net, or the *resubmit* transition of the SubmissionWorker net. In the same way killings (channel *:ck()*), failures (channel *:f()*), submission (channel *:s()*), and output retrieving (channel *:cg()*), have to be synchronized with a corresponding transition in another net.

The integration of the documentation and the code with the formalism of the nets has allowed us to identify a bug in the way job states are modified. In particular, the net allows some transitions that are not actually activated by any

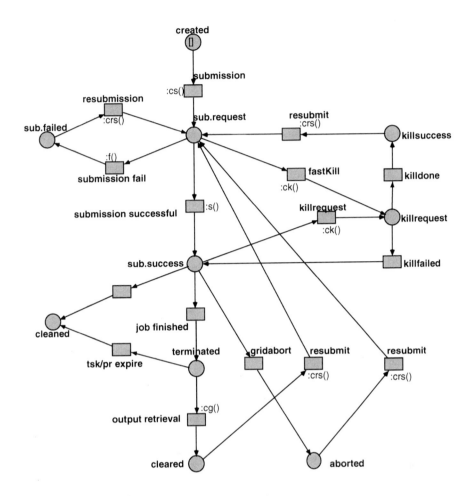

Fig. 6. The Job net

event observed by the system (bug 1). For example let us consider the unlabeled transition between the *sub.success* and the *cleaned* places in Figure 6: the latter denotes that a job has been abandoned because the user security credentials are expired and the Grid will not manage processes whose owner cannot be recognized. A malicious code interacting with the clients in place of the proper server could move jobs arbitrarily to this terminal state. The fix for this bug consisted in a review of the code managing the job state automata in accordance with what is stated by the presented Job net. Also, the pre-conditions that allow a client to perform a *kill* request over the jobs are not granted properly (bug 2): jobs can be killed when they are in states where the killing is dangerous. For example, a user could run into a condition where a failed job cannot be resubmitted as the system requires to kill it. That means the job is in a deadlock, as a failed job cannot be killed on the Grid. In term of Job net, the lack of synchronization between *killdone, killfailed* transitions and the server-side components has been identified as the cause of this bug. More details on the misbehavior of kill request feature are considered in the following.

4.3   TaskRegister

The TaskRegister component, shown on the left of Figure 7, duplicates the task and jobs structures that have been created at the client side and alters all the object attributes in order to localize them with respect to the running environment of the server, taking care also of security issues (like user credentials delegation) and files movement (check the existence of input). We modeled this cloning by means of the *reference semantics*: the TaskRegister component receives from the client a copy of the reference which points to the Task.

The component is able to handle more tasks simultaneously thanks to a pool of threads implementing the net of Figure 7. The first transition that is fired is *submission*, which is synchronized with the transition in the system net that receives the task reference from the CRABClient. Then four operations which can fail are executed on the task. These include local modification of the task with respect to the server environment, the user's credential retrieval (also known as delegation), the setting of the server behavior according to what the credentials allow to do and, finally, the checking that the needed input files are accessible from the Grid. If the registration fails the only possible operation available is *archiveTask* which deletes the reference to the task from the task register component. If the user has the privileges to execute the jobs in the task, and if the inputs needed by the task are available, then a range of jobs is selected from the task and passed to the CRABServerWorker by firing the *toCSW* transition (again under the supervision of the system net).

The modeling and the simulation of the TaskRegister net has highlighted some relevant defects and bugs. In case of failure the TaskRegister component was not able to set properly the status of the jobs in a task to fail. In fact, in the model all the transitions *fail* in the TaskRegister component (Figure 7) do not have any downlink. This reflects the fact that if the registration process fails for a task then the state of this task is not updated correctly. This macroscopic lack in the system design implied different side effects. The server was not able to discriminate whether to retry automatically the registration process or to give up and notify the user about the impossibility to proceed (bug 3). In addition, the system could not tell if the registration has been attempted previously. This implies that the client transfers the input data every time a registration failure appears, with a waste of network resources (bug 4). Both the defects have been solved by introducing the proper synchronization between the *fail* transition in the component with *submission failed* in the job net. Mapping the synchronization into the server code has granted that the status of the jobs is set to the correct failure state and that the submission counters are properly incremented (being implementative details the counter is not shown in the Job net). With this modification the server becomes aware that a first try has been executed and also network transfers are exploited more efficiently. Another bug has been identified thanks to the study of the synchronization among the transitions for

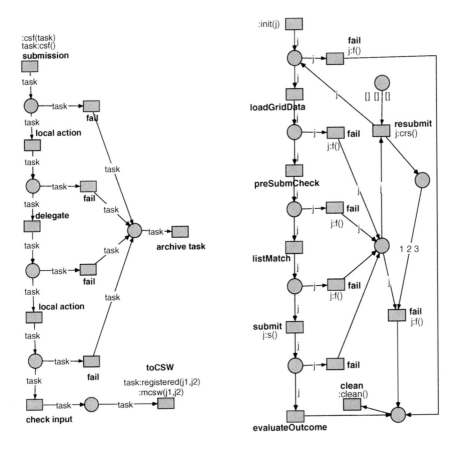

Fig. 7. TaskRegister and SubmissionWorker nets respectively

the client, the jobs and the TaskRegister nets. In detail, the handling of the *kill* commands presents some issues. If a user requires to kill some jobs while the task is being registered, the system cannot distinguish properly which jobs have to be killed and therefore it applies an over-killing strategy by halting the whole task (bug 5). The perceived effect of this bug is that when a user asks for the halting of a specific job, its whole task is terminated. This happens because the code performs some sort of synchronization with the Task net instead of having rendezvous with the related transitions into the lists of killing jobs. Transition *prematureKill* in the Task net (Figure 5) models this scenario.

The killing of Grid jobs is a demanding action, both in terms of network communications and in terms of coordination among the different services involved in a Grid. Furthermore the killing of an analysis job is a permitted but infrequent action. For these reasons the CRAB developers have decided to suppress this early job termination feature in order to avoid the latter bug. Now users are allowed to kill jobs only once they have been actually submitted to the Grid. This additional constraint let to avoid the conditions that bring to the emergence also of bug 2. In this way the defect is avoided and the bug can be considered as fixed.

4.4   CRABServerWorker, and SubmissionWorkers

In our model the result of a submit operation is that the CRABServerWorker component, shown in Figure 8, receives a structured token in the place *accepted*. If the submit was the first, transition *newTaskRegistered* is fired after the task has been registered by the TaskRegister component by means of transition *toCSW*, which is synchronized with transition *newTaskRegistered* through the overall system. If the submit is not the first, the task has been already registered, therefore transition *subsequentSubmission* is fired. After receiving the range of jobs, the CRABServerWorker component schedules these jobs for the execution on the Grid infrastructure. The practical effect of this component is to break the task into lists of jobs in order to improve the performance thanks to bulk interactions with the Grid middleware. The Submission Worker thread spawned by the component monitors the actual submission process of the jobs. We have modeled this fact by creating a Submission Worker net for each one of the jobs in the list. Indeed, transition *triggerSubmissionWorker* creates a new Submission Worker assigned to the variable *sw* and synchronizes it with a transition labeled *init*.

The thread is responsible both for tracking the submission to the Grid infrastructure, and for resubmitting jobs when a failure occurs. Failures can occur for different reasons: network communication glitches, unavailable compatible resources. Some types of failures are recoverable and in those cases the Submission Worker automatically tries to resubmit the job a three times. This value can be configured in the code, but in the model we only used the actually employed value of three. If the failure persists the job is permanently marked as failed. The net shown on the right in Figure 7 is our model of the submission worker component.

The study of the synchronization between the job and the Submission Worker nets allowed us to identify another bug in the code. The *submission success* transition in the job net (Figure 6) synchronizes with the *submit* Submission Worker's transition (right of Figure 7). In fact, in the model the job's transition has an uplink named *:s()*, and the Submission Worker's transition has a corresponding downlink named *:s()*. This means that the CRAB Server marks the submission as successful just after the interactions with the Grid. Actually the network latencies could delay the propagation of the job failure message (bug 6) and, therefore, the correct rendezvous should be enacted between *submission success* and *evaluateOutcome*.

4.5   Details on the Models Derivation and Simulation

The model was derived from the code by analyzing both the official documentation and the source code of the system. The Job net is directly built from the documentation. A finite state automata which describes the Job is reported explicitly. After that, simply by using pattern matching we analyzed the source code relevant for the submission use case by searching for interaction with jobs.

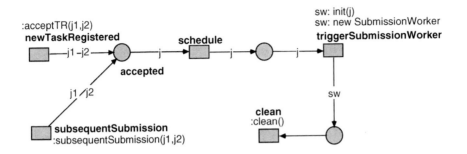

Fig. 8. The CRABServerWorker Net

Each source module is modeled as a net (e.g. CRABClient) by analysing their source code and the logs. In particular, the components located inside a server (TaskRegister, CRABServerWorker, SubmissionWorker) have been modeled by considering the execution flow of their event dispatch loop: the publish & subscribe paradigm is implemented as a loop polling for new events to process at regular intervals. By following the execution flow that every kind of message can activate in a component, the sequence of procedures and message publications have been used to depict the transitions of the corresponding net. Local processing (e.g., intra-component methods and functions) corresponds to a transition, while publishing of new events and modifications of objects through reference semantic have been modeled with synchronized transitions.

For example, the interactions with the Job nets are modeled using the RENEW uplink/downlink mechanism. A modification of the status of a job in the code is modeled as a pair of synchronized transitions in the model itself: one in the job net and one in the net that models the component changing the job status.

To ensure that the model is an accurate representation of the software, we made several task submissions with the CRAB tool and monitored the status of the jobs during the evolution. In detail, by following the logs of every submission performed by the server in a period of a week (i.e., approximatively one hundred submissions) we simulated the steps of the submission on the nets. The logs includes different parameters setup that brought to error condition, like jobs lacking of input files, job submitted by users with expired credentials, and jobs killed before the completion of task registration process.

Using these real system logs, we simulated the submission process by firing the transitions (i.e., method's call in the log) in the model, taking care that the status of the job net is consistent with what the user saw at terminal during the actual job submission to the Grid. When an exception appears in the log, we stop the simulation and consider the places in the nets to identify the causes of the error condition. The bugs presented in this section has been identified by considering the causes of the failure on the nets only, avoiding to look at the actual code of the system. Once a solution has been identified for a bug, the CRAB developers have been contacted in order to apply the fix.

5   Towards Formal Verification

In the study we have just presented, a formal approach was used to validate a system that has already been implemented. Building a model of the system and simulating its behavior by means of a computer aided tool was what allowed us to find problems in the implementation of the CRAB server. However, another great advantage of modeling a system with formal methods is the possibility to apply *automatic* analysis techniques to extract information about the system, like invariant analysis, and model checking.

In order to apply some of these techniques, the formal model must respect specific prerequisites. For example, most algorithms for model checking a concurrent system require a finite state space. Nets-within-nets models which satisfy this last requirement are hypernets [2] and their generalization [4], which can both be expanded to 1-safe Petri nets [3,20]. This expansion guarantees the possibility of applying all the analysis techniques of this well known class of Petri nets to hypernets.

The first idea was to use such a class of nets to model the CRAB server, but because of the absence of modeling limitations and verification features in RENEW, and because of the high complexity of the system, we preferred to use a slightly more powerful version of hypernets. However, it can be interesting to come back to the class of hypernets in order to have the certainty that the state space is finite. To do this the following fixes are necessary:

- Transitions which create or delete tokens must be deleted in some way. For example, transition *crab -create* of the CrabClient net cannot create an unbounded number of tasks anymore, but an input place which contains as many tokens as the maximum number of allowed tasks must be added.
  This is not a big problem. As a matter of fact the computers disks space is limited, and consequently so are the number of tasks which can be created by a user.
- Hypernets use a *value semantics*, which means that a net cannot have two references to it. Nevertheless, in our model some transitions duplicate the references to a net. For example, CRABClient transition *crab -submit (first)* duplicates the reference of the task bound to variable *task*, and TaskRegister transition *toCSW* makes a copy of two jobs of the task (that is the reason for the dashed lines in Figure 2).

  Therefore, to be able to use hypernets we need to remove all the transitions which duplicate references in the model. This has an impact in the way the system is modeled. The main change is that the client cannot modify the status of jobs directly interacting with them, but it has to send a message to the server which will take care of changing jobs status. For example, the intention of killing a Job can be achieved by the *CRABClient* net by sending a "black token message" to the TaskRegister which will modify the status of the interested job.

  If from one hand this approach complicates the model, on the other hand it helps in controling the boundedness of the model. Infact, duplication of references is somehow dangerous if the intention is to keep the state space bounded. Loosely speaking, the risk is of an uncontrolled growth of the references of a net without a corresponding deletion of these references. Moreover, another good point of the value semantics is that although modeling the interactions between a client and the server by means of a shared reference is convenient, it is not what really happens in the system where the client sends a message to a server, which is who really modifies the state of the job.

Even though analysis of properties is not available with the current version of the model because of the issues just discussed, the advantage of using a reference semantics, from a modeling point of view, helped us finding several design defects in the implementation of the CRAB server.

Future works will be focused on restricting the model to a hypernet, to verify properties like invariants and to apply model checking techniques. In fact, RE-NEW helped us to model the system with the net-within-net paradigm, however it does not support formal verification. The reformulation of the model according to the hypernet formalism will let us overcome the limitation of the modeling tool. Restricting the model to hypernets is not the only way to have a limited state space, but a formal proof is available using hypernets thanks to the 1-safe expansion [3,20].

6   Conclusions

High Energy Physics experiments like CMS needs large scale Grid application to perform distributed data analysis, and software tools like CRAB have been developed to protect users from the architectural complexities of the distributed infrastructure. In this paper, we considered the fundamental use case of the submission of user data analysis to the Grid of the CRAB tool. Because of the complexity of the software architecture, the use case has been modeled using the nets-within-nets paradigm. Every component of the CRABServer involved in this use case has been modeled in the hierarchy of the nets and compared to the behavior expected by its users.

The approach followed for the modeling of the CRAB Server submission chain is a particular case for a quite general class of Grid systems. All the Grid middlewares rely on jobs that are represented by finite state automata and that are concurrently managed by the different services involved in the Grid. In addition, the intermediate action of a broker like the CRAB Server is becoming a common pattern with the diffusion of scientific gateways: programmatic portals that abstract the user applications from the complexities of the distributed infrastructures acting as back end.

The adoption of the nets-within-nets paradigm has provided a natural and effective way to model subtle interactions among the different net levels. It would have required a significantly greater effort to discover the same problems with a flat net approach (the identification of the components involved in a bug would have been more complex).

From the simulation of the model a number of bugs and design defects emerged. This has led the developers to improve the overall quality of system implementation in the subsequent releases that the users now adopt. Two groups of bugs have been identified: bugs related to wrong coding of the expected behaviors (bug 1, bug 2, and bug 4) and bugs where the specific adoption of nets-within-nets formalism has highlighted synchronization problems among the entities (bug 3, bug 5, and bug 6).

More in detail, the reason that makes the nets-within-nets paradigm suitable for modeling Grid systems like CRAB, is that the hierarchical structure of the system is represented in a natural way in the model. There is a client, and there is server which have several components. Moreover there are tasks which are made of jobs. All the interactions between nets at different levels are modeld in an explicit way. The risk of a flat approach is of loosing the direct modeling of all the possible interactions among different nets at different levels that we have for example in our model. For this motivation we chose to use the RENEW tool for the experiment discussed in this paper. Therefore, even though only a localized small caze were modeled in this paper, other use cases, like handling the splitting of tasks in jobs, or managing the job queue of Grid sites, can of course be effectively modeled with RENEW which also offers the possibility of use contruct typical of coloured Petri net.

The class of nets used to model this system is a more powerful version of hypernets, using the reference semantics instead of the value semantics, and allowing creation/deletion of tokens. It is possible to restrict the model to a proper hypernet by sacrificing its readability (some places and some transitions must be added) and restricting its behavior (transitions which makes nets unbounded must be deleted). Then, by means of hypernets and their expansion to 1-safe nets, it will be possible to use all the techniques defined for the class of 1-safe nets for analyzing the system.

A plugin of RENEW that allows to draw and to analyze a hypernet has been developed [21]. We plan to use this plugin to make automatic verification of properties of the system.

References

1. Alt, M., Hoheisel, A., Pohl, H.W., Gorlatch, S.: A Grid Workflow Language Using High-Level Petri Nets. In: Wyrzykowski, R., Dongarra, J., Meyer, N., Waśniewski, J. (eds.) PPAM 2005. LNCS, vol. 3911, pp. 715–722. Springer, Heidelberg (2006)
2. Bednarczyk, M.A., Bernardinello, L., Pawłowski, W., Pomello, L.: Modelling Mobility with Petri Hypernets. In: Fiadeiro, J.L., Mosses, P.D., Yu, Y. (eds.) WADT 2004. LNCS, vol. 3423, pp. 28–44. Springer, Heidelberg (2005)
3. Bednarczyk, M.A., Bernardinello, L., Pawłowski, W., Pomello, L.: From Petri hypernets to 1-safe nets. In: Proceedings of the Fourth International Workshop on Modelling of Objects, Components and Agents, MOCA 2006, Bericht 272, FBI-HH-B-272/06, pp. 23–43 (June 2006)

4. Bernardinello, L., Bonzanni, N., Mascheroni, M., Pomello, L.: Modeling Symport/Antiport P Systems with a Class of Hierarchical Petri Nets. In: Eleftherakis, G., Kefalas, P., Păun, G., Rozenberg, G., Salomaa, A. (eds.) WMC 2007. LNCS, vol. 4860, pp. 124–137. Springer, Heidelberg (2007)
5. Bratosin, C., van der Aalst, W., Sidorova, N.: Modeling Grid workflows with Coloured Petri nets. In: Procs. of the 8th Workshop on Practical Use of Coloured Petri Nets and CPN Tools, CPN 2007, pp. 67–86 (2007)
6. CERN. Worldwide LHC Computing Grid, http://lcg.web.cern.ch/lcg/public/ (accessed May 2010)
7. Choppy, C., Dedova, A., Evangelista, S., Hong, S., Klai, K., Petrucci, L.: The NEO Protocol for Large-Scale Distributed Database Systems: Modelling and Initial Verification. In: Lilius, J., Penczek, W. (eds.) PETRI NETS 2010. LNCS, vol. 6128, pp. 145–164. Springer, Heidelberg (2010)
8. Codispoti, G., Cinquilli, M., Fanfani, A., Fanzago, F., Farina, F., Kavka, C., Lacaprara, S., Miccio, V., Spiga, D., Vaandering, E.: CRAB: a CMS Application for Distributed Analysis. IEEE Transactions on Nuclear Science 56(5), 2850–2858 (2009)
9. Cortadella, J., Reisig, W. (eds.): ICATPN 2004. LNCS, vol. 3099. Springer, Heidelberg (2004)
10. Darwin, I.F.: Checking C Programs with Lint Nutshell Handbooks. O'Reilly Media (1988)
11. Foster, I., Kesselman, C.: The Grid 2: Blueprint for a New Computing Infrastructure. Morgan Kaufmann Publishers Inc., San Francisco (2003)
12. Foster, I., Kesselman, C., Nick, J.M., Tuecke, S.: Tuecke. Grid services for distributed system integration. Computer 35, 37–46 (2002)
13. Guan, Z., Hernandez, F., Bangalore, P., Gray, J., Skjellum, A., Velusamy, V., Liu, Y.: Grid-Flow: a Grid-enabled scientific workflow system with a Petri-net-based interface: Research Articles. Concurr. Comput.: Pract. Exper. 18, 1115–1140
14. Hoffmann, K., Ehrig, H., Mossakowski, T.: High-Level Nets with Nets and Rules as Tokens. In: Ciardo, G., Darondeau, P. (eds.) ICATPN 2005. LNCS, vol. 3536, pp. 268–288. Springer, Heidelberg (2005)
15. Hoheisel, A., Der, U.: Dynamic Workflows for Grid Applications. In: Procs. of the Cracow Grid Workshop 2003, p. 8 (2003)
16. Köhler, M., Farwer, B.: Object Nets for Mobility. In: Kleijn, J., Yakovlev, A. (eds.) ICATPN 2007. LNCS, vol. 4546, pp. 244–262. Springer, Heidelberg (2007)
17. Köhler, M., Rölke, H.: Properties of object Petri nets. In: Cortadella, Reisig (eds.) [9], pp. 278–297
18. Kummer, O.: Referenznetze. Logos-Verlag (2002)
19. Kummer, O., Wienberg, F., Duvigneau, M., Schumacher, J., Köhler, M., Moldt, D., Rölke, H., Valk, R.: An extensible editor and simulation engine for Petri nets: Renew. In: Cortadella, Reisig (eds.) [9], pp. 484–493
20. Mascheroni, M.: Generalized hypernets and their semantics. In: Proceedings of the Fifth International Workshop on Modelling of Objects, Components and Agents, MOCA 2009, Bericht 290, pp. 87–106 (September 2009)
21. Mascheroni, M., Wagner, T., Wüstenberg, L.: Verifying reference nets by means of hypernets: a plugin for renew. In: Proceedings of the International Workshop on Petri Nets and Software Engenering PNSE 2010, Bericht 294, pp. 39–54 (June 2010)
22. Taktak, S., Kristensen, L.: Formal Modelling and Initial Validation of the Chelonia Distributed Storage System. In: Riekki, J., Ylianttila, M., Guo, M. (eds.) GPC 2011. LNCS, vol. 6646, pp. 127–137. Springer, Heidelberg (2011)

23. Taylor, I.J., Deelman, E., Gannon, D.B., Shields, M.: Workflows for e-Science: Scientific Workflows for Grids. Springer, Heidelberg (2006)
24. The CMS Collaboration. The CMS Experiment at CERN LHC. J. Inst., 3, S08004 (2008)
25. The TLS Group. The Large Hadron Collider Conceptual Design. Technical report, CERN (1995); preprint hep-ph/0601012
26. Valk, R.: Nets in Computer Organisation. In: Brauer, W., Reisig, W., Rozenberg, G. (eds.) APN 1986. LNCS, vol. 255, pp. 218–233. Springer, Heidelberg (1987)
27. Valk, R.: Petri Nets as Token Objects: An Introduction to Elementary Object Nets. In: Desel, J., Silva, M. (eds.) ICATPN 1998. LNCS, vol. 1420, pp. 1–25. Springer, Heidelberg (1998)
28. van Hee, K.M., Lomazova, I.A., Oanea, O., Serebrenik, A., Sidorova, N., Voorhoeve, M.: Nested Nets for Adaptive Systems. In: Donatelli, S., Thiagarajan, P.S. (eds.) ICATPN 2006. LNCS, vol. 4024, pp. 241–260. Springer, Heidelberg (2006)

Incremental Process Discovery

Marc Solé[1,2] and Josep Carmona[2]

[1] Computer Architecture Department, UPC
msole@ac.upc.edu
[2] Software Department, UPC
jcarmona@lsi.upc.edu

Abstract. *Process Discovery* techniques provide an automatic shift between a trace or automata model into an event-based one. In particular, the problem of deriving Petri nets from transition systems or languages has many applications, ranging from CAD for VLSI to medical applications, among others. The most popular algorithms to accomplish this task are based on the theory of regions. However, one of the problems of such algorithms is the space requirements: for real-life or industrial instances, some of the region-based algorithms cannot handle in memory the internal representation of the input or the exploration lattice required. In this paper, the incremental derivation of a basis of regions and the later partitioned basis exploration are presented, which allow splitting large inputs in fragments of tractable size. The theory of the paper has been implemented as the new tool `dbminer`. Experimental results on medium-sized benchmarks show promising reductions in the time required for process discovery when compared to other region-based approaches.

1 Introduction

The complexity of software and hardware systems is reaching a point of no return where it is almost impossible to have a formal description of everything that happens in a system. Desirable aspects, like *heterogeneity, fine granularity*, and *concurrency*, among others, contribute to increase the complexity in a magnitude that makes it impossible to resort to traditional specification practices to capture the behavior of a system. This is a real impediment for applying *formal methods* to analyze nowadays software/hardware environments, because the existence of an abstraction that summarizes the important behavior is only possible if a significant part the design stage is devoted to specification.

Process Mining naturally arose to solve this problematic situation. It considers three main dimensions: *discovery, conformance* and *extension* [1]. In particular, the techniques for the discovery of formal models from system logs limit the need for human intervention to formally specify the behavior implemented. Hence, the keystone of process mining is process discovery. In this paper we will provide techniques within this dimension.

Process discovery can be oriented to *control-flow* (discover the causal relationships between the activities), *data* (determine data patterns for several purposes)

K. Jensen, S. Donatelli, and J. Kleijn (Eds.): ToPNoC V, LNCS 6900, pp. 221–242, 2012.
© Springer-Verlag Berlin Heidelberg 2012

or *social* (find the structure of the human collaboration to carry out processes). In this paper we focus on control-flow process discovery: the input of the methods presented in this paper is a set of traces (a log) or an automata, representing (part of) the behavior underlying a system, and the output is an event-based formal model (in our case, a Petri net [2]) that represents the behavior seen in the input (but maybe more). In the last decade, several algorithms for control-flow process discovery have appeared. The first algorithm is the α-algorithm [3], which is based on detecting ordering relations in the log. Although having low-complexity, the α-algorithm can only discover a very restricted class of behaviors, i.e. *Workflow nets*. To extend the class of behaviors to account for, a genetic approach was presented in [4], which unfortunately can have problems in dealing with inputs of medium/large size.

The introduction of the theory of regions [5] in the early nineties enabled a new area of research that strives for transforming language or state-based representations into event-based ones. This transformation, known as *synthesis*, was initially devoted to derive a Petri net whose reachability graph was bisimilar or isomorphic to the input transition system. The variant of synthesis considered in this paper, discovery, has weaker requirements: the language of the derived Petri net must be a superset (maybe proper) of the language of the input transition system [3]. This is a reasonable goal, since logs typically represent a fraction of the whole behavior of the system, (*i.e.* are *incomplete*).

The theory of regions is interesting in the context of process discovery for three important reasons: i) there is no limitation on the types of behaviors to discover[1], ii) the set of traces in the log is a subset of the behavior of the Petri net derived (under some circumstances, the extra behavior allowed is minimal [7]), and iii) the region-based algorithms can be guided to search for particular patterns in form of Petri net classes [8,9].

Many research has been carried out since the introduction of regions, specially of theoretical nature, which has brought a better understanding of the theory [10,11,12,13], and has provided meaningful extensions to make it more general [14,15,16,7]. As a consequence of the aforementioned theoretical work, tools based on the theory of regions started to be available by the end of the nineties [17,18] and still new ones are developed nowadays [16,7]. These tools are the outcome of bridging the gap between the theory and practice, and many of them are used extensively in the academic domain, whereas few are used in industry. The reasons for the limited success of these tools in industry might be:

1. The algorithms involved are complex, i.e. in general polynomial with the size of the input [10], that might be prohibitive for large inputs, and the use of efficient data structures like BDDs [19] or heuristics only alleviates the problem.
2. No scalable techniques have been presented that may allow dividing the problem of region-based derivation of Petri nets.

---

[1] In [6] one can find very simple logs for which the α-algorithm is unable to derive a Petri net covering its traces, whilst region-based algorithms on the same log derive a Petri net that accepts the traces in the log.

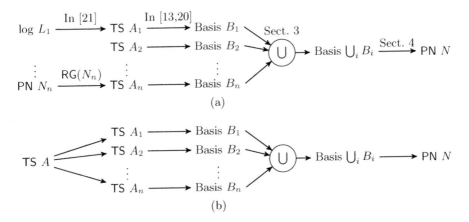

Fig. 1. Two forms of Incremental Process Discovery: (a) Computing the region basis from several components and distributed generation of a PN. (b) Splitting of a large TS into fragments of manageable size and application of the approach.

In this work we provide the theoretical basis for deriving scalable strategies that may allow handling large specifications. More concretely, as space requirements are typically the bottleneck for some of the tools listed above, in this paper we present an incremental technique that allows splitting the input into several smaller parts. Moreover, we show how the theory of regions can be extended algorithmically to combine the regions of each part in order to derive the regions of the whole input.

The theory presented will be oriented for the problem of discovery: given a set of objects describing behaviors (like a Petri net, a transition system or an event log) $O_1, O_2, \ldots, O_n$, we want to obtain a Petri net N such that $\mathcal{L}(N) \supseteq \bigcup_{i=1}^{n} \mathcal{L}(O_i)$. The traditional way to solve this problem is to generate a transition system A_i for each O_i, join all these A_i to create a single transition system, and then apply a region-based technique to derive a Petri net from a transition system [18,9].

In this paper we explore a different approach. Instead of working with a monolithic transition system, we use the fact that a transition system can be represented by a basis of regions, such that any other region is a linear combination of the regions in the basis (a recent publication shows an efficient technique to accomplish this task [20]). Then, bases can be combined to obtain a region basis for the whole system, from which we can derive the Petri net N.

The general picture of the approach of this paper is outlined on Fig. 1(a). Some arcs are labeled with an indication of the section or the reference where the conversion/operation is explained. Basically the first step is to convert inputs that are not transition systems into a transition system, and then compute a region basis from which a PN can be generated.

Another possible application of the techniques presented in this paper is shown in Fig. 1(b), where a large TS is split into smaller subsystems of manageable size, with the only restriction that all the subsystems must include the initial state and be connected.

The paper is organized as follows. We start by giving the necessary background in Sect. 2. The process of combining a set of bases to produce a unique basis for the whole system is explained in Sect. 3. A description of the generation of a PN from a region basis is given in Sect. 4, which is compared to related work in Sect. 5. Our generation algorithm has been implemented in a tool that is experimentally tested and compared to other applications in Sect. 6. Finally, Sect. 7 concludes this paper.

2   Background

2.1   Finite Transition Systems and Petri Nets

Definition 1 (Transition system). *A transition system (TS) is defined by a tuple $\langle S, \Sigma, T, s_0 \rangle$, where S is a set of states, Σ is an alphabet of actions, $T \subseteq S \times \Sigma \times S$ is a set of (labelled) transitions, and $s_0 \in S$ is the initial state.*

We use $s \xrightarrow{e} s'$ as a shortcut for $(s, e, s') \in T$, and we denote its transitive closure as $\xrightarrow{*}$. A state s' is said to be *reachable from state* s if $s \xrightarrow{*} s'$. We extend the notation to transition sequences, i.e., $s_1 \xrightarrow{\sigma} s_{n+1}$ if $\sigma = e_1 \ldots e_n$ and $\forall i : 1 \le i \le n, (s_i, e_i, s_{i+1}) \in T$. We denote $\#(\sigma, e)$ the number of times that event e occurs in σ. Let $A = \langle S, \Sigma, T, s_0 \rangle$ be a TS. We consider connected TSs that satisfy the following axioms: (i) S and Σ are finite sets, (ii) every event has an occurrence and (iii) every state is reachable from the initial state.

The *language* of a TS A, $\mathcal{L}(A)$, is the set of transitions sequences feasible from the initial state. For two TSs A_1 and A_2, when $\mathcal{L}(A_1) \subseteq \mathcal{L}(A_2)$, we will say that A_2 is an *over-approximation* of A_1.

Definition 2 (Union of TSs). *Given two TSs $A_1 = \langle S_1, \Sigma_1, T_1, s_0 \rangle$ and $A_1 = \langle S_2, \Sigma_2, T_2, s_0 \rangle$, the union of A_1 and A_2 is the TS $A_1 \cup A_2 = \langle S_1 \cup S_2, \Sigma_1 \cup \Sigma_2, T_1 \cup T_2, s_0 \rangle$.*

Clearly, the TS $A_1 \cup A_2$ is an over-approximation of the TSs A_1 and A_2, i.e. $\mathcal{L}(A_1) \cup \mathcal{L}(A_2) \subseteq \mathcal{L}(A_1 \cup A_2)$.

Definition 3 (Petri net [2]). *A Petri net (PN) is a tuple (P, T, W, M_0) where the sets P and T represent disjoint finite sets of places and transitions, respectively, and $W : (P \times T) \cup (T \times P) \to \mathbb{N}$ is the weighted flow relation. A marking is a mapping $P \to \mathbb{N}$. The initial marking M_0 defines the initial state of the system. A PN is called* pure *if, for each place p and transition t, it holds that $W(p, t) \cdot W(t, p) = 0$.*

A transition $t \in T$ is *enabled* in a marking M if $\forall p \in P : M(p) \ge W(p, t)$ holds. Firing an enabled transition t in a marking M leads to the marking M' defined by $M'(p) = M(p) - W(p, t) + W(t, p)$, for each $p \in P$, and is denoted by $M \xrightarrow{t} M'$. The set of all markings reachable from the initial marking M_0 is called its Reachability Set. We say that N is k-bounded if, for all reachable marking M and all place p, it holds that $M(p) \leq k$. The *Reachability Graph* of N, denoted $\mathsf{RG}(N)$, is a transition system in which the set of states is the Reachability Set, the events are the transitions of the net and a transition (M_1, t, M_2) exists if and only if $M_1 \xrightarrow{t} M_2$. We use $\mathcal{L}(N)$ as a shortcut for $\mathcal{L}(\mathsf{RG}(N))$.

2.2   Generalized Regions

The theory of regions [5,12] provides a way to derive a Petri net from a transition system. Intuitively, a region corresponds to a place in the derived Petri net. In the initial definition, a region was defined as a subset of states of the transition system satisfying a homogeneous relation with respect to the set of events. Later extensions [14,22,7] generalize this definition to multisets, which is the notion used in this paper.

Definition 4 (Multiset, k-bounded Multiset, Subset). *Given a set S, a multiset r of S is a mapping $r : S \to \mathbb{Z}$. The number $r(s)$ is called the* multiplicity *of s in r. A multiset r is k-bounded if all its multiplicities are less or equal than k. A multiset r_1 is a subset of r_2 $(r_1 \subseteq r_2)$ if $\forall s \in S : r_1(s) \leq r_2(s)$ holds.*

We define the following operations on multisets:

Definition 5 (Multiset operations)

Maximum power	$\text{pow}(r) = \max_{s \in S} r(s)$
Minimum power	$\text{minp}(r) = \min_{s \in S} r(s)$
Scalar product	$(k \cdot r)(s) = k \cdot r(s)$, for $k \in \mathbb{Z}$
Scalar sum	$(r + k)(s) = r(s) + k$, for $k \in \mathbb{Z}$
Sum	$(r_1 + r_2)(s) = r_1(s) + r_2(s)$
Subtraction	$(r_1 - r_2)(s) = r_1(s) - r_2(s)$

The operations described above have algebraic properties, e.g., $r + r = 2 \cdot r$ and $r_1 - k \cdot r_2 = r_1 + (-k) \cdot r_2$.

Definition 6 (Gradient). *Let $\langle S, \Sigma, T, s_0 \rangle$ be a TS. Given a multiset r and a transition $s \xrightarrow{e} s' \in T$, its* gradient *is defined as $\delta_r(s \xrightarrow{e} s') = r(s') - r(s)$. If all the transitions of an event $e \in \Sigma$ have the same gradient, we say that the event e has* constant gradient, *whose value is denoted as $\delta_r(e)$.*

Definition 7 (Region). *A region r is a multiset defined in a TS, in which all the events have constant gradient. We say that r is* normalized *if $\text{minp}(r) = 0$. Similarly, it is* non-negative *if $\text{minp}(r) \geq 0$.*

Fig. 2(a) shows a TS. The numbers within the states correspond to the multiplicity of the shown multiset r. This multiset is a region because both events a and b have constant gradient, i.e. $\delta_r(\mathsf{a}) = -2$ and $\delta_r(\mathsf{b}) = -3$. The region is normalized since its minimum power is zero.

There is a direct correspondence between non-negative regions and the *feasible places* of a pure PN with respect to the language of a TS.

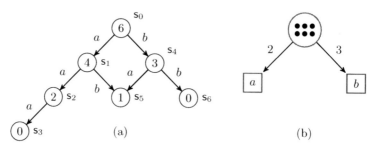

Fig. 2. (a) Region in a TS: $r(s_0) = 6, r(s_1) = 4, \ldots, r(s_6) = 0$, (b) corresponding place in the Petri net.

Definition 8 (Feasible place). *Given a* TS $A = \langle S, \Sigma, T, s_0 \rangle$ *and a pure* PN $N_p = \langle \{p\}, \Sigma, W, M_0 \rangle$, *we say that place p is feasible (w.r.t. $\mathcal{L}(A)$) if $\mathcal{L}(N_p) \supseteq \mathcal{L}(A)$. Every non-negative region r of A corresponds to a feasible place p such that $M_0(p) = r(s_0)$, and $W(p, e) = -\delta_r(e)$ if $\delta_r(e) < 0$, and $W(e, p) = \delta_r(e)$ otherwise.*

Intuitively, feasible places are places that can be used to construct a PN that will always include the language of a TS A, since the addition of a feasible place p with language $\mathcal{L}(N_p)$ to a PN N yields a net N' such that $\mathcal{L}(N') = \mathcal{L}(N) \cap \mathcal{L}(N_p)$, and all feasible places p satisfy $\mathcal{L}(N_p) \supseteq \mathcal{L}(A)$. Fig. 2(b) shows the feasible place corresponding to the region shown in Fig. 2(a). The place contains six tokens since $r(s_0) = 6$ and, for instance, it has an outgoing arc to transition a because $\delta_r(a) = -2$.

Any region r can become normalized by subtracting $\text{minp}(r)$ from the multiplicity of all the states.

Definition 9 (Normalization). *We denote by $\downarrow r$ the normalization of a region r, so that $\downarrow r = r - \text{minp}(r)$.*

Definition 10 (Gradient vector). *Let r be a region of a TS whose set of events is $\Sigma = \{e_1, e_2, \ldots, e_n\}$. The gradient vector of r, denoted as $\Delta(r)$, is the vector of the event gradients, i.e. $\Delta(r) = (\delta_r(e_1), \delta_r(e_2), \ldots, \delta_r(e_n))$.*

Proposition 1. *Gradient vectors have the following properties:*

$$\Delta(r_1 + r_2) = \Delta(r_1) + \Delta(r_2) \qquad \Delta(k \cdot r) = k \cdot \Delta(r)$$
$$\Delta(r + k) = \Delta(r) \qquad \Delta(r_1 - r_2) = \Delta(r_1) - \Delta(r_2)$$

Regions can be partitioned into classes using their gradient vectors.

Definition 11 (Canonical region). *Two regions r_1 and r_2 are said to be equivalent if their gradient is the same, i.e. $r_1 \equiv r_2 \Leftrightarrow \Delta(r_1) = \Delta(r_2)$. Given a region r, the equivalence class of r, is defined as $[r] = \{r_i | r_i \equiv r\}$. A canonical region is the normalized region of an equivalence class, i.e. $\downarrow r$.*

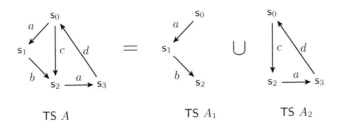

Fig. 3. TS A is split into two subsystems A_1 and A_2

Example of canonical regions are provided in Fig. 4, where two TSs are shown in which some regions have been shadowed. For instance, the canonical region $r_0 = \{s_1, s_2\}$ has gradient vector $\Delta(r_0) = (1,0)$. A PN built from the set of minimal canonical regions has the same language as a PN built using all the regions [22,12], thus it yields the smallest overapproximation with respect to the language of the TS [7].

Definition 12 (Subregion, Empty region, Minimal canonical region).
r_1 *is a subregion of* r_2, *denoted as* $r_1 \sqsubseteq r_2$, *if, for each state* s, $\downarrow r_1(s) \leq \downarrow r_2(s)$. *We denote by* $\emptyset$ *the region in which all states have zero multiplicity. A minimal canonical region* r *satisfies that for any other region* r', *if* $r' \sqsubseteq r$ *then* $r' \equiv \emptyset$.

3   Combining Region Bases

In this section we detail how region bases of different TSs can be joined, yielding a region basis of their union. We will illustrate the theory with the running example shown in Fig. 3. In this case, we assume A is a very large TS that cannot be easily handled, hence it is split into two smaller subsystems, namely A_1 and A_2, so that $A = A_1 \cup A_2$.

3.1   Basis of Regions

Definition 13 (Region basis). *Given a* TS, *a region basis* $B = \{r_1, r_2, \ldots, r_n\}$ *is a minimal subset of the canonical regions of* TS *such that any canonical region* r *can be expressed as a linear combination of* B *(i.e.* $r = \downarrow(\sum_{i=1}^{n} c_i \cdot r_i)$, *with* $c_i \in \mathbb{Q}$, $r_i \in B$).

Bernardinello *et al.* proved that any TS has a region basis [22]. Region bases are interesting because, as the following theorem states, their size is usually small.

Theorem 1 ([22]). *Let* $\langle S, \Sigma, T, s_0 \rangle$ *be a* TS. *The size of the region basis is less or equal to* $\min(|\Sigma|, |S| - 1)$.

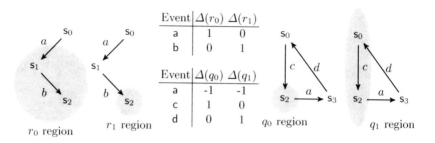

Fig. 4. Region basis for A_1 (left) and A_2 (right)

3.2   Region Compatibility

Given two systems described by their region bases, we want to obtain the region basis of their union TS. The work more closely related is [6], in which it is described how the set of regions in the joined system can be obtained from the regions of the component systems. This is achieved by introducing the concept of compatible (standard) regions. In this section we first review and extend this concept of compatibility to generalized regions.

Definition 14 (Compatible TSs). *Two TSs A_1 and A_2 are compatible if they have the same initial state.*

Def. 14 is more general than the one in [6], where the number of shared states is restricted to one (the initial state). For instance, systems A_1 and A_2 of Fig. 3 are compatible according to this definition, but not using the definition in [6], since they share states s_0 and s_2.

Definition 15 (Compatible regions, offset). *Two regions r_1 and r_2 from two compatible TSs $A_1 = \langle S_1, \Sigma_1, T_1, s_0 \rangle$ and $A_2 = \langle S_2, \Sigma_2, T_2, s_0 \rangle$ are said to be compatible if:*

- *$\forall e \in \Sigma_1 \cap \Sigma_2, \delta_{r_1}(e) = \delta_{r_2}(e)$, i.e. they have the same gradient for all common events, and,*
- *$\exists k \in \mathbb{Z} : \forall s \in S_1 \cap S_2, r_2(s) - r_1(s) = k$, i.e. the difference in multiplicity of each shared state is equal to a constant, that we call the offset between r_1 and r_2, denoted as $\mathrm{off}(r_1, r_2)$.*

Two compatible regions are said to be directly compatible *if $\mathrm{off}(r_1, r_2) = 0$. Conversely, if $\mathrm{off}(r_1, r_2) \neq 0$, we say that the regions are* indirectly compatible.

An immediate consequence of Def. 15 is that, if there is only a single shared state, then any two regions with the same gradient for all common events are compatible. This is, for instance, the case when TSs represent execution trees and only the initial state is shared among them.

Two compatible regions can be made directly compatible by adding the offset to one of them.

Definition 16 (Directly compatible region). *Given two compatible regions* r_1 *and* r_2 *with* $\mathrm{off}(r_1, r_2) > 0$, *the directly compatible region of* r_1 *with respect to* r_2 *is* $r_1 \uparrow^{r_2} = r_1 + \mathrm{off}(r_1, r_2)$.

Definition 17 (Union of compatible regions). *Given two compatible regions* r_1 *and* r_2, *defined over sets of states* S_1 *and* S_2, *respectively, with* $\mathrm{off}(r_1, r_2) \geq 0$, *their union, denoted* $r_1 \sqcup r_2$, *is*

$$(r_1 \sqcup r_2)(s) = \begin{cases} (r_1 \uparrow^{r_2})(s) & \text{if } s \in S_1 \\ r_2(s) & \text{otherwise} \end{cases}$$

Note that, in order to simplify the presentation, Definitions 16 and 17 assume $\mathrm{off}(r_1, r_2) \geq 0$. This assumption is without loss of generality since, depending on the offset, one can compute $r_1 \sqcup r_2$ or $r_2 \sqcup r_1$ to obtain the union region. This is possible because the union of compatible transition systems is commutative (*i.e.* $A_1 \cup A_2 = A_2 \cup A_1$).

Proposition 2. *Given two compatible regions* r_1 *and* r_2 *of two compatible TSs* A_1 *and* A_2, $r_1 \sqcup r_2$ *is a region of* $A_1 \cup A_2$. *For each shared event, its gradient is equal to the gradient in* r_1 *or* r_2, *which are equal. For non-shared events of* A_1 *(A_2), their gradient is the gradient in* A_1 *(A_2). Moreover, every region of* $A_1 \cup A_2$ *is the union of two compatible regions* r_1 *and* r_2.

Proof. Assume $\mathrm{off}(r_1, r_2) \geq 0$. Region $r = r_1 \sqcup r_2$, where $r_1 \uparrow^{r_2} = r_1 + \mathrm{off}(r_1, r_2)$. The latter entails that, in a shared state s, the multiplicity is the same for $r_1 \uparrow^{r_2}$ and r_2, which is the multiplicity assigned to r. For non-shared states, on the other hand, the multiplicity assigned in r is the multiplicity of the region whose TS contains the state. Thus any arc (either going from a shared to non-shared state or any other combination) has a constant gradient, equal to the gradient of that event in the corresponding region. Result transfers to r_1 because $\Delta(r_1) = \Delta(r_1 \uparrow^{r_2})$. This completes the proof of the first part of the proposition.

Every region r of $A_1 \cup A_2$ is the result of $r_1 \sqcup r_2$ for some compatible regions r_1 and r_2. This is straightforward if we define r_1 so that, for all state s of A_1, $r_1(s) = r(s)$, and we do the same for r_2 and A_2. Now r_1 and r_2 are regions since r is a region. Moreover they are directly compatible since the gradients of the common events have to be the same (and equal to the ones in r) and they have the same multiplicities assigned to each shared state between A_1 and A_2 since both have the same multiplicities for these states as r has.   □

Example 1. In Fig. 5 we show one region of each subsystem of our running example. They are compatible, since the gradient of the single shared event a is the same in both regions. More specifically, they are indirectly compatible, since their offset is one.

The PN generation algorithm presented in Sect. 4 explores the regions space using non-negative regions, by taking advantage of some additional properties that these regions enjoy with respect to the union of compatible regions.

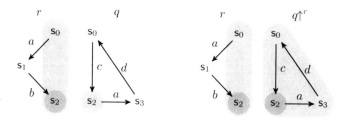

Indirectly compatible regions   Directly compatible regions

Fig. 5. Region r of A_1 and q of A_2, are indirectly compatible (left). Adding off(q, r) to q yields $q\!\uparrow^r$ which is directly compatible with r (right). The graphical notation to show k-bounded regions is by color tones: darker tones illustrate higher multiplicities (e.g., $r(s_2) = 2$) while lighter tones denote low multiplicities (e.g., $r(s_0) = 1$), and no tone represents 0 multiplicity (e.g., $r(s_1) = 0$).

Property 1. Given two compatible non-negative regions r_1 and r_2. If they are directly compatible then $r_1 \sqcup r_2$ is a normalized region, if and only if, one of them is normalized. If they are not directly compatible, but both of them are normalized, then again $r_1 \sqcup r_2$ is a normalized region.

Proof. If one of them is normalized and they are directly compatible no modification of multiplicities is performed, so the state with 0 multiplicity will keep this multiplicity and since regions are non-negative, then $\text{minp}(r_1 \sqcup r_2) = 0$. Conversely, if $r_1 \sqcup r_2$ is a normalized region and r_1 and r_2 are directly compatible, then all multiplicities of either r_1 or r_2 are greater or equal to 0, and since there is at least one 0 multiplicity, at least one of them must be normalized. If both are normalized but are not directly compatible, only one of them modifies its multiplicities and we have the same situation as before.   □

3.3   Incremental Algorithm for Obtaining a Basis

Suppose A_1 and A_2 are two TSs, and let r be a region of A_1 and q be a region of A_2. From Def. 15 we know that r and q are compatible if: (i) They have the same gradient for all common events and (ii) The difference in multiplicity of each shared is equal to a constant. To obtain a region basis for the union system $A_1 \cup A_2$ we start by writing the conditions (i) and (ii) in matrix form.

Let $\{r_1, \ldots, r_n\}$ be the region basis of A_1 and $\{q_1, \ldots, q_m\}$ the basis of A_2. This implies (see Def. 13) that $r = \sum_{i=1}^{n} x_i \cdot r_i$ and $q = \sum_{i=1}^{m} x_i \cdot q_i$, where x_i are variables that represent the coefficient used in the linear combinations. We can extend this result to their gradients: for instance $\Delta(r) = \sum_{i=1}^{n} x_i \cdot \Delta(r_i)$, which means that, for a particular event e_i, the gradient of this event in r can we written as $\delta_r(e_i) = \sum_{i=1}^{n} x_i \cdot \delta_{r_i}(e_i)$ and similarly for q. Thus, the fact that all common events must have the same gradient in both systems can be expressed (relabeling the indices of variables x_i to avoid unwanted variable sharing) as:

$$\forall e_i \in \Sigma_1 \cap \Sigma_2, \sum_{1 \le j \le n} \delta_{r_j}(e_i) \cdot x_j = \sum_{1 \le k \le m} \delta_{q_k}(e_i) \cdot x_{n+k}$$

This system of equations can be rewritten in matrix form as $M \cdot \boldsymbol{x} = \boldsymbol{0}$, where $\boldsymbol{x}$ is the column vector of variables x_i and M is the following matrix:

$$M = \begin{pmatrix} \delta_{r_1}(\mathsf{e}_1) & \dots & \delta_{r_n}(\mathsf{e}_1) & -\delta_{q_1}(\mathsf{e}_1) & \dots & -\delta_{q_m}(\mathsf{e}_1) \\ \delta_{r_1}(\mathsf{e}_2) & \dots & \delta_{r_n}(\mathsf{e}_2) & -\delta_{q_1}(\mathsf{e}_2) & \dots & -\delta_{q_m}(\mathsf{e}_2) \\ & \vdots & & & \vdots & \\ \delta_{r_1}(\mathsf{e}_c) & \dots & \delta_{r_n}(\mathsf{e}_c) & -\delta_{q_1}(\mathsf{e}_c) & \dots & -\delta_{q_m}(\mathsf{e}_c) \end{pmatrix}$$

where c is the number of common events in the system, $i.e.$ $c = |\Sigma_1 \cap \Sigma_2|$. We call this matrix the *gradient compatibility matrix* between A_1 and A_2.

Compatibility of regions requires also that the offset is the same for all shared states. To enforce such condition, assume that we shift all the regions in the bases $\{r_1, \dots, r_n\}$ and $\{q_1, \dots, q_m\}$ so that their multiplicity in the initial state is 0. Let us denote by r_i^0 and q_j^0 these shifted regions, formally defined as $r_i^0 = r_i - r_i(\mathsf{s}_0)$ and $q_j^0 = q_j - q_j(\mathsf{s}_0)$. Now any region obtained by combining the regions from the $\{r_1^0, \dots, r_n^0\}$ and $\{q_1^0, \dots, q_m^0\}$ bases will have a 0 multiplicity in the initial state. For instance, if $r^0 = \sum_{i=1}^n x_i \cdot r_i^0$ and $q^0 = \sum_{i=1}^m x_i \cdot q_i^0$, we have that $r^0(\mathsf{s}_0) = q^0(\mathsf{s}_0) = 0$. If we must enforce the offset to be the same in all shared states, then for each shared state s it must hold $r^0(\mathsf{s}) = q^0(\mathsf{s})$. This condition is equivalent to $\sum_{i=1}^n x_i \cdot r_i^0(\mathsf{s}) = \sum_{i=1}^m x_i \cdot q_i^0(\mathsf{s})$. This can be easily be written in matrix form as before by adding a row of the form $(r_1^0(\mathsf{s}) \dots r_n^0(\mathsf{s}) -q_1^0(\mathsf{s}) \dots -q_m^0(\mathsf{s}))$ for each shared state.

However, in many cases the multiplicities are guaranteed to be the same and the corresponding row is useless. Let us explain in which cases the corresponding row can be safely discarded.

The multiplicity in a region r of a given state s can also be computed as follows: assuming there is an event sequence σ such that $\mathsf{s}_0 \xrightarrow{\sigma} \mathsf{s}$, then $r(\mathsf{s}) = r(\mathsf{s}_0) + \sum_{\mathsf{e} \in \Sigma} \#(\sigma, \mathsf{e}) \cdot \delta_r(\mathsf{e})$. Consider two regions r and q from A_1 and A_2, respectively, such that they have the same gradients for all common events. Given that $r^0(\mathsf{s}_0) = q^0(\mathsf{s}_0)$, it is clear that $r^0(\mathsf{s}) = q^0(\mathsf{s})$ if there are event sequences σ_1 and σ_2 such that $\mathsf{s}_0 \xrightarrow{\sigma_1} \mathsf{s}$ in A_1, $\mathsf{s}_0 \xrightarrow{\sigma_2} \mathsf{s}$ in A_2 and $\forall \mathsf{e} \in \Sigma, \#(\sigma_1, \mathsf{e}) = \#(\sigma_2, \mathsf{e})$. If no such sequences exist, we say that the shared state s is *in conflict* since the multiplicity of s going through σ_1 or σ_2 could be different even if the gradient of all common events is the same in r and q.

Consequently, in these cases, we explicitly add the constrain that the multiplicity must be the same by creating a matrix C, called the *shared state conflict matrix* between A_1 and A_2, that, for each shared state s in conflict, contains a row of the form $(r_1^0(\mathsf{s}) \dots r_n^0(\mathsf{s}) -q_1^0(\mathsf{s}) \dots -q_m^0(\mathsf{s}))$. Since the multiplicity of all these states must be the same in r^0 and q^0, their subtraction must be 0. Thus, $C \cdot \boldsymbol{x} = \boldsymbol{0}$

Theorem 2. *Let A_1 and A_2 be two compatible TSs with region bases $\{r_1, \dots, r_n\}$ and $\{q_1, \dots, q_m\}$, respectively. Let M be their gradient compatibility matrix, C be the shared state conflict matrix, and $\boldsymbol{x}$ the column vector of variables x_1 to x_{n+m}. Consider an assignment to the variables in $\boldsymbol{x}$ such that $\binom{M}{C} \cdot \boldsymbol{x} = \boldsymbol{0}$ and some $x_i \neq 0$. This assignment identifies a region $r \sqcup q = \sum_{1 \leq i \leq n} r_i x_i \sqcup \sum_{1 \leq j \leq m} q_j x_{n+j}$ in $A_1 \cup A_2$.*

Proof. A non-trivial solution x (different from $\mathbf{0}$) defines two compatible regions, namely $r = \sum_{1 \leq i \leq n} r_i x_i$ and $q = \sum_{1 \leq j \leq m} q_j x_{n+j}$, in A_1 and A_2 respectively. These two regions are compatible according to Definition 15 if $M \cdot x = \mathbf{0}$, because for common events the gradient is the same and the offset is the same in all shared states if $C \cdot x = 0$. By Proposition 2, $r \sqcup q$ is a region of $A_1 \cup A_2$.   □

So the problem reduces to finding the solutions to a homogeneous linear system. Note that the system does not require to have solutions in the integer domain. In fact all the solutions are in $\mathbb{Q}$, since all the gradients are integers. Homogeneous linear systems have one trivial solution (*i.e.* $\mathbf{0}$) and infinite non-trivial solutions. Let y_i be all the non-redundant solution vectors, then any possible solution of the system can be obtained by linear combination of these solution vectors, since adding or subtracting $\mathbf{0}$ from $\mathbf{0}$ does not change its value. These y_i are a basis of the nullspace of $\binom{M}{C}$, and any solution x can be written as a unique linear combination $x = \sum_i \lambda_i y_i$, with $\lambda_i \in \mathbb{Q}$.

There are several well-known methods to obtain a basis for the nullspace [23], one of the easiest is to put the matrix in *reduced row echelon form*, determine the free variables, and then, for each free variable x_i, derive a vector of the basis by assigning 1 to x_i and 0 to the rest of free variables. The y_i columns correspond to the combination of regions of both systems that have the same gradient and guarantee that there is the same offset in all shared states. By computing, for each y_i, the union of the corresponding two compatible regions that each y_i yields, we do obtain a set of regions that is a region basis for the union TS.

Example 2. We will compute the region basis of the union of TSs A_1 and A_2 shown in Fig. 3. Two possible region bases for these systems are $\{r_0, r_1\}$ and $\{q_0, q_1\}$, shown in Fig. 4. The matrix M in this case is

$$M = \begin{pmatrix} 1 & 0 & 1 & 1 \end{pmatrix}$$

where columns (from left to right) correspond to regions r_0, r_1, q_0, q_1 and there is a single row that corresponds to the only shared event between A_1 and A_2, namely event a.

The set of shared states is $\{s_0, s_2\}$, thus the shared state conflict matrix C has just one row because only state s_2 is reachable from s_0 by firing a different multiset of events. Consequently $C = \begin{pmatrix} r_0^0(s_2) & r_1^0(s_2) & -q_0^0(s_2) & -q_1^0(s_2) \end{pmatrix}$. With matrices M and C we can now build

$$\begin{pmatrix} M \\ C \end{pmatrix} = \begin{pmatrix} 1 & 0 & 1 & 1 \\ 1 & 1 & -1 & 0 \end{pmatrix} \xrightarrow[\text{echelon form}]{\text{reduced row}} \begin{pmatrix} 1 & 0 & 1 & 1 \\ 0 & 1 & -2 & -1 \end{pmatrix}$$

which gives rise to an indeterminate system with two degrees of freedom. We can write $x_1 = 2x_2 + x_3$ and $x_0 = -x_2 - x_3$, so by assigning values to variables x_2 and x_3 we can generate all the possible solutions. Given these parameters the region solution will be $((-x_2 - x_3) \cdot r_0 + (2x_2 + x_3) \cdot r_1) \sqcup (x_2 \cdot q_0 + x_3 \cdot q_1)$. Using the parameter values $(1, 0)$, and $(0, 1)$ for vector (x_2, x_3) we do obtain the following regions in the joined system: $b_0 = \downarrow((-r_0 + 2r_1) \sqcup q_0)$ and $b_1 = \downarrow((-r_0 + r_1) \sqcup q_1)$. The set $\{b_0, b_1\}$ forms a region basis for the $A_1 \cup A_2$ system (see Fig. 6, where

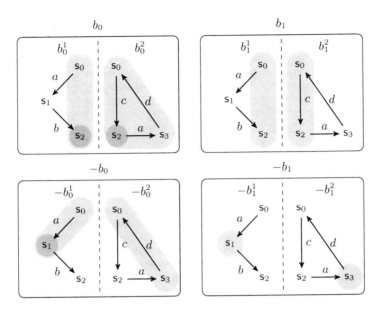

Fig. 6. Region basis $\{b_0, b_1\}$ (and their normalized complementary regions $\{\downarrow -b_0, \downarrow -b_1\}$) for system $A_1 \cup A_2$. Regions are partitioned so that $b_0 = b_0^1 \cup b_0^2$, where b_0^i is the part of b_0 in A_i.

they appear together with their normalized *complementary regions* or simply *coregions*, that is $\downarrow -b_0$ and $\downarrow -b_1$, that will also play a role in the PN generation procedure described in next section).

4   Generating a PN from a Distributed Basis

In [20] an algorithm was presented that allows finding minimal regions by careful exploration of the region space defined by the region basis. The fundamental idea is that the regions in the basis are initially assumed to be minimal, and then combinations of these regions can only yield a minimal region if the resulting region is non-normalized, since otherwise the region is a superregion of any of its component regions.

There are two important drawbacks of the technique presented in [20]. First, if the number of regions in the basis is not a small number, then the number of region combinations that one can use to explore the space of regions might be prohibitive. The algorithms presented in [20] bound this exploration by limiting the number of regions in the basis to be combined up to a given number (called *aggregation factor*). Second, the approach in [20] cannot be directly used if the number of states in the monolithic TS is too high to easily perform region operations in memory.

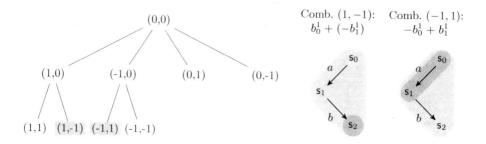

Fig. 7. Exploration of the region space. Each node represents a combination of the basis $\{b_0, b_1\}$ that will be explored. The shaded combinations are the ones for which A_1 yields a non-normalized region (shown on right), thus only these combinations would be checked in A_2.

The alternative we propose in this paper is to partition the region operations into the different component TSs, so that each time only the information of one of the systems is accessed. To achieve this partitioning, consider the region basis $\{b_0, \ldots, b_n\}$. We denote by b_i^j the part of region b_i that belongs to subsystem j. All the regions in the basis are assumed to be normalized, but the different b_i^j could be non-normalized, since they are defined so that, given i, all b_i^j are directly compatible (cf. Def. 15). For instance region b_0 in Fig. 6 is normalized, however b_0^2 is not.

Consequently a combination of the basis $\sum_i c_i \cdot b_i$ yields a non-normalized region only if, for each subsystem j, $\sum_i c_i \cdot b_i^j$ is a non-normalized region (by Property 1)[2]. Thus, the strategy is to test the basis combinations in the first subsystem, keeping only the combinations producing non-normalized regions. Then only these combinations are tested in the second subsystem, discarding the ones that yield a normalized region, and the process continues until all subsystems have been checked.

Finally, with only the surviving combinations, the subregion test (cf. Def. 12) is performed to guarantee that only the minimal regions are found. Again this test can be distributed among the subsystems, since $\sum_i c_i \cdot b_i \subseteq \sum_i c_i' \cdot b_i$ if, and only if, for each subsystem j, $\sum_i c_i \cdot b_i^j \subseteq \sum_i c_i' \cdot b_i^j$.

We illustrate this process using our running example. In Fig. 7 we can see a tree of combinations of the $\{b_0, b_1\}$ basis. Each node is a tuple $c = (c_0, c_1)$ describing the coefficients used to obtain a region r as $c_0 \cdot b_0 + c_1 \cdot b_1$. The second level of the tree corresponds to the regions in the basis and their coregions (as shown in Fig. 6). To bound the search space, assume we arbitrarily fix that the coefficients are only allowed to take values in the set $\{-1, 0, 1\}$.

---

[2] Since Property 1 only holds for non-negative regions, negative c_i coefficients are treated as markers for summing the normalized complementary regions (or simply *coregions*) of b_i. For instance $2b_1 - 3b_2$ will be actually computed as $2 \cdot b_1 + 3 \cdot \downarrow(-b_2)$. This way all regions are always non-negative and Property 1 can be safely used.

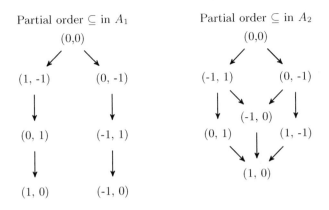

Fig. 8. Partial orders between combinations of regions in each subsystem, according to the subset relation on multisets ($\subseteq$)

From the four possible combinations in the third level, two of them yield already normalized regions in A_1, namely combinations $(1,1)$ and $(-1,-1)$. On the other hand, combinations $(1,-1)$ and $(-1,1)$ correspond to non-normalized regions in A_1, as shown in Fig. 7. Consequently only these two combinations will be checked in subsystem A_2. In this case, both regions, namely, $b_0^2 + (-b_1^2)$ and $-b_0^2 + b_1^2$, are also non-normalized in A_2. Thus these combinations correspond to non-normalized regions in $A_1 \cup A_2$, which means that they might be minimal regions (once normalized).

At this point we must check for minimal regions. The list of candidates includes all the regions in the basis (and their coregions), that is all the combinations in the second level, as well as combinations $(1,-1)$ and $(-1,1)$ that have been found during the exploration. To check for minimality, we create a partial order among all these combinations in each subsystem (see Fig. 8). A region is not minimal if there is a combination, different than $(0,0)$, that appears before it in all the partial orders. In our example, combinations $(1,0)$ and $(-1,0)$ are not minimal. Conversely, for instance $(-1,1)$ is minimal because, although combination $(0,-1)$ precedes it in A_1 (i.e. $-b_1^1 \subseteq -b_0^1 + b_1^1$), it is not longer true in A_2 (i.e. $-b_1^2 \not\subseteq -b_0^2 + b_1^2$). With the minimal regions found we build the PN of Fig. 9.

Algorithmic Details. For a set of subsystems $A_1, \ldots, A_n$ the corresponding pseudocode is shown in Algorithm 1. It starts by computing the distributed region basis for the union system $\bigcup_{i=1}^{n} A_i$ as described in Sect. 3. Then, the sets used for storing the combinations to explore are defined (lines 3 to 5). Set M will contain the combinations of the regions that are candidates to being minimal regions. Since the algorithm starts assuming that the regions in the basis and their coregions are candidates, M is initially populated with the corresponding combinations.

The cand(A_i) sets are used to keep track of which combinations have to be explored in each subsystem. Initially, only A_1 has pending combinations to explore, which correspond to the successor combinations of the combinations

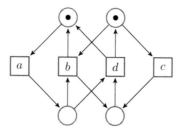

Fig. 9. Discovered PN

in M. The function $\mathrm{succ}(c, agg)$, given a combination c and an aggregation factor agg, returns all the new successor combinations of c obtained by assigning a non-zero value to a zero coefficient in c, but only when c has less than agg non-zero values. For instance, $\mathrm{succ}((-1,0),2) = \{(-1,1),(-1,-1)\}$ (see Fig. 7), while $\mathrm{succ}((-1,0),1) = \emptyset$.

The algorithm sequentially considers all A_i subsystems (line 7), starting from A_1, until there are no pending combinations for this system (line 6) and, hence, all combinations have been explored. Each A_i starts the exploration from the combinations in its $\mathrm{cand}(A_i)$ set, combinations that have been inserted in this set by the previous subsystem (see figure below) because they yield a non-normalized region in that subsystem and, thus, also in all previous subsystems.

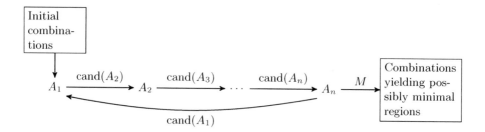

Note that the $\mathrm{cand}(A_i)$ sets contain triples which, in addition to the combination, include the *floor* of the combination and the minimum power of the region (considering only the systems up to A_i). The *floor* value allows normalizing the region obtained from a given combination, so that regions operations are always performed on normalized regions. For instance imagine that combination $(1,-1,0)$ yields a non-normalized region. If we do not normalize it, any descendant combination like $(1,-1,1)$ will surely be non-normalized. However, we are only interested in the descendants that are non-normalized if we consider that the region of the combination is normalized.

The innermost loop of Algorithm 1 shows the processing that occurs in a particular A_i subsystem. A candidate combination is selected and removed from the set (lines 8 and 9) and its corresponding region is computed, taking into account previous normalizations by subtracting the *floor* variable (line 10).

Algorithm 1. Distributed region exploration

1: **function** EXPLORE_REGIONS($\{A_1, \ldots, A_n\}, agg, k$)
2:     $\langle \{b_1^1, \ldots, b_p^1\}, \ldots, \{b_1^n, \ldots, b_p^n\} \rangle \leftarrow$ distributed_basis$(A_1, \ldots, A_n)$
3:     $\forall i : 2 \leq i \leq n$, cand$(A_i) \leftarrow \emptyset$
4:     $M \leftarrow \{ \boldsymbol{c} \mid \exists j : |\boldsymbol{c}(j)| = 1 \wedge \forall i \neq j, \boldsymbol{c}(i) = 0 \wedge i, j \in \{1 \ldots p\}\}$ ▷ Initial candidates
5:     cand$(A_1) \leftarrow \{ \langle \boldsymbol{c}', 0, \infty \rangle \mid \boldsymbol{c}' \in \text{succ}(\boldsymbol{c}, agg) \wedge \boldsymbol{c} \in M \}$ ▷ Initial comb. to explore
6:     **while** cand$(A_1) \neq \emptyset$ **do**
7:         **for** $i \leftarrow 1$ **to** n **do**
8:             **for all** $\langle \boldsymbol{c}, \text{floor}, m \rangle \in$ cand(A_i) **do**
9:                 cand$(A_i) \leftarrow$ cand$(A_i) \setminus \{\langle \boldsymbol{c}, \text{floor}, m \rangle\}$
10:                $r \leftarrow \left(\sum_{j=1}^{p} \boldsymbol{c}(j) \cdot b_j^i \right) -$ floor
11:                $m \leftarrow \min(m, \text{minp}(r))$
12:                **if** $m > 0$ **then**   ▷ r is non-normalized
13:                    **if** $i < n$ **then**   ▷ Handle to next subsystem if we are not in A_n
14:                        cand$(A_{i+1}) \leftarrow$ cand$(A_{i+1}) \cup \{\langle \boldsymbol{c}, \text{floor}, m \rangle\}$
15:                    **else**   ▷ $\boldsymbol{c}$ yields a non-norm. region in all A_i
16:                        $M \leftarrow M \cup \{\boldsymbol{c}\}$ ▷ Add to candidate to minimal
17:                        cand$(A_1) \leftarrow$ cand$(A_1) \cup \{\langle \boldsymbol{c}', \text{floor} + m, \infty \rangle \mid \boldsymbol{c}' \in \text{succ}(c, agg)\}$
18:                    **end if**
19:                **else**   ▷ If $\boldsymbol{c}$ yields a normalized region, continue search in A_i
20:                    cand$(A_i) \leftarrow$ cand$(A_i) \cup \{\langle \boldsymbol{c}', \text{floor}, m \rangle \mid \boldsymbol{c}' \in \text{succ}(c, agg)\}$
21:                **end if**
22:            **end for**
23:        **end for**
24:    **end while**
25:    **return** M ▷ Combinations yielding possibly minimal regions
26: **end function**

At this point, the normalization of the region is tested, by looking at the minimum power of the region (considering only the subsystems up to A_i), which is stored in variable m (line 11). If r is non-normalized and we are not in A_n, then the combination is handled to the next subsystem by adding the combination to the cand(A_{i+1}) set, to see if it is still non-normalized there. If we are in A_n, then the combination proved to be non-normalized in all subsystems, thus the complete region is non-normalized and, hence, candidate to being a minimal region. In this case, the combination is added to M, and the descendant combinations are scheduled to be checked in A_1. Note that since the region was already non-normalized, the *floor* of these descendant combinations is updated accordingly.

The result of Algorithm 1 is a list of candidate combinations (in M), from which only the ones whose maximum power is less or equal to k are kept, where k is a user-defined parameter. For these combinations we must check which ones actually yield minimal regions. To perform this check, we start from the first subsystem and we compute, for each candidate combination, which of the other combinations yield a subregion (in that subsystem). We pass the list of subregion combinations, for each combination, to the next subsystem. There, we scan through the list keeping only the combinations yielding a subregion in the current subsystem as well. Finally, when the last subsystem is processed, we keep only the regions of the combinations that have an empty list.

From the set of minimal regions that are k-bounded we can directly construct a pure PN. It can be proved that, if the aggregation factor is not used to limit the combinations search space, and by allowing the coefficients to take their values from an appropriate set of values, the resulting PN is the net with the smallest possible language built from k-bounded regions. For this it only has to be shown that the algorithm explores all the k-bounded regions, since by selecting the minimal regions in this set we do obtain a net as restrictive as using all the regions in the set.

On the other hand, although this theoretical guarantee might be of interest, both the presented algorithm and the one in [20] allow the user to define an aggregation factor and to arbitrarily limit the coefficients used in the combinations. This helps in coping with the inherent complexity of the analysis at the price of loosing the guarantee. However, as we will see in Sect. 6, it is frequently the case that moderate aggregation factors yield PNs of the same quality as other region-based approaches.

5   Related Work

In [6] an incremental approach was suggested based on the observation that any region of the union of two transition systems can be expressed as the union of regions of those systems. However there are important differences with our proposal.

First, the method in [6] was limited to standard (non-generalized) regions and TSs that could only share the initial state. In this work we have suppressed both restrictions, which allows generating PNs with arc weights and the use of arbitrary partitions of a TS. The latter is important since compact conversion methods that convert a log into a TS [21,20] typically do not yield TSs which can be easily partitioned if only the initial state can be shared among the partitions.

Second, in [6] the complete set of regions of each component transition system must be stored (either in memory or disk) in order to compute the set of regions of the union. In this work we propose a faster methodology based on the fact that the complete set of regions can be succinctly represented by a basis of regions. That is, instead of comparing the regions in each subsystem to find compatible regions, we compute a region basis for the union TS that is able to directly generate all compatible regions without having to generate all the regions of each subsystem.

Finally, we have implemented our proposal in a tool available at [24] that has been tested with several large benchmarks (see Sect. 6).

Regarding other region based approaches, the PN generation algorithm we propose derives from [20]. However the algorithm from [20] only works for monolithic TSs, thus it is not viable for large TSs that do not fit into memory. Similar limitations affect other approaches based on the theory of regions like [9] and [25].

6   Experiments

In order to validate the incremental discovery approach, we have implemented the proposed algorithm in a tool called dbminer [24], and we have tested it for some medium-sized benchmarks. In particular we have compared our approach with the following tools: (i) rbminer [26], which implements the equivalent mono-lithic approach and the one closer to our work. (ii) a plug-in in the well-known ProM toolset [27] that uses a heuristic approach based on integer linear pro-gramming (ILP [25]), and (iii) the well-known α-algorithm, also implemented in ProM. All the results were obtained on a PC with an Intel Core Duo at 2.10Ghz and 2Gb of RAM, running the 2.6 Linux kernel.

The benchmarks used in our experiments are summarized in Table 1. These logs are described in [25] and are publicly available at [28]. Each benchmark corresponds to a log from which a transition system can be derived, e.g., using the techniques in [21]. For each log we provide the number of different events it contains ($|\Sigma|$), the number of cases (number of sequences) of the log, the average number of events per case (column ev/case), and the number of states of the corresponding TS when the log was converted using the sequential conversion of [21] (column $|S_s|$). Although more efficient conversions are possible when using a region-based approach [20], we deliberately chose such an inefficient translation to obtain larger TSs. This means that the reported performance of rbminer and dbminer in these experiments is severely penalized with respect to ILP or the α-algorithm, which do not have a TS as an input but simply the log.

Table 1. Medium-sized TSs used for process discovery

Benchmark	$|\Sigma|$	cases	ev/case	$|S_s|$
a22_5	22	900	18	9867
a32_1	32	100	25	2011
a32_5	32	900	25	16921
t32_5	33	1800	78	64829

Table 2 provides the running time (row *Time*, figures are in seconds) and memory consumption (row *Mem*, values are in megabytes) of the four tools when they are used to discover a PN from the logs (or the corresponding TSs). For dbminer we used the following splitting procedure to create the subsystems: first the log was lexicographically sorted and then split into ten fragments as balanced as possible, which were then converted into TSs using the sequential conversion. The memory values for the ProM plug-ins were computed using the visualVM profiling application, but should be taken with caution since they include the footprint of ProM and its graphical front-end.

Comparing the results for rbminer and dbminer, surprisingly for a technique trading space for time, we can see that dbminer has better running times but almost the same memory usage. This phenomenon is related to the fact that the benefits of splitting a TS in subsystems are more relevant when the TS is big, as otherwise the overhead of the technique can be greater than the savings.

Table 2. Comparing the efficiency of several process discovery tools and the quality of the discovered PNs

Bench.	Metric	ILP	rbminer	dbminer	α
a22_5	Time	23	33	14	1
	Mem	345	8	7	102
	ETC	0.73	0.73	0.73	0.73
	Recall	1.00	1.00	1.00	1.00
	Score	0.73	0.73	0.73	0.73
a32_1	Time	25	67	54	2
	Mem	155	6	11	120
	ETC	0.52	0.52	0.52	–
	Recall	1.00	1.00	1.00	0.00
	Score	0.52	0.52	0.52	0.00
a32_5	Time	112	401	265	1
	Mem	431	12	16	156
	ETC	0.59	0.59	0.59	0.58
	Recall	1.00	1.00	1.00	0.98
	Score	0.59	0.59	0.59	0.57
t32_5	Time	9208	1740	1028	2
	Mem	546	32	30	156
	ETC	0.39	0.39	0.39	–
	Recall	1.00	1.00	1.00	0.00
	Score	0.39	0.39	0.39	0.00

However this only happens precisely in the cases where the amount of memory required is very low, and we expect to see important memory savings when much larger TSs are used.[3]

Regarding the mining quality of the discovered nets, Table 2 provides also some quality indicators. In particular, for each benchmark we give: (i) the ETC metric [29], which evaluates the amount of additional behavior allowed by the net, being 1 an indicator that no additional behavior is present decreasing to 0 as more additional behavior is incorporated; (ii) the *recall* of the log, *i.e.* the fraction of sequences of the log also present in the language of the discovered net, and (iii) the *score*, which is computed as the product of the two previous values, to ease the comparison between the nets. We indicate with a "–" that some metric was not defined. In particular the ETC metric is not defined when the recall is zero. In such cases, we have defined the score as zero, since not a single sequence in the log belongs to the language of the generated net.

In these experiments, we have also compared with the well-known α-algorithm. This algorithm is much faster than region-based approaches, specially for large benchmarks. However, in terms of quality, region-based methods obtain better results, since the α-algorithm can yield PNs that exclude substantial parts of the behavior of the log. For instance, in benchmarks a32_1 and t32_5 the PNs

---

[3] For instance, in a preliminary experiment with a synthetic TS with more than one million of states, dbminer showed a 50% memory reduction with respect to rbminer.

discovered by the α-algorithm are not able to reproduce a single trace of the log, while region-based approaches never exclude behavior.

All in all, the results show that dbminer obtains nets of similar quality when compared to other region-based approaches, but with a better running time than the equivalent monolithic approach, an improvement that we expect to be larger when the naive strategy to check the minimality of candidate combinations is changed by some smarter blocking technique.

7 Conclusions and Future Work

In this paper we have extended the theory developed in [20] to devise an incremental algorithm for process discovery. The algorithms described have been implemented in the tool dbminer, and the experimental results reported demonstrate the capability of the tool in reducing the running time required for process discovery.

As future work, alternative algorithms for testing minimality of the candidate regions might be investigated, in order to reduce the complexity of the distributed algorithm presented in this paper, and we would like to conduct additional experiments on really massive transition systems obtained from large real-life logs.

Acknowledgements. This work has been supported by projects FORMALISM (TIN2007-66523) and TIN2007-63927. We thank the anonymous referees for the valuable comments and suggestions.

References

1. van der Aalst, W.M.P.: Process Mining. Springer, Heidelberg (2011)
2. Murata, T.: Petri Nets: Properties, analysis and applications. Proceedings of the IEEE, 541–580 (April 1989)
3. van der Aalst, W.M.P., Weijters, T., Maruster, L.: Workflow mining: Discovering process models from event logs. IEEE TKDE 16(9), 1128–1142 (2004)
4. van der Aalst, W.M.P., de Medeiros, A.K.A., Weijters, A.J.M.M.T.: Genetic Process Mining. In: Ciardo, G., Darondeau, P. (eds.) ICATPN 2005. LNCS, vol. 3536, pp. 48–69. Springer, Heidelberg (2005)
5. Ehrenfeucht, A., Rozenberg, G.: Partial (Set) 2-Structures. Part I, II. Acta Informatica 27, 315–368 (1990)
6. Dongen, B.F.V., Busi, N., Pinna, G.M., van der Aalst, W.: An iterative algorithm for applying the theory of regions in process mining. In: FABPWS, pp. 36–55 (2007)
7. Carmona, J., Cortadella, J., Kishinevsky, M.: New region-based algorithms for deriving bounded Petri nets. IEEE Transactions on Computers 59(3) (2009)
8. Bergenthum, R., Desel, J., Lorenz, R., Mauser, S.: Process Mining Based on Regions of Languages. In: Alonso, G., Dadam, P., Rosemann, M. (eds.) BPM 2007. LNCS, vol. 4714, pp. 375–383. Springer, Heidelberg (2007)
9. Carmona, J., Cortadella, J., Kishinevsky, M., Kondratyev, A., Lavagno, L., Yakovlev, A.: A Symbolic Algorithm for the Synthesis of Bounded Petri Nets. In: van Hee, K.M., Valk, R. (eds.) PETRI NETS 2008. LNCS, vol. 5062, pp. 92–111. Springer, Heidelberg (2008)

10. Badouel, E., Bernardinello, L., Darondeau, P.: Polynomial Algorithms for the Synthesis of Bounded Nets. In: Mosses, P.D., Nielsen, M. (eds.) CAAP 1995, FASE 1995, and TAPSOFT 1995. LNCS, vol. 915, pp. 364–383. Springer, Heidelberg (1995)
11. Hoogers, P.W., Kleijn, H.C.M., Thiagarajan, P.S.: An event structure semantics for general Petri nets. Theor. Comput. Sci. 153(1&2), 129–170 (1996)
12. Desel, J., Reisig, W.: The synthesis problem of Petri nets. Acta Inf. 33(4), 297–315 (1996)
13. Badouel, E., Darondeau, P.: Theory of Regions. In: Reisig, W., Rozenberg, G. (eds.) APN 1998. LNCS, vol. 1491, pp. 529–586. Springer, Heidelberg (1998)
14. Mukund, M.: Petri nets and step transition systems. Int. Journal of Foundations of Computer Science 3(4), 443–478 (1992)
15. Darondeau, P.: Deriving Unbounded Petri Nets from Formal Languages. In: Sangiorgi, D., de Simone, R. (eds.) CONCUR 1998. LNCS, vol. 1466, pp. 533–548. Springer, Heidelberg (1998)
16. Bergenthum, R., Desel, J., Lorenz, R., Mauser, S.: Synthesis of Petri nets from finite partial languages. Fundam. Inform. 88(4), 437–468 (2008)
17. Caillaud, B.: Synet : A synthesizer of distributable bounded Petri-nets from finite automata (2002), http://www.irisa.fr/s4/tools/synet/
18. Cortadella, J., Kishinevsky, M., Lavagno, L., Yakovlev, A.: Deriving Petri nets from finite transition systems. IEEE Trans. on Computers 47(8), 859–882 (1998)
19. Bryant, R.: Graph-based algorithms for Boolean function manipulation. IEEE Transactions on Computer-Aided Design 35(8), 677–691 (1986)
20. Solé, M., Carmona, J.: Process Mining from a Basis of State Regions. In: Lilius, J., Penczek, W. (eds.) PETRI NETS 2010. LNCS, vol. 6128, pp. 226–245. Springer, Heidelberg (2010)
21. van der Aalst, W., Rubin, V., Verbeek, H., van Dongen, B., Kindler, E., Günther, C.: Process mining: a two-step approach to balance between underfitting and overfitting. Software and Systems Modeling 9, 87–111 (2010)
22. Bernardinello, L., Michelis, G.D., Petruni, K., Vigna, S.: On the synchronic structure of transition systems. In: Structures in Concurrency Theory, 69–84 (1995)
23. Schrijver, A.: Theory of Linear and Integer Programming. John Wiley & Sons, Chichester (1986)
24. Solé, M.: dbminer, http://personals.ac.upc.edu/msole/homepage/dbminer.html
25. van der Werf, J.M.E.M., van Dongen, B.F., Hurkens, C.A.J., Serebrenik, A.: Process Discovery using Integer Linear Programming. In: van Hee, K.M., Valk, R. (eds.) PETRI NETS 2008. LNCS, vol. 5062, pp. 368–387. Springer, Heidelberg (2008)
26. Solé, M., Carmona, J.: Rbminer: A Tool for Discovering Petri Nets from Transition Systems. In: Bouajjani, A., Chin, W.-N. (eds.) ATVA 2010. LNCS, vol. 6252, pp. 396–402. Springer, Heidelberg (2010)
27. van der Aalst, W.M.P., van Dongen, B.F., Günther, C.W., Mans, R.S., de Medeiros, A.K.A., Rozinat, A., Rubin, V., Song, M., Verbeek, H.M.W(E.), Weijters, A.J.M.M.T.: ProM 4.0: Comprehensive Support for *real* Process Analysis. In: Kleijn, J., Yakovlev, A. (eds.) ICATPN 2007. LNCS, vol. 4546, pp. 484–494. Springer, Heidelberg (2007)
28. Eindhoven University of Technology: Process mining wiki, http://www.processmining.org
29. Muñoz-Gama, J., Carmona, J.: A Fresh Look at Precision in Process Conformance. In: Hull, R., Mendling, J., Tai, S. (eds.) BPM 2010. LNCS, vol. 6336, pp. 211–226. Springer, Heidelberg (2010)

Providing an Agent Flavored Integration for Workflow Management

Thomas Wagner, José Quenum, Daniel Moldt, and Christine Reese

University of Hamburg, Faculty of Mathematics, Informatics and Natural Sciences,
Department of Informatics
http://www.informatik.uni-hamburg.de/TGI/

Abstract. This paper discusses an application of software agents to improve workflow management systems, with a practical emphasis on Petri net-based systems. The properties of agent technology will be used to gain advantages within the workflow management systems on both a conceptual and practical level. In this paper we discuss the theoretical background of our work, the conceptual idea and approach, and one possible practical implementation. As a central practical means we use reference nets, a high-level Petri net formalism. These nets are used to model both agents and workflows, which results in a clean and natural integration of both technologies.

Keywords: High-level Petri nets, workflow management systems, multi-agent systems, software architecture.

1 Introduction

Workflows and *Workflow management systems* (WFMS) have been very attractive research topics in the last decades [20,25,23]. They provide means to further understand, unambiguously specify and analyze business processes within organizations. According to the state of the art, several heterogeneous WFMS can be combined to perform a specific complex task that cuts across various organizations. A systematic, structured approach to these interorganizational workflows requires great care both from the modeling and implementation perspectives.

Among the rising software paradigms, the concept of *agent* is a preeminent one. In the last decade, agents have been touted as a most appropriate paradigm to support the design and implementation of decentralized and distributed applications/systems, which yield intelligent behavior and require a great deal of interoperability. A decentralized application implies an application which consists of autonomous entities. Clearly, these are among the properties one seeks while developing an approach for interorganizational workflows. Using agents to design and implement distributed applications across a network is, in itself, not new. However, the autonomy of the various subparts is difficult to capture in the overall collaboration of agents. As such, agent approaches cannot be generalized for the design and implementation of collaborative applications across

K. Jensen, S. Donatelli, and J. Kleijn (Eds.): ToPNoC V, LNCS 6900, pp. 243–264, 2012.
© Springer-Verlag Berlin Heidelberg 2012

various organizations. Concepts such as workflows, which render a clear view of the business processes within and between organizations, need to come into play.

Consequently, both agents and workflows possess features beneficial to interorganizational workflows. A clear distinction between the two can be made on account of their focused perspective. Workflows emphasize the behavior and processes of and within a system. Agents focus on the entities and their relationships, which constitute the structure of the system. Both of these perspectives are needed to effectively model and implement interorganizational workflows. Combining these perspectives by integrating the two technologies is the ultimate goal of our research.

In this paper we discuss the introduction of software agents and their related concepts into workflow management. This constitutes an important part of our overall research. By offering a structured integration of agents into workflows to provide enhanced workflow management, we take a major step towards a complete, mutual integration of the two concepts.

Introducing agents into WFMS is not counterintuitive. By virtue of being autonomous, sociable and intelligent, human and artificial agents share many similarities. Moreover, human agents' operational mode can be viewed as a set of independent yet interoperable entities. From that angle, a human agent can be viewed as an agent system. Finally, since human agents have to coordinate the various tasks they are involved in at a certain point in time, they can be regarded as a WFMS. We take this human analogy, especially its duality, to show that both agents and workflows can be joined in a complex system.

Generally speaking, WFMS can benefit from agents in various regards. In this paper, we discuss seven key areas, including distribution, autonomy and intelligence. In order to make the resulting approach appealing to new technologies, we structure our assumptions and ideas into a reference architecture, which we believe lays the foundation for more specific and advanced systems to support collaboration within and between organizations. We do not claim that our current implementation is as powerful as the existing commercial tools. However, thanks to the Petri nets formalism we use, our implementation holds the potential to properly handle concurrency, robustness and resilience in the future.

The discussions in this paper feature clearer articulations of ideas and intuitions presented in [28,29,30]. More than all these papers, we elaborate on the underpinnings of the conceptual role agents can play in the new approach. Finally, we discuss the implementations and provide a practical example. This paper constitutes an extended version of [26].

The remainder of the paper comes as follows. Section 2 describes the technical and theoretical background of our work. Section 3 gives an overview of our overall architecture. Section 4 examines the conceptual view of our approach, while Section 5 discusses one specific implementation. In Section 6 an example is presented to illustrate the prototype. Related work is discussed in Section 7. Finally, Section 8 draws conclusions and directions for the future.

2   Frameworks and Formalisms

Each of the key concepts in this paper, agents and multi-agent systems on the one hand and workflows on the other hand, is represented using the reference Petri net formalism [22]. This formalism follows the philosophy of *nets-within-nets* introduced by Valk [33]. Different net instances can dynamically interact with one another via references. Reference nets use *Java* as an inscription language, manipulate various types of data structures, and, like many other types of high-level Petri net formalisms, offer several types of arcs. Finally, they use synchronous channels [5] to synchronize with other nets or Java objects. The treatment of Java objects and net instances is transparent, so that both kinds of artifacts can be exchanged arbitrarily. Moreover, in the Petri net community, tool support is a general trend. Therefore, the RENEW tool (**RE**ference **NE**ts **W**orkshop (see http://www.renew.de)) has been developed to support quick prototyping of systems or parts of systems using the reference net formalism. RENEW provides an editor to specify and draw the nets, as well as a simulation engine to test and validate them. The reference net formalism is discussed in detail in [22].

Agent-oriented software engineering deals with software systems consisting of a number of entities, called agents. These systems are called multi-agent systems (MAS). Similarly to objects in the object paradigm, the overall functionality of a system is provided by agents. However, agents possess a number of advanced properties over typical objects. It is generally accepted that agents possess a certain degree of autonomy in their environment and communicate with one another asynchronously. Furthermore, certain agent types can exhibit, for example, mobility (i.e. agents can migrate to other environments and continue their execution) and intelligence (i.e. agents can exhibit reasoning and adaptability). A general introduction into the field of agents can be found in [37].

In this research, MAS are designed following MULAN's (**MUL**ti-**A**gent Nets) structure [17,31]. MULAN has been extended with CAPA (**C**oncurrent **A**gent **P**latform **A**rchitecture) in order to comply with FIPA's (**F**oundation for **I**ntelligent and **P**hysical **A**gents (see http://fipa.org)) (communication) standards to support concurrent execution [8,9]. In so doing, CAPA agents can easily interact with any type of FIPA compliant agents. MULAN and CAPA describe the various components of a MAS using reference nets, which can be executed using the RENEW tool. The reader should thus note that not only do we offer a formal ground to reason about the behaviors of agents, but we also provide an execution environment for MAS.

Inspired by the *nets-within-nets* concept, MULAN's structure is a four-layer architecture used to describe a MAS. These layers respectively describe the overall MAS, the agent platforms (the direct execution environments for the agents), the agents and their behavior, the protocols.

Workflows are aimed at automating and facilitating business processes [13]. Workflow management systems (WFMS) execute and manage these workflows, so that human or automated resources can carry out the individual tasks making up the process. Our particular work is based on the principles of workflow nets, a specialized Petri net formalism described in [34]. Implementation-wise our work-flow nets are reference nets making use of a special task transition introduced in [14]. This special transition implements and encapsulates the facilities for requesting and confirming/canceling a task in one single transition.

3   Overall Architecture

The contributions presented in this paper are part of a larger ongoing effort. The systems described in the following sections can be classified within the overall architecture described in [27]. The goal of this architecture is to integrate agents and workflows, both on a technical and conceptual level. The architecture consists of five tiers[1], built on top of each other. Each tier itself is a layered architecture, which combines various aspects of both technologies. Each tier modifies the structure of its own layered architecture compared to the previous tier and in doing so enables new or improved aspects to be used.

Starting from either a pure workflow or agent system, the architecture grad-ually evolves into a novel integrated unit system, which equally benefits from both original concepts. The main motivation in building this architecture lies in the shortcomings of each individual concept as is discussed in detail in [27,36]. In short, agent technology can struggle with offering a clear behavioral view of a system. Especially in large, distributed systems, capturing and representing the interactions between agents can become difficult. However, agent technology excels at representing the structural state of a system. Identifying and repre-senting the different entities and their states is quite natural. The opposite holds for workflow technology. Workflows can easily describe the behavioral view of a complex system. Overall processes and their active, completed and future tasks can be identified and captured easily. But the entities, their relations between each other and their states are very hard to represent. Both technologies offer their particular "views" on a system. A structure-oriented view for agents and a process/behavior-oriented view for workflows. In combining both technologies we can integrate these views into one new system which supports both a clean structural **and** behavioral view.

First Tier. The first tier is our starting solution to address the limitations of both technologies. It involves either a pure/classic agent management system (AgMS) or a WFMS. Such systems exclusively use workflow or agent technology to provide their functionality. This means that there is no integration between the two. The architectural view of this tier (see Figure 1) offers two layers. The bottom depicts the adopted management system (either agent or workflow), on top of which an application lies. This application follows, as its main conceptual basis, the perspective provided by the bottom management system. Examples of

---

[1] The notion of tiers in this architecture denotes a kind of step-by-step refine-ment/enhancement on the way to the overall goal of integration. The tiers can be viewed as the layers of the overall *abstract* architecture but they do not correspond to layers within a *concrete* architecture.

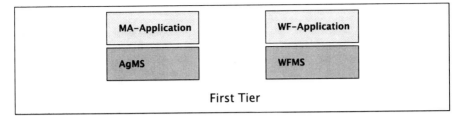

systems, which can be classified into this tier, are MULAN and CAPA as AgMS on the agent side and WIFAi [32] as a WFMS on the workflow side. It should be noted that even advanced, sophisticated systems, like the ADEPT WFMS [6] are classified into this tier, even though they tackle and already solve similar issues as addressed by us. However, these systems follow different approaches and since our goal is to integrate *agents* and workflows, these systems fall into this tier.

Second Tier. In the second tier, one of the two paradigms is used to realize the other. In other words, we use agents to design a WFMS, and vice versa use workflows to design an AgMS. Because of this, there are two variations of the second tier: one with agents in the background, the other with workflows in the background. The architectural view of this tier (see Figure 2) offers three layers.

Using the management system at the bottom, an intermediate layer is built. This layer implements a management system for the alternative concept, using the functionality offered by the bottom layer. For example, if the bottom layer is an AgMS, then the intermediate layer is a WFMS implemented by agents. On top of the intermediate layer applications can be built. However, this application layer can *only* use the concept provided by the intermediate layer. So, if the intermediate layer is a WFMS implemented by agents, the application can only use the WFMS-functionality offered by that layer and *not* the agents offered by the bottom layer.

The transition from the first to the second tier of the overall architecture is made through the intermediate layer. Using the first tier to realize a management system one can then use that management system to implement new systems. In other words the application of the first tier is turned into the intermediate layer on top of which a new application can be built.

Compared to the first tier, the advantage is a limited integration of the two concepts. The limitation exists due to the fact that agents and workflows are still handled quite distinctly. The concept from the bottom layer *only* affects the intermediate layer in the background of the application. As such no direct influence on the application can be observed in this tier. However, indirectly, systems of this tier still benefit from the other. For example, distribution, interoperability, etc. are facilitated in WFMS using agents.

At this point the overall architecture could be split into two different branches, one for each of the two variations of the second tier. However, in this paper we

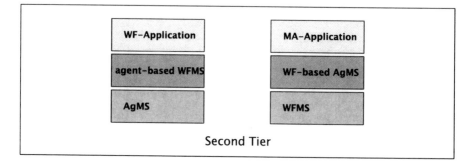

Fig. 2. Architecture of the second tier of the overall architecture, modified from [27]

only consider the branch which is based on the variation using agents to realize a WFMS. Examples for this kind of systems are detailed in [10,11,15]. The other variation is quite rare and will thus not be examined any further.

Third Tier. In the third tier both agents *and* workflows can be used together for application development. This opens up the possibilities greatly, since it expands the potential functionality and is quite flexible. Any degree of integration between agents and workflows can be achieved in this tier. However, this integration happens on an arbitrary level and is completely unstructured. The relation and integration between agent and workflow needs to be potentially re-invented for each application. This is a major limitation of this tier, since systematic and structured integration is key to successfully combining agents and workflows. Consequently it becomes very difficult to harness the power of this tier, especially the efficient design of complex systems. The required structure to the integration is only added in the subsequent tiers of the overall architecture. As such, the third tier can be considered of more of a transitional nature. The application developer experience of this tier might be considered similar to the use of the Microsoft .NET framework including the Workflow Foundation, where the usual structural view of objects and modules is enriched by a process oriented add-on (see [4]).

The architectural view of the third tier can be seen in Figure 3. In addition to the interface between the application and intermediate layer, this tier allows direct access from the application layer to the bottom AgMS. In practice, the application can thus use both the interfaces offered by the core AgMS and the agent-based WMFS (*AgWFMS*, the intermediate layer introduced in the second tier). Therefore, the key functionality of the AgMS is combined with that of the AgWFMS.

Fourth Tier. In order to obtain the structured integration missing in the third tier, we need to take one step back. By restricting the immense possibilities of the third tier we gain the means for defining an explicit structure for the application layer. This is achieved by adding an *integration layer* between the management systems at the bottom and the application layer on top (see Figure 4).

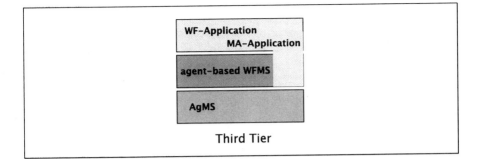

Fig. 3. Architecture of the third tier of the overall architecture, modified from [27]

The integration layer can access the entire functionality of both management systems. It combines and integrates the agents and workflows into clearly structured constructs, which it offers to the application. However, only *one* perspective (agents or workflows) is directly supported when modeling on the application layer. This is necessary, since an understanding of a structural integration for both associated perspectives individually is required for the final tier of the overall architecture. In this way this tier also provides an abstraction and thus a higher level of modeling.

The renewed focus on either agents or workflows as the exclusive main abstraction for application development in this tier results in two variations for this tier: One offering agents to the application (called *workflowagents*; left hand side of Figure 4), the other one offering workflows (called *agentworkflows*; right hand side of Figure 4). As stated, the integration layer provides exclusively WFMS or AgMS functionality, but uses *both* technologies in the background. This means that an agent application possesses parts and aspects of workflows and vice versa in the other variation. Consequently, the two concepts, agent and workflow, begin to blend together. Agents can exhibit certain workflow properties, workflows can exhibit certain agent properties. This results in a much more powerful means of supporting one of the two concepts. The implicate properties of workflow functions implemented by and using agents allow for a more powerful (i.e. abstract) modeling, since some properties of the agents can be transferred to the workflows. Modelers do not have to model, for example, mobility issues explicitly, if the agents already support this. On the other side, agents can make use of a WFMS-like handling of processes, which finally constitute the agent's behavior.

It is worth noting that, even though we are again using either workflows or agents as the main modeling paradigm at the top layer, the main difference between this tier and the second tier is that we no longer have one concept realizing the other. Rather, we obtain a successful combination of both, i.e. agents and workflows working side by side and benefiting from each other. The agentworkflow variation of this tier (workflows as the main abstraction being supported by agents) is the main focus of this paper and will be discussed in detail in the following sections.

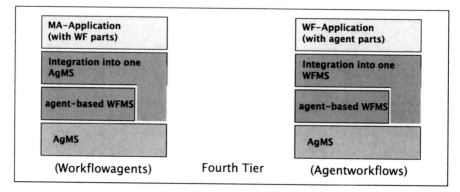

Fig. 4. Architecture of the fourth tier of the overall architecture, modified from [27]

Fifth Tier. This tier introduces the concept of *unit*, an abstraction to any entity involved in the design of the system. Units offer the facets of both agents and workflows. This is achieved by completely integrating and combining the functionalities of AgMS and WFMS. More precisely, both structured integrations from the fourth tier need to be incorporated into one single system. This results in both corresponding perspectives being available for a novel type of management system, a *unit management system* (UMS). The UMS has to be able to handle all agent and workflow functions that might be required from the units, as well as be able to "translate" aspects of agents into workflows and vice versa. The relationship between agent and workflow facets of units needs to be defined clearly and supported by the UMS. Because of this, it is a far more complex system than both the individual integrations acquired in the fourth tier.

The architecture of the fifth tier can be seen in Figure 5. The integration layer of the fourth tier has been split into two parts, of which UMS represents the upper part. Since one can no longer clearly differentiate between agents and workflows, the application layer is simply called unit application, also referred to as agent/workflow applications in [27]. In merging both agent and workflow concepts into a single unit concept, both the structural view (from the MAS) and the behavioral view (from the workflows) are available at the same level of abstraction. One can switch between the views depending on momentary needs. If a unit needs to be considered as a structural entity, the agent view is selected. If it needs to be considered as or in the context of processes, the workflow view is selected. In this way the facets of both concepts can be used in combination, without sacrificing the ease-of-use of the individual concepts. Both views are available during runtime and design time, so that maximum flexibility and versatility is provided.

The fifth tier achieves what we set out to do in our motivation. It offers both a structural and behavioral perspective on a system, while maintaining and combining the beneficial properties of agents and workflows. In doing so it addresses the shortcomings of each individual technology and opens up new and improved means to model complex systems. The fifth tier is the ultimate goal of our research.

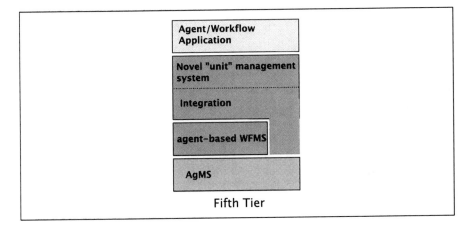

Fig. 5. Architecture of the fifth tier of the overall architecture, modified from [27]

4   Conceptual View

This section will discuss our conceptual approach to improving workflow management with agent technology. We argue that common properties of agents, like mobility, autonomy, proactivity and especially the encapsulation of workflow instances in agents, can greatly benefit workflow execution. Our goal is to use these aspects of software agents to our advantage regarding the execution, modeling and management of workflow instances.

As described in the previous section, this is just part of a larger ongoing research effort to integrate workflow and agent technology. This particular area of discussion can be classified within the fourth tier of the overall architecture. More precisely, all descriptions in this and the following sections relate to the *agentworkflow* variation of the fourth tier. To clarify the designation we consider agentworkflows to be workflows, which, through an agent/workflow integration in the background as proposed in the fourth tier, exhibit agent-like properties. The purpose of our work with agentworkflows is to achieve a structured integration of agents and workflows. This is one of the two perspectives required for the fifth tier of the overall architecture. However, with agentworkflows we also achieve a more powerful means for modeling workflows in the process. The conceptual approach to this endeavor, as well as its advantages and limitations, will be discussed in this section. A more practical presentation of a prototype implementing part of our conceptual approach will follow in Section 5.

One of the core ideas behind our approach is to encapsulate workflow instances through autonomous software agents. With this it is possible to transfer properties of that software agent directly to the workflow instance. In other words, the clear separation between agent and workflow begins to fade. This is a key concept of the overall architecture and is important for the fifth tier. Another important aspect of our approach is to also consider other entities of the workflow management system as agents. Having the general functionality of the WFMS be provided by agents is already part of an AgWFMS of the second tier. In our approach agents can be used to realize any of the elements (e.g. tasks, users, resources) of the workflow as well. In [24], for example, we used agents to realize activities. Thanks to the agent technology, the resulting WFMS does not only focus on the behavior of the system, as was the case in the previous tiers of the overall architecture, it also emphasizes the structure of the system. This paper focuses on the aspect of encapsulating workflow instances through agents. Other aspects are considered but will not be discussed in further detail.

We will now examine some of the principal and conceptual areas and aspects in which workflows can benefit from agents. The following points will directly cover some agent properties and their particular advantages, but will also include some general observations.

Encapsulation. In general, the encapsulation of one or more workflow instances through agents can be seen as a prerequisite to opening up many of the possibilities offered by the agent-oriented paradigm. Without this concept it would be hard or even impossible to transfer other agent properties over to the workflow instances. Nonetheless, the encapsulation also improves the workflows in more ways than that. For example, the encapsulation provides the workflows with a clearer identity within the overall system. They can now be identified in the same form as the other elements (agents) of the system. This unified approach makes it easier to monitor, observe and analyze the system, which in turn makes maintenance and enhancement more efficient. A disadvantage of the encapsulation is that the number of agents active at one time is possibly, drastically increased, depending on how the encapsulation is handled. This may pose problems on less powerful systems, which simply cannot handle this number of agents or the communication between them. However, since agent architectures are generally built to efficiently handle communication, this should not pose a significant problem in practical use.

Mobility. By allowing workflows to gain agent mobility they benefit in a variety of possibilities. In the context of software agents mobility describes the capability of a software agent to discontinue its execution within one execution environment (agent platform), migrate to another environment and continue the execution there, starting off from its previous state. For agent-workflows this means that the execution of a workflow can be discontinued on one instance of an executing WFMS and continued on another. Practically, this can be used if certain resources needed for the execution of a workflow are not available on every platform. This can include particular (groups of) users or critical data available, for security or efficiency reasons, only on certain platforms. Another use case for this property is to have a workflow instance migrate not because certain resources are needed, but because its home platform is beginning shutdown or because another platform carries less of a workload than the home platform. Consequently, this use of mobility can lead to improved flexibility, efficiency and fault tolerance.

Autonomy. One of the key concepts of the agent paradigm is that agents are autonomous entities. This means that, to a certain degree, they are independent from their environment and can choose for themselves whether to execute an action or not. In the context of agentworkflows this property can be used in a number of ways. It can, for example, be used as a kind of access control to critical data for which an agent is responsible. This can be a workflow instance but also other entities like activities or the handling of users. Another use of this becomes relevant if combined with mobility. An agent migrating to another platform to access certain data or perform certain actions can do this relatively independent from the other agents and software constructs of that platform, if, of course, it has all the necessary permissions.

Intelligence. Intelligence in software agents can be used to describe a multitude of aspects. One major aspect is the ability of certain agents to proactively decide, by themselves, which actions to take. In the context of workflow management this can be used to predetermine which users should be offered certain tasks, taking variables like workload or related tasks into consideration. At this point reactivity of agents also comes into play. Software agents can react to events in their environment and adapt according to the situation. For example, if there is an error during the execution of a task the agent could observe this and retry the action with changed parameters. Another very interesting aspect where intelligence, proactivity, reactivity and adaptiveness can be used is the adaptivity of workflow instances. Changing workflow instances and even entire workflow definitions according to changed circumstances (temporary or permanent) improves the flexibility and versatility of a WFMS. The realization of this can be handled through variable and late binding of (sub-)workflows and tasks, coupled with certain, agent-internal reasoning mechanics.

Distribution. The agent paradigm naturally supports the design of distributed software systems. This is facilitated by the asynchronous message communication and the autonomy of the individual agents. By relying on agents as the main building blocks of a WFMS, it is easy to use these predispositions for the distribution of the system. The communication of different parts of the system can be handled through asynchronous messages, which are flexible and versatile. Extending on this idea opens up even more possibilities of using distribution to the advantage of workflows. Especially interorganizational workflows (i.e. workflows being executed by a number of separate organizations) can benefit from a distributed WFMS, since their critical or private information should not be stored in a centralized location.

Interoperability. The FIPA communication standards are accepted by many widely-used agent frameworks. Adhering to these standards guarantees interoperability between the different involved software systems, independent of agent architecture or framework. This can be translated into workflow management based on agents as well. In this case different WFMS of different providers can work together, as long as they can process the data structures that are exchanged. This aspect is especially important in the context of interorganizational workflows, since it allows some freedom of choice for the different WFMS in the companies. But also in more general use cases interoperability can be used to an advantage. A FIPA-compliant WFMS can request data from any other FIPA-compliant (non-WFMS) system. This improves the WFMS's versatility and possible support for external tools. Another aspect which is related to this point and distribution, is the openness of the system. Through interoperability and distribution it is possible to create flexible and dynamic open systems to which different WFMS can connect to, complete some tasks, and then disconnect again. Open systems can provide users with functionality that is otherwise difficult to obtain without specialized software solutions.

Structure. This point is related to the motivation behind our overall architecture. As illustrated in the previous section, we reason that workflow systems can struggle in adequately describing the structure of a complex system. They focus on the behavior and excel at representing this aspect. Agent systems on the other hand possess a strong focus on the structure. By joining the two in the ways described in this paper we begin to combine this structural view given by the agents with the behavioral view of the workflows. This is mostly related to the encapsulation aspect discussed above, but encompasses a more abstract view. By relying on agents one can easily describe the current state of an entity including its current location (in regards to distribution), knowledge and behavior. By adapting this for workflow instances this can already help provide the structural view needed within a distributed system. If the agentworkflow idea is taken even further and every aspect of the system modeled through agents, the structural view becomes even more useful. The location (in regards to distribution) of every resource, user and workflow can be determined and displayed. On an abstract level we gain a consolidated structural perspective on the workflow system. This perspective is quite helpful in understanding and enhancing a system. It also constitutes a major part of the necessary prerequisites for achieving the fifth tier of our overall architecture and a complete integration of agents and workflows.

All these properties especially unfold their full potential if used in combination. Each one of these properties and aspects possesses some advantages individually, but in composition with the others, new and improved possibilities can be achieved. For example, using mobile agents in a distributed environment of many interoperable agent platforms is more advantageous than forcing the same agent system onto all involved partners. Equally, an autonomous, intelligent agent can decide for itself, if a migration is reasonable or not and initiate the action accordingly. Using these properties together also strongly improves interorganizational workflow management and execution. While interoperability and distribution already favor this field, the other properties are also useful, especially in collaboration. For example, mobility allows for the transmission of data in a natural way, while encapsulation allows for the clear separation of critical data and assignment to different organizational entities.

The main disadvantage of our approach is that the realization and handling of these improved workflows is more complex than handling regular workflows. The reason for this is mainly that the new and improved possibilities are difficult to harness. It can, if used in the wrong way, affect execution in a negative way or even, in the worst case, prohibit correct execution at all. However, if used correctly and efficiently, they offer clear, distinct advantages to workflow execution in general. They offer novel ways of modeling many parts of workflows and can increase efficiency in use.

While discussing the conceptual view in this section we have shown that our approach offers many advantages. However, it is difficult to realize and handle. For the realization we have chosen technologies based on Petri nets. One problem of the conceptual approach is that entirely different kinds of entities (agents and workflows) have to be combined in a meaningful way. By choosing Petri nets as a common basis we can partially circumvent this problem, since it is easier to combine the two kinds of entities if they possess the same basis at the lowest level. On the other hand, this choice has the problem of not being widely spread and available. However, certain aspects, like concurrency and displaying behavior, are very easy and natural to model using Petri nets. In the next section we will discuss one prototypical implementation of our conceptual approach using Petri nets. This prototype already covers some of the properties described above.

5   Implementation

In this section we will present a prototypical implementation of our agentworkflow approach. We use Petri net based technologies to achieve a common basis for the integration and combination of workflow and agent technologies. In particular, we use the MULAN and CAPA architectures for our agents and workflow nets for our workflow functionality (see Section 2). The starting point of the practical work is an AgWFMS of the second tier of the overall architecture. This AgWFMS has been described in detail in [35]. It relies solely on agents to provide the functionality but does not mix the agent and workflow concepts enough to be considered an agentworkflow system.

Before going into the details of the implementation we will briefly discuss how the different properties observed in the conceptual section can be mapped onto Petri nets and consequently our workflows and agents. Since discussing these aspects in a reasonable extent would go far beyond the scope of this paper and since extensive work on this has already been performed and published, we will limit ourselves to referring to other papers. The mobility aspect has been extensively studied, especially in the context of nets within nets, for example in [3,19,18]. The autonomy and intelligence of Petri net agents have been discussed in the context of MULAN in [31]. The encapsulation aspect has been examined for object-oriented nets in [1]. Interoperability and openness have been explored in [21]. The final aspect, the structural view of combining agents and workflows, was discussed in [27].

The practical approach, called *structure-agentworkflow* (*S-AgWf*), extends the regular AgWFMS. The resulting system is called AgWFMS* in the following. It allows for the definition and execution of distributed workflow instances. More precisely, the workflow instances are now hierarchical workflows with nested

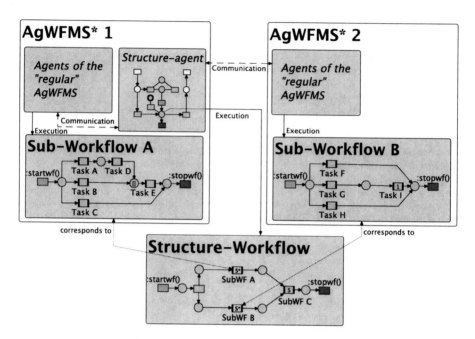

Fig. 6. Principle approach of the S-AgWf

subprocesses as defined by the WfMC [13]. As a consequence the entire system consists of a number of CAPA platforms, which all execute instances of the extended AgWFMS*. The different AgWFMS* instances, which are complete and independent MAS, are known to one another and messages can be exchanged between them. A more detailed description of the S-AgWf approach can be found in [36].

The basic principle of the S-AgWf can be seen in Figure 6. One agent encapsulates one workflow instance. This agent, called *structure-agent*, possesses an internal workflow, the *structure-workflow*. When the structure-agent for a new workflow instance is started, it receives the definition of the structure-workflow from the database agents of its home AgWFMS* and instantiates the workflow net. When this initialization is finished, the execution of the structure-workflow automatically begins. The tasks[2] of the structure-workflow correspond to sub-workflows. Sub-workflows can only be executed on certain AgWFMS* instances within the overall system. The criteria to tell which AgWFMS* instance is suitable is stored within the data of the task and can be extracted by the structure-agent. Whenever a task becomes active, the structure-agent assigns itself as the executor of that task. In this way the underlying workflow net executes the same way as in the AgWFMS and remains encapsulated. Once this is done

---

[2] In the workflow nets of [14] used by us tasks are represented as transitions with thick vertical bars, called task-transitions. Tasks in a structure-workflow representing sub-workflows are also drawn as transitions with thick vertical bars and the letter *S* marked in the centre.

the structure-agent queries a special agent of its own platform for a list of all the known AgWFMS* instances currently active. It then compares this list to the information extracted from the task and chooses a suitable AgWFMS* instance. If no suitable system is currently active or known in the collection of AgWFMS* the (human) initiator of the overall workflow is queried whether to try again or abort the workflow. If a suitable system is found the interface-agent of the chosen AgWFMS* instance is contacted by the structure-agent. The structure-agent asks the interface-agent to instantiate the sub-workflow locally (i.e. as a *regular* workflow of that AgWFMS*) and transmits all relevant parameters, like input data etc. Authentication and verification of the structure-agent's identity is assessed and the sub-workflow is then executed like any other workflow in the regular AgWFMS. Once it has reached the end of its execution the responsible structure-agent is informed and any (optional) results are sent back. The results are transmitted into the structure-workflow net and the structure-agent completes the task, so that its execution can continue. The execution of tasks and subsequent instantiation and execution of sub-workflows is continued, until the end of the structure-workflow is reached. The initiator of the overall workflow is then informed and the structure-agent can handle the termination of the workflow and itself.

In the example in Figure 6 two sub-workflows are currently executed on the two different AgWFMS* platforms. The structure-agent responsible for the structure-workflow is communicating with the agents of the two AgWFMS* platforms in order to initiate the execution and receive results. When both sub-workflows are finished, the structure-agent will start a final sub-workflow (*SubWF C*), before it can conclude the execution of the structure-workflow.

This realization of the agentworkflow concept offers distinct and practical advantages, but also still suffers from some limitations. The possibility to distribute the execution of workflows is a huge advantage for the otherwise centralized AgWFMS. The support of nested subprocesses allows for interorganizational workflows to be defined and executed. Since the details of the local workflows are not needed globally, the sub-workflows and any critical data they may contain are only known to the local parties. This satisfies the need of interorganizational workflows to secure and conceal confidential and valuable information.

The main limitation of this particular, specialized implementation of the agentworkflow concept is its still centralized nature. If the platform of the structure-agent is disconnected or fails, the entire workflow fails. This could partially be rectified by adding mobility to the structure-agent. It could then easily migrate to another platform, if it discovers any changes in its home platform that might hinder its execution.

The pre-defined relationship between agents and workflows within this system combines the structural aspect of agents with the behavioral aspect of workflows, as is the goal in the fourth tier of the overall architecture. The two concepts agent and workflow begin to merge together, since in this system a workflow is an agent and partly vice versa[3]. The practical advantages this particular system gains from this merge mostly consist in a groundwork for further enhancements. Agent autonomy may, for example, be used to give the structure-agent more control over the workflow instance (e.g. choice over where sub-workflows are executed), which could result in added flexibility. Relating to flexibility, it is also possible to adapt the S-AgWf approach to feature flexible workflow execution in its sub-workflows. By allowing the structure-workflow to incorporate variable bindings to its tasks, these variables could control which sub-workflow would finally be executed on the chosen AgWFMS*. For example, a process represented by a sub-workflow might need to adhere to certain, mutually exclusive protocols, depending on the properties of the case at hand. This might require different sub-workflows altogether for the same task in different workflow instances. This problem could be tackled by using variable inscriptions on the tasks of the structure-workflow. However still, the instances within the S-AgWF system as presented in this paper already possess certain degrees of distribution (structure-agents communicate with other AgWFMS* platforms in order to execute their structure-workflow), interoperability (the structure-agents exchange FIPA-compliant messages, so it is possible to exchange the AgWFMS* platforms with other WFMS if they adhere to the interface) and encapsulation (the structure-workflow is clearly encapsulated by the structure-agent).

6   Example

In this section we will briefly discuss a simple example of a structure-agentworkflow in an interorganizational setting. The structure-workflow and one of the sub-workflows can be seen in Figure 7. Workflow nets like these consist of regular Petri net places and transitions, as well as a few special elements. A workflow net starts with a transition connected to a synchronous channel labeled *:startWf(input)* and ends with a transition connected to a synchronous channel labeled *:stopWf(output)*. Note that the **input** parameter provides data for the execution of the workflow, while the **output** returns the result. The tasks are represented as the special task-transitions from [14]. They are marked with an *S*, if they are tasks of a structure-workflow corresponding to a sub-workflow. The "regular" Petri net transitions within the figure represent (abstract) operations on the variables and data within the workflow. Usually they would/could feature more complex net structures as well as synchronous channels to receive outside information. However, to retain readability of the net for this paper we have chosen to abstract from a detailed view in favor of a simplified version. For the same reason we omitted the technical inscriptions on the example workflow net, which would be needed for the actual execution of the workflow.

---

[3] The "partly vice versa" refers to the fact that the structure-agents directly represent their workflow instances and thus *can* be considered workflows themselves. However, generally speaking agents in the S-AgWf approach are not workflows. This perspective is added in the *workflowagents* variation of the fourth tier of the overall architecture and the subsequent fifth tier.

Structure–Workflow: Order item

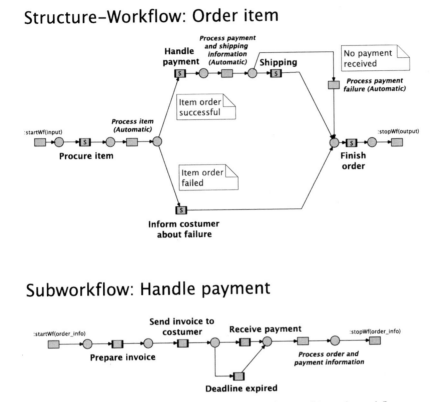

Subworkflow: Handle payment

Fig. 7. Example of a structure-workflow and one of its sub-workflows

Figure 7 represents a workflow for processing and handling an incoming order in a generic company offering many items. Items ordered by costumers need to be procured first (this includes locating it in a warehouse or ordering out of stock items), after which payment and shipping is handled. If the procurement of an item fails or payment is not received, the workflow skips to the end and is cancelled (also included in the "Finish order" task). Each of these complex tasks is modeled as a sub-workflow. We consider a main company to be in charge of this workflow with most of the sub-workflows being executed internally. Only the "Shipping" task is handled by a third party (e.g. a parcel service). Even though, this is the only "real" interorganizational aspect of the workflow, the relating principles can be applied to the other sub-workflows as well. As item procurement, payment and costumer relation are usually handled in different departments, they can be viewed as separate organizational entities. In this way, all sub-workflows are executed by different "organizations". Consequently the related sub-workflows heavily feature the encapsulation and distribution aspects described in the previous sections.

A sub-workflow, *Handle payment*, is shown in the lower part of Figure 7. It represents the process of preparing and sending the invoice to the costumer and then processing payment. If the costumer fails to pay by a certain deadline, the order will be cancelled (upper branch in the structure-workflow).

Though the workflow of Figure 7 is a simple example, it serves to illustrate the modeling of workflows in the S-AgWf system quite well. The depicted workflow is completely handled by the structure-agent. It controls, manages and executes the structure-workflow and its sub-workflows. This form of integration makes it possible to translate the distribution and encapsulation aspects of the conceptual approach into our prototype. If further aspects of agentworkflows, like intelligence and mobility, are considered, it becomes clear that even these already versatile ways only scratch the surface of the overall approach and its potential.

7   Related Work

The idea of using the agent concept to support the execution and management of a workflow, or even to structure the activities of an agent as a workflow is not new. In this section we discuss prior research contributions which have explored agent and workflow management systems together.

In [2], Burmeister et al introduce a goal-oriented approach to support business process representation. The main objective is to cope with agility in business process execution and management. BDI agents as well as goal-orientation and task decomposition form the background of the approach. It provides a modular goal-oriented and context-based process model, where starting from a goal (which can be refined into subgoals) one can finally identify a plan as a concrete execution model. Also, agents are used as assistants or guides to the actual users in charge of driving the task through the process.

Another important contribution is the work in [16], where Jennings et al resorted to an agent-based system to manage workflows of business processes. Using the agent concept provides a more appropriate solution to reactivity, semantics, extensibility and heterogeneity needed in workflow management systems. In using agents to manage the execution of workflows, data distribution is taken care of in a more natural way. Also, the problem-solving capabilities of the resulting system are extended. Other aspects such as richer interactions, as well as the autonomy and integrity of the organizational structure are enhanced.

Other works have also investigated the idea of combining agents and workflow management systems. For example, [12] introduced the agent concept to support the design of processes using a reasoning mechanism.

Overall, most of the aforementioned approaches seek to address a particular aspect of workflow management. And they achieve their goal generally by resorting to the agent technology. These pieces of work depart from our approach in the conceptual sense that our work attempts to address the issue of possible integration between workflow management systems and the agent technology. Moreover, our approach is versatile since one can use agents to address the limitations of traditional central workflow management systems, or use workflows and their management approaches to further represent the activities an agent is in charge of.

8   Conclusion

In this paper, we made a strong case for a systematic introduction of agent concepts into the management of workflows. In our quest to develop a systematic approach to integrate agent and workflow technology, we proposed an overall reference architecture. The architecture consists of five distinct tiers. These different tiers gradually combine the agent and workflow concepts. This effort culminates in the fifth tier, where both concepts exist alongside each other in a unified perspective.

In order to achieve this fifth and final tier, a structured integration of agents and workflows for each of the associated perspectives individually needed to be developed. We presented this structured integration for the perspective of workflows, called *agentworkflows*, in this paper. The approach can be classified within the fourth tier of the overall architecture and the implementation we presented already realizes some of the approach's features. We pointed out key aspects in which agents can be used to improve workflows and their management. These aspects all provide advantages for the execution of general workflows. But especially considering interorganizational workflows their impact is even more significant. Introducing these concepts into workflow management allows for the effective implementation of many use cases occurring in the interorganizational context. The prototype we presented begins to address this, marking first steps in practically applying our conceptual approach.

To achieve the final tier of our overall architecture the next step is to provide the perspective for the agents. In the approach, called *workflowagents*, the integration layer of the fourth tier provides agents as the main abstraction for application development. However, the agents heavily feature workflow properties. The most prominent area affected is the behavior of agents, internal and external. The external behavior, the interactions between agents, can be modeled by workflows quite naturally. The agents can then be seen as the resources executing the tasks of the workflow. Clearly, following that perspective, workflows could, for example, bring their systematic and proof-driven approach to complex task execution into the agent system. However, this is just a small aspect of the workflowagent approach.

From the lessons learned from both approaches, we expect to collect the amount of information that enables us to design a full-fledged approach which offers the best of *both* agent and workflow technologies in one single system, i.e. the fifth tier. Such an approach will balance out the shortcomings of each technology. With the support of high-level Petri nets as a foundational formalism, we are guaranteed of combining structure and behavior in one representation.

References

1. Becker, U., Moldt, D.: Objekt-orientierte Konzepte für gefärbte Petrinetze. In: Scheschonk, G., Reisig, W. (eds.) Petri-Netze im Einsatz für Entwurf und Entwicklung von Informationssystemen. Informatik Aktuell, pp. 140–151. Springer, Heidelberg (1993)

2. Burmeister, B., Arnold, M., Copaciu, F., Giovanni, R.: BDI-Agents for Agile Goal-oriented Business Processes. In: AAMAS 2008: Proceedings Industry and Application Track, pp. 37–44 (2008)
3. Cabac, L., Moldt, D., Wester-Ebbinghaus, M., Müller, E.: Visual Representation of Mobile Agents – Modeling Mobility within the Prototype MAPA. In: Duvigneau, Moldt (eds.) [7], pp. 7–28
4. Chappell, D.: The Workflow Way: Understanding the Windows Workflow Foundation. Microsoft corporation whitepaper. Chappell & Associates (2009)
5. Christensen, S., Hansen, N.D.: Coloured Petri Nets Extended with Channels for Synchronous Communication. In: Valette, R. (ed.) ICATPN 1994. LNCS, vol. 815, pp. 159–178. Springer, Heidelberg (1994)
6. Dadam, P., Reichert, M., Rinderle-Ma, S., Göser, K., Kreher, U., Jurisch, M.: Von ADEPT zur AristaFlow BPM Suite - Eine Vision wird Realität: Correctness by Construction und flexible, robuste Ausführung von Unternehmensprozessen. EMISA Forum 29(1), 9–28 (2009)
7. Duvigneau, M., Moldt, D. (eds.): Proceedings of the Fifth International Workshop on Modeling of Objects, Components and Agents, MOCA 2009, Hamburg, FBI-HH-B-290/09 in Bericht. University of Hamburg (September 2009)
8. Duvigneau, M., Moldt, D., Rölke, H.: Concurrent Architecture for a Multi-agent Platform. In: Giunchiglia, F., Odell, J., Weiß, G. (eds.) Proceedings of 3rd International Workshop on Agent-Oriented Software Engineering, AOSE 2002, Bologna pp. 147–159. ACM Press (2002)
9. Duvigneau, M., Moldt, D., Rölke, H.: Concurrent Architecture for a Multi-agent Platform. In: Giunchiglia, F., Odell, J., Weiß, G. (eds.) AOSE 2002. LNCS, vol. 2585, pp. 59–72. Springer, Heidelberg (2003)
10. Ehrler, L., Fleurke, M., Purvis, M., Savarimuthu, B.T.R.: Agent-based workflow management systems (WfMSs) - JBees: a distributed and adaptive WfMS with monitoring and controlling capabilities. Information Systems and E-Business Management 4(1), 5–23 (2006)
11. Freßmann, A., Maximini, R., Sauer, T.: Towards Collaborative Agent-Based Knowledge Support for Time-Critical and Business-Critical Processes. In: Althoff, K.-D., Dengel, A.R., Bergmann, R., Nick, M., Roth-Berghofer, T.R. (eds.) WM 2005. LNCS (LNAI), vol. 3782, pp. 420–430. Springer, Heidelberg (2005)
12. Hall, T., Shahmehri, N.: An Intelligent Multi-Agent Architecture for Support of Process Reuse in a Workflow Management System. In: 1st International Conference on the Practical Application of Intelligent Agents and Multi-Agent Technology, pp. 331–343 (1996)
13. Hollingsworth, D.: The Workflow Reference Model. Workflow Management Coalition. Verfügbar auf, http://www.wfmc.org/reference-model.html
14. Jacob, T.: Implementierung einer sicheren und rollenbasierten Workflowmanagement-Komponente für ein Petrinetzwerkzeug. Diploma thesis, University of Hamburg, Department of Computer Science, Vogt-Kölln Str. 30, D-22527 Hamburg (2002)
15. Jennings, N.R., Norman, T.J., Faratin, P.: ADEPT: An Agent-Based Approach to Business Process Management. ACM SIGMOD Record 27, 32–39 (1998)
16. Jennings, N.R., Norman, T.J., Faratin, P., O'Brien, P., Odgers, P.: Autonomous Agents for Business Process Management. Int. Journal of Applied Artificial Intelligence 14(2), 145–189 (2000)
17. Köhler, M., Moldt, D., Rölke, H.: Modelling the Structure and Behaviour of Petri Net Agents. In: Colom, J.M., Koutny, M. (eds.) ICATPN 2001. LNCS, vol. 2075, pp. 224–241. Springer, Heidelberg (2001)

18. Köhler, M., Moldt, D., Rölke, H.: Modelling Mobility and Mobile Agents Using Nets within Nets. In: van der Aalst, W.M.P., Best, E. (eds.) ICATPN 2003. LNCS, vol. 2679, pp. 121–139. Springer, Heidelberg (2003)
19. Köhler, M., Rölke, H.: Modelling mobility and mobile agents using nets within nets. In: Moldt, D. (ed.) Proceedings of the Second Workshop on Modelling of Objects, Components, and Agents (MOCA 2002), University of Aarhus, Department of Computer Science, August 26-27, vol. 561, pp. 141–157. DAIMI PB, Aarhus (2002)
20. Köhler-Bußmeier, M.: Hornets: Nets within Nets Combined with Net Algebra. In: Franceschinis, G., Wolf, K. (eds.) PETRI NETS 2009. LNCS, vol. 5606, pp. 243–262. Springer, Heidelberg (2009)
21. Köhler-Bußmeier, M.: SONAR: Eine sozialtheoretisch fundierte Multiagentensystemarchitektur. In: Lüde, R.V., Moldt, D., Valk, R. (eds.) Selbstorganisation und Governance in künstlichen und sozialen Systemen. Reihe: Wirtschaft – Arbeit – Technik, vol. 5, ch. 8-12, Lit-Verlag, Münster (2009)
22. Kummer, O.: Referenznetze. Logos Verlag, Berlin (2002)
23. Markwardt, K., Moldt, D., Reese, C.: Support of Distributed Software Development by an Agent-based Process Infrastructure. In: MSVVEIS 2008 (2008)
24. Markwardt, K., Moldt, D., Wagner, T.: Net Agents for Activity Handling in a WFMS. In: Freytag, T., Eckleder, A. (eds.) Proceedings of 16th German Workshop on Algorithms and Tools for Petri Nets, AWPN 2009, CEUR Workshop Proceedings, Karlsruhe, Germany (2009)
25. Moldt, D.: Höhere Petrinetze als Grundlage für Systemspezifikationen. Dissertation, University of Hamburg, Department of Computer Science, Vogt-Kölln Str. 30, D-22527 Hamburg (August 1996)
26. Moldt, D., Quenum, J., Reese, C., Wagner, T.: Improving a Workflow Management System with an Agent Flavour. FBI-HH-B-294/10 in Bericht, pp. 55–70, University of Hamburg, Department of Informatics (June 2010)
27. Reese, C.: Prozess-Infrastruktur für Agentenanwendungen. Agent Technology – Theory and Applications, vol. 3. Logos Verlag, Berlin (2010) Dissertation, http://www.sub.uni-hamburg.de/opus/volltexte/2010/4497/
28. Reese, C., Ortmann, J., Offermann, S., Moldt, D., Markwardt, K., Carl, T.: Fragmented Workflows Supported by an Agent Based Architecture. In: Kolp, M., Bresciani, P., Henderson-Sellers, B., Winikoff, M. (eds.) AOIS 2005. LNCS (LNAI), vol. 3529, pp. 200–215. Springer, Heidelberg (2006)
29. Reese, C., Wester-Ebbinghaus, M., Dörges, T., Cabac, L., Moldt, D.: A Process Infrastructure for Agent Systems. In: Dastani, M., Fallah, A.E., Leite, J., Torroni, P. (eds.) MALLOW 2007 Proceedings. Workshop LADS 2007 Languages, Methodologies and Development Tools for Multi-Agent Systems (LADS), pp. 97–111 (2007)
30. Reese, C., Wester-Ebbinghaus, M., Dörges, T., Cabac, L., Moldt, D.: Introducing a Process Infrastructure for Agent Systems. In: Dastani, M., El Fallah, A., Leite, J., Torroni, P. (eds.) LADS 2007. LNCS (LNAI), vol. 5118, pp. 225–242. Springer, Heidelberg (2008)
31. Rölke, H.: Modellierung von Agenten und Multiagentensystemen – Grundlagen und Anwendungen. Agent Technology – Theory and Applications, vol. 2. Logos Verlag, Berlin (2004)
32. Tarullo, M., Rosca, D., Wang, J., Tepfenhart, W.: WIFAi - A Tool Suite for the Modeling and Enactment of Inter-organizational Workflows. In: IEEE/INFORMS International Conference on Service Operations, Logistics and Informatics 2009, SOLI 2009, pp. 764–769. IEEE (2009)

33. Valk, R.: Concurrency in Communicating Object Petri Nets. In: Agha, G., De Cindio, F., Rozenberg, G. (eds.) APN 2001. LNCS, vol. 2001, pp. 164–195. Springer, Heidelberg (2001)
34. van der Aalst, W.M.P.: Verification of Workflow Nets. In: Azéma, P., Balbo, G. (eds.) ICATPN 1997. LNCS, vol. 1248, pp. 407–426. Springer, Heidelberg (1997)
35. Wagner, T.: A Centralized Petri Net- and Agent-based Workflow Management System. In: Duvigneau, Moldt (eds.) [7], pp. 29–44
36. Wagner, T.: Prototypische Realisierung einer Integration von Agenten und Workflows. Diploma thesis, University of Hamburg, Department of Informatics, Vogt-Kölln Str. 30, D-22527 Hamburg (2009)
37. Wooldridge, M.: An Introduction To MultiAgent Systems, 2nd edn. John Wiley & Sons Ltd. (2009)

A Graphical Approach to Component-Based and Extensible Model Checking Platforms

Michael Westergaard[1,*] and Lars Michael Kristensen[2]

[1] Department of Mathematics and Computer Science,
Eindhoven University of Technology, The Netherlands
m.westergaard@tue.nl
[2] Department of Computer Engineering, Bergen University College, Norway
lmkr@hib.no

Abstract. Model checking is applied for verification of concurrent systems by users having different skills and background. This ranges from researchers with detailed knowledge of the inner workings of the tools to engineers that are mostly interested in applying the technology as a black-box. This paper proposes JoSEL, a graphical language for specification of executable model checking jobs. JoSEL makes it possible to work at different levels of abstraction when interacting with the underlying components of a model checking tool and thereby supports the different kinds of users in a uniform manner. A verification job in JoSEL consists of tasks, ports, and connections describing the models to verify, the behavioural properties to checked, and the model checking techniques to apply. A job can then be mapped onto components of an underlying model checking tool for execution. We introduce the syntax of JoSEL, define its semantics, and show how JoSEL has been used as a basis for the user interface of the ASAP model checking platform.

1 Introduction

Model checking [1] using state space methods is a highly automatic technique for validating the correctness of concurrent systems, and a multitude of model checking tools have been implemented. To address the inherent state explosion problem of model checking, a large number of reduction techniques have been devised. Reduction techniques typically exploit specific characteristics of systems to represent states more efficiently or store only a subset of the states, but no reduction technique performs well for all systems. Many reduction techniques can be parametrised, and the chosen parameters can greatly affect the performance of the model checker. A useful model checker must allow the user to select from a large number of *components* of the model checker implementing various reduction techniques and set parameters for each. Furthermore, new reduction techniques are continuously being developed, and a model checker must be *extensible* such

---

* Supported by the Technology Foundation STW, applied science division of NWO and the technology programme of the Dutch Ministry of Economic Affairs.

K. Jensen, S. Donatelli, and J. Kleijn (Eds.): ToPNoC V, LNCS 6900, pp. 265–291, 2012.

that it is easy to incorporate new techniques. This means that it must be possible for developers to augment the model checker, and users must be able to access new techniques in a uniform way.

Model checkers can be used in at least three settings: by researchers (who develop reduction techniques), by students (who learn about model checking and reduction techniques), and by engineers (who analyse systems). The three kinds of users have different backgrounds and approaches to using model checkers. Researchers may need fine-grained control over all parameters, they know in detail how the techniques work, and they often need to experiment with new reduction techniques and compare their performance with existing ones. A student in the process of learning, initially knows little about model checking techniques and wishes to experiment without preexisting intuition about the techniques. An engineer normally does not learn the techniques in detail so the model checker should preferably be a push-button technology. Sometimes, an engineer may need to fine-tune a few parameters. This means that users of a model checker work on different levels and need different abstractions. It is thus desirable that a model checker makes it possible to hide details of the supported techniques, but also to fine-tune details when required.

A model checker consists of several components. Examples of components are storages (for storing reachable states), queues (containing states that need to be processed), queries (e.g., written in a temporal logic) that express behavioural properties, and hash-functions for states stored in hash-tables. Based on the usage scenarios outlined previously, we specify requirements for a language for composing components in a model checking job. First, it must be possible to specify how components are composed into a job, but the user should not have to specify how to execute a job. Hence, the tool must be able to schedule the execution directly from the specification provided by the user. Second, the focus of the language should be on how components interact, not on the inter-component exchange format which is up to component developers and irrelevant from a user perspective. Third, the language should be extensible to accommodate new variations of existing techniques and integration of new techniques. In particular, the language must treat all components of the underlying model checking platform uniformly and not promote any parts of the model checker as special, including the core state space exploration algorithms. Fourth, it should be possible to hide components to allow inexperienced users to focus only on the components relevant to reach their objective. Finally, the language should facilitate modifications of predefined templates created for use by non-experts.

The contribution of this paper is to propose the verification Job Specification and Execution Language (JoSEL) aimed at supporting users with different background when applying and experimenting with model checkers and addressing the requirements identified above. A verification job in JoSEL consists of tasks, input/output ports, and connections. A job typically specifies one or more models, properties to verify, and model checking techniques to apply. The tasks correspond to software components of an underlying model checker and the input ports of a task specify required parameters of the corresponding component.

The output ports of a task specify the results produced when the component is executed. Output produced by one component can be used as input for other components by connecting the corresponding tasks using connections. JoSEL is independent of any concrete model checking tool, but to execute a verification job, tasks must be mapped onto components of a concrete model checking tool. This can be done in a manner which is fully transparent to the user, and in this paper we show how this is implemented in the ASAP model checking platform [18]. JoSEL in ASAP has been used for comparing newly developed methods (research, [7, 6]), and for teaching advanced state space methods to graduate students in addition to forming the basis for several master's theses (teaching). This shows that it fulfils the first two of its goals. To facilitate use in an industrial setting, ASAP provides a selection of predefined templates for commonly occurring model checking jobs.

JoSEL should be viewed as a uniform and flexible graphical alternative to hard-coding the supported model checking techniques into dialog boxes in a graphical user interface or relying on complex command-line arguments or pre-processing of the code to manipulate the parameters of the model checker. To allow users to abstract away details that may not be required for everyone, JoSEL has macro tasks that basically represent a set of tasks and their interconnections. If a macro has a meaningful name, it is possible to ignore the details of the *compound task* it represents. Still, it is easy for users to manipulate the details if needed. To make specifications created in JoSEL less prone to human errors, we assign types to the input and output ports of tasks. Finally, in JoSEL the user does not have to be concerned with the order in which tasks are executed, as a dependency analysis can automatically schedule the components. It is important to stress that this paper is not concerned with the internal implementation of the components provided via the underlying model checking platform, e.g., how the underlying data-structures are implemented and behavioral properties are checked. This is deliberate as JoSEL is designed to provide a black-box view on the components provided via the underlying checking platform, and instead emphasizes the input and output of the components and how the components are connected and configured in model checking jobs.

The paper is structured as follows: Section 2 introduces the basic concepts of JoSEL and defines the syntax of the language. Section 3 explains how jobs are executed by giving an operational semantics for JoSEL. In Sect. 4, we use a selection of representative examples to illustrate how JoSEL is used in the ASAP model checking platform. We sum up our conclusions in Sect. 5 which also provides a detailed comparison with related work.

2   Creating JoSEL Specifications

The Job Specification and Execution Language (JoSEL) combines concepts known from existing visual specification languages for modelling dataflows (such as dataflow diagrams) and workflows (such an UML activity diagrams). We do not use these languages directly as we aim at a language tailored for specification of verification jobs. In particular, we want the model checking job specifications to be executable, be able to distinguish the inputs and outputs consumed and produced by instances of tasks, and instantiate and synchronise tasks based on input and data content. The process-centric and temporal parts of JoSEL is similar to UML activity diagrams with a main difference being that JoSEL does not provide explicit and visual fork and join constructs. Concurrency and synchronisation is expressed by the semantics that define what input data must be available for task instance creation. Furthermore, JoSEL is not equipped with choice construct. The data-centric part of JoSEL combines dataflow diagrams (as known from structured analysis) and the concept of multiple input/outputs as found, e.g., in the pin concept of UML activity diagrams. A difference in this respect, is that JoSEL defines different kinds of input and output ports that influence the temporal flow of data and in turn task instantiation. Furthermore, we introduce a concept of synchronisation history mappings to control task instantiation. The primary aim of JoSEL is to specify the structure of components, i.e., it is at a level just below standard programming in the large [3] approaches. These approaches typically assume a clear separation between the different tasks, where in a funtionally oriented model checking platform, a task may provide a data-structure for use by other tasks. This means that the values produced by tasks are not only simple data types, but functions for generating new objects at the destination. This is not compatible with many programming-in-the-large languages, where the focus is on independent services and their exchange of data in a service oriented architecture. One example is BPEL [14] which focuses on standards for exchange of information. However, the XML documents mandated by the BPEL standard cannot represent how a data-structure is to be instantiated and used efficiently. Additionally, many existing programming-in-the-large languages use explicit control structures for iteration, whereas JoSEL takes a declarative approach where iteration and synchronisation is inferred.

To introduce JoSEL, we use an example of a verification job for verifying two safety properties of a model. The two properties are that the model contains no dead-locks (states without enabled transitions), and that it is impossible to reach a state where a certain buffer overflows. We assume that dead-lock freeness is a standard property built into the underlying model checking tool, and that the buffer overflow property can be expressed as a state predicate in a propositional logic. Executing this job consists of systematically traversing all reachable states of the model and storing already encountered states in a storage. If a violation is found, i.e., if we encounter a dead-locked state or a state where the buffer has overflowed, an error-path leading to the violating state should be reported. The example job is presented bottom-up. In practise, it is rarely required to specify all parts of a model checking job from scratch as most building blocks would be available beforehand.

2.1 Tasks

The basic executable unit in JoSEL is a *task*. A task is represented by a rounded rectangle, and Fig. 1 shows a task named Instantiate Hash Table Storage.

Fig. 1. A task with one input port and one output port

The purpose of the task in Fig. 1 is to instantiate the hash table storage required for the verification job. Associated with a task T are two kinds of *ports*: *input ports* (denoted I) and *output ports* (denoted O). Input ports specify the input data required for a task and are by convention located on the left side of a task. Output ports specify the output data produced by a task and are located on the right side of a task. Ports are represented by triangles; input ports point into the task, symbolising values going into the task, and output ports point out of the task. The name of a port is written inside the task, next to the port itself. The task in Fig. 1 has one input port (Hash Function) and one output port (Storage). This specifies that to obtain a storage (the output port) that stores states in a hash table, a hash function must be provided (the input port).

Associated with each port is also a *port mode function PM* mapping each port to a port mode which is either unit, iterator, or collection. The port mode describes how data are consumed (input ports) and produced (output ports). A *unit port* only produce/consume one value, whereas iterator and collection ports can consume/produce more than one value. We explain port modes in more detail in Sect. 3 when discussing the execution of tasks. Iterator and collections ports have a special tag positioned next to them (which we introduce later) whereas absence of a tag implicitly indicates a unit port.

Associated with a task is additionally a *port type function* τ mapping each port to a port type belonging to a set of types Σ. The port type of an input (output) port specifies the kind of data that can be provided to (produced at) the port. The actual types allowed are implementation specific, but can, e.g., be strings, integers, files, or more complex data-structures like hash-tables, representations of models and state space graphs. The type of each port is not reflected in the graphical representation. The main reason for omitting the types from the graphical representation is simplicity of the graphical representation, but tools implementing JoSEL are free to explicitly reveal the types if desired. The syntactical definition of a task is given below.

Definition 1. *A **task** is a tuple $T = (I, O, PM, \Sigma, \tau)$ where:*

1. *I is a finite set of **input ports**,*
2. *O is a finite set of **output ports** such that $I \cap O = \emptyset$,*
3. *$PM : I \cup O \to \{unit, iterator, collection\}$ is a **port mode function** that assigns to **port mode** to each port,*
4. *Σ is a set of **port types**,*
5. *$\tau : I \cup O \to \Sigma$ is a **port type function** that assigns a **port type** to each port.* □

2.2   Jobs

For a task capable of generating a hash function, we would like to specify that the hash function produced should be passed to the Instantiate Hash Table Storage task. A *job* J consists of a set of tasks $\mathcal{T}$ connected by a set of *connections* $\mathcal{C}$ describing how the output produced by one task is provided as input to other tasks. A connection is a pair (c_O, c_I) that connects an output port c_O of one task with an input port c_I of another task. A connection is represented by a line from the output port to the input port. Figure 2 shows an example of a job, where the output port of Instantiate Hash Function is connected to the input port of Instantiate Hash Table Storage. In this case Instantiate Hash Function generates a hash function for a specific model provided via the Model input port. The hash function is passed to Instantiate Hash Table Storage, which generate a storage for storing states of the model given to Instantiate Hash Function.

Output ports can be connected to input ports with the same type or a supertype (so the recipient can consume the value). Furthermore, we require that the directed graph induced by the tasks and connections in a job is acyclic to ensure completion (termination) of the job (provided that the individual tasks completes). As we require that input ports are always to the left and output ports are to the right of the task, this naturally leads to a flow from the left to the right of the job. The syntactical definition of a job is given below.

Definition 2. *A **job** is a tuple* $J = (\mathcal{T}, \mathcal{C})$ *where:*

1. $\mathcal{T} = \{T_i = (I_i, O_i, PM_i, \Sigma_i, \tau_i)\}_{1 \le i \le n}$ *is a finite set of **tasks** satisfying $i \ne j \Rightarrow P_i \cap P_j = \emptyset$, where $P_i = I_i \cup O_i$,*
2. $\mathcal{C} \subseteq \mathcal{O} \times \mathcal{I}$ *is a set of **connections** (where $\mathcal{I} = \bigcup_{T_i \in \mathcal{T}} I_i$, $\mathcal{O} = \bigcup_{T_i \in \mathcal{T}} O_i$) satisfying that the directed graph induced by tasks and connections is acyclic,*
3. *For all $c_O \in O_i$ and $c_I \in I_j$ with $(c_O, c_I) \in \mathcal{C}$, $\tau_j(c_I)$ is a supertype of $\tau_i(c_O)$.*

□

We allow multiple connections to originate in an output port and multiple connections to end in an input port. This is, e.g., useful if we want to use the value produced at an output port in multiple tasks, if we want to consume values from multiple sources, or create an instance of a task for values calculated by different tasks. It is possible for tasks in a job to have *free ports*, i.e., ports that are not assigned using connections. The set of free input ports of a job J is denoted $Free_I(J)$. A job is *closed* if it has no free input ports, otherwise it is *open*. The job in Fig. 2 is open as the input port Model of Instantiate Hash Function is free.

Fig. 2. A job consisting of two tasks for obtaining a storage

2.3   Macro Tasks

To support different levels of abstraction, we introduce *macro tasks*. A macro task is a high-level representation of a job with free ports. A macro task typically represents a component intended to be re-used in different settings and does not have all parameters defined immediately. For example, we may want to reuse the job from Fig. 2 in different job descriptions, as it provides a way to obtain a storage that is able to store states of a given model. Instead of copying the entire job, we draw a special macro task. A macro task is represented like an ordinary task except that we draw its outline using double lines. An example of a macro task can be seen in Fig. 3 (top). To specify the input and output ports of a macro, we introduce *exported ports* (exported input/output ports) which states that when a job is used as a macro, this port should be available to the user of the macro. Exported ports are drawn using a double outline, as in Fig. 3 (bottom), where Model and Storage are exported. Next to an exported port, we write the *exported name* of the port which is chosen by the user and it is often the same as the name of the underlying port. The macro task in Fig. 3 (top) represents the job in Fig. 3 (bottom). The exported name becomes the name of the port in the macro. We require that the set of exported input ports includes all the free input ports of the job; that the exported input ports are contained in the set of input ports of the underlying job; and that exported output ports are contained in the set of output ports of the job. Port modes and types of exported ports are inherited from the port modes and types of the ports in the underlying job. The syntactical definition of a macro task is provided below.

Definition 3. *Let $J = (\mathcal{T}, \mathcal{C})$ be a job with $\mathcal{T} = \{T_i = (I_i, O_i, PM_i, \Sigma_i, \tau_i)\}_{1 \le i \le n}$. J can be represented by a **macro task** which is a task $M = (I, O, PM, \Sigma, \tau)$ where:*

1. *I is a set of **exported input ports** such that $Free_I(J) \subseteq I \subseteq \mathcal{I}$, where $\mathcal{I} = \bigcup_{T_i \in \mathcal{T}} I_i$,*
2. *O is a set of **exported output ports** such that $O \subseteq \mathcal{O}$, where $\mathcal{O} = \bigcup_{T_i \in \mathcal{T}} O_i$,*
3. *$PM(p) = PM_i(p)$ for all $p \in P \cap P_i$ and $1 \le i \le n$, where $P = I \cup O$ and $P_i = I_i \cup O_i$,*
4. *$\Sigma = \bigcup_{1 \le i \le n} \Sigma_i$ and $\tau(p) = \tau_i(p)$ for all $p \in P \cap P_i$ and $1 \le i \le n$.* $\square$

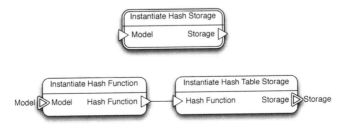

Fig. 3. A macro task (top) and the corresponding job (bottom)

2.4 Hierarchical Jobs

In our example, we have until now constructed a means to store states of a given model (cf. Fig. 3). We now hierarchically construct the remainder of the verification job for checking the two safety properties. The next step is to construct a job for checking a safety property of a model. Such a job is shown in Fig. 4. The job has a Waiting Set Exploration task which outputs an Exploration that can be used to traverse all states, stores all states we have already visited in a Storage, and stores all discovered but not yet processed in a Waiting Set. The Waiting Set Exploration task is parametrised to allow flexibility as is evident from the input ports of the task. For example, we can use a Storage storing states in a hash-table or on external storage (disk), or we can use a different Waiting Set to impose a different traversal order. The types of ports make sure that only storages and waiting sets that are usable can be connected. Our previous macro task from Fig. 3, Instantiate Hash Storage, takes care of creating a storage, and the task Instantiate Queue takes care of instantiating a specific waiting set (here implemented as a queue) which imposes a breadth-first traversal of the states. As the Model has to be used both for the Waiting Set Exploration and as input for instantiating the storage and waiting set, we use a Pipe task, which just lets its input flow unaltered to the output port. For the Pipe task we have used the ability to connect an output port to multiple input ports. The result of the Waiting Set Exploration is an Exploration, an instantiation of a state space exploration algorithm, which can be used by the Safety Checker task to check properties. The Instantiate Queue, Waiting Set Exploration, and Safety Checker are all components of the underlying ASAP model checker. In Fig. 4, four exported ports Model, Properties, Answer, and Error trace are shown. They belong to the corresponding macro task to be introduced shortly.

The Safety Checker task in Fig. 4 takes care of checking a given property. It produces an Answer (a boolean value specifying whether the property did hold) and an Error Trace to violating states (if any). As a property may have more than one violation, the task may produce multiple error traces. We use port mode *iterator* for the Error Trace port as we produce error traces as violating states are found instead of waiting until we have found all traces. This allows us to report the error traces to the user immediately. Iterator ports are annotated with a "..." tag. The Answer port has iterator port mode as it is possible to provide an answer before having explored the entire state space (if we find just one violation, the property does not hold universally), and using this port mode allows us to report this to the user immediately. We could have used port mode

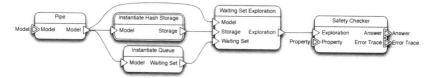

Fig. 4. Specification of a verification job for checking a safety property

collection (indicated with a { } tag) for the Error Trace port instead, signifying that we may return multiple results. With a collection port, the results would then only be reported after a complete traversal, i.e., upon completion the job.

To check the two safety properties for a model we create the job in Fig. 5, which constitutes the *root job* of our example verification job. Figure 5 is a snapshot from the implementation of JoSEL in ASAP. The Safety Checker macro task represents the job in Fig. 4. In addition, we have tasks to create an instance of a safety property for checking dead-locks (No Dead States), and to create an instance of a safety property from a user-supplied file (the two Input tasks and the SML Safety Property task) for checking buffer overflow. Both of these properties are input to the Safety Checker task. This illustrates sending more than one result to a single port. Additionally, we have tasks to create an instance of a model from a user-supplied file (the top left Input task and Instantiate Model). The model is also passed to the Safety Checker. Furthermore, we want to generate a report which specifies whether the properties were violated and, if so, how we can reach a state where the property is violated. At our disposal we have a Simple Report macro task which can generate such reports. This task is passed the values produced by the Safety Checker macro task. The Simple Report macro task is able to update the report as answers arrive, so we can see partial results during the calculation. For this reason the Results port has mode iterator, indicating that starting the task does not require all values being available. If the report could not show results incrementally, we could instead have used collection mode here. We can abstract from the actual implementation of the Simple Report macro and need only be aware that it creates a report and displays the values passed to it.

Our example shows that JoSEL can express rather complex jobs at different levels of abstraction. The top-level view (Fig. 5) allows us to specify which properties to check of which model and what to do with the results. The next level (Fig. 4) allows us to determine the traversal strategy (by specifying the waiting set implementation) and how to store states (by specifying the storage implementation). At the lowest level (Fig. 3) we can change the hash function used to store states in a hash table and similar low-level details. The three levels together form a *hierarchical job* as defined below.

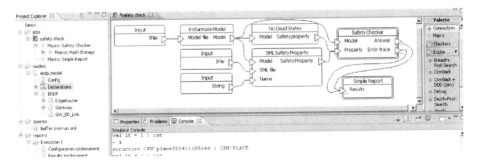

Fig. 5. The JoSEL model checking job for the two safety properties in ASAP

Definition 4. *A **hierarchical job** is a tuple $H = (\mathcal{J}, J_r, \mathcal{T}, SJ)$ where:*

1. *$\mathcal{J} = \{J_i = (\mathcal{T}_i, \mathcal{C}_i)\}_{1 \leq i \leq n}$ is a finite set of jobs such that $\mathcal{T}_i \cap \mathcal{T}_j = \emptyset$ and $\mathcal{C}_i \cap \mathcal{C}_j = \emptyset$ for $i \neq j$,*
2. *$J_r \in \mathcal{J}$ is a distinguished **root job**,*
3. *$\mathcal{T} = \{T_k = \{I_k, O_k, PM_k, \Sigma_k, \tau_k\}\}_{1 \leq k \leq m}$ is a set of macro tasks such that for all $T_k \in \mathcal{T}$ there exists a $J_i \in \mathcal{J}$ such that $T_k \in \mathcal{T}_i$,*
4. *$SJ : \mathcal{T} \to \mathcal{J}$ assigns jobs to macro tasks such that SJ is onto $\mathcal{J} \setminus \{J_r\}$, T_k is a macro task for $SJ(T_k)$ for all $T_k \in \mathcal{T}$ (cf. Def. 3), and the graph induced by $\mathcal{J}$ and SJ is a tree rooted in J_r,*
5. *For $J_i, J_j \in \mathcal{J}$ with $i \neq j$, $(\mathcal{P}_i \setminus \mathcal{P}'_i) \cap (\mathcal{P}_j \setminus \mathcal{P}'_j) = \emptyset$, where $\mathcal{P}_i$ are the ports of tasks of J_i and $\mathcal{P}'_i$ are the ports of macro tasks of J_i.*   □

Item 1 ensures that the individual jobs have disjoint tasks and connections. Item 3 ensures that each macro task belong to a job. Item 4 states that all jobs (except the root job) are represented by a macro task, and that the graph with nodes being the set of jobs and with edges determined by SJ is a tree. Item 5 ensures that only exported ports are shared between jobs. The requirement in item 4 demanding a tree structure could be relaxed to requiring an acyclic graph. This, however, complicates the semantical definition as we then have to introduce the notion of job instances. A hierarchical job is *closed* when its root job is closed.

3   Execution of JoSEL Specifications

We now specify how the jobs are executed by defining the semantics of the JoSEL language. A hierarchical job (cf. Def. 4) can be automatically flattened by recursively replacing macro tasks with the underlying jobs. Hence, it suffices to consider flat jobs in the formal semantics. Furthermore, we are not concerned with the detailed internal behaviour of tasks (i.e., the components of an underlying model checking platform) only that values are provided to input ports and produced at output ports.

A task may be *instantiated* zero, one or more times depending on the values provided to the task on input ports and the input port modes. A port of type unit can only consume a single value. If more than one value is provided to a unit port, a *task instance* is created for each value. The basic idea in the semantics of JoSEL is to instantiate each task such that whenever a task is instantiated, all preceding tasks (tasks with a connection to an input port of the task in question) have been instantiated and *completed* (excluding tasks providing values to iterator input ports). This approach is sound since we require that jobs are acyclic and hence it is possible to execute them according to a topological ordering while storing values produced at output ports as needed.

As a running example in this section, we use the slightly modified version of the model checker from Fig. 5 in Fig. 6 (ignore the dashed ovals and large numbers for now). The Model File input port of Instantiate Model is now connected to two Input file tasks and will be provided with a value from each. This means that the Instantiate Model will be instantiated twice and each instance will produce

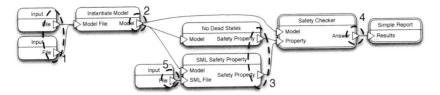

Fig. 6. Example model checking job and synchronisation points

a value on the Model output port. Both of these values will be *transferred* to the No Dead States and the SML Safety Property tasks which means that each of these tasks will be instantiated twice (once for each value received).

To formally capture the output ports on which instantiation of a task depends, we introduce the concept of a *synchronisation point* which for an input port is the set of output ports to which it is connected.

Definition 5. *Let* $J = (\mathcal{T}, \mathcal{C})$ *be a job,* $\mathcal{T} = \{T_i = (I_i, O_i, PM_i, \Sigma_i, \tau_i)\}_{1 \leq i \leq n}$, *and* $\mathcal{O} = \bigcup_{T_i \in \mathcal{T}} O_i$. *A* **synchronisation point for an input port** $\iota \in I_i$ *of a task* T_i *is defined by:* $SP(\iota) = \{o \mid (o, \iota) \in \mathcal{C}\}$. *The set of* **synchronisation points for a task** T_i *is defined by* $SP(T_i) = \{SP(\iota)\}_{\iota \in I_i}$, *and the set of* **synchronisation points for** J *is defined by* $SP(J) = \bigcup_{T_i \in \mathcal{T}} SP(T_i)$. □

In Fig. 6, we have marked and enumerated all five synchronisation points using a dashed oval and a number. In Fig. 6 the synchronisation point of the input port Model of No Dead States is the output port Model of Instantiate Model. The synchronisation point of input port Property of task Safety Checker (number 3) consists of the output ports Safety Property of task No Dead States and Safety Property of task SML Safety Property. It can be seen that different input ports may have the same synchronisation point. An example is the three ports named Model of No Dead States, SML Safety Property, and Safety Checker which all have synchronisation point number 2. Continuing with the example in Fig. 6, the Safety Checker task receives two values on the Model input port and four on the Property input port (two from each of No Dead States and SML Safety Property). This means that with a naive approach the Safety Checker must be instantiated 8 times (once for each combination of values received on input unit ports). However, one of these combinations consists, e.g., of a value for a Model X produced by one instance of a Instantiate Model (on output port Model) with a Property produced by SML Safety Property (on output port Safety Property) based upon a second Model Y produced by the other instance of a Instance Model. As it makes no sense to check a property specified for one model on another model, we need to control what values are used to instantiate tasks. In this example, we only want to start the four instances of Safety Checker that makes sense (each model with the two corresponding properties).

To control the instantiation of tasks we introduce *synchronisation history maps* that are used track the values produced at synchronisation points and which for each task instance specifies the values that gave rise to this task instance. A synchronisation history map is a partial mapping from synchronisation points to values. For example, the task Instantiate Model is instantiated twice with two different synchronisation history maps, $\{1 \mapsto A\}$ and $\{1 \mapsto B\}$, where A and B denote the values provided by two Input tasks and 1 is the number of the synchronisation point. This is shown in Fig. 7 where synchronisation history maps are written in grey boxes on the tasks whose instances they belong. In this case, we have also written names of the values produced below the dashed line in each box (the latter notation is possible in this example but not in general, as an output port may belong to multiple synchronisation points). For tasks with no input ports (and hence no synchronisation points), the synchronisation history mapping is undefined on all synchronisation points. This is the case for all Input tasks in Fig. 6 (where we have only specified the value produced by the task).

Before instantiating a task we add all values from input ports to the history mapping for the synchronisation points associated with the input port on which the values were received. An example of this is the No Dead States and SML Safety Property tasks that are instantiated twice and each instance has an associated history mapping which extend the synchronisation history maps with the values received from Instantiate Model. For the two instances of SML Safety Property the history mapping is also extended with the value provided via the SML File input port (synchronisation point 5). The four values produced by the instances of the No Dead States and SML Safety Property tasks are provided to the Property input port of Safety Checker together with the two values provided via the Instantiate Model task on input port Model.

The history mappings of the provided values can be used to ensure that we only instantiate the Safety Checker task for combinations of models and properties that match. As an example, the history mappings associated with values provided on input port Property of task Safety Checker by No Dead States specifies in the entry associated with synchronisation point 2 whether the value originates from Model X or Model Y. When instantiating the Safety Checker each of these values should only be used in combination with values provided on input port Model that maps synchronisation point 2 to the same model (X or Y). In this way we can exclude instances of Safety Checker where, e.g., the Model is X and the Property is for Model Y.

More generally, we only instantiate task with combinations of values for which the synchronisation history maps are *consistent*, i.e., where they agree on the synchronisation points where they are defined. The consistent history maps are then combined to form the synchronisation history mapping for the task instance. Finally, we associate the history map of a task instance with each value produced by that task instance. The example above demonstrates that we need the entire history of values produced by preceding task instance as we may otherwise lose history needed to compare the origin of two values. The following definition formalises the notion of synchronisation history maps and consistency.

Definition 6. *For a job $J = (\mathcal{T}, \mathcal{C})$ with $\mathcal{T} = \{T_i = (I_i, O_i, PM_i, \Sigma_i, \tau_i)\}_{1 \leq i \leq n}$, a **synchronisation history map** for J is a partial function $h : SP(J) \to \mathcal{V}$ where $\mathcal{V} = \bigcup_{T_i \in \mathcal{T}} \bigcup_{V \in \Sigma_i} V$ is the set of all possible output values of tasks. $\mathcal{H}(J)$ denotes the set of all synchronisation history maps for J.*

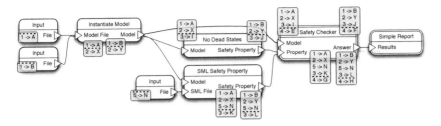

Fig. 7. Example model checking job and synchronisation history maps

Two synchronisation history maps $h_1, h_2 \in \mathcal{H}(J)$ are **consistent** *if $h_1(s) = h_2(s)$ for all synchronisation points $s \in SP(J)$ where they are both defined. For two consistent synchronisation history maps $h_1, h_2 \in \mathcal{H}(J)$, we define the union $h_1 \cup h_2$ as $(h_1 \cup h_2)(s) = v \iff h_1(s) = v \vee h_2(s) = v$.* □

The Report task in Fig. 7 is only instantiated once even though it receives four values, one from each of the four instances of Safety Checker. This is because the input port of Results is of type iterator. Input ports of type iterator (or collection) never affect the number of times a task is instantiated, as they can consume any number of values. Thus, the number of times a task is instantiated is (at most) the product of the number of values the task receives on input ports of type unit.

We introduce an *execution environment* to capture the state of a JoSEL specification during execution. A task instance is characterised by a pair consisting of a task and a synchronisation history map specifying the values used for input unit ports. In the definition of execution environment, we use a concept of *completion*. A task instance is completed when it will not produce furter values on its output ports (in reality when the component of the underlying platform is done processing). A task is completed if all its instances are completed and no additional instance of the task will be created. An output port of a task is completed when the task is completed and an input port is completed when all connected output ports are completed and all values transferred.

Definition 7. *An* **execution environment** *for job $J = (\mathcal{T}, \mathcal{C})$ with $\mathcal{T} = \{T_i = (I_i, O_i, PM_i, \Sigma_i, \tau_i)\}_{1 \leq i \leq n}$ is a tuple $E = (R, C, V)$ where:*

1. *$R \subseteq \mathcal{T} \times \mathcal{H}(J)$ is a set of running task instances,*
2. *$C \subseteq (\mathcal{T} \times \mathcal{H}(J)) \cup \mathcal{T} \cup \mathcal{I} \cup \mathcal{O}$ is a set of completed task instances, tasks and input/output ports, and*
3. *$V : \mathcal{I} \cup \mathcal{O} \to 2^{\mathcal{V} \times \mathcal{H}(J)}$ is a mapping assigning to each input and output port a set of values and associated synchronisation history maps.*

The **initial execution environment** *for J is the tuple $(\emptyset, \emptyset, V_\emptyset)$, where $V_\emptyset$ maps each port to the empty set.* □

In the following we assume that we are given a job $J = (\mathcal{T}, \mathcal{C})$ with $\mathcal{T} = \{T_i = (I_i, O_i, PM_i, \Sigma_i, \tau_i)\}_{1 \leq i \leq n}$. For a task T_i, we denote by $\text{unit}_i = \{i_{ui} \in I_i \mid PM_i(i_{ui}) = \text{unit}\}$ (input unit ports of T_i), $\text{iterator}_i = \{i_{ii} \in I_i \mid PM_i(i_{ii}) = $

iterator} (input iterator ports of T_i) and collection$_i$ = {$i_{ci} \in I_i \mid PM_i(i_{ci})$ = collection} (input collection ports of T_i). Furthermore, we assume that all values produced at outputs are globally unique. We can accomplish this in an implementation by making each value a pair of the actual value and a unique identifier.

The semantics of JoSEL is specified as six inference rules to be introduced in the following. We have have numbered the lines in the inference rules for ease of reference when explaining them. The first three rules describe the start, execution and completion of task instances: (start) describes conditions for starting a new instance of a task, (iterator) describes production of values on iterator output ports during execution of a task instance, and (complete$_i$) describes the completion of a task instance. The last three operational rules are for bookkeeping and transferal of values along connections: (complete$_t$) describes when a task is completed, i.e., will never be instantiated again, (transfer) describes transferal of values from output ports to connected input ports, and (complete$_p$) describes when no more values will be provided to an input port.

Starting a Task. Creation a task instances is specified in the (start) rule below. Tasks are instantiated as soon as all required inputs are available. For input ports of type unit, this means that one or more values for the port must be available; the task is instantiated once for each value **(1)**. For input ports of type collection, this means that all tasks connected to the port must have completed **(2)**. Input ports of type iterator do not put any restrictions on starting a task instance as values will be provided as they are produced. This means that the Safety Checker is instantiated as soon as a matching model/property pair is produced and the Report can be instantiated immediately (as Results has type iterator and it has no other ports). Finally, the history maps for values on input port must be consistent **(3)**. The combined history map becomes the history map of the task instance and the task instance about to be created must not be running or previously completed **(4)**. A newly created task instance is added to the set of running task instances **(5)**.

$$
\begin{array}{cr}
i_u \in \text{unit}_i \implies (v_{i_u}, h_{i_u}) \in V(i_u), & \textbf{(1)} \\
\text{collection}_i \subseteq C, & \textbf{(2)} \\
h_{i_u}, h_{i'_u} \text{ are consistent for all } i_u, i'_u \in \text{unit}_i, & \textbf{(3)} \\
h = \bigcup_{i_u \in \text{unit}_i} h_{i_u}, (T_i, h) \notin R \cup C & \textbf{(4)} \\
\hline
(J, (R, C, V)) \to (J, (R \cup \{T_i, h\}, C, V))\textbf{(5)}
\end{array}
\qquad (\text{start})
$$

Iterator Output During Task Instance Execution. Output from ports of types unit or collection is produced when a task is completed. Ports of type iterator may produce output at any point after the task instance has been created, which is useful if we wish to provide partial answers prior to task instance completion. For example, in the safety checker in Fig. 5, the ports Answer and Error trace are of type iterator. We produce Error traces as we find violations of the safety property, so users may decide to abort computation to fix an error and not run the job to completion.

Rule (iterator) below specifies the creation of a value on an iterator output port o of a running task instance (1), where we assume that v is a value produced by the task instance on the port (recall that we are not concerned with the internal behaviour of tasks). The rule updates the value mapping V such that the produced value becomes associated with the port (2).

$$
\frac{(T_i, h) \in R, o \in O_i, PM_i(o) = \text{iterator} \wedge v \in \tau_i(o), \quad (1)}{V'(p) = \begin{cases} V(o) \cup \{(v, h)\} & \text{if } p = o \\ V(p) & \text{otherwise.} \end{cases} \quad (2) \\ (J, (R, C, V)) \to (J, (R, C, V'))(3)} \quad \text{(iterator)}
$$

Task Instance Completion. The (complete$_i$) rule specifies when a task instance is complete, where we assume that v_p is a value produced on the unit port p and V_p is a set of values produced on a collection port p. Completing a task instance (1) requires that all iterator inputs are completed (2), a value of correct type is available for each unit output port (3), and a set of values for each collection output port (4). The value mapping is updated to reflect the values produced on unit and collection ports (5) and the task instance is moved from running to completed (6).

$$
\frac{
\begin{array}{ll}
\{(T_i, h)\} \in R, & (1) \\
\text{iterator}_i \subseteq C, & (2) \\
v_p \in \tau_i(p) \text{ for all } p \in O_i \text{ with } PM_i(p) = \text{unit}, & (3) \\
V_p \subseteq \tau_i(p) \text{ for all } p \in O_i \text{ with } PM_i(p) = \text{collection}, & (4) \\
V'(p) = \begin{cases} V(p) \cup \{(v_p, h)\} & \text{if } p \in O_i \wedge \tau_i(p) = \text{unit}, \\ V(p) \cup V_p \times \{h\} & \text{if } p \in O_i \wedge \tau_i(p) = \text{collection}, \\ V(p) & \text{otherwise.} \end{cases} & (5)
\end{array}
}{(J, (R, C, V)) \to (J, (R \setminus \{(T_i, h)\}, C \cup \{(T_i, h)\}, V'))(6)} \quad \text{(complete}_i\text{)}
$$

Task Completion. Task completion is specified in the (complete$_t$) rule below and requires that all input ports of the task is completed (1) and that all consistent instances of the task are completed (2)-(4). In addition to completing the task this also completes all output ports of the task (5).

$$
\frac{
\begin{array}{ll}
I_i \subseteq C, & (1) \\
(T_i, h) \in C \text{ for all } h = \bigcup_{i_u \in \text{unit}_i} h_{i_u} & (2) \\
\text{for some } (v_{i_u}, h_{i_u}) \in V(i_u) & (3) \\
\text{with } h_{i_u}, h_{i'_u} \text{ consistent for all } i_u, i'_u \in \text{unit}_i & (4)
\end{array}
}{(J, (R, C, V)) \to (J, (R, C \cup \{T_i\} \cup O_i, V))(5)} \quad \text{(complete}_t\text{)}
$$

Value Transfer. The values transferred (provided) to an input port is the union of all values produced at the synchronisation point of the port, i.e., all connected output ports. We therefore have three ways of receiving more than one value on an input port: if the port is connected to a unit port of a single task that is instantiated more than once, if the port is connected to unit ports of multiple tasks, or if it is connected to a port of type iterator or collection, and the connected task produces an iterator or a collection containing more than one value. Transfer of a not previously transferred value and its history mapping (v, h) along a connection from output port o to input port i **(1)** is specified in the (transfer) rule below. The rule updates **(3)** the value mapping for the input port i to record in the associated history mapping that the value was provided via synchronisation $SP(i)$ **(2)**. It should be noted that the rule implicitly encapsulates and extracts from collections and iterators as necessary.

$$
\frac{(o, i) \in \mathcal{C}, (v, h) \in V(o), (v, h') \notin V(i) \text{ for all } h' \in \mathcal{H}(J), \quad \textbf{(1)} \qquad V'(p) = \begin{cases} V(p) \cup \{(v, h \cup \{SP(i) \mapsto v\})\} & \text{if } p = i, \\ V(p) & \text{otherwise.} \end{cases} \quad \textbf{(2)}}{(J, (R, C, V)) \to (J, (R, C, V'))\textbf{(3)}} \quad \text{(transfer)}
$$

Input Port Completion. Completion of input ports follows the (complete$_p$) rule below which for a not yet completed port requires that all output ports have been completed **(1)** and all values have been transferred from the port in the associated synchronisation point **(2)**. The result of applying the rule is that the port p is added to the completion set **(3)**.

$$
\frac{p \in I_i \setminus C, (o, p) \in \mathcal{C} \implies o \in C, \quad \textbf{(1)} \qquad (o, p) \in \mathcal{C} \wedge (v, h) \in V(o) \implies \exists h' \in \mathcal{H}(J).(v, h') \in V(p) \quad \textbf{(2)}}{(J, (R, C, V)) \to (J, (R, C \cup \{p\}, V))\textbf{(3)}} \quad \text{(complete}_p\text{)}
$$

We start the execution of a JoSEL specification by (conceptually) flattening the specification and execute it starting from the initial execution environment according to the above rules. If a hierarchical job is closed, so is the corresponding flattened job, guaranteeing that all tasks are instantiated. Some times more than one of the operational rules may be applicable, in which case we choose one nondeterministically. It should be noted that our semantics does not allow a task instance to complete before it has received all input values from iterator ports (i.e., they are not allowed to ignore values). This can be relaxed but makes the rules more complex. We have chosen not to do so such that the semantics given corresponds to the implementation in ASAP. The reason for only using the synchronisation history maps with unit ports is that there is no canonical way to introduce them for collection and iterator ports. As an example, the Simple Report in Fig. 6 can be instantiated either once, twice or four times, depending on which part of the synchronisation history maps we consider (one if we ignore the model and property, two if we ignore one of them, and four if we ignore both). As all cases in the above example are meaningful, we decided not to restrict the semantics in this respect. A future refinement of the semantics may, however, restrict executions by taking the history maps into consideration for iterator and collection ports.

4   Application of JoSEL in the ASAP Platform

JoSEL is an integral part of the ASAP model checking platform [18] and in this section we describe the issues addressed when using JoSEL in ASAP. ASAP supports checking safety properties and liveness properties (specified using LTL) of models (specified by, e.g., coloured Petri nets or in the DVE language) by means of a wide range of methods (including bit-state hashing, hash-compaction, full state spaces, the comback method, the sweep-line method, and methods using external storage) (see [18] for details). ASAP builds on the Eclipse Rich Client Platform (RCP) allowing us to extend the tool using plug-ins and common Eclipse frameworks. The object model for JoSEL is implemented using the Eclipse Modeling Framework (EMF), The graphical editor for construction of JoSEL specifications is implemented using the Eclipse Graphical Modeling Framework (GMF), which makes it very easy to generate graphical editors for EMF models. JoSEL is independent of the ASAP model checking platform, and the effort needed to integrated with another modular platform is expected to be on par with the effort described below for ASAP. In fact, parts of the ASAP tool are independent of the underlying platform. This includes a representation, visualizations, and various exporters of generic graphs as well as the reporting mechanism described at the end of this section.

4.1   Tasks

JoSEL itself does not specify which tasks are to be available, this depends solely on the underlying model checking platform. Tasks in ASAP are available for common utility purposes (such as providing inputs in the form of strings, integers, booleans, files, and the Pipe task from Fig. 4), state space methods (such as various model loaders, storages, explorations, and checkers for different classes of properties), and various high-level non-state space related operations (such as drawing graphs and creating reports). Tasks are available during construction in a palette as shown on the right of Fig. 5.

Exposing a component in the underlying platform amounts to providing an implementation of a new task in the JoSEL editor. This consists of defining its interface (input/output ports) and internal implementation. The internal implementation is a standard Java method that is executed when the task is instantiated and which typically invokes components on the underlying platform. Defining a task in ASAP consists of making a sub-class of a generic task. All the boiler-plate code needed for integration is handled automatically by EMF. A programmer has to specify the interface (typically in the order of five lines of code), the name of the task (one line of code), and a method implementing the execution of the task (this typically ranges one to more than a hundred lines of code). Naturally, the latter method is the most demanding part, but the complexity depends primarily on how user-friendly a task should be. A programmer can chose that a task should provide no user-interaction, in which case the implementation is simple (less than ten lines of code). Alternative, a task can provide intermediate results and feedback (such as a progress bar) or allowing a user to manually cancel an ongoing task (requiring twenty to a hundred or more lines of code). Once a programmer knows how to integrate JoSEL tasks, a concrete integration can typically be done in a matter of hours. For example, the Instantiate Queue task in Fig. 4 comprises 90 lines of code (12 of which are written manually), Waiting Set Exploration comprises 98 lines (17 hand-written), and Safety Checker 166 lines (74 hand-written. The latter task supports intermediate status information such as the number of states checked, and allows the user to cancel exploration prematurely via the GUI. Tasks can be added to ASAP using the plug-in mechanism of the Eclipse RCP. For example, the task for using the sweep-line method is completely independent of the rest of the tool and all functionality is supplied by a removable plug-in. We use Java types for port types and the Java sub-classing relation for inducing super-types.

4.2   Scheduling and Task Execution

The JoSEL scheduler is responsible for executing tasks the correct number of times according to the JoSEL semantics. The implementation of a task is only responsible for handling a single execution with the concrete parameters. Our Java implementation for execution of JoSEL specifications aims to increase concurrency on a single machine and observes that starting many threads that are just waiting to be executed is relatively inexpensive on modern platform. The idea is to create a thread for each port, for each task, and dynamically instantiate threads for task instances. The threads for tasks take care of starting threads for task instances according to the (start) rule and for cleaning up according to the (complete$_i$) and (complete$_t$) rules. We have separate kind of threads for input and output ports; threads for output ports collect values from task instances and send them to input ports according to the (transfer) rule, and threads for input port collect data from output ports and notify task threads when no more values are produced according to the (complete$_p$) rule.

This allows us to rely on Java's scheduler for threads, thereby exploiting the available CPUs on the machine. The threads taking care of communication are light-weight and provide no measurable overhead to the execution (as most of the time, they just wait for data from another thread), and threads for handling the actual execution of tasks are only started when all information is available.

4.3   On-the-Fly and Off-Line Analysis

The examples we have seen until now use an on-the-fly approach to checking properties, where we check the property during state space exploration. This is efficient for checking a single property once, but less efficient if we wish to check multiple properties that we may not know beforehand. Here, it it more efficient to first generate the entire state space (assuming that we have sufficient memory) and subsequently traverse the generated state space to check the property. This is often referred to as *off-line analysis*.

The On-the-fly Safety Checker in Fig. 4 uses an Exploration as input value. An exploration is able to execute a function for each state of the state space, and corresponds to a visitor in an object oriented language or a fold function in a functional programming language. An exploration is a traversal of a state space which is independent of the algorithm used. In ASAP it is easy to specify off-line analysis: we have a task for producing a representation of the state space from an Exploration and another task for traversing this representation, thereby producing a new Exploration. An example of the off-line checker can be seen in Fig. 8. Here we have a Off-line Analysis task that takes an Exploration value as input and produces a new Exploration value. The two exploration values are not the same, however: the second one produced is backed by an explicit representation of the state space (actually the ML Graph which is also exposed) and is much faster to traverse. This means that if we are checking two properties, we only generate the state space once but traverse it twice. We also expose a Graph Model, which can be used as any other model, except it is much faster to traverse, as it is also backed by an explicit underlying data-structure.

4.4   State Space Reduction Techniques

ASAP supports several reduction techniques. Some reduction techniques supported are implemented by simply adding a new storage task whereas some require that we also add a new exploration task. When doing on-line analysis, we do not retrieve states from the storage, but only check whether a state has been seen before. We can therefore use one-way compression of states in the storage. Two prominent methods for doing so are the hash-compaction [19] and bit-state [9] (also known as super-traces), and double-hashing [4] methods. Hash-compaction does not store the entire state descriptor, but instead uses a hash function to generate a smaller hash-value that is stored instead. This may lead to collisions, so we can only prove presence of errors, not absence. Hash-compaction in ASAP is implemented as a storage, as shown in Fig. 9 (left), where we have replaced the Hash Table Storage from earlier with a Hash Compaction Storage. The fragment needs a hash function (like in Fig. 2) in order to work. Bit-state hashing is related to hash-compaction, but instead of storing the hash-value, an array with an entry for a bit for each possible hash-value is allocated, and a bit is set when a hash-value is encountered. ASAP supports the more reliable double hashing method, which is a variant that uses multiple hash functions automatically generated from two base hash functions using a linear combination. This reduces collisions at a very small cost in time and no extra cost in space.

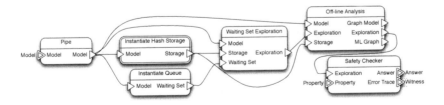

Fig. 8. Example of a job for off-line analysis in ASAP

Fig. 9. Hash-compaction (left) and double hashing (right) in ASAP

The use of the task providing access to the implementation of double hashing is shown in Fig. 9 (right). In addition to two hash functions it also requires two integers: the number of combinations, and the size of the bit array to allocate.

As mentioned, the hash compaction method suffers from hash collisions, which makes it impossible to prove absence of errors. The comback method [7] is able to resolve such hash collisions by additionally storing a spanning tree for the state space, making it possible to reconstruct a full state descriptor from a hash value at a cost in both time and space. An example using the comback method in ASAP shown in Fig. 10. It is a bit more complex than the two previous methods, as we not only have to store states differently, we also have to maintain the spanning tree, which is why we additionally have introduced the ComBack Exploration. It which wraps the given exploration and ensures that a spanning tree is also generated. The fragment needs a hash function and an integer indicating the size of a cache in order to work.

A completely different approach is not to focus on storing states efficiently, but to delete them from memory when they are no longer needed. One such method is the sweep-line method [11]. Here, a progress measure is used to syntactically identify when a state is no longer needed. It does so by assigning a progress value to each state so that a state with a higher progress value never (or only rarely) has edges to states with lower progress values. That way, when we have explored all states with progress value lower than a given number, we can safely remove all states with this progress value from memory. Support for the sweep-line method is illustrated in Fig. 11. The sweep-line method requires a Progress Measure (here as an exported port) in addition to the usual input for an exploration, but does not require a Waiting set, as the sweep-line method by definition imposes a least-progress first traversal.

We have looked at several reduction techniques and while they have different implementation, they appear (almost) the same to a user, as shown in Fig. 12. From the macro tasks, we see that only the Sweep-line Safety Checker has a

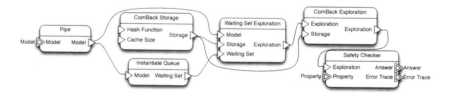

Fig. 10. Application of the comback method in ASAP

Fig. 11. Application of the sweep-line method in ASAP

Fig. 12. Top level macros for different reduction techniques in ASAP

different interface, as it requires a progress measure. The uniform way in which the macros have been constructed makes switching between methods easy.

4.5   LTL Model Checking

All examples we have considered until now deal with checking safety properties, i.e., properties whose correctness can be determined by looking at each state in isolation. ASAP also supports model checking of liveness properties using linear temporal logic (LTL) [16]. The standard approach for checking LTL is to take an LTL formula, translate it to a Büchi automaton, which can then be synchronised with the state space generated from a model. The resulting product automata can then be used to check violations by searching for a loop with an accepting state. Loops are typically found using nested depth-first traversal of the product. This can be performed on the fly, so we do not need to generate the state space or the product before performing the nested depth-first traversal.

We have chosen to make the JoSEL specification for checking LTL in ASAP (shown in Fig. 13) closely reflect the conceptual procedure for checking LTL. At the top, we have Instantiate Model from our safety checkers loading a model. Below that, we have the Load LTL macro, which takes a Formula File containing the formula to check as input. The Model parameter is used to ensure that the formula matches the model. The task Construct Product does not actually construct the product (just like the Waiting Set Exploration does not actually generate the state space), it instead constructs a representation of the transition relation for the product automaton. Nested DFS implements nested depth-first search using the provided transition relation, and produces an output specifying whether the property was satisfied and any error traces (if applicable). Output from the search is sent to a standard report.

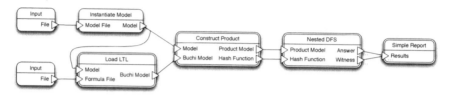

Fig. 13. An LTL model checking job in ASAP

4.6   Profiling

When experimenting with state space analysis, a researcher often has to compare a newly developed method with other methods. This typically includes measuring the time and memory spent by the algorithm. Instead of adding profiling as a primitive in ASAP, we have decided to expose it using the mechanisms already available in JoSEL. If we were to implement profiling in a conventional programming language, one way of doing so would be to create proxy code wrapping the code to be profiled. The proxy would delegate each call to the original code and measure how long it took. We use the same approach in ASAP. Here, we wrap essential data-structures (e.g., a storage), in a profiled version of the component. In Fig. 14, we see a fragment of a JoSEL specification for profiling the Hash Storage by wrapping it in a Profiled Storage. This makes it possible to implement profiling once for all implementations of a data-structure and do so in a coherent way. We have implemented both time and memory profiling in this manner. In the example, we similarly wrap the Exploration and send all profiling data to the report, where it appears along with other information about the execution.

Fig. 14. Profiling in ASAP

4.7   Reporting

While JoSEL describes what to analyse and how to do so, it does not by itself provide a way to present the results of executing a model checking job. It is desirable to be able to present the results of an executed JoSEL specification in a way that is easy to understand and manage. For this purpose we the have concept of a *report* for an execution of a JoSEL specification. A report can in its simplest form be a standard report listing the answers to a set of standard behavioural properties as known from, e.g., CPN Tools [2]. In addition, our approach also makes it possible for users to add information to the report and to display, e.g., details about the reduction techniques used.

To generate reports, ASAP uses a standard report generator framework from Eclipse called the Business Intelligence and Reporting Tool (BIRT). BIRT relies on an underlying database containing data to be shown and a *report design* specifying how data should be shown. Adding results from the execution of a JoSEL specification to a database should naturally be handled automatically, and in order to make it easy to visualise data, we also automatically generate a sensible standard report design.

Collecting Data for the Database. A key element is to collect data from a job execution without making the user worry about what data to gather. We want this to be completely automatic and extensible. We therefore let each JoSEL task add pieces of information about the execution that they posses. Using the safety checker in Figs. 4 and 5 as examples, the Instantiate Queue tasks knows that traversal is going to be breadth-first. The On-the-fly Safety Checker knows for how long processing went on, the Waiting Set Exploration knows how many states it processed, the Instantiate Model knows which model was used (it gets that as input parameter), the No Dead States and SML Safety Property know which property was analysed (the latter gets the name of the property as parameter). As each task instance knows part of the information about the execution, we need to gather this information in a consistent way (for example, we have two instances of On-the-fly Safety Checker, one for No Dead States and one for SML Safety Property, and need to match the execution time from the correct instance with the correct property). Using the synchronisation history map of the value received in Simple Report, ensures access to all values and ensures that values are consistent, so so we can add it to the database as a single run. This means that in an execution as the one in Figs. 4 and 5 only information relevant to this execution is recorded and we can easily add more data to a run by simply using more tasks. As an example, the Sweep Line Exploration in Fig. 11 can add information about how many states were generated and what the peak number of states stored in memory was.

Automatic Report Design Generation. With an underlying database in place, we now need to extract it to generate a suitable report. One option is to rely on users to do this manually using one of the graphical designers shipping with BIRT. For most users this is too cumbersome, and we therefore generate such report designs automatically, but without preventing advanced users from creating their own designs. The idea is to generate a report automatically from descriptions of *fragments*. A report fragment is a very small part of a report, which describes a single section or subsection of the report. A fragment could for example display the number of nodes generated or the name of the model in question, but it could also be more elaborate and display a trace from the initial state to an error state – or even show a chart with the execution time of the analysis as function of a parameter of the model. A fragment describes which parameters must be available for the fragment to be relevant. This way we do not show an empty section containing error traces if a model has no errors. As an example, we show no section describing the progress measure and peak number of states unless the sweep-line method is used, and no profiling section if profiling was not used. An example report for an execution of a job checking a property on a model using hash-compaction is shown in Fig. 15. Here we have checked a safety property named buffer overrun on a model named erdp, generating 58133 states in 1.801 seconds.

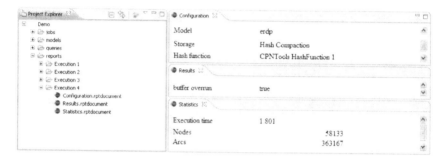

Fig. 15. Example report generated for execution of JoSEL job using hash-compaction

5   Conclusion and Future Work

In this paper we have developed a graphical approach to specification and execution of verification jobs in model checking. We have shown how the proposed JoSEL language provides a uniform and flexible mechanism for accessing and configuring the components of an underlying model checker platform, ranging from the core components implementing the state space algorithms to components supporting profiling and reporting. Furthermore, we have presented a set of representative examples illustrating how JoSEL has served as a basis for the user interface of the ASAP model checking platform.

In the introduction, we introduced five requirements (and two requirements inferred from those) for a language for composing model checkers, namely the ability to specify composition, the ability to automatically find an appropriate execution order, extensibility, the ability to abstract away components that are not important to the task at hand, the ability to make minor modifications to pre-existing templates, treating all components equally to support extensibility, and a focus on composition of components rather than on the actual data-exchange between components. The seven requirements are shown in Table 1, where we summarise how a number of related composition languages and tools adhere to these requirements. We discuss the table in further detail below.

A prominent model checker is SPIN [10], where components are selected by providing compiler switches. Some of the switches can be selected in the graphical user interface Xspin, but some switches can only be found by looking at the source code. SPIN automatically executes the components in a correct order, but compiler switches sometimes interact in unsupported ways. Another approach is SAL [15], which is basically an interchange format for model checkers along with implementations of wrappers for a number of model checkers. Each of the components can be run on a model and the results can be used by other components. The user must run components manually or via a script, Makefile or custom language like SVL [8], which all provide textual languages for composition with great extensibility. By using procedure-like constructs, these can allow abstraction to a certain extent, but rarely in a way that is easy to grasp for a beginner. Furthermore, textual languages require either a good editor or that the user remembers all keywords and components. Some textual languages can automatically devise an execution order, but the textual nature of the languages imposes an order (the one in the script) and it may be confusing if the execution order differs from this order. Other composition languages, like OsMoSys [17] or HLA [13] mainly focus on composing different modelling languages, and not on the actual model checking phase.

Graphical languages exist as well, such as workflow specification languages, but they are not tailored to model checking, and we find that a language designed specifically for model checking is preferable. An example of a language for this purpose is jETI [12], whose main objective is to easily compose web-services. jETI does not, however, make it easy to specify several similar tasks as it is more tailored to a "write once, run many times"-paradigm rather than slight modifications of templates. Bogor [5] is a model checking platform similar to ASAP and is also extensible. It does not use a general-purpose language for composition, but rather configuration dialogs for certain tasks (like our On-the-fly Safety Checker), which makes it difficult to introduce completely new methods and run methods in parallel automatically. JoSEL addresses all our requirements. It is built for composing components and takes care of the order of execution automatically. Furthermore, it is easy to add new tasks to JoSEL and all tasks are treated equally. JoSEL is designed with abstraction in mind via macro tasks and it is easy to substitute one task with another task having the same interface. Finally, the main focus of JoSEL is composition, and data interchange is left up to component developers. It is clear that using two or more of the listed tools together may be an advantage. One could, for example, let SAL take care of the interchange of values and use JoSEL for composing the SAL components or introduce JoSEL into Bogor, removing the settings dialogs and using JoSEL to compose the Bogor model checking components.

Table 1. Comparison of approaches to construct model checkers from components

Tool	Requirement						
	Specify composition	Automatic execution order	Extensible	Abstraction	Minor modifications	No special parts	Focus on composition
SPIN	(✔)	✔			✔		
SAL	(✔)				(✔)	✔	
Shell-script, Makefile, SVL	✔	(✔)	✔	(✔)	(✔)	✔	✔
OsMoSys, HLA	(✔)	✔	(✔)				✔
jETI	✔	✔	✔	✔		(✔)	✔
Bogor	✔	✔	(✔)		✔	✔	(✔)
JoSEL	✔	✔	✔	✔	✔	✔	✔

Future work includes considering extensions of the JoSEL language. We have chosen not to make control structures part of the language, as most can be implemented as special tasks. One such example is an If task, which takes as input a boolean value Test and an arbitrary value Value. Depending on the value of the test, the value is transmitted either to a Then or an Else output. Some control structures cannot be implemented in this way, however. One interesting language extension is to allow cyclic connections, so we iteratively can improve a verification result. This is interesting for implementing incremental improvement of approximative reduction techniques. The reason for not just doing this that it would be easier for users to make mistakes in specifications. It would also be interesting to add a way to terminate a task or a set of tasks. This has interesting applications to, e.g., state-of-the-art model checking, in which we start model checking with several model checking techniques. As soon as the first technique provides a definitive answer we terminate the execution of the rest. One issue is to find a good graphical representation for this mechanism. Another interesting direction is to investigate scheduling across multiple machines. By extending JoSEL with annotations describing the time- and space-wise cost of a task and the produced values, we may be able to intelligently distribute data to the appropriate machines, taking into account that it may sometimes be more efficient to re-calculate data than to transmit it.

References

1. Baier, C., Katoen, J.-P.: Principles of Model Checking. MIT Press (2008)
2. CPN Tools webpage, www.cpntools.org
3. De Remer, F., Kron, H.: Programming-in-the large versus programming-in-the-small. SIGPLAN Not. 10, 114–121 (1975)
4. Dillinger, P.C., Manolios, P.: Fast and Accurate Bitstate Verification for SPIN. In: Graf, S., Mounier, L. (eds.) SPIN 2004. LNCS, vol. 2989, pp. 57–75. Springer, Heidelberg (2004)
5. Dwyer, M.B., Hatcliff, J., Hoosier, M., Robby: Building Your Own Software Model Checker Using the Bogor Extensible Model Checking Framework. In: Etessami, K., Rajamani, S.K. (eds.) CAV 2005. LNCS, vol. 3576, pp. 148–152. Springer, Heidelberg (2005)
6. Evangelista, S.: Dynamic Delayed Duplicate Detection for External Memory Model Checking. In: Havelund, K., Majumdar, R. (eds.) SPIN 2008. LNCS, vol. 5156, pp. 77–94. Springer, Heidelberg (2008)
7. Evangelista, S., Westergaard, M., Kristensen, L.M.: The ComBack Method Revisited: Caching Strategies and Extension with Delayed Duplicate Detection. Transactions on Petri Nets and Other Models of Concurrency 3, 189–215 (2009)
8. Garavel, H., Lang, F.: SVL: A Scripting Language for Compositional Verification. In: Proc. of FORTE. IFIP Conference Proceedings, vol. 197, pp. 377–394. Kluwer (2001)
9. Holzmann, G.J.: An Analysis of Bitstate Hashing. Formal Methods in System Design 13, 289–307 (1998)
10. Holzmann, G.J.: The SPIN Model Checker. Addison-Wesley (2003)

11. Kristensen, L.M., Mailund, T.: A Generalised Sweep-Line Method for Safety Properties. In: Eriksson, L.-H., Lindsay, P.A. (eds.) FME 2002. LNCS, vol. 2391, pp. 549–567. Springer, Heidelberg (2002)
12. Margaria, T., Nagel, R., Steffen, B.: Remote Integration and Coordination of Verification Tools in JETI. In: Proc. of ECBS, pp. 431–436. IEEE Comp. Soc. Press (2005)
13. Morse, K.L., Lightner, M., Little, R., Lutz, B., Scrudder, R.: Enabling Simulation Interoperability. Computer 39(1), 115–117 (2006)
14. OASIS WSBPEL TC. Web Services Business Process Execution Language Version 2.0, http://docs.oasis-open.org/wsbpel/2.0/OS/wsbpel-v2.0-OS.html
15. Shankar, N.: Combining Theorem Proving and Model Checking through Symbolic Analysis. In: Palamidessi, C. (ed.) CONCUR 2000. LNCS, vol. 1877, pp. 1–16. Springer, Heidelberg (2000)
16. Vardi, M., Wolper, P.: An Automata-Theoretic Approach to Automatic Program Verification. In: Proc. of IEEE Symposium on Logic in Computer Science, pp. 322–331 (1986)
17. Vittorini, V., Iacono, M., Mazzocca, N., Franceschinis, G.: The OsMoSys Approach to Multi-formalism Modeling of Systems. Software and Systems Modeling 3(1), 69–81 (2004)
18. Westergaard, M., Evangelista, S., Kristensen, L.M.: ASAP: An Extensible Platform for State Space Analysis. In: Franceschinis, G., Wolf, K. (eds.) PETRI NETS 2009. LNCS, vol. 5606, pp. 303–312. Springer, Heidelberg (2009)
19. Wolper, P., Leroy, D.: Reliable Hashing without Collision Detection. In: Courcoubetis, C. (ed.) CAV 1993. LNCS, vol. 697, pp. 59–70. Springer, Heidelberg (1993)

Author Index